OF

LOWER

CALIFORNIA

The Last of the Conquistadors
JUNÍPERO SERRA

Books by Omer Englebert
ST. FRANCIS OF ASSISI, translated by Edward Hutton
THE WISDOM OF FATHER PECQUET, translated by Katherine Woods
THE LIVES OF THE SAINTS, translated by Christopher and Anne Fremantle
THE HERO OF MOLOKAI, FATHER DAMIEN, translated by Benjamin Crawford
SAINT ADVENTURERS

OMER ENGLEBERT

THE LAST OF THE CONQUISTADORS
Junípero Serra
(1713-1784)

Translated from the French by Katherine Woods

HARCOURT, BRACE AND COMPANY · NEW YORK

Imprimatur: GREGORIO ALFARO, Vic. Gen.
Tijuana, Baja California, 31 de mayo 1954.

LIBRARY OF CONGRESS CATALOG CARD NUMBER: 56-7917

PRINTED IN THE UNITED STATES OF AMERICA

CONTENTS

ILLUSTRATIONS

The Last of the Conquistadors
JUNÍPERO SERRA

One

*Majorca, or the First Thirty-five Years
in the Life of Junípero Serra*
[1713-1749]

At the period when Junípero Serra spent the first half of his life
there, the Island of Majorca (in the Balearic Islands, a part of
Spain) counted no less than 317 churches and about 500 secular
priests in an area of 1,352 square miles and 140,000 people. The
city of Palma alone possessed some twenty communities of women
and eleven large convents for men. Every locality, however un-
important, had its hospital, its orphan asylum, and its old people's
home. The most widely disseminated of all the religious organi-
zations, the Franciscan Order maintained some fifteen flourishing
houses of religion, and supplied the Lullian University with its
best professors.

The Mallorcans had been refined and matured by the Greco-
Latin civilization more than twenty centuries before. They were
already trading with the Greeks under Pericles, and were winning victories in the Olympic Games; as masters of the sling, especially, they had no rivals. They had passed successively under
the domination of Carthage, of Rome, of the Barbarians, and of
the Moors; in 1229 they had set up their country as an independent kingdom; in 1334 they had surrendered to the power of the
King of Aragon; and in 1479 they had been united to the crown
of Spain.

Christianized as early as the first century after Christ, the inhabitants of Majorca in the eighteenth century were all still practicing Catholics. They greeted one another with the words *Amar
a Dios!* (Let us love God!), a salutation which, thanks to Junípero, was the first to be used in Upper California. They were
almost all people of natural ability. Corrupt and evil men were
rare among them, as is shown by the fact that hangings numbered

3

only about ten a year. Both laymen and clergy by the hundreds took university degrees. There were many scholars and poets, and there were even astrologers. The vocations of sailor and missionary were at all times followed by the men of the island. The names of two Franciscans who were natives of Majorca are still cited from medieval days; the apostate Anselme Turmeda (1352-1432), who became a son-in-law of the Sultan of Tunis; and the great Raymond Lull (1235-1315), poet, mystic, and martyr, a man of genius if there ever was one.

In this beautiful corner of the globe, with its delightful climate, agriculture and stock raising flourished; the most delectable fruits were to be gathered; all kinds of fish were there for the catching; orange, almond, and olive trees, and grape vines, too, grew in abundance.

It was at Petra, twenty-five miles from Palma, the island's capital, that Junípero was born, at about one o'clock in the morning of November 24, 1713. He was baptized the same day, under the name of Miguel (or Miquel) José, in the parochial church of St. Peter, and he received confirmation there on May 26, 1715. The home of his infancy, since preserved as a relic, consisted of four rooms, some attics, and a storeroom. His native town, with a population of about two thousand, possessed ten water mills and one windmill; its chief patroness was the Virgin Mary, who was invoked under the title of Our Lady of Good Harvests.

Antonio Serre [1] and Margarita Ferrer, his wife, had five children, three of whom died at an early age; in addition to Miguel José, the one who lived to maturity was his sister Juana (or Juanita), three years younger than he. Antonio Serre made his living sometimes as an agricultural worker and sometimes as a quarryman. Both he and his wife were members of the Third Order of St. Francis. Margarita Ferrer was much given to prayer, and was wont to reiterate her conviction that we are on this earth to carry out the divine will. Although they did not know how to read and write, they were both of them rare and fine human beings, with souls of an untarnished nobility, never sullied by the intrusion of a base thought. Junípero could not have been better brought up if he had been the son of a prince.

---

[1] The Majorcan *Serre* becomes *Serra* in Catalan and *Sierra* in Spanish. At first Junípero signed himself "Serre," then "Sierra" and finally "Serra." His paternal grandmother was named Juana Abram, which gave rise to the belief that he may have had Jewish ancestors.

From the time he was able to walk, he went regularly with his parents to the Franciscan church of San Bernardino attached to the convent of the same name, and close by his home. "Antonio Serra was very much liked by the friars," his biographer Palou writes, "and they received his son in their college. Here Miguel José had his primary schooling and then his classical education, shining particularly as a Latin scholar. Gifted with an engaging voice and a good ear, he was a member of the choir, and sang in choir with the community. Even at this early period he had that quality of earnestness tempered by a gracious kindliness, which belonged to him always."

From the school of the San Bernardino convent at Petra he went on to that of the convent of St. Francis at Palma to begin his work in philosophy. He lived with a canon in the town, and in his free time worked for him as a house servant. From this pious priest he learned to recite the breviary, and the two recited it together.[2] It was during this scholastic year (1729-30) that he applied to Father Perillo, Provincial of Majorca, for admission to the Franciscan Order.[3] At first he was turned away, for his height was still only that of a child and his generally frail appearance seemed an augury of poor health. But his teachers pleaded his cause so earnestly that Father Perillo changed his mind and opened the door of the novitiate to the postulant.

The youth found himself assigned then to the convent of Jesus-without-the-Walls in a suburb of Palma. There, on September 14, 1730, Miguel José put on the Franciscan habit: a tunic of rough cloth worn next to the skin, a brown monk's frock with a cowl, a white cord with three knots forming a belt, and sandals on feet

---

[2] The breviary, or divine office for the day, is composed of the following hours: matins, lauds, prime, tierce, sext, nones, vespers, and compline. The private recital of the office takes about an hour; when several people recite it together, as the Franciscans do in choir, it takes about two and one-half hours.

[3] The Franciscan Order was founded by St. Francis of Assisi (1182-1226). Composed in part of men vowed to the life of religion who become priests (clerics), and in part of those likewise taking religious vows but not taking Holy Orders (lay brothers), it is divided into *provinces*, each of which groups together a certain number of *convents*. As head, it has a *Minister General*, who lives in Rome and is assisted by a council or *Definitory General*. Each province is governed by a *Provincial Minister*, assisted by his council or *Provincial Definitory*. At the head of each convent is a *Guardian*, assisted by his council or *Discretory*. The members of the Definitory are called *Definitors;* the members of the Discretory are called *Discretos*. Members are addressed as "Brother" (in Spanish, *Fray*)—at least among themselves—as St. Francis called his foundation the Order of Friars Minor ("lesser brothers"). When ordained priests, they are called by the term of respect "Father."

otherwise bare. From this time on, his life was that then led in the Franciscan convents of Spain. From six to seven hours of each day were devoted to prayer. The daily schedule was generally as follows: from midnight to 2 A.M., recitation of matins and lauds in chorus, followed by mental prayer; 6 A.M., the rising hour, prayer, prime and tierce, Mass, breakfast; 11 A.M., sext and nones, examination of conscience; 12 noon, midday meal, recreation, siesta; 4 P.M., vespers and compline, prayer; 7 P.M., evening meal, evening prayer, bed. What time remained was employed by the lay brothers in manual labor, by the clerics in study, teaching, and preaching. It was in his reading of the history of the great missionaries of his Order, during his novitiate, that Junípero reached the determination to go one day to convert the American Indians. He dreamed of following in the footsteps of a great missionary recently (1726) canonized—St. Francis Solano (1549-1610), who had traveled through Peru, Chile, and northern Argentina, playing the violin and, alone and singlehanded in his efforts, baptizing some hundred thousand Redskins.

At the conclusion of his year of probation, Miguel José made his religious profession on September 15, 1731, pronouncing the vows of poverty, chastity, and obedience, and adopting, by design, the name of Brother Juniper, the beloved companion of St. Francis, whom the *Fioretti* show us to have feigned lunacy in order to share the humiliations and abasements of the Saviour. For our Junípero, the vow of poverty was no insurance against all risk of destitution, nor was his profession of the religious life an enrollment that would encourage a distinguished ecclesiastical career. We must note here—so as not to have to repeat it a hundred times in the following pages—that on this day he took an inner vow to strive ever toward saintliness, and to be "poor in spirit," as the *Poverello* had been. It is known that St. Francis, carrying out the Gospel teachings to the letter, regarded money and all other material goods of this world as no more than dirt. It is known also that he found "the perfect joy," and left to mankind an example of which the blessings will never be lost. It was this same conception and realization of poverty, in the literal Gospel sense, which made it possible for Junípero to be what he was and to do what he did.

"To wish to succeed after the world's fashion is to fail," said Jesus, "whereas to lose one's life in God is to gain it." In fact, those who pursue riches, honors, and pleasure never have enough of what they seek; nor are they ever really able to say their "Our Father" rightly. How can they petition God to give them their "daily bread" when they are trying to pile up a reserve stock that would last them a century? How can they pray that His will may be done when they have their personal plans of happiness worked out in advance? And how can they ask to be delivered from evil when it is the favors of Mammon to which they aspire? To seek after the good things of this world, therefore, is to condemn oneself to be abandoned by God, and to doom oneself to restless agitations and vain demands, to bitterness, to fear, often to utter powerlessness. But the man who is "poor in spirit," regulating his desires according to the dispositions of Providence and placing all his hope in it, is never frustrated; his chains fall from him, his soul is free, his prayer is answered, he finds succor for his grief and pain; the hundredfold return that the Saviour promised is bestowed upon him, for him the Gospel miracle is performed—since his humility, his patience, his inner peace render him invulnerable to the blows of fate, equal to any circumstance, ready to accept all tasks that may be laid upon him, capable of moving mountains if need be. . . . It is thus that we see Junípero, who was a happy man in spite of his sufferings, and who, in spite of persecution, succeeded in bringing to fulfillment one of the noblest undertakings that man could ever have attempted for his neighbor's good.

So it is by no means surprising that his profession in the religious life should have marked for him, as he used to say, the most beautiful day of his life. "He never spoke of it without tears in his eyes," Palou wrote. Not for anything in the world would he have failed to celebrate its anniversary. *"Omnia bona pariter cum illa"* (All good things came to me with it), he would say. "I, whom the master of novices used to consider only strong enough to serve at Mass—I found myself all of a sudden in just as good health as the others. I, who was so small that I could not reach up to turn the pages on the lectern—I suddenly grew to be as tall as you see me now." Not that God performed an exaggerated miracle: in 1943 it was confirmed by measurement of his bones that Junípero's height never came to more than five feet two inches.

After making his profession he left the convent of Jesus-without-the-Walls for that of St. Francis, which was in the center of the town and housed about one hundred fifty members of the Order. There he spent seventeen years, the first six in study, the ten following in teaching philosophy and theology. Palou, who lived at the convent of St. Francis from 1740 on, and who wrote twelve thousand lines about his master, devoted only sixty lines to this epoch of his life.

Junípero was admitted to minor orders on December 21, 1731. He became a subdeacon on December 18, 1734, a deacon on March 17, 1736, and a priest several days before Christmas, 1737. His superiors soon advised him to teach philosophy. He pursued his teaching until 1743, when, "wearing the cap of a doctor of theology," his biographer writes, "he progressed to the *Catedra de Prima del Subtil Maestro*," which is to say that he was entrusted with the course in higher dogmatics according to Duns Scotus, the most distinguished chair in the University of Palma. This University, established by Raymond Lull, carried out the philosophical and theological teaching of the Franciscan Duns Scotus, the "subtle Doctor," whom specialists generally consider the most original philosopher of the Middle Ages, and whose theological system differs from that of St. Thomas Aquinas. For long years Junípero won as dazzling victories over the Thomists as the Thomists, in the Dominican convents, were winning over the Scotists. "He acquitted himself with erudition and profundity in this position," Palou writes, so that he was "as highly appreciated in university circles as by his colleagues." Among these last there are two whom we shall often meet again: Fray Francisco Palou and Fray Juan Crespi, both natives of Palma, who were never to leave their master until they were separated by death.

At the San Felipe Neri library in Palma there is an eight-hundred-page manuscript entitled *Compendium Scotisticum*, which contains Junípero's teachings. It has never been published. For his preaching, Junípero needed only the Gospel. That Gospel Junípero preached to the people of Majorca during the academic vacations, which were about four months long. Between 1739 and 1748 his name is mentioned twenty-seven times in the Register of Sermons at St. Francis. He was sought after for Lenten sermons and scheduled lectures. His easy eloquence, his resonant voice, and his fiery earnestness made Father Serra the great orator of the island. Palou calls attention to the panegyric of Raymond Lull which Junípero delivered at the university's patronal celebration on January 25, 1749. "Everyone was full of admiration," he writes. "With my own ears I heard one of his listeners, a professor and brilliant preacher who was himself a little jealous of my master, exclaiming, 'There is a sermon that deserves to be printed in letters of gold!'"

But, like his classroom courses, Junípero's public addresses were never printed at all. That is not too much to be deplored, for his originality and his zeal found their goal and expression elsewhere. In fact he was tired of commenting on Duns Scotus and preaching to the converted sinners of Majorca. He felt a kind of remorse because he was not yet among the Indians and, as he used to say "weeping" to Francisco Palou, because "he had let himself be distracted by academic studies from the resolution of his novitiate."

He would soon be able to carry out that resolve.

Toward the end of 1748 Father Rafael Verger, a professor at the university, learned that Father Mezquia, special representative of San Fernando, was in Spain recruiting missionaries for Mexico. He had even been reliably informed that a friar from Majorca wanted to join them. He passed this news on to his friend Francisco Palou, who took as great an interest in it as he did himself. Both of them made discreet efforts to find out who the colleague in question was but they did not succeed.

San Fernando de Mexico was one of those "apostolic colleges" of Spanish America especially dedicated to the conversion of the Indians who were still in a state of savagery. Founded in 1731, it sent a special representative to Spain every ten or fifteen years, charged with the task of recruitment. This time San Fernando's enlistment officer had orders to bring back thirty-three missionaries.

There was good reason to fear that the superiors of the Province would be opposed to Father Verger's leaving Majorca, since he was a professor whom it would be difficult to replace. "As for me, who was much less necessary and who could try my luck," writes Palou, "I nevertheless did not wish to do so without first consulting my beloved master. So I was getting ready to go and see him, when he himself came knocking on the door of my cell. I had hardly opened my mouth when the tears sprang to his eyes. 'Deeply sorrowful as I was over undertaking this great journey alone, I should have set out all the same,' he said. 'But I resolved to make two novenas to ask God, if it be His will, to give me a comrade. Now that they are finished, I had come to suggest that you accompany me, feeling confident that you would not refuse. . . .' We agreed to begin taking preparatory steps immediately, without breathing a word to anyone."

It was in February, 1785, in the Mission of San Francisco, that Francisco Palou wrote these lines. Thirty-six years had passed— thirty-six years in which he had been "happy to be a missionary." And this happiness, he adds, "I attribute to the prayers of my revered Father Lector Junípero. And I make the formal declaration of this here and now, so as not to be lacking in gratitude."

The man whose word would decide for or against their going to Mexico was Father Velasco, Commissioner General of the Indies. He spoke in the name of the King, and when once he had sent an authorization for a friar's departure to another field, the provincial authorities had nothing to do but submit.

In behalf of himself and Francisco Palou, Junípero wrote secretly to the Commissioner of the Indies. His letter had been sent from Palma at the beginning of January. Father Velasco's reply was received in February, and it was not encouraging. "The delegate of San Fernando has made up his contingent," it said. "There is not one more place available. I will keep a note of your two names, however, and transmit them to Father Mezquia in case there are any defections."

As it turned out, there were. When Father Mezquia arrived at Cadiz with his thirty-three recruits, five of them, Andalusians who had never beheld the sea, took fright at the sight of it. The thought of getting into one of those walnut shells that might well be going to the bottom of the ocean was enough to strip them of their missionary vocation, and they went back home, preferring to continue their quest for salvation on dry land. Father Mezquia made haste to send Junípero the two authorizations he had asked for.

It so happened that this year Junípero was preaching the Lenten sermons at St. Peter's in Petra, his native parish. He had left his friend Palou about the twentieth of February, warning him to watch the mails. Now on Palm Sunday, March 30, on the way to church for the blessing of the palms, Palou encountered a special messenger sent by Father Mezquia. He was the bearer of an envelope containing two authorizations and a letter. In the letter the recruiting agent from San Fernando expressed his surprise that Junípero and his friend were not yet at Cadiz. What was happening? This was the second time that he had sent for them. Had the first authorizations gone astray? Palou learned later that they had been, so to speak, spirited away. Unwilling to accept the loss of a man like Junípero, the Provincial had found it best to hold back Father Mezquia's envelope—at least until the ship should be on the way to Mexico. That would be ten years gained. . . .

Palou showed the "letters patent" to the Provincial, and set out at once for Petra. That same evening Junípero was, like himself, in possession of the diploma that made him a member of the College of San Fernando. He jumped for joy on receiving it. "Hurry!" Father Mezquia was saying. "We must not lose the next sailing on account of you." Since no boat was leaving Palma before April 13, however, Junípero finished his Lenten services as if nothing had happened.

On Easter Sunday, April 6, he preached before his father and mother for the last time, in the church where he had been baptized. On Thursday, April 10, forcing back his tears, he went—as at every separation—to kneel at their feet and ask their blessing. He took more time than usual, held them in a longer embrace, especially his sister Juanita. Then he left the beloved home of his childhood, without telling them that he would never return.

Two

From Palma to Mexico City
by Way of Cadiz and Veracruz
[1749-1750]

The two friends sailed on Sunday, April 13, on an English cargo boat that was to call at Malaga. The farewells in the convent of St. Francis had been moving. Kissing the feet of their confrères, the men who were going away asked the community's forgiveness for the transgressions and bad example of which they had been guilty. The Guardian, Junípero's former professor of philosophy, was weeping so that he could not speak a word. He seized Junípero's hand, and did not let it go until they reached the outer door. Meanwhile, at the last moment, three of the Fathers begged Junípero, in an undertone, to make note of their names to Father Mezquia, in case there should still be need of replacements; among them were Fray Rafael Verger and Fray Juan Crespi.

The crossing from Palma to Malaga took fifteen days. As soon as they went aboard, Junípero had said to his companion, "I do not want you to give me those titles of 'Doctor,' 'Master,' and the like any longer: from now on, we are equals." Of this, Palou writes: "It grated on me at first, as it grated on me to see that on all occasions he behaved as if he were the lesser of us two. People noticed this, and some of them observed, even aloud, that this was a scholar such as was rarely to be seen, who had so much humility, and who gravitated naturally toward saintliness."

To picture the following scene, it must be noted that Junípero's traveling companion was a foot taller than he. And to believe in the episode we are going to set down from that companion's record, it must be remembered that Francisco Palou, author of the ten-volume *Chronicle of the California Missions*, is the most upright of historians, never reporting anything inexactly.

12

The captain of the freighter on which they had taken passage was an Englishman who abominated Spanish monks. Bible in hand, he at once began to lecture our travelers and henceforth left them no peace. Junípero entered into the game in good faith. For every verse quoted by the heretic, he would cite him two that were better. When the other returned to the attack, Dr. Serra would reply with texts and syllogisms that might have worked wonders at the Lullian University, but on the deck of a cargo boat only succeeded in unleashing the captain's wrath and profanity. The captain would then retire, under pretext of ship maneuvers; but he would soon reappear, armed with new texts, and they would go back to the dispute—from which the captain emerged in a state of wild fury. The night having restored his strength, he would be back again in the morning to renew the combat. "He came back to it so often," Palou writes, "that he hardly left us time to recite our breviary. One day at the height of his rage he threatened to throw us into the sea, adding that he was going to go straight on to London without calling at Malaga.

" 'Into the sea?' I answered. 'Just try to throw us into the sea! And if you do not stop for us at Malaga, I will call upon my King, who will complain to yours; and you will find yourself roosting on the gallows-tree in London!' "

This intervention by the tall and powerful Palou ended the religious controversy for that day. But the next day at nightfall it began again. As Junípero was walking on the deck absorbed in meditation, the captain came along with a new text. He had made sure that Palou was not there; besides, he had probably been drinking. What was it that led Junípero, by way of refutation, to tell him that his Protestant Bible was not good, being incomplete and badly translated? However that may be, the brutal creature, losing all self-control, seized the little friar by the throat and began to scream: "Recant, recant, petty monk of Satan! Recant, or I'll strangle you and throw you to the fishes!" He had such a strangle hold, indeed, that the victim fainted; then he went off and left him there, unconscious on the deck.

When Junípero came to himself, he went down to wake Palou. "I think," he said, "that the gold and silver and all the treasures we are going to seek in the Indies may well come our way before ever we reach Malaga." He was speaking as a martyr who sees the hour of final torture drawing near. "For the rest," he added, "I have nothing to reproach myself with: it was the captain who began and wanted to continue the discussions. I had to answer him, since the honor of the holy Faith was at stake."

The disciple blushed with shame at having slept so soundly while his master was being strangled. "We stayed up all night, ready for any eventuality," he writes. Nothing more happened, however, for the reason that the sturdy Palou was never one step away from the undersized Junípero after this, and that even the most impassioned apologists do not lose the instinct of self-preservation to that extent.

After a pause of five days at the Franciscan convent in Malaga, the travelers embarked on a Mallorcan freighter that landed them at Cadiz on the seventh of May.

Father Mezquia gave them a great welcome: these were two precious recruits who had come to him, and who, besides, were bringing him three more. . . . Actually, the contingent for San Fernando fell short of being complete: the five deserters had been followed by others; of the thirty-three volunteers there were no more than nineteen left. To the embarrassed enlistment agent, Junípero gave the names of Fathers Crespi, Vicens, and Verger; these came hurrying from Palma, thus bringing the number of departing missionaries to twenty-four. Nine were still needed to attain the figure fixed by the royal ordinance; the difficulty met with in getting them together held back the actual departure until August 29.

Meanwhile, the old couple in Barracas Street in Petra were now realizing that they would never see their child again, and there was no end to their weeping. Junípero wrote to them a great many times during that period—three and one-half months—of waiting. As they could not read, he addressed his letters to his father's cousin, Fray Francisco Serra, a priest in the San Bernardino convent in Petra. The following letter, written in the Mallorcan language, is the only one that has been found; we reproduce half of it:

To Father Fray Francisco Serra:
This is my letter of farewell. We are all packed. In four days the *Villasota* will have weighed anchor and we shall have left Cadiz.

My dear, dear friend, words cannot express what I am feeling at this hour of separation. I know that my parents are in mortal grief;

at this moment I commend them to you once more, and tell you again that it is you upon whom I rely for their comforting. Ah, if it were only possible for me to make them share my own immeasurable happiness, they themselves would urge me on! Could they dream, indeed, of a nobler vocation for their son than that of apostolic missionary?

Advanced in age as they are, and with their days numbered, the life that remains to them on this earth is only a moment in relation to eternity. Brief, alas, would have been the consolation which my presence would have given them. Would it be reasonable, and in conformity with the will of God, to cling henceforth to that? It is better to renounce seeing each other again in this world, so that we may deserve to be united forever in heaven.

Tell them, make them realize, that I suffer deeply in no longer being near them, as I once was, to solace their old age. But they know that what is essential must come before all else; and what is essential is for us to carry out the divine will. God alone, indeed, is responsible for my going away; it is His love alone which has snatched me beyond reach of their tenderness. May this same love so inspire them that they may generously accept our separation! Their confessor will say this to them again; may they listen well to his counsel: they will derive from it that holy patience, that resignation to the divine will, which will restore their souls' serenity; and they will feel that the Lord has never called down such a blessing upon their home. By grace of repeating to themselves, as I repeat to them, that it is Our Lord and no one else who is the author of their ordeal, they will come to find, at last, that His yoke is easy, and their tribulation will be transformed into a calm happiness.

Since nothing in this world is worthy of our finding affliction in its loss, is it not better to concentrate our endeavors on fulfilling God's will and preparing ourselves for a good death? With a righteous death, everything is saved; without a death in righteousness, all is lost.

May they come to esteem themselves happy, these dear parents of mine, in having a son who, unworthy and a sinner as he is, prays at the altar for them every morning, with all his heart, imploring that God will give them the necessities of life, patience in trials, resignation to His holy will, the grace to live in peace and friendship with those about them, and, when at last God's summons comes, the grace of a sanctified death! In thinking of me—my beloved parents, and also my little sister Juanita and my brother-in-law Miguel—may they devote themselves wholly to beseeching God that I may become a good priest and a good friar. . . .

You remember, my dear Father, what you said to me some fifteen years ago, when, having received extreme unction, you believed your-self close to appearing before God? . . . I recall your words as if they had fallen this very moment from your lips; and with them I recall the promise I made to you, as you asked me, then: "Always to be a good son of St. Francis." Very well, then! It is to carry out your will, which is also the will of God, that I am now on the way to Mexico.

My dear Mother, as for you, I know that this is what you too have always asked of God for me, in your prayers. He has answered them already, in setting me upon the path on which I have entered. Be happy then, beloved Mother; and when you suffer say again, with your son, "Blessed be God! May His holy will be done!"

After thus addressing himself to his parents, he turned next to Juanita. She, too, had been near death some time before. "In God's restoration of her health," he wrote, "it is made evident that He intended her to be the mainstay of our old parents."

May she, and her husband with her, show patience, respect, and com-passion toward them; may they two live together as a good husband and wife who love each other; may they bring up their three chil-dren well; may the entire family continue in the practice of piety, going regularly to church, keeping close to the sacraments, assidu-ously making the Stations of the Cross.

And now we are parting, promising, as we do so, to pray for one another a very great deal. God will be the close protector of us all; He will give us His grace in this life and His glory in the life to come. Farewell then, my cherished Father! farewell, my fond Mother! farewell, little sister Juanita! farewell, Miguel, my dear brother-in-law! You will be able, each and all of you, to count upon the deep feeling in the heart of the one who is going away. Farewell! Farewell!

After these farewells to the members of his immediate family, he again addresses his cousin, Fray Francisco:

Farewell to you, Father Serra, my very dear colleague! Henceforth my letters will be of necessity less frequent; but you love my parents and they love you. That is why I commend them to you again, to you first of all; I commend them also to the loving-kindness of the Father Guardian, the Father Vicar, and the Father Master of Novices. If the last-named two could be present at the reading of this letter, I am sure that this would give pleasure to my parents and would add to their solace. . . .

Your affectionate friend in Our Lord,
Fray Junípero Serra, very unworthy priest.

This letter throws clear light upon Junípero's entire existence. Into his farewells to those he most cherished in this earthly life he put all his ethics, his aesthetics, his science, and his philosophy, the depths and the substratum of his soul. In his eyes nothing existed except what was eternal; to him, this world was not an end in itself; time and space had meaning and value only as they offered ways of doing, and of loving, the will of God. These divine intentions were revealed to Junípero in the Gospel, in the commands of his superiors, and in the ineluctable course of events. In actual fact, we shall never see him occupied with any other purpose than to carry out God's will with his whole heart.

The departing missionaries were divided into two groups, of which the first, comprising a President and twenty friars, sailed on the *Villasota* on August 28. Junípero and Palou were in this company.[1] The crossing from Cadiz to Veracruz took a hundred days. In addition to the Franciscans, seven Dominicans and a number of other passengers were aboard. "There were a lot too many," writes Palou, who was always to remember the discomforts and vexations of the voyage.

The worst hardship was the shortage of drinking water. "For two weeks," writes Junípero, "our rations were reduced to a quarter of a litre [about one-half pint] every twenty-four hours. There were moments when my throat was burning so, I would have drunk slime." We know this because he tells of it in a letter he wrote his cousin Fray Francisco Serra from Veracruz; but he never complained on the ship. "One would have said he was the only person who was not suffering from thirst," Palou writes. To those who wondered at him and would ask him his secret, he replied, "I have observed that the best way of saving one's saliva is to eat little and talk still less."

This torture came to an end with the arrival at Puerto Rico, where the *Villasota* lay at anchor from the eighteenth to the thirty-first of October.

Our missionaries had first gone to the Hermitage of the Immaculate Conception, on the Ramparts. After that, Junípero was the guest of the Servants of Mary. On the very first evening he had been besought to "address a word of spiritual consolation"

---

[1] The following description of Junípero is given in the passenger list: "Medium stature, swarthy complexion, dark eyes and hair, scant beard."

to the faithful who came to recite the Rosary with the hermit in the chapel. "I bring you word," he said to them, "that for the consolation of your souls we are going to preach a great mission for you. It will continue as long as the time is granted us." Then he urged those present to take good advantage of this privilege.

"What is this, this mission?" demanded the President, who had asked him to occupy the pulpit.

"Did you not ask me to bring them consolation?" the orator responded. "Now what is better for that than a good mission?"

The sermons began the next day. They were so successful that the cathedral was filled to overflowing. They lasted for a week. Most of the Puerto Ricans had not made their confession since the last mission, preached nine years before by Spanish Franciscans likewise on their way to San Fernando at the time. Now the confessionals were always full. "We went into them as early as three or four o'clock in the morning," Junípero wrote to his cousin Fray Francisco on December 14, 1749, "and we remained there until midnight." The general satisfaction found expression in an extraordinary generosity. "In spite of the contract, the captain had refused to feed us at a port of call. The populace supplied the deficiency. The Mallorcans of the town especially distinguished themselves. Learning that there were compatriots of their own among us, they brought fruit, preserves, candles, lemonade, money to buy meat, and a hundred other things in profusion. We still had some left when we reached Veracruz. I assure you that our colleagues sang the praises of the people of Majorca on that occasion!"

The Andalusian mountaineers who had gone back home had not been mistaken as to the dangers in store for the *Villasota*. Twice the ship just escaped foundering. The first time was in the Puerto Rico roadstead on October 31. "As we were leaving the harbor," Junípero writes, "the wind drove us on the reefs, where we thought we would sink like a stone. We were still in barely two fathoms of water. When the cannon boomed to sound the alarm, there was general lamentation in the town, where it was believed that we were lost. The Governor sent all the boats to our rescue; they took us ashore, and we spent the night in the town's central square. The next day (All Saints') we went aboard again, and the vessel made its way off without any accident."

They were in greater peril a month later: "We had arrived off Veracruz, when a north wind reached the proportions of a cyclone and threw the *Villasota* back toward the open sea. For days it drifted at the mercy of the storm. On the night of December 3 it was thought to be lost, and many of the passengers prepared for death: the mainmast appeared to be split; the hull was breaking up; the pumps no longer sufficed to draw the water from the bunkers; the crew, in a state of complete distraction, were calling upon the captain to let the ship go aground on the coast—in this way, they said to him, a few lives at least might be saved."

It was then that the friars aboard made a vow. Each one wrote the name of a saint on a card; the cards were placed in an urn; they all recited aloud the orison of the Holy Ghost and that of all the saints; then they drew lots. Junípero had written the name of St. Francis Solano; Francisco Palou, that of St. Michael; it was the name of St. Barbara, whose feast day it was, that was drawn from the urn. "We all cried, '*Viva Santa Barbara!*' Soon the sea grew calm and a favorable wind blew across our sails, bearing the vessel straight into port. Everyone including the sailors believed that we had been saved by a miracle. We carried out our vow on the tenth of December before we separated. On that day Dominicans and Franciscans sang a solemn Mass in honor of St. Barbara in the church of St. Francis in Veracruz. The Dominican Prior officiated, and the special sermon was entrusted to my incapacity."

We have two records of this ocean crossing; Palou's, in his *Vida*, and Junípero's, in his letter of December 14, 1749, to his cousin Fray Francisco. The two reports agree, except on two points that actually amount to one.

Speaking of the "discomforts and vexations of the voyage," Junípero says that "there were only a few. The most serious thing of all," he adds, "is that I did not manage to bear them with patience." Francisco Palou declares, on the contrary, that his master "was always even-tempered and smiling, that he never uttered the slightest complaint, that his patience was the wonder and admiration of everyone." On the night of December 4, when all believed themselves lost, Junípero alone, Palou writes, "preserved a complete serenity. I asked him, 'Then you are not afraid?' 'I was a little afraid at the beginning,' he answered, 'but the thought of the ideal that is leading us to the Indies got the better of my fright at once.' "

More remarkable still is the way the mission was reported by the one and the other of the two men. "No one failed to take advantage of this opportunity of putting his conscience in order," Palou writes. "It was an extraordinary success; and, by general opinion, the credit for it belonged to the revered Father Junípero."

Palou, who spoke thus in 1785, would not have expressed himself otherwise in 1749, when he was sending on information to his colleagues and friends in Palma. Junípero was unwilling on any account to have such reports get about; so his letter focused things otherwise.

"It was decided," he wrote, "that the sermons in the cathedral should be preached alternately by the Father President and myself. An undeserved honor was thus done me, which embarrassed me very much. Between his preaching and mine there was the same difference as there is between gold and straw, fire and snow, day and night. When the Father President spoke, the entire congregation would be given over to tears and sighs. When it was I in the pulpit, you would not have perceived the slightest sign of emotion, although I might be treating of the most moving subjects and putting all my force into my voice. Everybody was struck by this, and it was a good mortification for my pride. The truth is that I lack that inner flame from which are born the speeches that can enflame men's hearts. Have pity on me, I beseech you; bestow your charity upon me in asking God that I may love Him with all my strength, and become worthy of so sublime a ministry."

Humility is that unworldly virtue which is most striking in Junípero. He must be expected always to speak like this of himself. And this was no mere mannerism of style in his writing: like the saints, he believed what he was saying, and he wanted others to believe it.

Had he an inferiority complex?

The man who is afflicted with an inferiority complex is in despair over his nothingness, tries to forget it, goes through life wanting to persuade others that he is something he is not. Thence comes his touchiness, his vanity, his hunger for titles and decorations, his need of ostentation and, sometimes, of vengeance.

The saint is humble, which is a very different thing. Measuring the abyss which separates the creature from the Creator, and recognizing gifts from on high in all that the creature has; aspiring to be perfect as the Heavenly Father is perfect, and refusing, for his own part, to be above his Master—for these reasons and a hundred others which he finds in meditation and in prayer, the humble in heart holds himself to be nothing. But he knows that the others are nothing, also, and he does not wish for their praise. In addition to being without value, such praise seems to him to be without justice, since it pays honor to man for what belongs to God. As for that passion he has for making himself the least of men, this comes from the fact that, not passing judgment upon his brothers, he believes them to be better than himself, feeling certain that if they had been granted such richness of grace as he they would have profited more richly from it. Forgetful of himself, the man who lives according to the Gospel thinks only of others, that he may serve them, and of God, his only love, his sole happiness.

We shall see, for the rest, whether Junípero's humility kept him from undertakings and successes from which a great many proud men would have drawn back and in which they would have failed!

Two hundred sixty miles, as the crow flies, separate Veracruz from the City of Mexico; but the distance by road is made almost a third longer by four mountain ranges, of which the highest points (Ciblatepetl, Macultepec, Malinche, and Popocatepetl, giant peaks with snow-clad summits) soar respectively to a height of 19,762, 14,661, 14,700, and 19,558 feet.

Without waiting for the mule-train sent by the Viceroy for the new arrivals, Junípero set out on foot, accompanied by a colleague from Andalusia. "They took their breviaries with them as their only luggage," writes Francisco Palou, who had recently been so ill as to be near death, and, although slowly recovering his health, was unable this time to go with his master. For half the distance the road at this period was no more than an Indian trail, which would at times climb into the clouds and at other times be lost in low marshlands.

To persuade his missionaries always to rely upon God, Junípero used often to recall three episodes of that journey. . . .

The black darkness of night had fallen when our travelers, at the end of a long day's march, came to the bank of a stream swollen to flood-tide by the melting snows. Finding no fording place that would make it possible for them to reach the next village, they said a prayer. It was no sooner finished than they thought they noticed the outline of a man in movement on the opposite bank.

"By the Blessed Virgin, is that a Christian who is passing there?" Junípero called out.

"It is a Christian!" a man's voice answered. "What can I do for you?"

"We are looking for the ford; do you know where it is?"

"Go back up the stream with me; I will take you to it."

He led them, forthwith, to his own fine *hacienda*. This was far away, and it would have been hard to explain how this gentleman happened to have left it at such an hour to go wandering about in such a place. When Junípero questioned him about this, his answers were evasive. He welcomed his guests heartily. When they set out on their way again in the morning they saw that there was frost over everything. What would have become of us, they asked each other, if we had had to spend the night out-of-doors? . . .

On the following day, after walking fifteen miles under a broiling sun, they sat down in a wilderness, with their throats on fire. And just then, out of the blue, so to speak, a horseman appeared.

"Where are Your Reverences going?" he asked.

They named the *hacienda* where they were counting on spending the night.

"That is still a long distance away," the horseman said. "Anyway, eat this pomegranate—it will do you good."

They shared it for fun, for they would have needed a dozen apiece! Yet it did suffice to quench their thirst. . . .

It was again a man on horseback who came to their aid the next day. Underestimating the length of the day's march, they had allowed a beggar to rid them prematurely of their store of provisions; and now, so faint they could go no further, they were resting on a grassy slope when a horseman brought his mount to a stop beside them.

"Take this!" he said, and handed them a corn loaf, half raw.

At first they did not dare taste this mess, for fear of being sick. Then hunger constrained them to bite into it. It was so good one would have said it was a bit of the best pastry, made of semolina and cheese; and it restored effective strength to their limbs for the rest of the day.

At Jalapa they lodged at the Franciscan convent, a kind of fortress built on a peak where the view extended some seventy-five miles over the sea. They passed through Perote, perched at an altitude of 3,280 feet, and through Las Vergas, 1,640 feet higher; they traversed fertile plains, deserts, valleys, gorges, vast and wonderful forests; they climbed hill slopes and abrupt rises, went over passes where the glacial wind blew at hurricane force; and at last they reached Puebla, where they spent Christmas night with their Franciscan confrères.

It was between Cholula and Amecameca, on this journey, that an accident occurred which was to have curiously lasting results. In his sleep, Junípero was bitten in his left foot by a scorpion. He aggravated the injury by scratching the sore, with the result that the poison spread up into his leg; he became half crippled for the rest of his life because of it; it was often believed that he was even stricken by cancer, and we shall see that on a number of occasions he almost died. But he did not wish it to be spoken of, and when anyone did mention it, he would cut him short with *"No es cosa de cuidado!"* (It is not of the slightest consequence; there is no reason for bothering about it.)

Two days after the accident, he succeeded in dragging himself as far as the City of Mexico. On the evening of December 31, the two travelers arrived at the sanctuary of Our Lady of Guadalupe. They spent the night in prayer there, and the next day, the first of January, 1750, they went into the church of San Fernando. It was the hour of sext. Junípero was heartened and inspired by the grave serenity of the friars in reciting the office: "We have come from far away, and trials have not been wanting," he said to his companion, "but to belong henceforth to so fervent a community is to be well recompensed for our pains."

Three

The Discovery and Conversion of Mexico

In an area of 1,700,000 square miles, Mexico, or New Spain, had at that time a population estimated at 6,000,000, made up as follows: 70,000 Spaniards, 1,100,000 Creoles, 2,400,000 Redskins (or Indians), and as many half-breeds.[1] These statistics are undoubtedly inaccurate; there must have been more pure-blooded Indians, but no one knew how many. Any census-taker who risked going to count them without strong military support, at least in certain regions of Texas, Sonora, and the Apache country, would never have come back alive.

Roughly, the land of Mexico extended from the fourteenth to the thirty-eighth parallel, from Guatemala to the present city of Santa Fe. It comprised two "kingdoms," two "governments," and nine "provinces." The two kingdoms were those of Mexico (Mexico, Tlaxcala, Puebla, Oaxaca, Michoacan) and Nuevo Galicia (Jalisco, Zacatecas, Colima); the two governments were those of Nuevo Biscaya (Durango, Chihuahua) and Yucatan (Merida, Tabasco, Campeche); the nine provinces, with lines badly defined in the northern section, were Nuevo León, Tamaulipas, Texas, Coahuila, Sinaloa, Sonora, Nayarit, Santa Fé, and Lower California. To these nine provinces, Junípero was to add a tenth, the most beautiful of all: Upper California.

It seems that, a year after Christopher Columbus reached America, Pope Alexander VI divided between Portugal and Spain the territories that these two countries had discovered or were yet to discover. The bull *Inter Cetera*, of June 28, 1493, drew a line

[1] The term "Creole" is used to denote whites born of Spanish parents in Mexico; the "half-breeds" were Indians (Redskins) with some Spanish blood. Believing that it was the Indies which were discovered in the discovery of America, the Spaniards gave the name "Indians" (*Indios*) to the men they found there, with the result that in their language the same term is applied to the Indians of America and those of Asia. In English, those of Asia are called, rather, Hindus.

from one pole to the other, passing 250 miles to the west of the Azores and Cape Verde; what lay to the east of this imaginary line was Portugal's, the rest belonged to Spain. The following year, the Treaty of Tordesillas moved the "line of demarcation" 675 miles to the west; the King of Portugal thus gained Brazil. A half-century later, Francis I of France demanded to be shown the clause in the "last will and testament" of Adam which excluded the French from the apportionment of the globe. But France and England, occupied with their wars of religion, had let the hour go by, and the Emperor Charles V held sway henceforth over three-fourths of the American continent.

It was Cortez who had brought him Mexico.

Born at Medellín, Spain, in 1485, and arriving in San Domingo in 1504, Hernándo Cortez had set out from Cuba on February 10, 1519, with eleven boats, a hundred sailors, five hundred eight soldiers, sixteen horses, thirty crossbows, ten bronze cannon, four falconets, and thirteen arquebuses. On April 21 he landed on the beach of Ulua; the next day (Good Friday) he founded the town of Veracruz nearby, in honor of the True Cross, and on November 8 he made his entry into the City of Mexico. Driven out of it the year after, he reoccupied what was left of it on August 13, 1521, and on that day Spain established itself there for three centuries to come.

"Nothing like this has been done in all history," he wrote Charles V. How many tribes existed at that time in the country of Mexico? Sixty? Six hundred? In the sense in which Palou and Crespi understood the word, there were hundreds; for they themselves counted as many as forty as late as 1780, between San Diego and San Francisco alone. At all events, if every Redskin in 1519 had thrown even a handful of earth on the invaders, they would have been smothered to the last man. In addition to his horses, his arquebuses, and his cannon, however, Cortez had the genius of the founders of empire, and companions of prodigious valor. One of them, Bernal Diaz, took part in 119 combats. Cortez had cut off everyone's retreat by running his boats aground.

Their mounts, their guns, and even their beards inspired awe in the Indians, who, as is known, had hardly any hair on their chins. The white men were taken for demigods, and Cortez, their leader, for no other than Quetzalcoatl, an ancient Toltec divinity who had one day disappeared with the assurance that he would come back. But neither Montezuma nor the high priest of Vichilobos [2] actually wished for his return. From Mexico City they sent Cortez discs of gold as large as wagon wheels, hundreds of pounds of precious fabrics, jewels, and slaves, while calling upon him to go back, with his company, to where he came from. Cortez assured Montezuma's envoys that he came to bring greetings from the King, Don Carlos, to their master, and swore by his beard that he would not leave until he had fulfilled his mission.

Montezuma was "king" or "emperor" of the Aztecs, a cannibal people from the north who for the last hundred fifty years had occupied the central part of Mexico. Their rule extended, more or less effectively, from the fifteenth to the twentieth parallel. They had picture-writing and a rudimentary but fairly flourishing industrial life, practiced polygamy and homosexuality, and had developed a religious and military organization on a communal basis. The capital of the "kingdom," built on a lake, was magnificent; the servility of the people was beyond all bounds. It had been said that their reflections were nurtured on "the thought of death"; we shall see that it was rather "the thought of causing death" that obsessed them. The mere state of being drunk would impel them to kill; that is why Aztec law made drunkenness a capital crime for persons under seventy. Cunning, industrious, and good warriors, the Aztecs extorted tribute from many tribes, wresting from them gold, food supplies, soldiers, and victims to Vichilobos and his infernal fellow deities. "There is not one year," the High Cacique of Campoal told Cortez, "in which Montezuma does not take four thousand youths from us, to be offered to his gods." The alliances the conquistador formed with these subjugated tribes contributed enormously to his victory.

Cortez deceived everyone except his King; he kept Montezuma a prisoner, put his successor Coauhtémoc to death, rebuilt the City of Mexico after destroying it, succeeded in bringing all the territories dominated by the Aztecs under his own rule. After an unlucky expedition into Honduras he had to go to Spain in 1527 to

[2] It was the Spaniards who called him this, and also gave the title of "king" and "emperor" to Montezuma. Before their arrival Mexico was called Tenochtitlán; Vichilobos was called Huitzilopochtli, and Montezuma, their military chief and "lord of lords," bore the title of Tlacatecuhtli. His second-in-command, whom he appointed himself, was head of the police and the government officials, and at the same time priest of Cihuacahuatl, the mother of Vichilobos. The Aztecs spoke "Nahuatl."

defend himself against his enemies. The King, to whom he had sent great piles of gold, named him Marquis del Valle and "Captain General . . . of the southern seas." Returning to Mexico and now as rich as Croesus, Cortez fitted up ships at his own expense and launched out on the Pacific in search of new lands. His only discovery was of Lower California, where he was not able to maintain his position. New legal proceedings forced him to return to Spain in 1540; but this time he was forbidden to set foot again in the country of Mexico. Then he took part with his sons in an expedition to Algeria, and came back in very poor health; whereupon he arranged bequests for charity, provided for the future of all the children, legitimate and illegitimate, that had been born to him, and prepared for death, which came to him in 1547.

Charles V, who had refused the governance of Mexico to Cortez, organized the new "kingdom" immediately; and it was all so well arranged and regulated that the system established then was still in force during Junípero's time.

The country was divided basically into *municipia* directed by *alcaldes;* these were subject to the provincial governors, who, in turn, owed obedience to the Viceroy. The Viceroy was deputy for the sovereign, and governed in his name. He was Captain General of the Army, which in Junípero's time was made up of eight thousand foot soldiers and two thousand cavalrymen; he was Vice Patron of the Church, and he presided over the *Junta,* or *Audiencia.* "He can do everything," the Edict of Establishment declared, "except what is forbidden." He was appointed for three years, but the King could extend his term; as a matter of fact, four years was the average term of the sixty-two Viceroys who followed one another in the Palace in Mexico City from 1535 to 1821.

"The Viceroys pass and the *Audiencia* remains," it was said. Composed of some fifteen eminent personages—"fiscal agents," "public prosecutors," "advocates in criminal law"—the Junta (*Real Audiencia,* or *Junta de Real Hacienda*) sat several times a week, dispensed justice, dealt with ecclesiastical and financial questions, and could take exception to certain decrees proposed by the Viceroy. It constituted his council, and checked the administration of his office; it took his place while awaiting his arrival, or when he died. The council and the Viceroy were bound, moreover, to "work in complete accord for the glory of God, the maintenance of the rights of the King, and the welfare of his subjects."

At long intervals a Visitor General sent by the King would appear to see what was going on and to take such measures as might be fitting; the powers with which he was endowed were a restriction on those of the Junta and the Viceroy.

Finally—and soaring, so to speak, above all the others—there was the Council of the Indies, at Madrid. Established in 1524 and originally composed of four members, it had twenty-nine in Junípero's time. Everything that had to do with the lands overseas came within its province; it was this Council, particularly, which worked out the provisions of the Law of the Indies in pace with such needs as might arise, and made the important appointments; it was this Council that the King consulted, as a court of last resort, before making decisions.

As the right of conquest, for the Spaniards, was justified only by the duty of conversion, the missionaries had followed closely in the path of the conquerors.

The first missionaries to Mexico were three Flemish Franciscans: Jan Dekker (Juan de Tecto), Jan van den Auwera (Juan de Aora), and the celebrated Pedro de Gante, bastard cousin of Charles V. They were joined in 1524 by twelve Spaniards—"the Twelve Apostles"—who founded the convent of St. Francis in Mexico City. The third Franciscan mission, composed of twenty friars, landed in 1529: Sahagun, the greatest expert in Aztec matters, belonged to this missionary band. In 1526, twelve Dominicans had arrived, of whom five died almost immediately and four took ship again; the three who remained were placed under the direction of Father Betanzos. Seven Augustinians made their appearance in 1536.

Something happened then which had never come to pass since the time of the Apostles—or even, it seems, since the beginning of the world: this was indeed the first time that human beings should have looked upon other human beings and taken them for beasts. It happened, so, among these evangelists who had hurried here from so far away: there were those who declared that there was no reason for evangelization; and this because the Mexican natives were not men. Such, if we are to believe his accusers, was the opinion of the Dominican Betanzos.

What was the basis of his reasoning, which unleashed a tempest

and provoked the intervention of the Pope? That question must
be asked, and answered.

"Everywhere," wrote Bernal Diaz, "in the villages through
which we passed between Veracruz and Mexico, there were temples and oratories where human sacrifice had taken place; there
were as many of them as there are churches and chapels in Castille." Everywhere, too, Cortez and his soldiers noticed large cages,
made of rows of stakes, in which young men and girls were awaiting the day of their immolation. They were well fed; they were
given hot baths; care was taken, by providing them with mates,
that the vexation of continence should not hinder their fattening
process. The richer a landowner was, the more cages he had near
his house. In the town of Cholula, where an ambush had been
prepared, the invaders saw the urns that were awaiting *them,* as
well as the salt, garlic, and tomatoes that would be used in cook-
ing them.

They were completely enlightened when, compelled to show
them his gods, Montezuma led them to the great pyramid of Mexico. It rose above the sacred citadel where, under the direction of
the high priest, five thousand priests, officiating priestly helpers,
and young clerics exercised their sacred functions. The visitors
climbed the 114 steps that led to the sanctuary of Vichilobos, god
of war, and of Tezcatepuca, goddess of the moon.

There, at the top, was the slaughterhouse.

Above the slightly convex tables of stone, and upon the men
bent double who serve as altars, in the midst of dances and chor-
uses of joy, the priest with his long hair and his wide-sweeping
black robe is at work. Assisted by the men who are holding the
victim in position, he lays the chest open with one great stroke
of his obsidian knife, snatches out the heart, presents it, palpitat-
ing, to Vichilobos, then throws it on the brazier where the in-
cense burns. He smears with blood the snout of the god, sprinkles
with blood the walls of the sanctuary, wipes his bloody hands on
his robe and runs them through his hair; then he begins again,
while the victims roll over and over to the bottom of the great
stairway, to be carved up there by his colleagues. The thighs and
other choice parts are set aside for the devout public, the entrails
for the snakes, jackals, and other sacred animals; the denuded skulls
are hung in festoons on poles. A cave has been discovered which
contained 135,000 of them.

The slaughter is never interrupted, for Vichilobos is insatiable, and the same is true of his neighbor Tezcatepuca, and likewise of the other divinities of the great temple, the smaller temples, and the private oratories. On festival days—and the Aztec calendar is full of them—it is by hundreds and by thousands that the victims are butchered. In 1487, at the time of the dedication of the new temple, the human sacrifices numbered, some say 72,344, others say 80,400, the most moderate estimate is 20,000—and this in four days. In ordinary times, it is enough to offer from twenty to forty thousand victims in a year. When there is a plethora of fresh meat, it is cut into thin strips that are dried for preserving.

"There was no banquet that would not call for human flesh," writes Bernal Diaz. The devotees had it consecrated beforehand; the others dispensed with that. Torquemada avers that twenty thousand children a year were immolated in the City of Mexico. Like the wolves that do not eat each other, the Aztecs did not feed upon the flesh of their fellow countrymen. That is why they never stopped going out to war, to lay in provisions elsewhere. Their law permitted them, however, to sacrifice slaves, so that among the rich, at least, there was never a shortage.

It was these horrors that moved Betanzos to assign the Indians of Mexico to the kingdom of the lower animals. It was not possible, he said, to apply to them the definition of man: *animal rationalis,* "a being endowed with reason and goodness."

Obviously, every man has his outbreaks of unreason and ferocity: in war, for example. And even in time of peace there is the murderer and the sadist. But war, like anger, is a seizure; and the sadist is a monster. The human species is not defined by its anomalies and its monstrosities. Now, these were an everyday matter for the Indian; what to man is exceptional and inadmissible was to him the normal state of affairs. Look at him, indeed, feeling the habitual need to carve up his fellow creature, delightedly chewing up and swallowing his flesh; taking a vow to clothe himself in his skin until it rots away and falls thus from his shoulders; leaning down to enjoy the spasms of the child and young woman whose hearts are being wrested from their bodies; knifing his best friend when he is drunk and his subconscious is unfettered, as others, in such moments, laugh, sing, weep, and have only too great a tendency toward maudlin sentimentality. . . .

Recognize the fact, then, that cruelty, which arouses remorse in the breast of man, was for the Indian the supreme sensual pleasure, which filled the sum of his desires and brought him rest. And do not say that the fault lies with Vichilobos! The gods always reflect the aspirations of those who discover or invent them. Vichilobos was the Aztec expressing his true nature, which, once more, had nothing in common with the nature of humanity.[3] Betanzos concluded that, inasmuch as the Indian's soul was not "reasonable and immortal," the creature was not qualified to receive the Faith. As this missionary was also a prophet, he foretold the imminent disappearance of this zoological species; and as he was a good man at heart, he asked that in the meantime the Redskins should be kindly treated.

Among the fifty priests then in Mexico, how many were there who shared this opinion? A half-dozen, perhaps. But it was eagerly adopted by many Spaniards who were interested only in taking advantage of the Indian women and robbing the Indian men. It became so much a part of current speech that, in Junípero's time, the whites were still called *la gente de razón* ("the people endowed with reason"), to distinguish them from the Redskins.

The Franciscans waged a unanimous war against this extravagant thesis. They, for their part, saw the Indians as men possessed of the devil, who should be wrested at the earliest possible moment from his power. This was also the opinion of the first conquerors. "Great Emperor," said Cortez to Montezuma, "how is it that the profound reflections of your sublime genius do not bring you to the recognition of your errors? By my beard, I swear to you that Vichilobos and your other gods are devils." He himself and his companions were so convinced that they were dealing with demoniacs that, for fear of touching the devil, they made their chaplain Father Olmedo exorcize and baptize the Indian women before they used them for their pleasure.[4]

[3] It is we ourselves who formulate the minor premise of Betanzos' syllogism, which rests upon authenticated facts. Olmedo and the Franciscans also made use of it in their reasoning; but it served them as a demonstration of demonic possession. The work of the Jesuit José Acosta (born in 1539) shows clearly that in the middle of the sixteenth century it was still generally believed that the Aztecs were possessed of the devil.

[4] We do not take it upon ourselves to justify Father Olmedo, a friar of the Order of Our Lady of Mercy, who was universally revered in his lifetime, and universally mourned when he died in Mexico City in 1524. As for Father Betanzos, A. M. Carreño has attempted to prove that he has been traduced, and that he never alleged that the Indians were fundamentally incapable of reason. (Cf. *Fray Domingo de Betanzos*, by Alberto Mario Carreño [Mexico, 1934];

The Junta let it be said that the Indians were possessed, but it did not tolerate the theory that judged them animals. On May 4, 1533, the Prosecutor Salméron wrote to Charles V: "The devil has carried off a great victory in entering into the skin of this Betanzos. . . ." On May 11 and 15, and again on August 8 of the same year, Bishop Fuenleal, President of the Junta, besought the King to intervene in the matter. His three letters may be summed up as follows:

The theology of Betanzos is doing us appalling harm. Not to speak of the fact that it is an offense to God and Your Majesty, it encourages the Spaniards to treat the Indians like beasts. Moreover, this Dominican does not know their language, and it is from lack of zeal, so as not to have to convert them, that he sticks to his error. It is the Franciscans who are right, and everyone can bear witness that their apostolate is obtaining magnificent results. We are greatly in need of apostles; but, for pity's sake, may the Council of the Indies send here only those friars whom it knows! And, let it be said in passing, may the four Dominicans who have returned to Spain be obliged to remain there!

They did remain there. Others came, who were possessed of admirable zeal and excellent judgment. Betanzos had to keep silent and change his views. Moreover, there began to be a great deal of talk about an intervention embarrassing to his theology, to say the least. . . .

On December 9 and four times after that, the Blessed Virgin Mary had appeared, it was said, to Juan Diego, an authentic Redskin, no doubt a former cannibal, who attended the Franciscan

Divulgación Historica [Mexico], May, June, and July, 1940; and "Pope Paul III and the American Indians," by Dr. Lewis Hanke, *Harvard Theological Review*, XX, No. 2 [1937].) Whatever may be said, however, of the theologian whom some claimed as their support in regarding the Mexicans as mere animals, it remains no less true that this opinion took a hold on men's minds, since the Pope deemed himself in duty bound to condemn it, and the Spanish theologians (notably the Dominican Vittoria) in duty bound to refute it.

Fathers Olmedo and Betanzos are not the only members of holy orders of whom we shall have to give a rather ill report in the course of this narrative. We shall encounter others, both Franciscans and Dominicans, who behaved in equally bizarre fashion. To avoid being shocked, the reader must remind himself: first, that these friars had, like all of us, sinned in Adam; secondly, that their intentions were good: the glory of God, the salvation of souls, love of their order and desire for its glory, etc.; thirdly, that their confrères did not act in the same way, and therefore one cannot hold the order responsible for their conduct; fourthly, that all this occurred two centuries ago and assuredly nothing of the sort could happen today.

church of Tlatelolco. The Virgin asked that a chapel be built to her at the place since known as Guadalupe. The Archbishop of Mexico City, the Franciscan Zumarraga, stood guarantee for the miracle, and the oratory was set up. The event had reverberations that grew greater from day to day. Since the Mother of the Saviour was inviting the natives to prayer, was that not proof that their place in Heaven was as clearly appointed as the Spaniards'? And that the priests should guide them to it?

Following this came an intervention from Pope Paul III, in the papal bulls *Veritas ipsa* and *Sublimis Deus*, of June, 1537, which said:

There are certain ones who claim that the Indians, not being qualified to receive the Faith, are meant to be at the service of man like domestic animals. This doctrine comes from the devil, who makes use of it to salve the conscience of those who want to enrich themselves at any cost. As Our Lord, in sending forth His apostles, directed them to teach and baptize *all* nations, the truth is that there is no people on earth which has not the right of keeping its own goods, and which is not called to salvation.

Now that the question of the nature and predestination of the Indians had been settled, it was for those among the men in Mexico who had taken the vows of religion to devote themselves to making Christians of them. Their success was astonishing in its swiftness. "We have nine convents, and I, for my part, have built more than a hundred churches and chapels," wrote Father Pedro de Gante in June, 1529. And in June, 1531, Zumarraga sent word to Charles V: "More than twenty thousand idols have been destroyed."

Temples, pyramids, sculptures, images—all that recalled the idolatrous past—disappeared. The Indians were instructed and baptized by hundreds of thousands. As early as 1559 the Franciscans, who numbered 380, possessed eighty foundations; the Augustinians, who numbered 212, had forty; and the Dominicans, who numbered 210, had forty also. The Dominican missions were situated to the southeast of Mexico City; those of the Augustinians were in the south; those of the Franciscans covered the central part of the country, from the Gulf of Mexico to the Pacific Ocean.

The spiritual conquest, properly so called, continued for another score of years. It may be said that, toward 1580, the region that lies between the seventeenth and twenty-third parallels had been Christianized. This was the region in which the stock-breeders, sugar planters, and mine operators had settled, and where the soldiers maintained order. In the towns especially, Christianity put down deep roots.

Then the missionary impulse weakened, and three-quarters of the country were left almost fallow. This is not the place to seek the reasons. The fact remains that, broadly speaking, the Church of Mexico does not appear in conquering guise in the seventeenth century. The old Orders, recruited on the spot among the Creoles, devote themselves to their faithful congregations; the episcopal seats are occupied by nobles, come from their native Spain; the important parishes are administered by beneficiaries, and the others by needy officiants often more versed in the breeding of mules than in Latin; the communities, both of men and of women, are comfortably off; less so are the six thousand free priests whose ministry consists in saying Masses for the dead, at the rate of a hundred pesos a year.

Yet the Redskins that were still pagan had not been forgotten by everyone. The Jesuits were devoting themselves to those of Sinaloa, southern Sonora, and Lower California. The King had his mind on those of the Apache country and other regions of the north, who were receiving bad advice and good guns from the English and French. He decided to send soldiers to the Sonora-Texas frontier.

The royal solicitude coincided with one of those revivals of evangelical fervor to which the sons of St. Francis are periodically subject. Certain ones among them were determined to set out again for spiritual conquest. They were led, in this, by Father Antonio Liñaz, a Mallorcan, whom Pope Innocent XI authorized to establish "apostolic colleges" in Mexico.

These foundations, independent one from another, were an innovation in the Order. Drawing their recruits from all the Spanish Provinces and subject to none, they were directly answerable to the Commissioner General of the Indies. Each was governed by a "Guardian," elected for three years, with the assistance of his Council or "Discretory." They were made up of friars who were not afraid of death, and who pledged themselves to serve ten years in the missions. In 1683 Antonio Liñaz founded the first apostolic college, under the name of Santa Cruz, at Querétaro; others were established at Guadalupe-Zacatecas, Pachuca, Cholula, Orizaba, Zapopan, and elsewhere. That of San Fernando in Mexico City, of which we shall be speaking constantly from now on, came into being in 1731, the same year in which Junípero took his religious vows and decided to devote himself to the conversion of the Indians.

Four

Among the Pames of the Sierra Gorda

Five months after he had arrived at the College of San Fernando, Junípero was sent by its Guardian, Father Velasco, to work among the Pames of the Sierra Gorda.

This mountainous and tropical region, which lies 120 miles north of the City of Mexico, forms a rectangle some 250 miles long by 75 miles wide, halfway between Querétaro and the Gulf of Mexico; the Moctezuma River flows through it. If one were to divide this rectangle into three approximately equal squares, it would be in the central square, along the present Mexico-Laredo highway, that the five missions held by San Fernando would be found. Even today, the roads leading to these mountains are no better than trails; access to them is especially difficult in the rainy season, when the wooden bridges are washed away, and one must swim across flooded streams twenty feet deep.

The Jonaces and the Pames had been living there from time immemorial. Of the Jonaces, Captain Labra's report, in 1740, says: "After a century and one-half of experiment, the means of bringing them to submission has not yet been found. All the military expeditions undertaken against them have failed; Franciscans, Augustinians, and Dominicans have likewise wasted their time in efforts at evangelization. I have reached the conclusion that the Jonaces are impossible to convert."

This report did not keep San Fernando, founded nine years before, from making a new attempt that same year. "On the twelfth of July, 1740," writes Father Velasco, "having succeeded in getting together seventy Jonaces, I established the Mission of San José de Vizarran. By December, the number of my congregation had tripled. They behaved well for two and one-half years; then suddenly they put everything to fire and sword. They are

36

truly an accursed breed; six of them proved a match for fifty Spaniards. They were paid back in their own coin, however. The chiefs were captured, the population was massacred, and His Excellency the Viceroy had all their habitations burned. For our part, we were obliged to withdraw, and it was all over with our Mission."

There was no longer anything to be done about the Jonaces, since, thanks to His Excellency, the race was extinct. But there remained the Pames, who were scarcely any better: they plundered the distant *haciendas*, then burned them; they robbed travelers and merchants, then murdered them—according to a widely current Indian custom of always enjoying two pleasures at once, when possible, by committing two crimes instead of one. Then they would retire to their lairs in the mountains, inaccessible to the King's cavalrymen.

This barbarism, practiced so close to the capital, exasperated the Spaniards and brought shame upon the authorities. In 1744, General Escandon promised success where everyone so far had failed. He made his way into the country of the Pames with two "crews" of Franciscans: one belonging to the College of Pachuca, which he set up on the right bank of the Moctezuma and of which, therefore, we shall not have to speak farther; the other made up of ten Fernandinos, who were settled on the left bank. With Father Mezquia, he drew a line in the form of a trapezium, along the horizontal sides of which five missions were to be founded: Jalpan, Landa, and Conca in the south; Tancoyol and Tilaco in the north. It is thirteen miles from Jalpan to Conca, twenty-one miles from Jalpan to Tancoyol, twenty-four miles from Tancoyol to Tilaco, eight miles from Tilaco to Landa, thirteen miles from Landa to Conca. This trapezium, then, whose sides followed the gorges and the valleys, had a perimeter of seventy-nine miles. Escandon set up a *presidio* [1] at Jalpan, divided thirty escort soldiers among the four other posts, and then went back to Querétaro, leaving to the Fernandinos the responsibility for collecting, converting, and feeding the Pames.

They succeeded in assembling 7,406; by dint of self-sacrifice—eating nothing but corn—they set up five emergency churches and

---

[1] The name given by the Spaniards to the fortresses they established in regions reputed to be dangerous.

as many farms; but overwork and privation got the better of them
in the end: four of these sturdy men died, and four others, gravely
ill, were obliged to return to the College. To make matters worse,
two epidemics reduced the number of natives by two-thirds: 1,402
succumbed to the illness, and 3,507 ran away and refused to come
back, attributing the plague to the vengeance of the ancient cast-
off gods. The Fernandinos stood fast, however, and while waiting for reinforcements from Father Mezquia succeeded in persuading their confrères of Zacatecas and Querétaro to come to
their aid.

We have seen that Father Mezquia and his thirty-three recruits
had reached the City of Mexico in January, 1750. Among the new
arrivals, the Guardian Velasco chose ten who on May 31 set out
on the road to the Sierra. This team included, among others,
Fathers Juan Crespi, Paterna, and Cruzado, whose names will often reappear in this chronicle. In spite of his protestations of un-
fitness, Junípero was appointed Prefect of the Missions; to please
him, he was given the title of "Acting Prefect" only; Francisco
Palou was assigned to him as Vice Prefect.

Although they had mules at their disposal, the two friends covered on foot, by way of penance, the 170 miles that then separated Jalpan from the City of Mexico. The road went by way
of Querétaro; it was not too bad as far as that town; but the
passes, the swamps, and the heat made the rest of the route difficult, and the sores in Junípero's leg had reopened. On June 16,
he reached Jalpan, where he and Francisco Palou were to settle
down.

Situated at the foot of a mountain 11,300 feet high, and con-
sisting of about three hundred huts, the village of Jalpan grouped
together approximately a thousand of the 2,477 Pames who had
not fled back to their nomad existence. The other Pames who
had accepted a fixed abode were divided among the four remaining missions, each of which was in charge of two ministers. Junípero soon left his companion for several weeks, in order to visit
all his colleagues—a thing he did at least ten times in eight years.
As he believed that he was holding office only temporarily, he
was pained, after the Chapter meeting of 1752, by the receipt of
the License, or "Patent," which confirmed him in his official po-

sition as Prefect.[2] Before the Chapter met in 1755, he made a
point of sending the License back to the College, attaching a letter in which he argued as follows: "Either it is an honor to be
Prefect, and it is time someone else should enjoy it; or it is a
burden, and it is fitting that turns should be taken in carrying
it." This dilemma convinced no one, and until the day of Junípero's death the Discretos of San Fernando put as much stubborn
resolution into reappointing him Prefect as he did, every three
years, into sending them his resignation.

The methods the Fernandinos employed in the Sierra, and later
in California, were perfectly adapted to the curiously degraded
nature of most of the Indians in Mexico. How was one to civilize
these Redskins: dirty, boisterous, lazy, generally drunkards;[3] in
the habit of lying, cheating, stealing, killing; people who begged
without shame, enjoyed the sight of suffering, knew nothing of
the sentiment of honor or of gratitude, seemed susceptible only
to fear, and considered as their neighbors only the folk of their
own clan and kinship? Would it be enough to supply them with
A-B-C books and mechanical contrivances? Even in our day, if
all you do for one of them is teach him his letters and give him
an automobile, you will have one newspaper reader and motorist
the more, but not one savage the less; for he will be all the more
able, and more quick, to commit new offenses. Since civilization
is a matter of the inner being, and of an ethical standard, it was
only by transforming their soul and their conscience, through the
revelation of the true God and the observance of the Ten Com-
mandments, that one could change these malefactors into honest
folk. In addition, they must be imbued with the love of work,
so as to rescue them from idleness and the poverty in which their
perverse instincts flourished. Thus the spiritual and temporal task
that the Fernandinos accomplished among the Pames was to make
them workers and Christians.

To put these Indians to work, to feed them, and to keep them
near at hand, the friars themselves took up pick, saw, and ax, felling trees, clearing the ground, snatching from the forest wide

---

[2] The reference is to the triennial "Chapter" at San Fernando, when the friars
met for the election of the superior officers of the College.

[3] In his *Historia Antigua de México*, dedicated to the glorification of his
fatherland, the Mexican Jesuit Clavijero acknowledges that "half of his compatriots were addicted to drunkenness."

stretches of land that could be sown with grain. Former professor of philosophy, Francisco Palou was well acquainted with "first causes," the how and why of things; a former interpreter of Duns Scotus, Junípero could confound all the Thomists in the world. Both of them had yet to learn where, when, and how barley and wheat should be planted, or how many seeds of corn should be put into the ground per square foot—not to speak of the laws governing the breeding of cows and mules! Junípero's letters, which make mention of the *toro padre* and the *burro padre,* show how anxious he was to give his calves and mules only fine bulls and sturdy donkeys as fathers. In an immense vegetable garden, also, they grew lettuce, cabbages, melons, brown beans, lentils, and that Mexican pimento, called *chile,* which burns up one's mouth. They taught their neophytes [4] to cook vegetables, to stop eating their meat raw, and to make the *tortillas, atole, pinole,* and *pozole,* pancakes and porridges of maize on which their descendants are still nourished. They raised goats and sheep, and sheared them. They taught the women to spin, to weave, and to manufacture rugs and wicker trays and baskets.

It was by these means that they made villagers and farmers of the nomad Pames. In teaching them the habit of drawing from the soil resources that would raise their standard of living, they led them to love this earth which they cultivated, as their foster mother and their friend; and, wanderers as they had been, they no longer dreamed of leaving it.

"From the temporal point of view," Palou writes, "the regime in force brought the communities of the primitive Church back to life. . . ." All the people were working under the direction of the Fathers, and the Fathers provided food and shelter for all. Their farms grew richer and more prosperous from year to year; they came to possess plough oxen by hundreds, mules, cows, and sheep in abundance; their granaries were piled high with corn and wheat. To the natives who accepted it, they would give a plot of land, offering them also the oxen to cultivate it. But the Pames were slow to take over the management of their own affairs; the communal regime pleased them; they preferred to obey, and to

---

[4] The neophytes, or "new Christians," are those who have been recently baptized. The catechumens are those who are preparing for baptism. The apostates, for the Spaniards, were those who left the Mission and reverted to their pagan life and associations. The Law of the Indies regarded this desertion as an offense.

let the missionaries retain the responsibility of providing, and of thinking, for them.

From the religious point of view, everything went on a little as it did in the great monastic communities of an earlier day. "Every morning at sunrise," Palou continues, "the bell calls all the adults—neophytes and pagans—to the church. The recitation of the catechism, and of the prayer, is followed by a lesson; and then, in the huge patio, before the church, the distribution of supplies takes place. This is followed by the gathering together of the children of more than five years, the catechumens, and the candidates for marriage. The bell will summon them again a little before sunset, for the purpose of having them repeat what they learned in the morning. Every Sunday, adults and children attend High Mass, after which they come forward as their names are called to kiss the hand of the missionary, who thus checks on who is there."

It soon became apparent that the Pames were neither less religious nor less perfectible than the other children of Adam. The Law of the Indies prescribed that the Indians should be made to pray in Castilian. Junípero learned the idiom of the Sierra, of which his predecessors had been ignorant, and translated the catechism and liturgical texts into the Pame tongue; this obliged his congregation to pray in two languages, but it made it possible for them to understand what they said. When he arrived among them, not one was going to confession; but as they saw him, every Sunday before High Mass, going to confess to Francisco Palou in the choir, they went into the confessional in their turn, to acknowledge their sins in the Pame language.

He had them sing a great deal, take part in mystery plays, join in processions. At Christmas, he dressed the little Pames as angels, the young men as seraphim, the tribal chiefs as the Magi kings; and a succession of moving performances would take place before the crèche.

Every Friday during Lent, between the Stations of the Cross and the sermon of the Passion, a procession of penitence would lead the whole village to the Calvary on the hill. At the head of it walked Junípero, bearing a tall and heavy cross. "He carried it both ways, going and coming," Palou writes, "and I do not know how he did it—for I, who am stronger, would have been incapable of that." On Holy Thursday, he washed the feet of twelve old men, and then invited them, after the ceremony, to a good meal. On Good Friday, he took the church's great figure of Christ down from the cross, by means of an apparatus with pulleys, and laid it on a couch among flowers. That evening there was the procession of Our Lady Forsaken (*Nuestra Señora de la Soledad*); on Easter morning, at dawn, that of Jesus coming out from the tomb. Two months later, the Corpus Christi procession passed beneath ten arches of green branches, and paused at four magnificent temporary altars where, again become angels and seraphim, the actors in the Christmas festival would pour forth, in Pame and in Spanish, their declarations of love to the blessed Host. To all this must be added the torchlight parade in honor of the Virgin, which coursed through the village every Saturday evening, and the hundred or more sermons Junípero preached to his congregation in the course of every year.

It will be said, no doubt, that this was quite a program. But it was never too much for the Pames, nor did they grow tired of it. "In the old days," they said, "we did not understand, and we were hungry; that is why we did not like to pray. But now everything is changed!" For his part Junípero used to say, drolly, "It was through the stomach that the Faith entered their heads. . . ."

He helped them to build houses to take the place of their huts; they helped him to put up a church of freestone, in the Churrigueresque style, more than fifty yards long and more than ten yards wide. It is still standing, with its thick walls like those of a fortress, its high dome, its severe and graceful façade, its porch with the spacious patio in front. Juan Crespi built one as beautiful, though smaller, at Tilaco; he was both its architect and its overseer. Every village had its own. All are still in existence, as is likewise in existence—as the writer has verified—the transformation brought about at the same time in men's souls. "And if anyone asks me where the money came from to pay for all this," exclaims Palou, "I will answer that it was not the King who gave it; we never had more than our ridiculous *sinodos*, and our miserable fees for Mass. Our Lord Himself intervened, making it possible that once these labors were accomplished there should remain more pesos in the syndic's purse and more corn in our granaries than had ever been found there before." [5]

---

[5] Since the rule of the Franciscans forbade them to handle money, it was a man whom they could rely on, called the "syndic," who took charge of it in

The zeal of the Fernandinos was rewarded. God blessed their fields, their cattle, their finances, and especially those whom they called their children—those former demi-brutes who had become decent folk and Christians. The Pames ceased to steal and to kill; they now regarded as their neighbors those Spaniards of whom they had lately said that they wished not to go to Heaven so as to avoid encountering them there; they were tasting the joy of the man who owes the bread he eats to his own labor alone. As for those who had fled after the epidemics, almost half of them were won back again; the others had joined the nomad tribes of the neighboring Huasteca. "The fact remains," writes Palou, "that our five villages could henceforth rival in fervor the most Christian villages of Spain. At Jalpan, for example, from forty to a hundred Indians come to the holy table every Sunday."

Such rapid success aroused wonder everywhere, and credit for it was given in large part to Junípero. When the Fernandinos left the Sierra ten years later, the Viceroy was able to withdraw his soldiers from the region, and the Archbishop of Mexico to send his priests into it. Both gave public expression to their admiration, and the Court of Madrid proclaimed its satisfaction with what had been done.

The *gente de razón*, however—the men endowed with reason, and with greed—had realized that the Pames had become harmless now and even possessed savings. Had some of them not been encountered at the fair at Zimapan, selling rugs, wickerwork, and chickens? Some Spaniards obtained authorization to come and settle in the Sierra. But Junípero had the authorization taken away. He was not at that time suffering the contradictions and persecutions that later bore down upon him without respite. It was a matter of only two days for him to warn the College, which was a mere few steps away from the Viceroy's headquarters; in California, later, it would often take at least two years for him to appeal to the higher authority against his persecutors, and to receive a reply. By force of impassioned activity, thus, the good shepherd was able to keep his flock in the Sierra Gorda from being prematurely shorn and stripped.

their place. The syndic of San Fernando held the missionaries' purse, into which were put the *sinodos* that the King allotted them, their fees for Mass, and the donations of their benefactors. It was he, also, who paid for their purchases. At Sierra Gorda the *sinodo* was about 400 pesos a year.

He left them in September, 1758, when he and Palou were both recalled to take the place of two colleagues who had just been martyred by the Apaches. In his traveling bag, packed in with his underwear and his breviary, he carried with him the mother of the sun. . . .

The Pames, it must be understood, originally worshiped the sun and his mother. As the sun was present everywhere in visible reality, they made no images of him, nor had they dedicated altars to him; it was different with his mother, named Cachum, who was never seen, and of whom a representation was thus in order. The Pames had made this in the form of an alabaster bust of a woman, which was venerated atop a mountain in a sanctuary presided over by a sorcerer. Believed to have the power to bring on rain, exorcize the bewitched, and heal the sick, Cachum was also the patroness—and performer—of marriages. The betrothed couple approached her by a stairway cut in the rock, each carrying a piece of bark. Our illiterate lovers were supposed to have inscribed their names and their vows on this bark, and Cachum was supposed to read them. They threw the bark into a basket, made the goddess a present which her high priest received and made use of in her name, and then went back home, married and content.

When the sanctuary of the goddess had been burned by the soldiers, the sorcerer had hidden her bust in a cave for safekeeping, and he showed it only to pilgrims in whom he could have complete confidence. Then he himself lost his faith, or, at least, yielded to the importunities of the new Christians. He ended by giving them Cachum; they gave her to Junípero; and he, on his return to Mexico City, put her in the museum of the College, where she bore witness that only the religion of Christ held sway in the Sierra from this time forth.[6]

[6] We are following Palou's account here. According to a document in the National Museum of Mexico, however, it was in 1752, when Junípero returned to the College for several days, that he brought Cachum with him. But isn't it the document which is wrong, rather than Palou?

Five

Prevented from Going Among the Apaches, Junípero Becomes an Itinerant Missionary
[1758-1767]

"After an absence of eight years and several months, I have just returned to the College," Junípero wrote on September 29, 1758, to his nephew Miguel,[1] who had become a Capuchin friar, "but I am on the point of setting out again, for the Apache country, four hundred leagues from here."

The maps of the period show the "Apache country" as a region of about eighty thousand square miles, to the east of the Colorado River. But this territory contained far from all the Apache Indians. Whole tribes of them were to be found in the northern part of Sonora and in Texas. Like the Comanches, their allies of the moment, the Apaches of Texas had a taste for human flesh, but they did not eat it with garlic and tomatoes like the Aztecs.

"Liking red meat," writes Father Santa María, "they first scourge their prisoners with thistles and drub their skin with rough bark, so as to stimulate the circulation of the blood. Then they kill one of them, put him to roast on the fire, and begin to dance around it, uttering cries of delight. In turn, the dancers, men and women, step out of the circle to go take a bite at the victim and tear off a bit of the fleshy parts, always avoiding cutting into the large veins, for fear of draining out his blood. When the bones appear on one side, he is turned over on the other; when he is entirely stripped of flesh, he is replaced by a second victim, until the day's menu is wholly consumed. The liver, spleen, lungs, and other

---

[1] Miguel Ribot y Botellas, Juanita's son, was then 17. Having applied for admission into the Order of Minims (*minimus*, very small), he had been refused because of his short stature. He became well known as an architect and mathematician.

tender parts are kept for the toothless old people who would not be able to bite into anything else."

Being then occupied with the subjugation of the southwestern part of Texas, the Spaniards wanted first to bring the "Apaches of the South" to submission. When the Viceroy offered to have missionaries sent to them, these Indians promised that they would come and settle near the Fathers.

A presidio with a hundred soldiers under command of Colonel Parrilla was established on the San Saba River near the present city of Menard, Texas. Six missionaries arrived in April, 1757: two Fernandinos, Fathers Santesteban and Molina; and four Queretarinos, Father Terraros and three others. They constructed their mission eight miles from the Presidio, and then, in company with a half-score of neophytes and an escort guard of six soldiers, they waited for the southern Apaches. Three of the Queretarinos, tired of waiting, went back to their College.

Fathers Terreros, Santesteban, and Molina were just about to follow them when, on the morning of March 16, 1758, there appeared some thousand Indians, to the sound of war cries; their bodies were painted in a motley mosaic of red and black, and they were armed with arrows and lances, and with guns supplied to them by the French in Louisiana. These were not the southern Apaches the missionaries had been waiting for, but "Apaches of the North" and Comanches; the corporal of the guard declared, however, that he recognized them, and that they were inoffensive. They themselves averred that they had come as friends, and that they wished to become Christians; but they had first a score to settle, they added, with the Apaches of the South. Once that matter was attended to, they would come back to the Mission to receive Baptism. . . .

Reassured, Fathers Terreros and Molina stepped out of the enclosure to offer them gifts. At once the horde surged in through the opened door, dashed at the storerooms, and seized the horses and mules in the corral. But they had to have more for their military expedition; and they demanded that one of the Fathers should go with them to the Presidio, where thanks to him, they said, what they wanted would be handed over to them. Father Terreros offered himself to the sacrifice. "I believe that we shall all soon have entered into eternal life," he said, as he left his confrères.

He got on his horse. The moment he crossed the yard he was struck by gunshot full in the face. It was the signal for the massacre. Soldiers and neophytes were felled like trees; Father Santesteban was run through with lances and his head was cut off; Father Terreros, already dead, was also decapitated; the bodies of the two missionaries were cut to pieces immediately afterward; the Indians played ball with their heads, and smeared themselves with their blood, dancing, yelling, and looting the while.

Only Father Molina, though wounded in the right breast, was able to escape by a window, and, dragging himself along as best he could, to reach the Presidio after two days and two nights on the way. He learned there that the northern Apaches and the Comanches had swooped down, the night before, to steal two thousand head of cattle from Colonel Parrilla.

This incident was a rude blow to Spanish prestige. Should Texas have to be abandoned, as New Mexico had been in 1680? The Viceroy, Amarillas, ordered the presidios on the frontier to aid Parrilla in maintaining the position on the San Saba, and the Franciscans to re-establish themselves at Santa Cruz. The College of Querétaro once more supplied four friars, and San Fernando assigned Junípero and Francisco Palou to replace Fathers Santesteban and Molina.

"Both had left Spain with me," Junípero wrote his nephew, on September 29, 1756. "Father Molina has just come back here to be taken care of. As for Father Santesteban, killed on his knees in his bedroom, the crucifix in his hands, and praying for his executioners, he was discovered six days later by the Christians from the nearby Presidio. His torn body exhaled a gentle fragrance, fresh blood was flowing from his wounds, beneath his tattered clothing was found the small triple chain of iron with which he girded himself by way of penance. It is this dear and well-favored friend whom holy obedience sends me to replace—I who am so incompetent and such a sinner. But the all-powerful God can bring about great things through the agency even of the cipher that I am. I beg you, pray for your uncle, who has never ceased to pray for you. . . . Give my greetings of affection to your little sisters, and above all to your dear parents." [2]

[2] Junípero's parents, whom he no longer mentions, had died while he was in the Sierra, his father on May 5, 1753, and his mother on December 25, 1754.

Months passed. Colonel Parrilla had suggested pursuing the north-ern Apaches and killing off as many of them as might be neces-sary for the subjugation of their tribe. After this, he said, the southern Apaches would no longer hesitate to come and take up their abode at Santa Cruz. A great deal of time and patience was demanded for the carrying out of this plan.

Toward the end of the summer of 1759, however, it was learned in Mexico City that Parrilla had advanced 150 miles north of the San Saba, and that the rebels were fleeing before his troops. Then, on the sixth of October, came the news that the Apaches had turned at bay in a village where the French had helped them to put up a line of defense, and had inflicted a complete defeat upon the Spaniards after one day of fighting.

Misfortune decreed that the Viceroy Amarillas should die on the fifth of February. His successor had other business on hand; the northern Apaches began again to give chase to the Apaches of the South; and the work of restoring Santa Cruz was post-poned till a better day. Francisco Palou returned to Jalpan and became Prefect of the missions there. As for Junípero, "whose principle it was never to manifest his own preferences, obedience kept him at San Fernando."

We have little information on the nine years that followed. None of the letters that Junípero wrote between 1759 and 1767 have come down to us, and Palou, who at this period was far away from his master, gives only a few pages of the *Vida* to this part of his life.[3] What we do learn is that Junípero was at that time an itinerant missionary. He traveled through the dioceses of Mex-ico, Puebla, Valladolid (today Morelia), and Oaxaca, spending about four months of the year at the College, and the other eight in apostolic tours. These latter took him, many a time, more than a hundred leagues from the capital; but he always went on foot. "I have calculated that he walked more than two thousand leagues in seven years," Francisco Palou writes.[4]

[3] He does not even mention a little devotional book that Junípero published at this time: *La Prelada de San Fernando—Novena a la Concepción Inmaculada de Maria, Distribuida por las Neuve Letras de "Ave Pulcra"* (*The Queen of San Fernando, or Novena in Honor of the Immaculate Conception, Issued in Accordance with the Nine Letters of the "Ave Pulcra"*).

[4] A league is 2.65 miles.

In the diocese of Mexico, during the course of nine months, he carried the Gospel to Zimapan and the surrounding country, as well as to a large part of the Mezquital and the Huasteca. He preached two missions in the City of Mexico, which then had a population of 120,000 and possessed twelve parish churches—five for the *gente de razón*, and seven for other human folk. In the diocese of Puebla, he made his way along the coast of the Gulf of Mexico between Tampico and Veracruz. In the diocese of Valladolid he did notable evangelistic work on the Rio Verde.

His journeys in the tropical regions of Oaxaca were sometimes dangerous. The roads were, so to speak, in default. To return from the Tabasco coast into the interior, Junípero and his companions had to go up the Rio Miges in a canoe that was constantly attacked by alligators. It was at night that these creatures made the most menacing display of their ill will; but the lions and tigers that inhabited the surrounding jungles were no more reassuring; if our navigators had tried to sleep on shore they would have had to deal with them. For more than a week, therefore, they did not dare leave their boat. Trusting in the Gospel promise, however, Junípero feared neither wild beasts nor poisons. One day after saying Mass he learned that he had been served poisoned wine at the altar. He was urged to take an emetic, but he refused; and he felt no ill effects.

Among the many conversions brought about by his eloquence, the *Vida* mentions that of a notorious sinner who, in the middle of the sermon, rushed up into the pulpit, snatched the chain with which the preacher was striking himself, knelt before the high altar, and there, naked to the waist, began to scourge himself until the blood come, crying out the while, "It is not for this holy man, it is for me to offer expiation for sin!" He put such a fury of fervency into his self-chastisement that at last he fell to the floor unconscious. He was revived, received the last sacraments, and died on the spot.

Junípero was then, it is seen, scourging himself in the pulpit, as St. Francis Solano and St. Leonard of Port Maurice had done; bruising his breast with stones, like St. Jerome in the desert; or, when he preached on Hell, burning his skin with live coals, like St. John Capistrano. Perhaps some will not approve of this. But the saints have these inspirations; their sins, and the sins of others, afflict them so bitterly that they would like to wipe out the mark of them, even by shedding their blood. May the right-thinking people, generally indulgent toward their own shortcomings, forgive Junípero for a few saintly excesses that hurt no one but himself, and were never to be widely imitated!

Conspicuously formidable as he was in proclaiming the truth from the pulpit, he was at the same time full of patience and compassion in private or intimate talk.

Certain devout women liked to receive spiritual guidance in their homes, and particularly to receive the individual who gave it to them. "The revered Father, for his part," writes Palou, "would not consent to direct souls anywhere but in the confessional or the reception room. He did not accept the invitations and the dinners of society people. And they, far from holding this against him, only respected him the more, and were the more desirous of having him as their confessor."

During his sojourns at San Fernando, Junípero exercised the functions of Discreto, and also those of choirmaster. Although he did not know the sol-fa syllables, he was a natural musician, and he had kept his magnificent voice. He escaped on several occasions from the imminent peril of being appointed Guardian: sometimes he absented himself from the convent at the time of the Chapter; at other times it was the Chapter members themselves who changed their minds, preferring to hold him available in case the opportunity should be offered of establishing a new mission among the Redskins.

Enjoying great renown as a theologian, he could not avoid being made "Commissioner of the Holy Inquisition for New Spain and the Adjacent Islands." He had even to undertake a long journey in that capacity. It is known, however, that no heretic was condemned by him to the stake. He was especially concerned with hunting out the books of the Encyclopedists, which were beginning to circulate in Mexico. It was on this occasion that Junípero was led to look into Voltaire. He saw that this writer, among his obsessions, had the notion of doing away with monks, in order to oblige these followers of the religious life to become fathers of families and to "give useful citizens to the State." He wondered for a moment whether this absurd idea were going to win the favor of Court circles. "A lot better off they will be," he said, "when they have suppressed the vows of religion!" He was quite right in his satiric judgment, as is easily to be seen: for if the Spaniards had not had their monks and friars they would not have brought so many countries under their rule, and they would not today have the pleasure of reflecting that their language is spoken by almost two hundred million men.

Six

Junípero in Lower California
[1767-1768]

The date of July 14, 1767, may be fixed as that upon which Junípero Serra entered upon the historic role he had been called upon
to play: it was on this day that he set out for Tepic and Lower
California. This beginning is tied up with the suppression of the
Jesuit Order in the States of the Spanish Crown. Fray Junípero
had returned to the College two days before the above date,
hastily recalled, in accordance with the wish of the Visitor General, Galvez, from an apostolic tour in the Mesquital, about one
hundred fifty miles from Mexico City. Three weeks earlier, at
4 o'clock in the afternoon of June 22, Galvez had arrested the
178 Jesuits who were living in Mexico, in order to deport them
to Corsica by way of Veracruz.[1]

The King of Spain at this period was Charles III, who reigned
from 1759 to 1783. The Viceroy of New Spain was the Marquis
Charles de Croix. But from 1767 to 1771 the real master of New
Spain was José de Galvez.

Gifted with an imagination and an intelligence that were alike
admirable, as well as with an extraordinary capacity for work, a
man of just and broad vision who knew how to decide, organize,
and command, Galvez was modest, disinterested, courageous, and
possessed of a boundless devotion to the King, his benefactor. He
was born at Velez, Malaga, in 1721, of a poor family. A poet in
his youth, he studied law at Alcala, and served successively as
counsel to the French Embassy at Madrid, secretary to Prime
Minister Grimaldi, and Visitor General for Mexico (1767-71),

---

[1] The Jesuits were banished by all the Catholic sovereigns at this time. April
2, 1767, was the date on which the King of Spain decreed their expulsion from
his dominions. In 1773 the Franciscan Pope Clement XIV suppressed the Order
throughout the Church. It was restored by the Benedictine Pope Pius VII in
1814.

after which he became Universal Minister for the Indies, a post he held until his death in 1786. In this office he was, as people were wont to say, "the most powerful man of his time after the kings themselves." It was added that "some used to tremble at the mere utterance of his name, so stern was he with everyone, and so formidable to evildoers." He practiced a sincere piety, and remained faithful to the lessons of the old priest who had started him in Latin and paid for his education. When he was created Marquis of Sonora at the end of his life, he was still so poor that the King was obliged to reimburse him for the expenses of his ennoblement.

To go back now to July of 1767. At that time Galvez was not troubling himself in any way about Upper California. His horizon, in that direction, was bounded by the frontiers of the Spanish possessions: that is, it was limited to Sonora, where the Indians were in revolt, and to Lower California, which was believed to be threatened by a Russian invasion. He himself was planning to go at an early date into these two territories, which were both of great strategic importance.

The missions established in these regions had belonged to the Society of Jesus. Galvez had therefore directed the Franciscans of Querétaro and Jalisco to go and replace the Jesuits in Sonora, and those of San Fernando to do the same in Lower California. Sacrificing its reserves of men, and withdrawing the friars from the Sierra Gorda, which was on the point of passing to the secular clergy, San Fernando had succeeded in gathering together sixteen missionaries, including Junípero. Among them were Palou, Crespi, and Paterna, whom we already know, and others—such as Parron, Gomez, Viscaíno, Murguia, and Lasuen, whom we shall often meet in the pages that follow.

Now they were about to set out on their new adventure. And as a crowd of curious onlookers on the Plaza San Fernando was milling around the pack mules, the saddle horses, and the baggage, Father Andres, Guardian of the College, addressed those who were leaving. "Dearly beloved sons and brothers," he said, "you are going out to evangelize those distant regions which our Catholic Sovereign is entrusting to your zeal. May the blessing of God, and that of our Seraphic Father St. Francis, accompany you! The best thing that I could do for you was to place you under the direction of the Father Lector Junípero. In bidding you farewell, all that I ask of you is to obey him as you would myself, and never to forget me in your prayers."

After a journey of seven hundred miles which took five weeks, the caravan arrived on August 21 at Tepic, fifty miles from the port of San Blas. There the travelers found the Fathers from Querétaro and Jalisco, as well as the troops on their way to carry on the war in Sonora. The ships *San Carlos* and *San Antonio* (which was just being fitted out in the San Blas shipyards) were to transport them to their destination. At Tepic they found also the newly appointed Governor of Lower California, Captain Portola. Portola had been the first to traverse the five hundred miles that separate San Blas from Loreto, arriving in the Peninsula at the beginning of December, 1767, whereas Junípero and his companions only disembarked at the port four months later, on the first of April, 1768.[2]

Military, maritime, and religious capital of the country, the port of Loreto was the official residence of both the Governor and the Prefect of the Missions. There was also another personage there who will become quite familiar to us: Captain Rivera, Commandant of the military forces, who had been dawdling about in that locality for the past twenty years. Apart from the Government and Mission buildings, Loreto was no more than an agglomeration of Indian huts made of rude branches.

There were fifteen stations to be manned and equipped in the 992-mile length of this peninsula. To name them from south to north, they were San José, Santiago, La Paz, La Pasión, San Luis, San Javier, Loreto, Comondu, La Purisima, Mulege, La Guadalupe, San Ignacio, Santa Gertrudis, San Borja, and finally Santa Maria, situated at the twenty-ninth parallel. While waiting for the reinforcements that Father Verger, Commissary of San Fernando, had gone to recruit in Spain, only one officiating priest could be spared to each station. San Javier fell to Vice Prefect Palou, La Purisima to Father Crespi, San Borja to Father Lasuen.

---

[2] Since Lower California was considered the best mission field in Mexico, the Fathers from Jalisco wished to have it for theirs, and, by favor of the Viceroy, they did obtain it. They had scarcely arrived there when Galvez, who had been appealed to by San Fernando, made them re-embark for San Blas, whence, as originally decided, they were to go and rejoin their Querétaro colleagues in Sonora. It took several months to get the better of the intrigues of the Jalisco Fathers; that is why Junípero and his companions, not having been able to leave San Blas until March 14, did not reach Lower California until April 1.

Junípero took Loreto for himself, designating Father Parron as his associate.

It soon became apparent to the missionaries that, far from what they had been led to believe, they had not entered upon the Promised Land. They found the missions in a deplorable condition. Although they had been in existence since 1697, the date of the occupation of the peninsula, all of them together numbered only 7,149 Christians, including women and children, and many of those were still running around nude. Some of the stations, established in barren localities, had always been poor. The others had been looted since the Jesuits, driven out by Portola in December, had left them.

In fact Portola had, upon his arrival and while awaiting the coming of the delayed Franciscans, charged certain of the soldiers with guardianship of those missions, as the Indians would have completely plundered them otherwise. These soldier guardians took over the looting in their turn. Not to mention the cellars and granaries they emptied, they became voracious meat-eaters, and set themselves up as butchers on a wholesale scale. One of them slaughtered 600 head of livestock, another 400, a third 300. "Six months more of such 'administration,' " wrote Palou, "and there would have been nothing left at all."

The Indians had greeted the arrival of their new spiritual fathers with song and dance. Then they began to drop away when they ascertained that there was nothing much, any more, for them to be given or to take. The Franciscans were somewhat disheartened, not to say demoralized. With his left leg limping, Junípero set out to visit them, beginning his tour at the north. But, as early as the sixth of July, came Galvez, and prevented him from continuing; he left him neither peace nor respite from that time on. He was not a man to leave those he trusted in quietness; and he had things on his mind.

"I had quitted Mexico on April 9, 1768," Visitor General Galvez wrote. "A little before arriving at San Blas I received orders from His Majesty to parry, by appropriate measures, the attacks which it was believed the Russians were contemplating against the Peninsula. Had their fleets, coming from the Sea of Tartary, not been seen cruising in sight of Northern California? The Marquis de Croix was of the opinion that I should send an expedition to Monterey, using, for this purpose, the *San Carlos* and the *San Antonio*, which had been built to transport our troops to Sonora."

Galvez arrived in Lower California, then, with a new and great project in mind. While working on it, however, he did not lose sight of his first purpose, which was to make the Peninsula impregnable and to create sources of profit there for the Royal Treasury. He undertook reforms at once.

His couriers rode their horses around and about, throughout the countryside; they were never fast enough. His secretaries, also, were too slow. He wrote innumerable letters by his own hand; hundreds have been lost, but eighteen addressed to Junípero have been rediscovered. "Excuse my blots," he wrote in one of them. "This is the second I have made; but I am in such a hurry! I have so much business on hand that even though I devote the whole day and a large part of the night to it I do not succeed in getting the most urgent things attended to."

He established a naval academy for the education of seamen. He established a school of mines, and brought miners from Guanajuato to teach the natives to extract the precious metals. He loved the Franciscan missionary, and relied upon him to transform the Indians into laborers, sailors, tillers of the soil, pearl-fishers, trappers of otter and beaver. He himself set the example of hard work and integrity. He dreamed of making a fine town out of the encampment of Santa Ana, near La Paz, where he lived, and drew the plans for it with his own hand. He wanted the missions with a future to be developed; the others he suppressed. He did away with San Luis and La Pasión with a stroke of the pen, and moved their residents elsewhere. More than a third of the natives were thus displaced. Junípero approved these measures, which were not without their inconveniences, as may be surmised.

Father Ramos, minister at La Paz and future bishop, complained of the Guaicuros, thieving folk who were descending upon him by the hundreds. Galvez hurried off to bring them to their senses. They were called together in assembly and he made a speech to them; at the appointed time he went over to the residence for dinner. But the good meal prepared in his honor had vanished. Some of the Guaicuros had eaten it while he was exhorting their fellows on the respect due to others' property; in addition, they had rifled the kitchen and plundered the reserve stocks. Galvez at once had his soldiers set up a gibbet; and Father Ramos had all the trouble in the world to keep him from hanging the guilty Indians on it.

Punishments, proclamations, decrees, harangues, the plans and reforms of the Visitor General—they all came to nothing. In this State which has remained Mexican, which is larger than Portugal and Hungary, and abounds in natural resources, there have been scarcely three inhabitants per square mile, and far too few churches, even to our own day.[3]

Would matters have turned out differently if there had been a man of genius among the Dominicans who replaced the Franciscans in 1772? Or if Junípero, who believed in the future of this Peninsula, had been able to deploy his talents there? . . . But Junípero remained there for only one year; and, even then, Galvez prevented him, after the fourth month, from carrying out his special task as Prefect. It would seem that he went to Lower California only to found the California of the North.

[3] The situation is in process of changing. The towns of Ensenada, Tijuana, and Mexicali, along the United States border, have expanded with extraordinary rapidity in the past few years.

Seven

Galvez and Junípero Prepare for the
Conquest of Upper California
[1768-1769]

Who was the first to conceive of this extraordinary venture?

It had always been in Madrid's mind: Charles III himself often dreamed of going as far north as Alaska. But Spain had never crossed the thirtieth parallel, where Santa Maria Mission was situated, three hundred miles south of the present frontier between Mexico and the United States.

The thirty or forty maritime explorations that had pressed farther to the north had served merely to enrich the maps to the extent of three new names: San Diego, Santa Barbara, and Monterey. San Diego was a port, at the thirty-third parallel; the Santa Barbara Channel was an archipelago stretching between the thirty-fourth and thirty-fifth parallels (from the present town of Ventura to that of Concepcion); Monterey was a hill, at thirty-seven degrees of latitude. In 1603, Sebastian Vizcaíno had anchored near this hill for several days. He had published a favorable description of the place; fame had done the rest: in 165 years the "King's Hill" (*Monte Rey*) had become a high mountain, and the tiny roadstead one of the largest ports in the world.

It was to bar the way to Catherine the Great, therefore—or at least to thwart the designs attributed to her—that Spain all at once decided to occupy Monterey. Galvez, with the modesty and generosity that have been spoken of as characteristic, ascribed a share in the enterprise to the Marquis de Croix. In fact, the decision itself originated in Madrid, and everything would have come to grief if, as was De Croix's wish, the expedition had been confined to the dispatching of two boats to Monterey. Thanks to Galvez, the whole project was successful. He thought out the plan and made sure of its execution. It was thus to him that Spain owed the establishment of its power in Upper California, as it was to Junípero that it owed that power's maintenance. Without Junípero, as we shall see, the occupation would have lasted exactly nine months, after which matters would have reverted to the same state in which they were in 1602. José de Galvez and Junípero Serra are the two last great *conquistadores* in the annals of Spain.

When the Visitor General disembarked at La Paz on the sixth of July the broad general outlines of his plan had been well worked out. Not for one moment was his desire and will limited to building a fortress at Monterey, with half its guns pointed seaward against the Russians and the others aimed at the Indians in the back country. He was resolved to "conquer" that hinterland in the Spanish fashion, that is, to bring missionaries into it, with their liturgical equipment for the celebration of divine worship, and with their livestock. Soldiers would accompany them to watch over their lives. And in some fifteen years there would be a new Christian kingdom on this soil, and a race of new subjects for the Spanish sovereign.

As soon as he arrived at Santa Ana, he summoned Junípero, "the man of the Sierra Gorda," who was known to the official world, in Madrid and in Mexico, as the man who in ten years had pacified a region that two centuries of effort had not been able to subdue. But Junípero was more than two hundred fifty miles from Santa Ana; he was visiting the missions in the north; he would come when he had completed that circuit, and would pass through Santa Ana on his visit to the southern missions. . . .

"No! That is not the point at issue!" said Galvez. "The King has need of you. Come at once. We are going to found new missions."

Junípero's response convinced the Visitor General that he had found the collaborator he had dreamed of. He left him no further respite. "I beg you, Most Reverend Father, hurry!" he urged. "My very dear Señor, worthy of all my veneration, you will find board and lodging here. With me, you will be as in your own home. And do not linger on the way; come straight here; we must talk at length about everything."

Since the King himself lacked wealth, it was the revenues of the Pious Funds and the missions that were to bear the expenses of the undertaking. The Pious Funds, an excellent provision for its purpose, consisted of a capital of 1,257,000 pesos ($3,000,000 by present exchange) which the Jesuits had received from their benefactors for the maintenance of their missions in California.[1] The Franciscans complained loudly when they saw their stipends (*sinodos*, as they were called) reduced by three-fifths, and their livestock corrals plundered by Rivera. "This is going to bring about the ruin of all our Christian communities!" Francisco Palou groaned. Junípero appeased the Franciscans, and Galvez was grateful.

"My thanks to you," Galvez wrote to Junípero, "for the speed with which you have had my orders carried out. It is absolutely necessary to assist Captain Rivera in requisitioning as much as possible; the missions should supply livestock, provisions, and the rest. That, all told, ought to take care of the land expeditions as far as San Diego; once there, they can count on what the boats bring. . . . Your Most Reverend Fathership will, I assume, have had the things sent—the oil, dates, wine, vinegar, and brandy— which the ships are to take with them? You know that without vinegar and brandy the sailors are not to be dragged beyond the thirtieth parallel! For my part, I have just sent a long-boat, filled with everything I have been able to find, to Santa Maria for Rivera; I shall send him others soon. . . . I am burning to see the boats arrive; they are on the way, I hope! God send that they do not delay! A speedy passage will help send my courage up. . . . Has Your Most Reverend Fathership started? You are not finding the journey too hard? . . . I await you with impatience: we have so many things to arrange; there are still so many questions that I am leaving unsettled so that I may discuss them with you! . . . If you have not yet left Loreto, take the first boat that sails, I beg! Or would you prefer that I sent you mules and an escort? . . ."

Junípero left Loreto on September 28. "Two days later," he wrote in his *Journal*, "Rivera began his requisitions, at San Javier. There,

[1] A great-granddaughter of Caesar Borgia, Doña Maria de Borja, Duchess of Gandia, had paid over 120,000 pesos to the Pious Funds; that is why the Missions of San Borja and Santa Maria bore her name. In 1902 the International Court of Justice at the Hague was still arguing about the Pious Funds, to determine to whom, in the United States or in Mexico, what was left of them should be returned.

as at the other stations, he took what seemed good to him. One had to resign oneself to it, for the service of both Majesties." [2]

With suppurating ulcers on one leg, Junípero made his way southward, pausing at every mission. He arrived at the Visitor General's headquarters on October 29. The two men worked in collaboration until the tenth of January. Sometimes they were at Santa Ana, sometimes at La Paz. One is impressed, perforce, in noting the speed and the joy with which they labored. In addition to complete disinterestedness, what gifts as men of action each possessed! Forgetful of no single detail, turning what they had to unlooked-for advantage and creating out of the whole cloth what was lacking, both of them were endowed with such force of stubborn determination and such genius for adjustment that they would have been able, it seems, to change places with each other: Galvez going out to found missions, and Junípero to serve as Minister to Charles III.

In its major outlines, the plan they adopted was as follows:

To their knowledge, the territory which they called Upper California, New California, or Northern California—and which we now call California—began 375 miles north of Santa Maria (the thirtieth parallel), and extended over a distance of five hundred miles from the port of San Diego (thirty-third parallel) to the port of Monterey (thirty-seventh parallel). Fray Junípero wanted to establish ten missions there, one every fifty miles, so situated that the ministers would be able to aid one another, and, when they traveled, could find asylum with their comrades every other day. He would start, as soon as he arrived, with the establishment of three missions: one at San Diego, one at Monterey, and one, between the two, on the Santa Barbara Channel. The first would have as its ministers Fathers Murguia and Parron, the second Fathers Junípero and Crespi, the third Fathers Gomez and Viscaíno.

It was further decided that in the interjacent territory, extending from Santa Maria to San Diego, which was still neither known nor conquered and would continue to form part of Lower California, five other missions would be set up. There would then be

---

[2] That is, for the Majesty of God and the Majesty of the King. The Spaniards used this phrase habitually: they worked, struggled, fought "for both Majesties" —God and the King.

fifteen missions in all between Santa Maria and Monterey—which would add a region half as large as Spain to the domains of His Catholic Majesty Charles III. But all that could be done only when Father Verger returned from Europe with the fifty friars he was engaged in recruiting there.

The first three missions of the New Conquest were immediately baptized.

"What shall we call them?" Galvez said to Junípero. "I feel sure you agree with me that San Diego should keep that name. We are not going to dispossess a Franciscan and Spanish saint so sympathetic as Fray Diego of Alcala! So, then, we have first the San Diego Mission at San Diego. And next?"

"I have been wishing that one might be named for our great doctor St. Bonaventura."

"And I, too, love the Seraphic Doctor. To prove it to you, I herewith adopt his mission, personally. I will be responsible for the chalice, vestments, and all the other liturgical furnishings for the services of worship. You will see whether I am not as good a sacristan as you, and whether the treasury of St. Bonaventura, with the Jesuits' liturgical effects that I have found, will not be the finest of the three! . . . And where are we putting San Buenaventura? On the Channel? . . ."

"Yes, indeed, Excellency! The first mission of the Santa Barbara Channel will be dedicated to St. Bonaventura."

"As for the Monterey Mission, we will call that San Carlos, for one cannot do less than dedicate one to the King's patron saint," said the Minister of Charles III.

"Then our Seraphic Father St. Francis will have nothing?" Junípero, a little disappointed, asked.

"If he wants something, let him move us to discover a third port! . . . In that way he will get his mission," Galvez replied.[3]

But let us not anticipate. Before discovering the port of San Francisco, it was necessary above all to rediscover that of Monterey, and to forestall the Russians there.

For that, Galvez organized two expeditions: one was to go by sea, under the leadership of Commandant Vila; the other was to

---

[3] Actually, like St. Diego d'Alcala, St. Francis already had his port, at least on paper. In 1595 Sebastian Cermeno had dedicated to him the bay he had discovered north of the thirty-eighth parallel. But it was a question of rediscovering this bay, and however much St. Francis helped, the bay, the port, and the mission were his.

take the land route along the coast, under Portola's command. The march by sea would be carried out in the first place by the two ships, *San Carlos*, which was to sail from La Paz in a few days, and *San Antonio*, which would set out from Cape San Lucas in February. After them would come the *San José*, which would soon be ready to leave the yards, and which, when it sailed a little later, would carry as large a load as the other two together. The land expedition, for its part, would comprise two columns. The first, constituting the advance guard, would be commanded by Rivera; the second, to take its departure some weeks later, would be commanded by Portola. Each boat was to carry twenty-five soldiers, with the same number in each column overland. It was thought that the boats would take about four months to reach the port of San Diego, and that the land columns would hardly need more than two. Reckoning twelve and one-half miles a day, sixty days should suffice for the caravans to cover 325 miles between Velicata and San Diego. (Velicata, fifty miles north of Santa Maria, was the place where the livestock was assembled for the farms of the future missions. Rivera had to go as far north as that with his hundreds of cows, because there was no pasturage at Santa Maria and they would have starved to death; at Velicata, on the contrary, they could be easily and comfortably pastured until time for them to set out, with the troop columns, on the march to Monterey.)

Father Parron was to sail on the *San Carlos*, Fathers Gomez and Viscaíno on the *San Antonio*, Father Murguia on the *San José*. As for Father Crespi and Junípero, the first was to accompany Rivera, and the second, Governor Portola. On this point, a discussion arose between the Visitor General and the Father Prefect.

"I insist that you take one of the boats," Galvez said. "With all the journeys demanded by your mission visits—"

"Thanks be to God, I have been able to visit all the missions with the one exception of Mulege."

"You are tired, and your leg is worse than ever."

"I cannot do less than Father Crespi, who, at my request, is going by land."

"Father Crespi is ten years younger than you. He can get on a horse as well as anybody, and he is in good health. As for you, bad horseman that you are—"

"I admit you are right in that. But let us not talk of this any longer; it is the only matter in which I cannot agree with Your Excellency. I put my trust in God, and I rely upon His aid to get me to Monterey."

Galvez was relying upon God, also. By his decree of November 21, 1769, he had placed the expedition under the patronage of St. Joseph, in whose honor Mass would be sung in the future missions on the nineteenth of every month. He lent Junípero the banner of the Virgin which he took with him everywhere, and which the Father Prefect was to send back to him after raising it in Monterey. "How I should like to be setting out with you," he said over and over again, "to go and plant the cross, with my own hands, in this new kingdom!"

Meanwhile, in the port of La Paz, the loading of the *San Carlos* was proceeding feverishly. Everything that could be got on to the boat was being stowed there: large and small cannon, chests of powder; jars of oil and of brandy, casks of wine, sacks of beans and of meal, stores of smoked meat, dates, and hardtack; bells and liturgical equipment for future churches, agricultural implements for the future farms; seeds, cuttings of flowers and fruit trees; chickens, and a dozen pigs, which, with their short feet, would not have been able to follow Rivera's cows on the land route.

Galvez was proud of his ship. They had spoken so ill of it, those men who had no faith in the success of the venture! The Visitor General had had it dismantled, heaved over, fitted with a new keel. As tar was lacking, he had made a substitute, with his own hands, from *pitayo* sap. "This pious Christian worked like a ship's caulker," Palou wrote.

"Well!" he would say to Junípero. "Now that you have seen how it steers, what do you think of the infamous calumnies that have been hurled at our *San Carlos?* Confess that this little boat is a first-class ship, one of the best in the King's fleet, a ship that will one day deserve to be put on show in a golden case!"

On the sixth of January Junípero blessed the ship and the flags; he sang Mass on board; everyone received Communion; the Visitor General had seen to it that everyone should make his confession. After the Litany of the Blessed Virgin and the prayer to St. Joseph, Junípero preached a sermon; then Galvez preached another. "According to general opinion, mine was the better of the two," Galvez wrote to Palou. And Junípero, for his part, wrote, "It is a fact that His Excellency has literally set the crew and the troops on fire."

The embarkation took place on the evening of January 9, 1769. Aboard the ship were Commandant Vila, old Father Parron, the engineer Constanso (celebrated for his geodetic discoveries), the French doctor Pierre Prat, twenty-five Catalan volunteers commanded by Lieutenant Pedro Fages, and some Indian archers. Galvez delivered another address to them: he spoke of God, the King, and the Russians; he enjoined the men to obey their leaders; to all of them he said again that the King was counting upon them to defend the missionary, if need be, at the cost of their own lives.

Night fell upon the port. The next day, at dawn, the *San Carlos* spread its sails. Galvez and Junípero followed it with their eyes for a long time. Then they embraced one another, and, the same day, Junípero set out once more on the road to Loreto. They were never to see one another again.

On the fifteenth of February, it was the turn of the *San Antonio* to weigh anchor. It was commanded by the great seaman Juan Perez, who had distinguished himself on the route of the Philippines. "It sailed more heavily loaded than the *San Carlos*, and convoyed by the same blessings from Heaven," Galvez wrote to Palou. "I preached a sermon again, in my own fashion. The Fathers (Gomez and Viscaíno) stared with amazement when they saw me begin; then they started to weep and sigh like everyone else. No doubt they are going to report that I have revived the comedy of the devil in the pulpit of truth; I shall be the first to laugh at that; it is all the same to me, provided we succeed in our holy enterprise. Besides, I am so constructed that my courage increases in proportion to the difficulties I meet."

In the meantime, the land expedition was also getting ready to start out. Father Crespi left his Mission La Purisima on February 26, and arrived on March 22 at the Velicata encampment. There he found Rivera and his men about to make their confession to Father Lasuen, who had accompanied them thus far. Certain among them were in great need of confession; for example the famous "soldier administrators" whose consciences were burdened with so many slaughtered cows and emptied casks. For their purification and punishment, Galvez had enrolled them all in the advance guard, judging that the Indians' first arrows, if there were any, ought by rights to be for them. Everyone made his Easter confession and received Communion on Holy Thursday, March 23, and the next day the column got under way. In addition to about one hundred fifty mules, with horses, donkeys, and cattle that brought the number of animals up to four hundred, the caravan included Rivera and Crespi, as mentioned above; the engineer Canizares, twenty-five cuirassiers with our one-time "administrators" among them, and forty-two Indians armed with bows and arrows.

Since the Portola column was not going to leave Velicata for several weeks, Junípero was able to stay on at Loreto until Tuesday of Easter Week. He took advantage of this free time to draw up a report on the thirteen missions, which he left for Francisco Palou. At the beginning of March he had learned that the Dominicans had just obtained a royal Memorandum authorizing them to go into Lower California and take possession of the ten missions there. Before leaving Loreto, Junípero transmitted this curious piece of news to Galvez, who, by that fact, became still more hostile to the religious of that Order.

The Visitor General Galvez was himself on the point of leaving the Peninsula. He got everything ready for the sailing of the *San José*, and, on May 1, 1769, embarked for Sonora.

The year he spent there was a frightful time for him. Overworked, devoured by cares, responsibilities, anxieties, he first received no news of the expedition, and then what came was disheartening. Worry and sorrow were gnawing at him constantly. No one dared any longer to utter the word "California" in his presence. Four physicians were trying to cure him; there were moments when those about him trembled for his reason.

For that matter (people were saying) was it not already mad to have embarked upon such great undertakings with such slight means at hand? As for himself, he had to struggle on without respite, his mind sick and his body wracked: to charge down upon the Indians in revolt, to negotiate, to organize; and he was continuing, also, to pray and to hope. He knew what the men of his entourage were thinking, and he cared less than nothing for that. It was enough for him that his orders should be carried out. At Arispe, in March, 1770, he signed at the bottom of one of the numerous decrees that were brought to him: "José de Galvez, mad in this world. Pray God he may be happy in the world to come."

During May of 1770 he returned, cured, to Mexico, having pacified the rebellious districts and earned the title of Marquis de Sonora which the King granted him later on. In Mexico he met up with Father Verger, who was bringing his fifty recruits from Spain, and was about to be appointed Guardian of San Fernando: the prudent Father Verger, who, not venturing to say that Junípero was likewise a little mad, confined himself to declaring that "he ought to curb his zeal."

And so it often happens: the sensible and discreet call "madness" that little extra quantity of genius which has been denied to them, and which others, more favored by Heaven, make use of to accomplish wonders.

Eight

The Discovery of New California
[March 28 - July 1, 1769]

Junípero took leave of his Loreto congregation on Easter Sunday, 1769, one year after he had first come among them. Escorted by two cuirassiers, a few pack mules, and his faithful twenty-year-old muleteer José María, he left Loreto on the morning of March 28 and arrived that same evening at Francisco Palou's mission at San Javier. He stayed there three days.

"It was necessary for me to spend a little time with this dear friend," he wrote in his *Journal*. "To say nothing of the strong and old affection that binds us to one another, I had to acquaint him with the work I was leaving to him as my successor." [1]

When he saw his master, Palou wept. "I who had loved him for twenty-nine years," he writes, "I had never found him so ill; there were running sores on his leg and foot. Taking the ground that the state of his health might jeopardize the success of the expedition, I besought him to let me go in his place; but he cut short all my entreaties. 'That is out of the question,' he said. 'I have put my trust in God, and He will help me.' But my grief revived at the moment of departure: two men had to lift him to the saddle. . . .

" 'To our meeting in Monterey,' he said, 'where we shall soon find ourselves working together again!'

" 'Alas, no,' I answered, in sobs. 'To our meeting in eternity, dear Father Lector!'

" 'You pain me by speaking like that. You are lacking in faith. . . .'

[1] Entitled *Diario de Viage para los Puertos de San Diego y Monte-Rey*, this *Journal* is about 25,000 words long, and the original is preserved in the Archives of Mexico. It recounts the journey from Loreto to Velicata, and, following that, the expedition properly so called.

68

"He threw me one last glance, full of affection, and went jolting off on his mule. . . . I wrote at once to the Visitor General, asking that I might be assigned to take my master's place. His Excellency replied that he had discussed the question with him a number of times, without succeeding in making him change his mind.

" 'Moreover, I am very happy to see him taking part in the expedition,' he added. 'I deeply admire his faith, and I share his hope completely.' "

Galvez knew that Junípero sick would be a hundred times more useful than Palou well, if a day came when everyone had lost courage and given up, and there must be someone there who would remain strong in hope and action.

As for our traveler himself, he made his way steadily northward, astride his saddle from seven to eight hours and covering an average of thirty miles a day. It was so hot that from time to time he had to take refuge in a cave; many a night he slept outdoors; and he stopped at all the missions spaced out along his route.

From the first to the fourth of April, thus, he stayed at San José de Comondu; on the fifth, he arrived at La Purisima, Father Crespi's old mission; on the eighth, he was at Guadalupe with Father Sancho, whom we shall meet again as Guardian of San Fernando; on the fourteenth, he was at San Ignacio; on the eighteenth, at Santa Gertrudis; on the twenty-seventh, at San Borja with Father Lasuen.

"The affection in which I hold this dear friend kept me at his side for two days," he writes. "At his request, I promised to help him to rejoin us as soon as possible at Monterey."

He did help him in that, and was at first ill rewarded, as we shall see.

On the fifth of May he overtook Portola and Father Campa at Santa Maria, and on the thirteenth he arrived with them at Velicata, where the main body of the expedition was awaiting them.

The soldiers broke into cries of joy when the party came in sight. The next day, which was the Feast of Pentecost, the cross was planted at Velicata, and Junípero founded his first mission on pagan soil. He sang the Mass, to which the soldiers came armed, shooting off salvos during the entire service. Entrusted to Father Campa as minister, San Fernando de Velicata was attached to the missions of Lower California, which numbered thirteen, and of which Palou, who had been made Prefect, would assume the direction henceforth.

On the following day, Junípero was praying in his cabin when word was brought him of the arrival of a group of Indians, whom the gunfire had kept from approaching on the evening before. "What a joy!" he writes. "So the hour had come when, after so many years of waiting, I was about to see men who were ignorant of Christ, and who from this time on should be my friends. With a heart overflowing with gratitude, I bowed my head to the ground, to kiss the earth to which Providence had at last guided me."

It was his kiss of espousal to the Indian soil. He put his whole soul into it, giving himself irrevocably to the unprivileged and unloved race. "They have taken possession of my heart," he used to say of the Redskins. We shall see what love he bore them, to his last breath. . . .

"I went out," he continues. "In front of the hut were twelve Indians, naked as Adam before the fall, and completely at ease in this costume. I laid my hands on their heads as a sign of friendship, and gave each of them a handful of figs, which they ate. They brought us a bag of mescal buttons and four big fish, which were half rotten, since they had not thought of salting or cleaning them. . . . Father Campa gave them some raisins, Governor Portola added tobacco, and the soldiers had them eat as much as they wanted. Through an interpreter I announced to them that from now on a Father would be living in this place.

" 'There he is,' I said, pointing to Father Campa. 'Come to see him often; he will be your best friend.' Then I pointed to the soldiers. 'And these, too, will do everything they can for you,' I said. 'In return, I will ask you not to steal the livestock. If there is anything you lack, no matter what, come to the Father instead, and he will give you whatever he can.'

"These words pleased them, and they made signs to show their approval. Then Portola, going up to their chief, said to him. 'If up to now you have been chief by the will of the tribe, you will be chief henceforth by the authority of the King, our master; for, in his name, I appoint you Captain.' "

While waiting for the party to set out, the animals were pastured at San Juan de Dios, five miles north of Velicata, under Ortega's guard. It was there that Junípero experienced one of those sudden cures of which he was the object several times in his life. We read in his *Journal*:

"*May 17.* Shall I have to follow the expedition on a stretcher? I can no longer stand upright: my leg, from which I have suffered so much during the past year, is swollen to the middle of the calf, and covered with purulent abscesses. *May 18.* I could not go up to the altar. . . . *May 19.* I am well once more, and have been able to celebrate Mass. . . ."

This is the way Palou tells the story: "At Velicata, the founding of the Mission had made the revered Father so happy that he had forgotten his affliction. But during the next two days his pain became all but unbearable, and it was thought that the cancer was spreading through his whole leg.

"'It is now only too certain that you will not be able to go along with us,' Portola said to him. 'Would you like me to have you taken back to Velicata?'

"'I have put my trust in God, who has permitted me to reach this point,' Junípero answered, 'and who is able to take me to San Diego. If He wills that I should die on the way, let me be buried where I fall; it will be sweet to me to rest in pagan earth; but nothing in this world will persuade me to turn back.'

"The Governor did not insist further. He had a stretcher made, in which the sick man could lie down at full length, and which would be carried by the archers. Junípero was deeply grieved by the thought of causing his beloved Indians this extra fatigue, and he begged God to come to his rescue. He had a muleteer summoned—a man named Juan Coronel—and said to him:

"'My boy, would you not have some remedy to cure me?'

"'But, Father, I am not a physician,' the man answered. 'I only cure animals.'

"'Very well: let us assume that I am an animal, and treat me as you would one of your mules!'

"Juan Coronel took some tallow, pounded it down between two stones, rubbed herbs he had selected into it, fricasseed the mixture on the stove, and smeared it over the Father's infected leg and foot. And God attended to the rest, for, as His servant Junípero wrote me, he slept all night afterwards, and woke ready to climb into the saddle the next morning."

On May 21, Trinity Sunday, the bugles were blown at dawn. Junípero said Mass outdoors, urged good behavior upon every member of the company, blessed them all in the name of the Father, Son, and Holy Ghost; and then the long column got under way.

It was made up of twenty-five cuirassiers on horseback; thirty Indians who belonged to the Missions of Santa Maria, Santa Gertrudis, and San Borja; cooks, muleteers, common laborers, sappers to clear the road, and several interpreters, along with some hundred cows, 170 pack mules, and a number of donkeys. Portola and Junípero rode at the head, followed by a part of the military troop. Then came the long baggage train and the lowing herd of cows. The Indian archers on foot, officered by the rest of the cuirassiers, brought up the rear of the procession. The white men carried guns and swords; the Indians were allowed only bows and arrows. In open country the soldiers unlaced their cuirasses; in the valleys and forests they fastened them on again. Cuirass and buckler served them as protection against the flint-headed arrows of the Redskins.

The caravan progressed at the rate of about thirteen miles a day. The march lasted thirty-two days, and eight days were lost in stopping to rest and pasture the livestock. With no landmarks, being now out of sight of the sea and finding their way solely by the astrolabe, the column sometimes drew near the coast and sometimes moved away from it. They were often obliged to change their route in order to find water and grasslands, or because the mountains barred their path. Sergeant Ortega would go out on reconnaissances, indicating the road by messages left on stones; and when he had discovered a place to camp he would come back and tell Portola about it. "In this way he traveled over the road three times," Junípero writes.

Meanwhile, Junípero gave names, as they advanced, to places that seemed to deserve them, either borrowing the name of the saint whose day it was, or finding his inspiration in some special detail of the landscape or the journey.

This expedition brought that of Cortez to mind. It was a hazardous adventure, almost a wager with destiny, for these thirty

Spaniards to plunge into the unknown, among peoples of whose intentions—whether bloodthirsty or innocuous—they were ignorant. They all believed that they would have to do with the Apaches. "How many times, seeing Ortega vanish in the distance, have I trembled for fear he had disappeared forever!" Junípero wrote. The least unruliness or indiscipline among the men might have brought about the massacre of the entire caravan; and so Portola, just and kind as he was, excused nothing to anyone. For a female donkey that had come to grief he took stern measures against his own cook, depriving him of his arms, sentencing him to travel afoot, and making him pay four times the price of the injured animal.

It was soon borne in upon Junípero that his future friends and parishioners had little idea of propriety or cleanliness. "Up to this time," he writes, "all the natives had flown away like birds, but on the twenty-first of May an old Indian came up to the camp. It was the second time, moreover, that he had seen a white man: a little while before, a man dressed like myself (it was Father Crespi) had passed by here. 'I did not run away,' the old Indian said. 'I stayed to look at him, and I even spoke to him.' He was completely nude, and as the soldiers had given him a great deal to eat he all of a sudden, without the least embarrassment, squatted down before us and satisfied Nature's more substantial demands. When he had finished he got up, took a long breath, and went on with the conversation.

"We asked him if he would like to receive baptism. 'With great pleasure!' he replied. 'And since the Father is here, let him give it to me right away!' It was pointed out to him that he must first receive instruction, and he lent himself with good grace to the catechism lesson which the interpreters passed on to him. As a mail courier was setting out for Velicata the next day, I suggested that the old man should accompany him, so as to conclude his religious education with Father Campa. Did he go there? . . ."

The soldiers did not have to do battle, although certain tribes were showing themselves hostile. As the *Journal* continues, "On May 26, our archers seized a spy, whom they brought before me. He struggled like a demon, rolling over and over on the ground in spite of his shackles. We took him to the Governor's tent, where, for a bowl of porridge, he acknowledged what he was up to and told us that five clan captains were preparing an ambush against us. Portola pardoned him and sent him home, where-upon he disappeared with his bow, his quiver, and a band of green wool which he wore in his long hair as his sole article of cloth-ing. . . . Two days later—Sunday, the twenty-eighth—we were just finishing Mass when some forty natives appeared, yelling, making menacing gestures toward us, and calling upon us to go back where we came from. We tried to persuade them to with-draw in peace, but they only howled the louder and threatened us the more; they did not even draw back before four horsemen abreast who advanced against them. Was there going to be a fight? . . . Then two soldiers fired in the air, and all the Indians ran away as fast as their legs could carry them, as if thunder from Heaven were about to strike them down. They followed us at a distance, then, without coming down from the hills. As we were entering a defile, the soldiers put on their cuirasses again, the muleteers checked the percussion caps of their guns, and the whole column was on the alert. But we got through without in-cident."

Beginning with the first of June they had done with "naked hills and stony deserts." When they reached the latitude of 30° 30′, they found vines growing wild, and there was grass again; the Spaniards had the feeling that this was the beginning of New California. "Our animals have never fed so well," observes the *Journal*.

To crown his happiness Junípero caught sight, next day, of "all kinds of flowers, including the most beautiful of all—the rose of Castille. The branch of a rose bush is at this moment caress-ing the hand that is setting down these lines," he writes. "It has three full-blown roses, some buds which are about to open, and six roses whose petals have fallen. I bless Thee, Lord, for having created the rose of Castille!"

The projected missions, Junípero announced to Palou, would all be "excellent." And he added, "There is soil and water every-where. Even the mountains can be cultivated." Palou would have a wide choice when Father Verger's Spanish recruits arrived: for four missions that were to be established the *Journal* indicates some fifteen sites.

As for the Indians, one could imagine nothing better: "A tre-mendous harvest awaits us," Junípero writes. "All the good that is to be wished for will be done for these natives; when I questioned them they all, without exception, declared that they wanted to see me stay on among them." What fine characteristics, of every kind, they possessed! Those of San Solano were tall: "Nowhere would the King be able to find such handsome grenadiers!" Those of San Antonio were artists: they could "make pottery such as is to be seen only at Guadalajara." Those of San Juan Bautista were consummate tradesmen: "For a large handkerchief the soldiers offered them they would give two hampers of fresh fish, but when the handkerchief was small they would give only one hamper." And, withal, how likable they were: "The mothers would lay their nurslings in my arms. And very elegant, I declare, with their long hair plastered down with white clay! The men and boys are all as naked as when they left their mothers' breast; but what modesty there is among the women and girls! A good sign for the future is that—men and women alike—they love dress goods. They would jump into the fire to get a piece. They used to pull at my sleeve, to take my habit from me; they wanted to strip Governor Portola of his trousers. If I had given my homespun robe to all the people who asked me for it, we should have properly clothed inmates for a large convent of Indian Franciscans, I assure you! Some of them, it must be confessed, have a tendency to borrow without returning, and I have had the utmost difficulty, particularly, in retrieving my spectacles. But are they alone in coveting others' goods?"

Let no one expect Junípero ever to find any lack of attractiveness in the Redskins! For a man in love, his squinting fiancée has the most beautiful eyes in the world; for a mother, her erring son is the finest lad on earth. The passages in the *Journal* which have to do with the volunteers from Lower California are especially illuminating; as, for example:

"*June 5*, San Pacifico. An archer ran away last night. *June 14*, San Basileo. Nine made off today. *June 18*, San Gervasio. Of the three archers from San Borja who were staying, two are leaving us. . . ." Well, what of that? says Junípero. "They are probably afraid of being held at San Diego, and kept from going home." Being without power to recapture them, he sends them his blessing from a distance: "May God bless them for the services they have rendered us, and the trouble their departure is causing!" The unhappy man almost justifies them: "One must be in my place and see how badly they are fed, to judge their conduct fairly. . . ."

Portola, however, had not sent them supperless to bed that day. For, under the same date of June 18, the *Journal* recounts that "a mare gave birth to a nice little mule. The simple beast would not have been able to follow our march, so it was given as a present to the archers, who skinned it at once and ate it by the light of the campfires. It did them good, I hope!"

He contradicts himself with the same ease and freedom where the Indians of Upper California are concerned. "Their kindness toward us was such that one would have said they were friends of long standing. How many times were we obliged to refuse the presents they offered us!" Has he forgotten that he trembled for Ortega's life a hundred times, and that if it had not been for the cuirassiers' shots in the air the whole caravan would probably have been wiped out? It was nothing to him that the Redskins showed themselves to be ungrateful and hypocritical, or that they tried on several occasions to kill him: he did not cease to find them captivating. They were infinitely dear to him; he continued to trust them indefinitely; he loved them with that mystic love which God has for the sinner, always ready and waiting for him, and rejoicing more over one sinner that repents than over the ninety-and-nine righteous men who have not strayed from good-doing.

To those who had believed that the "country of Monterey" was a peninsula, cut off from the south by a strait, it was a great joy to find, on the sixth of June, that they could begin to doubt this. The strait, in fact, was an invention of the Jesuit Wenceslaus Linck, who had attempted in 1666 to explore the mouths of the Colorado River. He did not reach them; but his *Journal* avers, none the less, that the Colorado empties into the Pacific after flowing through the Gulf of California, thus forming, from the Gulf to the Ocean, a wide and impassible arm of the sea.

"Now on the afternoon of June 6," Junípero relates, "a Redskin detached himself from the group that was watching us from a distance. Our men gave him so much to eat that he consented to spend the evening and night at the camp. He knew all sorts of things about the Rivera column: it had camped on this very spot, and the natives had guided it toward the northwest; at the present time, it was on the seacoast. . . .

"On the tenth of June, leaving his friends who were keeping distrustfully apart, a native came to us, with a stick in one hand and a little bell in the other. We offered him things to eat; he refused them. We ate them in his presence; he did not want even to taste them. He was forced to swallow a mouthful of porridge; he threw it up at once. Finally he explained that he was the tribe's dancer, and that he must dance before eating. We gladly gave him permission to do so, and he began to dance and sing, circling around the *tortillas*, sugar, and meat that he had had laid out on the ground. I noticed that he changed his air for the different articles of food that he was 'exorcising.' Some soldiers who were standing guard beside him offered him figs and raisins. He signed to them to throw them on the pile, and continued to dance around it, shaking his little bell and doing juggler's tricks with his baton. Then he asked if he might go and dance around the mules and the pack-baskets, so that nothing might be omitted from his consecrations. . . . And now that everything was purified and blessed, he was ready to eat no-matter-what.

"If we authorized him to dance all along the road, and with the proviso that he could go back home if he didn't like us, he would agree to accompany us to San Diego. For he knew that that was where we were going and that a Father like me was there already, with soldiers, mules, and cows. It was only a four-and-one-half-day march from here, he assured us. I had been moved to affection for him; I was already seeing him baptized; I had even chosen his name—Pascal. Why did it have to be that just as we were setting out a soldier said something to him, I don't know what, that hurt his feelings? Then I saw my Pascal bounding off like a stag in the forest, leaving all our presents behind."

If Pascal was right, Junípero observes, the Jesuit Father was obviously wrong. But was Pascal right? For his part, he believed him; and he spent some time in the effort to prove the explorer mistaken in his calculations. God send that the strait did not exist, he sighed! Otherwise, "we shall never reach Monterey by land, and we shall have to retrace our steps. Well, we shall know to-morrow. . . ."

On June 16, from the top of a hill, six soldiers caught sight of the ocean, and saw the coast extending toward the north without interruption. On the evening of the twenty-seventh, an Indian appeared, clad in green cotton. "He was coming from Rivera; at San Diego he had seen Fathers like me, and two great boats. He would have got here sooner if he had not had to stop two days on the way, to go fishing." The next morning horsemen loomed up on the horizon: "They were ten soldiers whom Rivera was sending us with relay mounts."

"On the twenty-ninth of June," Junípero writes, "we made a halt near a hamlet whose inhabitants came to call upon us. The man we had seen in green clothes was with them, just as naked as the rest. He lived in one of these huts, he told us; when he had finished his errand to us he had taken off his costume to go back to his own place. . . .

"On the thirtieth, almost floored with fatigue, we would have liked to camp in the neighborhood of a village whose cabins we glimpsed.

" 'Do nothing of the sort!' cried Ortega. 'The people who live there are loathsome scum-of-the-earth. Just think, they offered us their women so as to get our clothing, and when we refused the deal they came near massacring us!'

"That was why we had to continue our march for several hours," Junípero adds, "in order to reach the point on the water which the sergeant had marked out, farther on. . . . But what does that matter now? We no longer feel the hardships of our journey; our hearts are filled with joy, as we think of all the dear friends whom we shall clasp in our arms tomorrow."

Alas! A great many of these were dead, and others were dying, when the column reached San Diego next day. It was Saturday, the first day of July, 1769.

Nine

*Junípero Prevents the Abandonment
of New California and Founds the Missions
of San Diego and Monterey*
[1769-1770]

What they saw and learned on arrival quickly dispelled the newcomers' joy. The *San Antonio* and the *San Carlos* were anchored
in the bay, and Rivera's men, who had reached here on May fifteenth, were camped on the shore. But the ships had become ghost
ships, and Rivera's men had buried thirty-one sailors already.

Galvez' orders had specified that the first boat to arrive should
wait as long as twenty days for the other, and then, with or without it, proceed toward Monterey. The first to arrive was the *San
Antonio*, under Juan Perez, which dropped anchor at San Diego
on April 11. Its period of waiting was approaching an end when,
on the twenty-ninth, the *San Carlos* was sighted on the horizon.
But the incoming ship was in difficulty; its crew could no longer
launch the longboat—or, rather, it no longer had a crew. The
men had been mowed down by the pestilence, or *mal de Loanda*.
And then, in taking aid to the *San Carlos*, the *San Antonio* had
been smitten by the infection, too.

"All but two of the *San Carlos* sailors are dead," Junípero
wrote Palou. "Of the twenty-five Catalan volunteers it was bringing, three are dead and the rest are dying. Eight men of the *San
Antonio*, likewise, have already succumbed. . . . Who knows if
it will not be the *San José*, the last to sail, that will be the first
to reach Monterey?"

The *San José* was shipwrecked, and was never heard from again.

"Making shift as best it can," Junípero continued, in a letter
of July 3, 1769, "the *San Antonio* is about to return to San Blas
to get provisions; from there it will also bring back two new

79

crews, which will make it possible for it and the *San Carlos* to complete their task. As for Governor Portola, he is now on the point of starting for Monterey; as soon as he has gone, I will set up the Mission."

The *San Antonio* hoisted sail for San Blas on July 9. On the fourteenth, Portola left for Monterey, taking with him Fages and Rivera, Fathers Gomez and Crespi, the engineer Costanso, a band of forty cuirassiers, some fifteen Indian archers, and six Catalan volunteers. He left only eight real soldiers at San Diego: two to guard the boat and six to protect the mission. He had none too many himself for vanquishing the Russians, if he should find them.

On July 16, the traditional great cross was planted on a hillock three miles from the harbor where the ship commanded by Vila and Canizares was rocking sadly on the waves. Junípero sang the Mass under a canopy of twigs; and the Mission of San Diego was founded. It took over the camp vacated by Portola and, protected by a stockade and two cannon, it consisted of the chapel, the friars' cabins, two large tents and several small ones. The large tents, serving as a quarantine hospital, were sheltering thirty-five plague-stricken patients; the small ones lodged, in all, twenty able-bodied men: six cuirassiers, nine Indian archers of doubtful loyalty, the physician Prat, a blacksmith, a carpenter, and two muleteers.

When the Spaniards had first put in an appearance, the Indians had rushed to cover, believing that their last hour had come. They had taken the *San Antonio* for a monster from the other world, the horses and mules for supernatural creatures, and the mounted soldiers for demigods engendered by these wonder-beasts and wielding thunder itself with their guns.

But when nothing catastrophic happened, they were emboldened; and when Portola had vanished from sight with the bulk of the military troop, they became aggressive. The men began stealing; the women would jeer at the guns, and dance about crying, "Poum! Poum!" when the soldiers fired in the air to chase away the pilferers. One night on the *San Carlos* Vila and Canizares surprised some natives in the act of cutting the cable and removing the sails of the ship. On two occasions, the Indians attacked the camp, and Junípero just escaped being killed.

On August 15, at about nine in the morning, they returned in greater numbers. Of the six cuirassiers, two were serving as body-guard to Father Parron, who had gone to say the Mass of the

Assumption aboard the boat; the other four were at Mass in the camp chapel. The aggressors, who had only been waiting for such a moment, jumped the parapet, rushed to the hospital tents, stripped the beds and took the linen, and tore off the sick men's shirts. Powerless to resist, the victims were nevertheless able to cry out. Their cries reached the chapel. The corporal dashed outside and sounded the call to arms. His three men ran out, snatching up gun, cuirass, and buckler. The carpenter hurried out also, and with him the blacksmith, who had just received Communion. "Long live the holy Faith!" he cried, as he flung himself upon the pillagers, "and death to these dogs of heathens!"

The natives, who numbered about thirty, now ran from the tents, ranged themselves in battle order, and began to let fly their arrows. They thought that they could readily dispose of the six men who stood facing them, and that the turn of the others would come next. They were amazed that the soldiers' bucklers should stop their arrows, that they themselves should not see the bullets coming, and that at every shot one of their men should fall. So, after a half-hour of combat, they fled, taking with them their wounded and five men killed, whom, according to their custom, they would burn.

Apart from the blacksmith and the carpenter, who received minor wounds from which they recovered, and Father Viscaíno, the third finger of whose right hand was injured, there was only one casualty to be mourned on the Spanish side—but how grievous that was to Junípero! "They killed my José María" he wrote to Palou on February 10, 1770. "He was attached to me, and he wanted to stay with me always. It was at the very beginning of the shooting that he came running into the cabin where I was praying, spitting mouthfuls of blood, his throat shot through by a poisoned arrow. 'Father, give me absolution quickly,' he groaned, 'for they have killed me.' I helped him to die righteously and in peace; for a quarter of an hour he suffered his death throes in my arms; then he breathed his last. I laid him on the floor of the cabin in a pool of blood, continuing to pray beside him, with my arms crossed on my breast, the crucifix in one hand, the image of the Virgin in the other. So long as the fight lasted I besought for myself the grace of a righteous death, if, as was likely, I was about to rejoin José María in eternity. I waited until darkness fell to bury him, for the Indians must not learn of the reduction in our numbers."

A few days later, the savages came to sue for peace, and to ask care for their wounded. Dr. Prat, himself still convalescent, cured them all. The Redskins seemed touched by his unselfish devotion to duty, and by the fact that the Fathers bore them no resentment. From then on, they presented themselves at the Mission unarmed, and their wives tried to do their part toward a complete reconciliation. Having noticed the Visitor General's painting of the Mother and Child in the chapel, these women thought that the emaciated Madonna had not the milk to feed her plump chubby-cheeked Baby, and that some of them would be able to supply it. The soldiers themselves, who seemed to love the little Jesus, would be susceptible to such attention, and the more ready, thus, to pardon their husbands. So then they would be seen thrusting their rounded breasts between the bars of the grill, waiting there with bared bosoms and asking, by means of gestures, that the Christ-child be brought to them to be suckled.

The mission remained, nevertheless, on the alert. The three friars' ministry among the Indians was reduced to nothing. Junípero was blessing graves: he buried—in addition to José María— four sailors, eight Catalan volunteers, and six Indian archers. One day he believed he was about to be able to baptize a little Indian girl: the corporal of the cuirassiers having promised to be godfather and to supply his goddaughter's clothing henceforth, the parents had given their consent to the baptism. Escorted by a part of the clan, they arrived at the chapel; Junípero put on surplice and stole; the corporal, in full uniform, took the little girl in his arms and held her, gravely, over the font. As she began to cry the moment the lustral water trickled down upon her, the Indians took it into their heads that she was about to die; they snatched her from the arms of the godfather and rushed away with her, leaving Junípero there with his silver conch in his hand.

This semi-baptism formed the sum of Junípero's apostolic efforts during the nine months of his sojourn at San Diego.

Since there was no work for him to do, he prayed, and he suffered. He was struck down in his turn by the *mal de Loanda*. In his cabin made of branches, he was shivering with cold. "It is glacial here," he had written to his Guardian on July 3, 1769. "My two under-tunics are in rags, although I took care to mend them during the journey. Might I ask you for others, the thickest possible?"

The tunics did not arrive. Nothing reached San Diego. The year 1770 began without the little company's receiving news of anyone, without the appearance of any boat, without any sign of life from Portola after six months' absence. What, indeed, had become of Portola and his column? Had they been massacred by the Redskins or taken captive by the Russians? . . .

Under the winter rain the men at San Diego were prey to morose reflection when, on the afternoon of January 24, shots sounded from some hundred yards away, setting the tents a-tremble and bringing everyone to his feet with a jump. The soldiers on guard replied by discharging their guns; they had recognized Portola's column. It advanced in its accustomed order: "At the head rode the Governor, the two missionaries, Pedro Fages and his six Catalan volunteers; then, carrying shovel, ax, and pick, came the Indian sappers whose task it was to clear the route; these were followed by four trains of mules with their muleteers, and cuirassiers to defend them; finally, driving the extra mounts ahead of them, appeared the rear-guard, composed of the rest of the Spanish soldiers and the archers, under Rivera's command."

A Mass of thanksgiving to St. Joseph was sung the next day. Those who were returning were grateful to him because they had lost no one and especially because they found a mission still here. "The nearer we came, the less we counted on it," Father Crespi wrote in his *Journal No. 3.* "We said to each other, 'Will those who have been spared by the plague not have been killed by the Indians?' Or, again, 'Will they not have gone away, when they saw that the boats were not coming?' And we, who had been so hungry that we had had to eat mules for meat, what was going to become of us if there were no longer provisions to be found at San Diego?" St. Joseph could also be thanked that they had seen no Russians on those two hundred leagues of coast, and especially that in searching for the harbor of Monterey they had discovered another, utterly beautiful, which, according to the promise made by Galvez and Junípero at La Paz, had been christened San Francisco.

The harbor of Monterey, alas, had eluded all quest. On his outward trip, Portola had planted the cross at the site indicated on the maps and had buried a parchment on which was written, "We have not found the harbor of Monterey." On the return journey he had set up another cross in the same place and buried a new piece of writing: "We have searched in vain for the harbor, as far as San Francisco." This was to notify the boats, if they should arrive. On February 13 the Governor wrote to the Viceroy: "Among the valuable results of this expedition of six and one-half months must be counted the certainty we have come to, that . . . the harbor of Monterey does not exist."

And the engineer Costanso noted in his *Journal:* "God forbid that one should venture to denounce as mistaken the experienced men of the sea who discovered the harbor of Monterey and extolled its beauty! . . . How, then, is one to explain how this famous harbor eluded our search? Must we conclude that it has been silted up, and that the centuries have blotted out the traces of it?"

These infallible men of the sea were, as is known, Sebastian Vizcaíno and his pilot Cabrero Bueno. In his book, *Navegación Especulativa y Practica*, Cabrero described a great mountain, a great harbor, and a great river emptying into this harbor. Was this enthusiasm or mirage? The fact remains that his mountain was a little hill, that his river—christened Carmelo by the Carmelites who accompanied him—was a gully filled with water only in the rainy season, and that in this twenty-mile-wide bay the winds blew as on the open sea. It was anything but surprising that Portola and his comrades should not have recognized this as the wonderful harbor of Monterey!

Junípero, who was gifted with an extraordinary geographical sense, could scarcely contain himself as he heard what the returning travelers had to say. "What!" he cried. "You went to Rome and did not find St. Peter's? For it is indeed at Monterey, thank God, that you have planted the cross." The expedition that had failed was a success in his eyes: he already saw a long chaplet of missions strung over the 750 miles from Velicata to San Francisco.

He had to dim the bright hues of his dream two weeks later when Portola, after making an inventory of the remaining food supplies, told him of the decision he had come to.

"You know that I am responsible for a hundred human lives," said the Governor, who himself had just been going hungry and eating the flesh of old mules. "As Rivera must return to look for livestock at Velicata, he will start at once, with twenty-four men.

When they are gone, we shall have enough food left to last until the end of April. By that date, then, we must be in a Christian countryside, and to accomplish this we must leave here on the
fifteenth of March, since we are a forty-day journey from Velicata. So here is the decision I have reached, in agreement with
the officers of land and sea: if the ships come into the harbor before March 14, I shall immediately set out again for Monterey;
but if they are not here by the evening of that day, we shall all
leave for Lower California on the morning of the fifteenth, with
the possibility of returning later, according to the orders we receive."

This was common sense, and Junípero made no objection. He
merely begged the Governor to postpone the date of withdrawal
until March 19, the feast of St. Joseph. "I am confident that the
patron of the expedition will not forsake us," he said. Portola responded by granting St. Joseph and Junípero five days of grace
instead of four, and the departure was put off from the fifteenth
to the twentieth.

In measure as the days passed, hope fell. Soon nothing was being spoken of except the approaching departure. The order for
it was posted in the camp. The *San Carlos* was leaving also; its
crew would be made up of a few survivors of the *San Antonio*,
who had now recovered, and some archers who were being taught
seamanship.

"What heartbreak it was for the revered Father Junípero to
assist in these preparations!" Palou writes. "They were saying, indeed, that they would come back; but would they want to, and
would they be able to? How many times had men promised to
come, since 1603? . . . These territories whose conquest, awaited
for centuries, had been made in the King's name—were they then
about to be abandoned? And was the cross of Christ that had
been planted there to be abandoned too? Finally, was it abandonment that was in store for those innumerable pagan souls who had
been close to being converted to the Gospel? . . . Junípero was
far from agreeing to that."

He made a decision that marks one of the supreme moments
of his life. He resolved to die beside this cross, among these pagans, rather than go away. He would wait alone. And if no boat
came, "if all human succor was denied him, he would trust himself wholly to the mercy of Providence. The men would leave

him a little corn, and when there was no more of that he would eat grass if he had to. But he would never desert." [1]

He secretly notified his colleagues of his determination, leaving them free to act as they would. The ordeal had been a severe one for them all. Only one took a heroic stand: Juan Crespi declared that he would share the fate of his master. Fathers Gomez and Parron decided to attach themselves to Portola, the first in order to return to Spain, the second to take up once more his ministry in Lower California. As for Father Viscaíno, he left with Rivera on February 11, in haste to let his injured finger heal, far from the Indians, in Mexico.

A few days after this, Junípero went aboard the *San Carlos*. Were all the officers knights, whom Spain had on these boats at that time? In any case, we shall encounter no others. Vila and Canizares were among those to whom Galvez had said in his sermon, "I entrust these messengers of Christ to you; watch over them as the apple of your eye." They were moved to tears by the confidence Junípero placed in them, and not for one moment did they contemplate leaving the two friars to the mercy of the Indians.

"Then we will stay, too," they said. "If the withdrawal takes place, you will come aboard the *San Carlos* on the twentieth of March, and we will wait together."

This arrangement was kept secret until the last moment. Among those who, every evening from the ninth of March on, attended the novena in preparation for the feast of St. Joseph, no one knew of it but Portola himself. The novena was concluded on the eighteenth. On the morning of the nineteenth, Junípero sang the Mass and preached. He preached hope. But who had kept hope, and on whom could he bestow it, among those who were listening? The rest of the day was spent in the final preparations for departure. Junípero prayed, suffered, and hoped. . . .

[1] Palou's account, upon which some have thrown undue doubt, is confirmed by all the recently discovered documents. We confine ourselves to three quotations: From a letter to the Guardian Andres, February 2, 1770, "For myself and Father Crespi, who does not wish to leave me, I ask your permission to remain here, relying upon the Providence of God even though food be lacking." From a letter of the same date to Palou, "Only one thing is talked of: that is to abandon all. But though the hope of seeing help come must vanish, I shall hold on to the end. So long as there is grass in the fields, Father Crespi and I will not go away." And from Armona's report to the Viceroy, August 2, 1770, "The entire expedition had decided to go away again on the twentieth of March."

Evening drew near. The sun would soon disappear beneath the waves. Was it setting for the last time upon the little colony of San Diego? . . . Suddenly, as Junípero's eyes searched the ocean, he caught sight of a white dot on the horizon. Then the dot became sails; soon it was a boat, which tacked about for some time and then vanished, driven by the east wind out to sea. But they had all been able to recognize the *San Antonio*, and the order to leave was canceled.

It is on this tardy hour of Monday, March 19, 1770, that, it seems, the founding of New California must be fixed.

After battling against head winds for four days, the sailing ship came alongside San Diego on the twenty-fourth of March.

Those who believe in the Gospel are not surprised that God should reward faith by moving ships, as well as mountains. But those to whom coincidence is enough to explain everything surely will find that a great deal of it was needed to produce Juan Perez on the horizon on the nineteenth of March and to enter the harbor on the twenty-fourth, for he did this entirely against his will.

It was the *San José* and not the *San Antonio* which should have put into port at San Diego, and which had a crew for the *San Carlos* aboard. Juan Perez' own orders were to proceed direct to Monterey, where Galvez believed Portola had by now arrived. He was on his way there, and had passed the thirty-fourth parallel, when he had to call in the Santa Barbara archipelago to take on water. There he learned from the natives that the Portola column had turned south again two months before. What was he to do? . . . Take provisions to a place where no one was? . . . He decided to go back on his tracks, so to speak, and unload them at San Diego. But at the last moment, not daring to disobey his orders, he changed his mind and set sail for the north. As he was leaving the Channel, however, he lost his anchor; it would be impossible, then, for him to moor off Monterey. That was how he had come back to San Diego, knowing that there, thanks to the *San Carlos*, he could lay up his ship.

The letter from Galvez which Perez delivered to Portola did not contain only felicitations. No more than Junípero did the Visitor General believe in harbors that disappeared and mountains that flew away. So the Governor bestirred himself assiduously to carry out his assignment. The ship unloaded part of its cargo, and on Tuesday of Easter week, April 17, Portola set out with some thirty men: seven cuirassiers, five archers, thirteen Catalan volunteers commanded by Pedro Fages, and a group of muleteers. Once more Father Crespi was accompanying the column, equipped with his astrolabe and his writing desk.

At San Diego Fathers Parron and Gomez were left to officiate at the Mission, and Sergeant Ortega with eight cuirassiers and some fifteen Indian archers from Lower California to defend it.

The *San Antonio* was also leaving. Junípero embarked upon it on the fourteenth of April, the day before Easter, together with Constanso and Dr. Prat.

The sea journey was uncomfortable and perilous. Driven back to the thirtieth parallel, off Velicata, by contrary winds at the outset, they did not reach Monterey until May 31. Portola had got there a week earlier. "This is indeed the famous harbor discovered by Vizcaíno in 1603; it has not changed," Junípero wrote to Palou on June 13, 1770. "As for saying why the first expedition did not find it, that is not my affair. The great thing is that we are there."

The establishment of the mission took place on the third of June, the Feast of Pentecost. "The altar was set up under the same oak beneath which Vizcaíno's chaplains had celebrated Mass 167 years before," Junípero wrote his Guardian on June 12. "Everyone arrived singing, while the bells hung from the old tree were ringing at full peal. The sea company came in the ship's long-boat; the Governor and his men came from their cantonment, which had been set up two leagues from the coast. I put on alb and stole. Kneeling before the altar, we sang the *Veni Creator*. A large cross had been laid out on the ground; we lifted it together and planted it upright in the earth. I blessed it; everyone prostrated himself in worship before it. I sprinkled holy water over the level ground surrounding the cross. At each new rite the bells would ring, the soldiers would fire their guns, the *San Antonio* would discharge a volley from its cannon. After the raising of the cross, the colors of our Catholic Sovereign were set floating in the breeze, amid repeated cries of 'Long live the Faith! Long live the King!' Then we buried, at the foot of the cross, a cabin boy who had died aboard the *San Antonio*. During the Mass, which I sang after this, the cannon continued their volleys at intervals. After the Mass, the officers took official possession of the land in the name of the King, one of them unfurling the royal standard, the others pulling up grass and overturning stones, the whole procedure being accompanied by cheers, the ringing of bells, the sound of guns and cannon. Then we all came together for a banquet on the beach."

A few days later, the men installed themselves on the ocean shore and there built the Presidio and the Mission of San Carlos. It was the second of the projected missions, but already Junípero was busy with plans for the third: San Buenaventura.

"As soon as we are supplied with the necessary escort," he wrote his Guardian in the letter of June 12, 1770, "Father Crespi and I will separate, one of us remaining at Monterey and the other leaving for the Channel. It will be no meager ordeal for the sinner that I am to live alone with Indians eighty leagues [two hundred miles] from any priest; but so long as I have health it shall not be said that by fault of mine I have retarded the conversion of the heathen and the execution of the plans of the King our lord."

Since Father Viscaíno had deserted this distant field, and Fathers Parron and Gomez were burning to do the same, Junípero asked the College to send him recruits. Although, of his four companions, three had quickly had enough of Upper California, Junípero still imagined, during July of 1770, that everyone was going to back up his efforts. These periods of illusion were to be rare: four or five at most in fifteen years! But now his happiness burst forth in the letters he wrote his friend Galvez: the austere and almost sixty-year-old Junípero displayed in them the exuberance and joy of a child.

In one of these letters he describes the celebration of the Corpus Christi festival, June 14, at Monterey. Juan Perez had made the tapers; his sailors had marked out avenues bordered by shrubs; they had the procession, with Portola marching at its head and all the soldiers following, in two ranks; the handsome candalabra recently sent by the Visitor General were made use of, and his picture of the Madonna presided over the ceremony; everybody sang the hymns, and the cannon thundered anew. "If you had only been among us, dear lord, for our joy and our consolation!" he wrote in this letter of July 2, 1770. "It was so beautiful that I, always so lukewarm, was deeply moved by the general devotion. And now that she has occupied Monterey with us, I am going to send you back your Madonna, as I promised you at La

Paz. Tomorrow we shall bid her farewell by singing the Mass before her for the last time; we shall pray her to protect those of this place who are remaining here and those of the *San Antonio* who are going away. Juan Perez will take her with him."

A few days after reading this letter, Galvez announced to the world that the Franciscans were holding religious processions north of the thirty-sixth parallel, and that Charles III had annexed new provinces to his empire. It was Portola who had brought him this news. Embarking on the *San Antonio* on July 9, he had landed at San Blas on the first of August and had arrived in the City of Mexico the following week.

Enthusiasm burst forth at once in the capital. New Spain was larger by a 750-mile coast. The mother country was celebrating one of her most glorious conquests. The cannon thundered; the great bell of the cathedral was set swinging, and all the bells of the parochial churches and convents answered it. There was a gala reception at Court, with the diplomatic corps appearing in full regalia. They had to reappear at the ceremony of thanksgiving held in the metropolitan church, where José Galvez prayed in the front row, at the right of the Viceroy.

The "Report" of the Monterey expedition, signed by De Croix, came off the press on August 16, and was circulated *urbi et orbi*. After the historical recital of the vain attempts made in the course of two centuries to occupy the famous harbor, Galvez extolled the success of Gaspar de Portola, and of the seamen who had had a part in the expedition. For the edification of Catherine the Great and the King of England he added—forcing the note a little—that Spain was solidly entrenched between the thirtieth and thirty-eighth degrees of north latitude.

"Two of His Majesty's vessels," he wrote, "lie at anchor in San Diego harbor at this moment. As for Monterey, there is a strong garrison there, abundantly supplied with artillery and munitions of war. Last month, when the *San Antonio* left this port, the Presidio and the Mission of San Carlos had food supplies for a year in their storehouses, without counting the provisioning that would be necessary for the establishment of the next Mission, San Buenaventura. As early as this coming October, the same vessel is to go back to Monterey, freighted with a tremendous cargo and carrying thirty Fathers from San Fernando who will be going to found other Missions in these rich and vast regions that lie between the Old California and the harbor of San Francisco.

"According to what is told us by Captain Portola and the missionaries who have explored these territories, they are peopled by Indians so peaceable that our Spaniards are as safe there as they are in Mexico. The Reverend Prefect of the Missions, who is on the spot, adds that these good natives have already promised to entrust their children to him, to be brought up in our holy Faith. This worthy and zealous friar has been so kind as to describe to us the solemn Masses which he has sung since the arrival of the two expeditions, and the magnificent Corpus Christi procession over which he presided on June 14 last. All this is a clear manifestation that God is with us, and that it is He who has brought our undertaking to a successful issue."

Naturally, the Visitor General was leaving the picture's dark spots out of his report of victory. He was not mentioning the losses: one hundred and fifty dead, with the crews lost in the wreck of the *San José;* nor the Indian uprising of the fifteenth of August; nor, especially, the order for withdrawal—which would doubtless have changed everything if it had been carried out.

It may seem surprising that he should not have specified, ·or pointed out by name, the two men chiefly responsible for the conquest. But Junípero had written to Mexico, "I do not wish that there should be any mention of me, except in relation to the blunders I may have committed." And, respecting the desire of his friend, Galvez had not named him—but he had refrained likewise from any mention of himself.

Ten

The Founding of San Antonio, San Carlos del Carmelo, and San Gabriel
[1770-1771]

We shall not see that admirable man Portola again.[1] He was replaced as Governor of California by Armona, then by Barri, both
of whom continued to reside at Loreto. But Junípero never had
any dealings with them, inasmuch as, from the outset, the chief
of the new conquest was the Commandant at Monterey. This
position had devolved upon the young lieutenant Pedro Fages,
who held it from July, 1770, to May, 1774.

Galvez could not have chosen anyone more perfectly calculated
to run counter to his ideas and values. Fages was one of those
men in whom a moral sense awakes to consciousness only when
it can no longer hurt their career; one of those semi-brutes whom
Spain made use of to put fear—and submission—into the hearts of
the cannibals of the frontiers. His soldiers hated him. In May and
June of 1769 they had seen him filling for himself two large chests
of chocolate and provisions intended for the men stricken by pestilence, stealing brandy that might have revived them, diverting to
his own stewpot all the chickens that Dr. Prat was setting aside
for them. These details are drawn from two *Reports* the noncommissioned officers addressed to the Viceroy. One reads in them
further:

"At Monterey, starting from July, 1770, he used to beat us,
the men and ourselves, with cudgels; he would force us to buy
from him, at three times their value, the figs and raisins in which
he was trading; he would make sick men go and cut down trees
in the rain, and would deprive them of their supper if they protested; he would put us all on half-rations even though food might

---

[1] He afterwards became governor of Puebla (Mexico).

be rotting in the storehouse. We had to live on rats, coyotes, vipers, crows, and generally every creature that moved on the earth, except beetles, to keep from starvation. We almost all became herbivorous, eating raw grass like our horses. How many times we have wished we were six feet under ground!"

This somewhat sadistic little tyrant also sought, it seems, to make Junípero knuckle under to him. Not succeeding as he had hoped, he began to oppose and harass the Prefect in every possible way. "In all fields, he strove to make trouble for us," Junípero wrote Francisco Palou on June 21, 1771. "As the door of our living quarters opened on the inner court of the Presidio, he kept the key in his pocket, so that he could shut us in and let us out as he pleased. . . . If I tried to speak of all these things, I should never get through. . . . How many times I have thought that his bullyings would end by being the death of me!"

Coming from a man who welcomed suffering as Junípero did, and who could endure it so staunchly, these words are evidence that Pedro Fages was really moved by malice at that time. "But what does suffering matter," the missionary adds in his letter, "if we finally succeed in accomplishing our spiritual ministry? That is the only thing that counts, after all!"

His greatest grief was precisely that of being trammeled and thwarted in his apostolic work. Galvez had announced to the world that the Mission of San Buenaventura would come into existence in, so to speak, a matter of hours. The Prefect of Monterey was only waiting for an escort guard to set out on the road. Now, as early as June, 1770, Captain Rivera had brought some forty cuirassiers and a hundred animals from Velicata. Nothing was lacking, then, for the establishment of San Buenaventura: nothing, save the good will of Pedro Fages.

"I have not been officially notified of the captain's arrival," he would reply to inquiries.

And as a matter of fact Rivera, furious over the promotion of the young lieutenant, was stubbornly refraining from announcing his return, so that for more than a year, actually, he played dead, with his idle soldiers and his cows, at San Diego.

Junípero was suffering from the complete paralysis of the work of his own Mission. Aside from being glued, so to speak, to the Presidio, and thus exposed to continual petty persecution from the Commandant, the Mission was as badly situated as it could possibly be. There were no Indians around there; and, failing arable land and water for irrigation, both agriculture and stockraising were out of the question. At the very beginning, Junípero had made up his mind to move the Mission to Carmel, three miles north of the Presidio; but for that he had to have the authorization of the Viceroy. While waiting to obtain this, he succeeded in attracting a few natives, who came to set up their huts nearby. He made friends with them, and baptized twenty or so. "They call me 'the old Father,' and every once in a while they bring me a quarter of venison," he wrote to Palou. He tried, too, to clear a plot of land and make a garden. To aid him in this, Portola had put four soldiers and a muleteer at his disposal. "They kept on coming to eat," he wrote, in the letter of June 21, 1771, "but they refrained henceforth from working. For lack of manual labor, in short, we have accomplished nothing at all."

To all the sorrows and vexations Junípero endured in the fourteen months he was at Monterey, one was added which was brought upon him quite involuntarily by the man of whom he used to say, "I have loved him since his childhood," the man who had so heroically refused to forsake him when everyone else was making ready to leave this countryside, that dear one of all his friends, Juan Crespi, beside whom he wished to rest in the grave.

Juan Crespi was an angel of innocence and virtue.[2] "He kept forever the simplicity of the dove," writes Palou, his fellow student. "From the days of our clerical studies, we had canonized him; we called him 'the Mystic' and 'the Blessed,' because his piety was so great. Sometimes an unobtrusive rap on our door would serve notice that the Blessed was making his round of repentance: kneeling on the threshold of each one's cell, he would have come to ask pardon for some unworthy example or offense which none of us had noticed. . . . When he had become a missionary, at Tilaco in the Sierra Gorda, there was no one more devoted to the Indians; among other things, he had built them a lovely church. . . . With a bad memory, however, he was not a master at preaching; so he would take a book with him to the

---

[2] The passenger list of the *Villasota*, on which he sailed from Cadiz on December 31, 1749, gives the following description of him: "Twenty-eight years old, short in stature, of light complexion, pallid, though somewhat florid, with blue eyes and black hair."

pulpit, and would humbly announce to his hearers that he was going to read a sermon by someone else."

In default of eloquence, Fray Juan handled the astrolabe with consummate skill; he was an expert in botany, astronomy, geodetics, hydrography, and other natural sciences; he would divine the conformation of lands where he had never set foot, and would draw beautiful maps of those he had traveled over. He was more of a poet than his teacher, as is seen in the seven volumes of the *Journal* he left behind.

But since he had been at Monterey, Juan Crespi, preyed upon by his own self-doubt, had been going through one of those strange crises that seem to annihilate the will of the most valiant souls. He was shivering with cold, coughing day and night, having trouble with his eyes, head, throat, chest, and suffering from continual migraine headaches. He who had been unable to live apart from his master was now talking only of leaving him. That was his duty, he insisted, for if he stayed here he would die, and God would not wish him to let himself die, voluntarily, at the age of fifty years. . . .

"You seem to be a little better today," Junípero would say to him.

"I shall never get well here," Juan Crespi would sigh in response.

"But the boats will be bringing the authorization to move the San Carlos Mission to Carmel."

"The climate of Carmel is even worse; I have made a study of it. Only the Santa Barbara Channel can save me."

"Very well! As soon as our colleagues arrive, you will go to found the Mission of San Buenaventura. But in that case we shall have to separate, since as Prefect, you know, I must remain where the Commandant is. Think it over again."

"Alas, I have been thinking it over for a year. God alone knows what it has cost me to come to my decision!"

Of the boats they had been expecting, only one came: the *San Antonio*, which dropped anchor off Monterey on May 21, 1771. Ten Fernandinos stepped ashore from it. They belonged to the group brought from Spain by Father Verger, and they had traveled from Mexico City to San Blas with their twenty colleagues who were assigned to Lower California.

Juan Perez also brought a large amount of mail. Fages found

in it the notification of his promotion to the rank of captain, as well as an order from the Viceroy directing him to co-operate in the immediate establishment of five missions, one south of the Santa Barbara Channel and four north, to wit: San Gabriel, between San Diego and San Buenaventura; San Luis Obispo and San Antonio between the Channel and Monterey; and finally Santa Clara and San Francisco, north of Monterey.

Junípero, who had received the same instructions from the Marquis de Croix, wrote in answer, on June 18:

"It is of no avail to discuss Santa Clara and San Francisco until the bay named for my Seraphic Father has been more fully explored. As for the three other missions of which you speak, and San Buenaventura—which, contrary to what you think, does not yet exist—I am about to begin work on them immediately. Of the ten friars who have recently arrived, six will soon embark with Don Pedro Fages on the *San Antonio*, two for San Diego to replace Fathers Gomez and Parron, who are going away. The four others have been assigned to San Gabriel and San Buenaventura. As soon as they have left, I shall transfer the San Carlos Mission to Carmel, as you have authorized, and I shall take the San Antonio and San Luis ministers to their posts. Then, with the escort the Captain has promised to send me from San Diego, I shall set out with him to establish the two southern Missions of San Gabriel and San Buenaventura."

The *San Antonio* brought Junípero, who had received no letters for two years, one from his former Guardian.

"I strongly urge," wrote Father Andres, "that from now on you limit your correspondence concerning the missions to the members of the Discretory, who alone are qualified to negotiate with the representatives of the Crown. If I had not held my ground firmly, the Visitor General would have taken from us all forty-nine of the Fathers who arrived from Spain last May; and that because you told him you needed a hundred missionaries in California. At such a rate, the College would have to support three hundred friars—an impossibility, as you well know!"

It was to Verger, who had replaced Andres as Superior of the College, that Junípero addressed his reply, on June 20, 1771:

"The principle of writing only to the Discretory, I always professed and followed in the Sierra Gorda. If I have written to the Visitor General, who was writing constantly to me, it is because

I have considered that I could not do otherwise: seeing that I had spent two months with him in preparing for the expeditions, we had to take counsel together afterward, it seemed to me, as to the places where the missions should be set up. To the Viceroy, likewise, I believed that courtesy commanded me to reply. Enclosed are copies of the last letters of these Excellencies, and of my answers to them. The fact is that I have no recollection of having written to any layman on the subject of the number of missionaries it would be advisable to send here.

"I now beg Your Reverence to dictate a line of conduct to me: I shall obey you in everything. If you forbid me to reply to the letters of Their Excellencies, I will not reply to them; if you forbid me to open their letters, I will not open them; and I shall not suffer from that in any way. If, on the contrary, you authorize me, for the good of the missions, to keep on with this correspondence, I shall continue to send you copies of the letters exchanged. I repeat to you what I wrote to your predecessor: 'I feel no more attached to the place where I now am than to any other. Whether I am asked to move on or to stay here, to found new missions or to go back to the old ones, or even if I should be recalled to the College, it is with joy and submission that I shall carry out your instructions. I therefore beg Your Reverence not to hesitate to command me, as seems good to you."

Having said this, he set forth his views in regard to the future: "To date, I have founded three missions, San Fernando de Velicata, San Diego, and San Carlos. Fray Francisco Palou has been entrusted with the establishment of five others. As for myself, I count upon having eight missions soon, but we should have sixteen at the earliest possible moment. They would exist, thus, along the entire coast; and since they would be separated by no more than a three-days' march, the friars could go from one to the other on foot, except for the crossing of the Gulf and the journey from Mexico to San Francisco. . . ."

He ended the letter with his customary refrain: "Once more, you are the one to decide and I am the one to obey. Give me your orders: you will see that I shall carry them out to the last detail."

This was his invariable attitude toward his superiors. He did not practice the "submission of judgment," which, it seems, was unknown at San Fernando. He did not bend his mind to thinking successively like Andres, Verger, Pangua, again Verger, again Pangua, and finally Sancho, the men who governed the College from 1768 to 1786. No more to Verger today than later on to Pangua does he say, "As soon as I learned that I was blamed, I at once felt guilty; as soon as I came to know your opinions, I immediately changed my own." Acknowledging that neither his memory nor his reasoning is infallible, he says what he judges to be true, so that he may bear witness to the truth and help his superiors, if they are mistaken, to discover it. Then, as a follower of the religious life, bound by its vow of obedience, he adds: "Your commands being for me as those of God, I will obey them promptly, completely, and joyously; for I love God, I love to carry out His will, and I am happy that He should give me the opportunity to do so."

Junípero's dreams were sound as the thoughts of others were in error. If he had confided those dreams to the Visitor General, there is no doubt that the latter would have made them his own, and it would not have taken decades, as it did, to bring them to fruition. But he ceased suddenly to correspond with Galvez. The day came when the College would have looked with favor upon the resumption of this correspondence. Palou was then urging his master to write to the all-powerful Minister. "If he is as powerful as you say he is," Junípero responded, "that is one more reason for not reminding him that I am still living. Let us pray that God will take other measures for saving us."

As a matter of fact, he had learned, in 1772, that his name had been mentioned in connection with a vacant bishopric, and since Galvez appointed many of the bishops, Junípero would not have wished to resume relations with him for anything in the world!

As Prefect, Junípero consulted the newcomers about their preferences, and so far as possible he made up his "teams" from friars who came from the same region and the same Franciscan Province.

"There are twelve of us Fathers here," he wrote to Francisco Palou on June 21, "and here is the list of our future missions and their ministers:

San Carlos: Junípero Serra and Juan Crespi.
San Antonio: Pieras and Sitjar, Mallorcans.
San Luis Obispo: Juncosa and Cavaller, Catalonians.

San Buenaventura: Cruzado and Paterna, our highlanders from Andalusia.

San Gabriel: Cambon and Somera.[3]

San Diego: Dumetz and Luis Jaume, Mallorcans.

He went on to speak of Juan Crespi's state of disturbance. The sick man was not—it had just come out—going to San Buenaventura, the climate of which had nevertheless been counted upon to assure his recovery. This was because he had not been able to make up his mind to leave his teacher, when the moment for decision came. "He told me," wrote Junípero, "that if I would not turn him off, all he desired was to remain with me. I replied that to me, likewise, nothing could give greater pleasure." Had his "crisis" then come to an end? Alas, it took another year and two journeys to cure him!

Meanwhile, Junípero wanted his friend to have good tobacco in his snuffbox. The man who supplied them was Señor Trillo of San Blas, and Francisco Palou used to serve as middleman. Now it happened that on the miraculous appearance of the *San Antonio* on March 19 that ship had brought tobacco which four experts unanimously pronounced to be execrable. Junípero had rebelled against Trillo's bill. Now he wrote:

For the peace of my conscience and the love of truth, I want to correct a mistake I made last year, in the matter of Fray Juan's tobacco. As a matter of fact, all four of us were mistaken. As soon as the boxes arrived at San Diego, Fray Juan opened one, and we sampled what was in it. All of us—Fathers Gomez, Parron, Crespi, and myself—declared that the snuff was like dust, that it was actually rubbish. Later on, when our reserves were exhausted, we opened another of Señor Trillo's boxes: the top layer seemed acceptable; the rest, very compact, seemed still better. In short, this tobacco now seems to us so good that we prefer it to what we received a month ago, although that was said to be of the best quality. I beg you, therefore, to place another order with Señor Trillo, and to make amends for any wrong my letter may have done him. Enclosed is a check for thirty pesos.

The letters to De Croix, Verger, and Palou were dispatched by the *San Antonio*, which set sail again for San Diego on July 7. As passengers for that port it carried Pedro Fages and the friars

[3] Angel Somera originally came from Michoacan (Mexico) and Benito Cambon from the province of Galicia (Spain).

whose imminent entrance upon their new duties Junípero was announcing in his letter to the Viceroy.

The following day, Junípero, with Fathers Pieras and Sitjar, set out southeast. Under guard of seven cuirassiers and some Indians from the Peninsula, they took with them eight mules, nine cows, a bull, two heifers, six calves, a sow, a male pig, a hen and her chickens.

At the end of a five days' march, and some sixty miles from Monterey, they came to a beautiful valley, which Junípero christened *Cañada de los Robles* (Valley of the Oaks). A little farther on, they paused on a magnificent stretch of level ground, watered by a stream that he named the San Antonio. He had the mules unloaded and the bells hung from an old oak tree, and then he began to ring them with all his might, and to call out, "Come, pagan brothers! Come and receive the Gospel of Christ which we are bringing you!" He was exalted, intoxicated, beside himself; never had he been seen in such a state.

"But, for pity's sake, don't exhaust yourself like that!" said Father Pieras. "You can see that there are no pagans around here!"

"Ah, let me ease my heart, I beg you!" Junípero retorted. "If I could only ring the bells so that they might be heard throughout the world! Or, at least, if all the pagans of this land might come running to answer their call!"

He sang the Mass under a canopy of twigs. As he turned, after the Gospel, to preach the sermon, he caught sight of an Indian behind the soldiers.

"In truth, we shall have a fine mission here," he cried, "for this Indian is the augury of many others, who will come, like him, to embrace the Faith."

Thus was founded, on July 14, 1771, the Mission of San Antonio, the only one, perhaps, which was never anything but a source of comfort to Junípero.[4]

The Prefect returned to Monterey almost immediately, to attend to the transfer of San Carlos Mission.

Without livestock, but with an escort of four soldiers commanded by Corporal Carrillo, he set out on the fifth of August for the stream that Vizcaíno's chaplains had christened Carmelo

---

[4] St. Anthony (San Antonio), Doctor of the Church, who was born in Lisbon in 1195 and died in Padua in 1231, joined the Franciscan Order during the lifetime of St. Francis of Assisi.

in 1603. He planted his tent some three miles south of the Presidio, between the beach of fine sand and the forest, where giant pines and centuries-old sequoias grew to a height of more than three hundred feet. Quite apart from the advantages it offered for agriculture and stockbreeding, the situation was entrancing. Framing the great bay, hills stretched out toward infinity, to lose themselves at last in the waves. . . .

Fages was far away, the soldiers were breathing freely, and they accomplished marvels. They accomplished so much, indeed, that the new San Carlos Mission was opened ten days later. Junípero sang the first Mass there on August 24, 1771. After this, Fathers Crespi, Cavaller, and Juncosa returned to Monterey, and Junípero remained without companions until Christmas. When, on December 24, Fray Juan came with a few converts from the old San Carlos Mission to install themselves in the new one, everything was ready to receive them. The Carmel ground plan of that time was described in a letter Junípero wrote Verger on August 8 of the next year:

"Surrounded by a stockade 75 x 50 *varas* [225 x 150 feet], and protected by ravelins at the four corners, the Mission consists of three buildings: in the first are the kitchens; in the second the dormitory for young girls; in the third Father Crespi's room and mine, the temporary chapel, an office, the Indians' great hall, and finally the storeroom, which alone measures 39 *varas* in length. Backing up against the surrounding wall, but outside it, are the barracks, completely protected by a stockade made, like our own, of huge and very tall poles. Nearby are the corral, the vegetable garden, and the Indians' cabins."

On July 14 the *San Antonio* had landed Pedro Fages at San Diego, together with the six Fathers—Dumetz, Jaume, Paterna, Cruzado, Cambon, and Somera. Fathers Dumetz and Jaume replaced Fathers Gomez and Parron at San Diego, when the ship embarked them a week later, with Rivera, for San Blas. As for the four others, it will be remembered that two of them, Paterna and Cruzado, had been assigned to San Buenaventura, and the remaining two to San Gabriel.

It was at San Buenaventura that the work was to be begun. Fages had made an appointment there with Junípero, and in order that the friar might come to keep it he had pledged himself to send him, from San Diego, the indispensable escort guard. When they met at San Buenaventura they would at once found the mission; then, leaving Paterna and Cruzado there, they would go on to establish San Gabriel, where Cambon and Somera were to be officiating ministers; after that, turning north again, they planned to found the Mission of San Luis Obispo, under the ministry of Cavaller and Juncosa, whom Junípero was to bring with him; and then they would go back to Monterey, having carried out the entire program outlined by the Viceroy.

But we shall see that although Fages had some fifty soldiers at his disposal at San Diego, Fages did not send the promised escort; that Junípero and his two companions were consequently unable to leave Monterey; and that the Mission of San Buenaventura, which Galvez had been proclaiming for a year as already in existence, was not to be founded even yet.

Tyrannical and bungling, the captain had not been eight days in San Diego when nine soldiers deserted, taking with them fifty mules, a muleteer, and some cattle. Fages implored Father Paterna to go in search of them. The friar rode at a gallop for two days and a night, and came upon them a hundred miles east of San Diego. Appealing to their religious sentiment and promising that they would be better treated in the future, he succeeded in taking them back.

Then the captain decided to establish the Mission of San Gabriel. "But you will go without me," he said to Fathers Cambon and Somera.

"And without the Father Prefect?" they asked.

"The Father Prefect will not come, because I have not been able to send him any escort."

The two missionaries left on August 5 with a guard of twelve soldiers and their livestock. They made a march of about a hundred miles, and on August 15 they arrived at the spot that had been indicated as the site of the San Gabriel Mission.

The soldiers had scarcely made camp when the Redskins came running up by hundreds, with piercing war cries. The women ran screeching behind them, urging them on to kill. The Spaniards had no interpreters to explain that they came as friends. Was it Cambon or Somera that had the idea of hastily placing the great *Pietà* of their future chapel upon an improvised altar? The attackers, never having seen painting, believed that this was a real mother holding her dead son on her knees. How beautiful she was, and how sad! . . . And no doubt these eighteen white men were her other sons? . . . The men threw down their weapons; the women drew near, weeping. They, especially, could not tire of gazing at the Virgin of Sorrows. What could they do for her? . . . They ran to get foodstuffs and fruits, and laid them at her feet; so at least she could eat, that lovely Lady of Affliction, if she was hungry. . . .

"Perhaps their naïveté was to be laughed at," Junípero wrote Bucareli, "but what goodness of heart it bore witness to! And how well qualified these souls seemed to receive the Faith!"

"The Mission of San Gabriel," Junípero continues, in his *Memorandum No. 4*, of May 21, 1773, "was inaugurated without me on the eighth of September, 1771, by the singing of Mass and the customary formalities. The Indians were so happy to see the missionaries arrive that they took more part in the felling of trees and the construction of the buildings than all the soldiers put together. Never was a foundation begun under happier auspices. The Mission could speedily have become self-sufficient and able to help some of the others. . . . Why did the clumsiness and despotism of Señor Fages have to make such a promising young plant wither, and ruin our hopes?"

Fages arrived at San Gabriel at the end of October. He had spent weeks in trying to recapture the soldiers who were again deserting from San Diego. Far from succeeding, he had just missed being killed by them; and it was once more the friars who brought him back his men. He presented himself at the head of a huge caravan of twenty-six soldiers, two hundred mules, and all the livestock intended for Carmel, San Luis Obispo, San Francisco, Santa Clara, and the Mission of San Buenaventura which he was about to establish with Paterna and Juncosa.

There were no Indians more peaceable than those of San Gabriel. That is what Fages was told by the experienced missionaries Cambon and Somera. The corporal in command of the escort guard, on the contrary, represented the natives as very dangerous. In truth, it was the corporal, easily frightened and incompetent, who was doing everything to make them dangerous: such as preventing them, against the Fathers' advice, from coming to the Mission in numbers of more than five at a time, and by permitting his men to rape the Indian women.

So it was that, on the twelfth of October, the Indians took up arms. A white man—one of the mounted soldiers who guarded the livestock—had assaulted the wife of their captain. The chief whose honor had been thus flouted let fly an arrow at the offender; it struck the white man's shield, he fired his gun and shot down the husband of his victim. At the sound of the shot, the Indian troop fled, and the corporal came running up with his men. They cut off the head of the slain Redskin, set it on a pole, and went out to plant this trophy before the gate of the Mission.

"At that precise time," writes Junípero in his *Memorandum No. 4*, "the Indian captain's son was right there: a child whom his father had just entrusted to the missionaries."

Thanks to the Fathers, calm was nevertheless restored; the Indians began once more to confide their children to the missionaries' care, and to frequent the Mission. But that was not what mattered to Fages: it was the corporal who frightened him, and not the Fathers who reassured him, that the Commandant listened to. He detached six of the twenty-six soldiers who had come with him, and added them to the twelve already there. Only twenty were then left to him. As it was necessary to have a guard of fifteen men in the dangerous region of San Buenaventura, and as the five remaining would not be enough to assure the protection of the immense caravan he was leading, Fages gave up the founding of San Buenaventura Mission, in spite of the appeals Fathers Paterna and Juncosa made to him on their knees.

At San Gabriel, thus, Fages was leaving eighteen soldiers with nothing to do and four missionaries held back from the exercise of their zeal. These latter—except for Somera, whose physical and mental condition was such as to require his departure—remained valiantly at their post, immured in their prison, waiting for God to come to their aid.[5] As for the soldiers, most of them were transformed for the time being into beasts. "Every morning," wrote Junípero, "they would go out in groups of six, on horseback, and spread far over the countryside. Accustomed to lassoing cows and mules, they would chase the native women and catch them in a running noose, and they would strike down their husbands with gunfire when these attempted to defend their own. . . . They went so far as to defile the few children whom the friars had gathered together at the Mission."

[5] Angel Somera departed for Lower California, from which he reached the College in 1772.

Fages journeyed north for 260 miles, and arrived at San Antonio on about the twentieth of November. "In this mission, which had had four months of existence," Junípero wrote, "everything was going according to our hopes. There, too, the Commandant brought about paralysis by a single move. Learning that the corporal and his men were displaying kindly consideration and activity in our behalf, he replaced them then and there by as many idlers, who did not lift a hand to anything. Fathers Pieras and Sitjar were obliged to become carpenters and muleteers; they had only the Indians to help them from this time on."

On the thirtieth of November, the proconsul Fages made his re-entry into Monterey at the head of his soldiers, his mules, and three herds of cows. He had left the San Luis herd at San Antonio; he delivered the Carmel herd to Junípero, but—in order that he might keep their milk—he refused to turn over to him the cows for Santa Clara and San Francisco. He was taking actual pleasure in frustrating Junípero's efforts and in persecuting him.

Yet on his own horizon one dark spot still remained: the soldiers who were continuing to desert. As he drank the milk that belonged to the little Indians of the missions, and chewed on his stolen figs, he was asking himself how he was to explain these desertions to the Viceroy. What would the Viceroy think of a Commandant who commanded in such a fashion that he would soon have no one left to command? . . . Fages solved the problem by notifying his chief, the Governor of Loreto, in his own way. He did it in a manner that caused Governor Barri, in his year-end report to the Viceroy, to say, in substance: If things are going badly in Upper California, and if the new conquest is in danger of being lost, it is the fault of the twelve Franciscans who are there, and especially of their Prefect, who urges them on to disobey Captain Fages, the King's worthy and capable representative. They go further, miserable wretches that they are, in preaching revolt to the soldiers. It is thus to Fray Junípero Serra, in short, that the desertions are due.

Eleven

The Founding of San Luis Obispo, New Postponement of the Founding of San Buenaventura, and Junípero Sets Out for Mexico City

[1772]

As soon as Fages returned to the Presidio, Junípero presented his request for six soldiers, so that he might found the Mission of San Luis Obispo, 125 miles south of Monterey. The Commandant, who was continuing to flog his men, suddenly felt a mother's affectionate solicitude for them, and refused to allow them to get wet. "We will wait," he said, "until the rainy season is over."

Junípero renewed his effort toward the middle of February, when the rains had stopped. Fages apparently considered that more rest was needed by the thirty-five soldiers who had been idling in the Presidio for such a long time, for he replied that they would not establish this mission until after the ships had arrived.

On March 25, Fages went off to explore the bay of San Francisco, taking Juan Crespi with him as cartographer. Junípero was hoping that this journey would aid in Father Crespi's recovery; but on the fifth of April, in the night, he reappeared at Carmel. Horsemen who had rushed up from San Diego had joined our explorers at the entrance to the bay, and the party hurried back to the Presidio. The word from Sergeant Ortega was that his storehouses were empty, that the soldiers of San Gabriel and San Diego were hungry, and that they would desert if they were not sent something to eat.

This scarcity was due to the disasters suffered by the three ships of the little fleet Galvez had created. If it had not been for the loss of the *San José* and the misfortunes that had come upon the *San Carlos*, nine shipments of food would have reached Upper California between 1769 and 1771; as it was, there had been only four. And now this year the *San Carlos* and the *San Antonio*, already delayed by head winds, had been unable, for once, to cast anchor at Monterey and had returned to discharge their cargoes at San Diego. It was only in August that they landed there, three months late.

It was decided that Father Crespi should accompany the convoy sent with relief supplies for the establishments in the south. Coming back completely recovered on the fifth of April, he had had another breakdown two days later. "Decidedly, it is all over with me if I stay at Carmel," he said to his master. Junípero suggested that he change places with Father Dumetz, who was not getting on well with Father Jaume at San Diego. Heartsick, Crespi agreed to this, and left Monterey on the thirteenth of April. Where, how, why, by what miracle, did he find once more his physical and mental balance? . . . Whatever the answer may be, he had scarcely arrived at his destination when he was permanently cured.

"In a letter the muleteers brought me," Junípero wrote Verger on August 8, 1772, "he besought me to recall him, promising henceforth to accommodate himself to the fog, the rain, the cold of Carmel, as well as to the vexations attendant upon the close proximity of the Presidio. He pleaded his cause with so much of humble repentance and so many earnest promises that I had not the heart to refuse. Before taxing him with behaving like a child, remember that for the past three years he has been more fatigued than the rest of us, since he alone has traveled more than all the others put together."

The judgment of Junípero's heart was right; for when Juan Crespi came back now to his master, he never left him again until they were separated by his own death.

Meanwhile, since the ships expected in April or May did not arrive, famine struck Monterey also. We have said that for eight months there had been thirty-five idle men there, of whom at least twenty should have served as escort soldiers on the road to San Buenaventura and San Luis Obispo. To feed his company of men who were living without working—on unearned increment, so to speak—the Captain made up his mind to take them on a bear hunt. It was precisely in the vicinity of San Luis that these animals were to be found, in such numbers, indeed, that since

1769 this region had been known as "The Valley of the Bears" (*Cañada de los Osos*). Fathers Cavaller and Juncosa were therefore expecting to be able to go to their posts at San Luis Obispo when the hunt took place.

"You will take us with you when you go?" they said to the Commandant, who was a Catalonian like themselves, and whom they believed to be their friend.

"Yes—that is, no. . . . I will come back for you when I have got my hunters settled," he replied.

"He set out with his hunters on the twenty-fifth of May," Junípero continues, in his letter to Verger. "He returned not long afterward, bringing a few loads of salted meat. On the twentieth of June he went off again, having once more refused to take the Fathers with him. He rejoined his men, whom he finally abandoned, telling them at last to shift for themselves as best they could. They are still down there, robbing the Indian men and raping the Indian women; several of them, having traded their uniforms for food, are running about naked; all are starving, and have got to the point of eating grass, the bears having gone long since to take up their abode elsewhere."

This letter had hardly been written when couriers arrived with news that the ships were off shore. They brought Fages a letter from the Viceroy which, at the time, he kept secret, but which, when he disclosed its contents two months later, produced the spectacular turn of events which we shall see.

"The two ships carry a plentiful cargo," Junípero wrote to Palou on August 18, "but we, as well as those of San Antonio, must go to San Diego to get our share. The ordeal will have been hard for the four missions. For months we have not said Mass except on Sundays, because of the lack of wine. Yet I have been able to keep my little boys in the Home for children. . . . But we have all suffered, and are still suffering. All we Spaniards have been hungry, except one, who has not ceased to eat well, and has boasted of it." Here one recognizes Pedro Fages, whose chocolate and raisins were still holding out. "The great news," Junípero went on, "is that we are on the eve of founding San Luis. After fourteen months of waiting and sorrowing, Fathers Cavaller and Juncosa are at last about to be able to set to work. I am starting out with the Captain in a few days."

He left Carmel on August 22, accompanied by his interpreter

Juan Evangelista, a fifteen-year-old Indian boy. He was reckoning on an absence of three months; he was away for almost two years. The caravan, under command of Pedro Fages, included some twenty soldiers and all the mules that the Presidio and the Mission were sending to carry the provisions brought by the boats. Father Cavaller was attached to the expedition, but not Father Juncosa, who had been left to officiate at Carmel until Father Crespi should return.

They reached San Antonio in two days. There, Junípero baptized a child, 124 little boys and four little girls having received Baptism already. A great many adults were asking to be baptized, also; but in their case the rite was put off until the time when, with the development of the mission farm, they would be able to live a settled life, and not be obliged to be away for months seeking subsistence in the mountains.

Made larger by the little herd of cows that Fages had left there nine months before, and by the San Antonio mule train, the column reached the Valley of the Bears after three more days. A few hours were enough for Junípero to find an excellent site for the Mission of San Luis Obispo.[1] Inaugurated on September 1, 1772, it became—thanks to Father Cavaller and to Father Juncosa, who joined him shortly—one of the richest missions in California. To begin with, however, it had only nine cows, 13 mules, 55 pounds of meal, 13 quarts of wheat, 110 pounds of chocolate, and a box of brown sugar. More than anything else, it was this brown sugar, for which the natives would exchange their products, which kept the Mission's founders alive during the first weeks.

The Commandant retrieved his bear-hunters, left six soldiers as escort guard at San Luis, and on September 2 got the caravan under way again. After a march of a hundred miles they came to a halt beside the ocean, at the southern extremity of the Santa Barbara Channel. This, Fages and Junípero selected as the site of the Mission of San Buenaventura, which they intended to establish on the return trip. On September 8 they arrived at San Gabriel.

Born in blood and mire, this mission had been abandoned by

[1] Son of the King of Naples, St. Louis of Anjou, or Louis the Bishop (*Luis Obispo*), was born in 1274, became a Franciscan, and died as Bishop of Toulouse in 1297.

its founders: Father Somera, ill and in bad nervous condition, had set out again for Loreto en route to Mexico City; Father Cambon, eager to admire the landscapes of Lower California, had, without leave, joined Father Dumetz, who was taking the tale of famine to Francisco Palou. Then Fathers Paterna and Cruzado, set down here by Fages the year before, had put their shoulders valiantly to the wheel. A fortuitous episode with the couriers had removed the most dissolute members of the first escort and their leader, and the new corporal had imposed decency, improved the buildings, and done away with the incongruous rulings of the early days. The Indian women, who had, so to speak, gone underground for six months, were beginning to show their faces again; the men were once more making their way to the Mission; and the children's refuge had several dozen young guests.

"Saddened by these signs of progress," wrote Junípero in his *Memorandum No. 4,* under date of May 21, 1773, "Fages resolved to remove the new corporal and recall his incompetent predecessor. I begged him to do nothing about that. But he responded with his habitual refrain, 'This subaltern is succeeding too well and is too much talked about for my authority not to suffer from him.' "

The column, which had been joined by Father Paterna and the mule train from San Gabriel, reached its destination on September 16. Junípero, who, with his abnormally short legs, had been in the saddle for fifteen days on an average of ten hours a day, was ill when he got to San Diego. Soldiers and sailors unloaded the ships. They began with the *San Antonio,* of which that great navigator Juan Perez continued to keep the command. The *San Carlos* now had Miguel Pino as captain, with Canizares still as pilot. On September 27 the first convoy set out on the road north, with provisions for San Luis, San Antonio, and Monterey. Fathers Crespi and Dumetz left with it. From now on, Father Dumetz was attached to the Mission of Carmel, where a third minister was necessary on account of the frequent absences which his responsibilities as Prefect imposed upon Junípero. He had just come back from the Peninsula with as large a store of provisions as his mules could carry, and with a flock of goats and ewes, the gift of Francisco Palou. They were the first to make their way into Northern California. As for Father Cambon, not having had time to see everything, he had not yet come back. To offset this loss,

Palou was making Junípero a present of three friars: Fathers Figuer, Uson, and La Peña. This last had just arrived with Father Dumetz; the other two were soon to follow.

Junípero was delighted to note the progress of the Mission of San Diego. "Nowhere have we made so many conversions," he writes in his *Memorandum No. 4.* "The men who tried to murder us in 1769 are now baptized and come daily to the catechism class. Although they are the most savage and ferocious among them all, these Indians outdo our Spaniards in sexual morality; Father Luis Jaume assures me, indeed, that adultery is unknown among them, and that an unmarried woman who becomes a mother is dishonored in the eyes of everyone and is severely punished by the chief of the clan. Here at least, thanks to the courtesy and helpfulness of Sergeant Ortega, we have been able to work."

Fages was betraying vexation. "You have done wrong in baptizing so many natives without knowing how you were going to feed them," he said.

"Then the right thing, Señor," answered Junípero, "is for you to give them a little of that corn of which there is so much on the boats while we wait for the next harvest."

"They shan't get a mouthful of it," he retorted. And Junípero adds, "In that, at least, he kept his word."

This scene formed a prelude to the decisive conflict that was about to break out.

The negotiations on the subject of San Buenaventura were not going well.

"As for me, I am ready," Junípero would say to the Captain. "I have the two ministers here at hand, Fathers Uson and Figuer; the livestock is at San Gabriel, and the necessary provisions have just been brought by the ships."

"But there are decisions which are my affair," Fages would answer, with an air of mystery.

It was to become acquainted with these and to get away from ambiguity and equivocation that, after a week of futile negotiation, Junípero wrote to the Captain on September 22:

Inasmuch as it is to me that San Fernando has entrusted the direction of the missions, and you yourself have orders to proceed to the establishment of San Buenaventura, I am informing you herewith of the conditions which, for my part, I judge to be necessary to the success of the enterprise. You will tell me to what extent it is possible for you to meet them:

First: Taking into account the number and the character of the natives of that region, it is thought in Mexico City that twenty-five men will be needed. I confine myself to asking you for twenty: to wit, fifteen cuirassiers, one muleteer, and four marines.[2]

Second: The marines and the muleteer are to be at the service of the Mission, exclusively.

Third: The muleteer you get must know his business, and not allow the mules to die and the harness to deteriorate through his incompetence.

Fourth: Seeing that San Buenaventura is much farther from the port than the other missions, I am asking for twelve pack mules instead of the eight generally supplied.

Fifth: In addition, there must be two saddle mules, well equipped.

Sixth: I ask that at San Buenaventura, as everywhere else henceforth, the provisions be divided into two clearly distinct shares: that of the Mission and that of the guard and the transient couriers. In regard to the latter, I wish it to be no longer the Fathers, but some subordinate in whom you have confidence, who will distribute their weekly ration to the soldiers. Thus the accusations that have been brought against us will automatically subside.

Seventh: If the escort guard is authorized to have an Indian from the Peninsula in its service, it is understood that it is for the presidio, and not for the mission, to supply him.

Eighth: Be so kind as to stipulate the work which devolves upon the escort, in founding a new mission; I must know what I can count upon them to do.

. . . These are the points on which I beg you to reply on this same sheet of paper. It is your place to examine and know what you can and will grant us. If your response is favorable, we shall go at once to found this mission which the Court believes to have been established long ago.

The Captain did not reply, however, until September 30, his period of mental incubation lasting, at this time, a week and a day. As the outburst of a choleric policeman, his letter lacked hardly anything except profanity.

. . . If the spiritual care of the missions is your concern [he said], it is with me that you must come to an understanding in order to

---

[2] So named because they helped in handling the ship during the voyage, these "marines" were laborers recruited for two years in the San Blas district.

establish them: me to whom the civil and military administration of the country has been entrusted.

First: Disregarding the opinions from Mexico which you invoke, I estimate that—supposing the foundation of San Buenaventura does take place—from twelve to fifteen cuirassiers will be sufficient as escort.

Second: It is understood that the marines will obey the ministers, but that they will remain at all times subject to my good pleasure and that of my representatives. It is also I whom they must recognize as judicial authority: I, Don Pedro Fages, Captain of Infantry, appointed by the Most Excellent Lord Marquis de Croix, confirmed in my office by the Most Excellent Viceroy Don Antonio Bucareli y Ursua.

Third: Among the available muleteers, the Presidio will select the best for itself, and the ministers will have their choice of what is left.

Fourth: I cannot assign any more mules to San Buenaventura than to the other missions.

Fifth: Instead of the two saddle mules it demands, the Mission will receive two saddles, which will be entered on its account.

Sixth: Since the Fathers do not like to practice charity in making themselves responsible for the allotment of provisions to the soldiers, I will designate some one else to do this.

Seventh: It will be the Mission's own Indian who must come every day to grind the corn needed by the soldiers, since they have no time for it.

Eighth: The work which devolves upon the soldiers, in the founding of a new mission, is as follows: they have first to construct a quadrangular stockade two and one-half *varas* [eight feet] high, with a "half-moon" or ravelin at each corner of the enceinte; after this they have to build the church and the Fathers' living quarters and storehouse, as well as their own barrack and guardroom. The rest is under the jurisdiction of my government, and I will attend to it when the time comes.

After seeing Fages again, and making sure that he understood him fully, Junípero wrote to him on October 3:

Whereas you have answered me verbally and in writing [that is to say; whereas I cannot count on fifteen cuirassiers; whereas instead of twelve mules you offer me eight, and in place of two mules with their saddles you offer me two saddles without their mules; whereas our servitors must work so as to permit your soldiers to rest, and will be at all times under the domination of your "justice" and the good pleasure of your corporals; whereas, in a word, you pledge yourself to nothing unless it be to interfere, so as to make a mess of everything, in our affairs], I give up, for the moment, the foundation that was planned. There is a passage in your letter, however, which I cannot let go by. . . .

This was paragraph number six, in which the petty usurer, the fig merchant, was setting himself up as a professor of ethics.

It is not for lack of charity, it is, on the contrary, for charity itself [writes Junípero], that we do not wish to distribute their rations to the soldiers. Certain ones among them have accused us of wasting food, and even of appropriating it for ourselves. Charity, which forbids scandal, obliges us to take measures to prevent continued defamation of that sort. The scandalous imputation will be automatically done away with by this step on our part.

In this letter, replete with rejection, Junípero was showing that he remained Prefect of the Missions. It unleashed the furious rage of Pedro Fages, who had believed his dictatorship to be assured ever since the arrival of the letter from the Viceroy which he had kept secret for two months. These friars whom he had represented as fomenters of desertion, and whom he was counting upon to serve as scapegoats for the soldiers' hunger—they were still preserving their independence, and he was outraged! After reflecting again for a week and a day, he made up his mind to serve notice on them that from now on their place was merely to be silent and obey. On the evening of October 11, he himself delivered to Junípero the following letter:

Very Reverend Father Fray Junípero Serra, Prefect.
My dear Señor:
Under date of November 30, 1771, the Most Excellent Lord Viceroy, Don Antonio Bucareli y Ursua, wrote to me:
"You will remind the Reverend Father Prefect Junípero Serra and his friars of their solemn obligation to preach to everyone the obedience which is due you, and themselves to give an example of it."
I am transmitting this text to Your Fathership, and I beg that you will notify the other Fathers of it.
May Our Lord deign to preserve you for a long life. . . .

These three lines, which Bucareli had written five weeks after taking office, had important and far-reaching consequences.

Junípero always spent much time in talking with God. Morning and evening, at Carmel, he would remain prostrated for long periods before the great cross, between the Mission and the sea. Very late in the night his window would still be lighted. "Then when does he sleep, and when does he stop praying?" the soldiers on guard would say. The night after he got this letter he prayed longer still. . . .

He was not asking that his own trials be ended, or that he might have the last word with a captain of infantry. What did it matter to him whether his suffering came from his left leg or from somebody named Pedro Fages, since he desired suffering? The Christ who was his model, had He cared who it was who spat upon Him and struck Him, when He was enduring these things as ransom for us? . . . What Junípero was beseeching from God was light. Entrusted by the College with the conversion of the Indians between the thirty-second and thirty-eighth parallels, what was his duty? What did the divine will require of him now?

It appears that he knew the answer the next morning, when he transmitted Fages' letter to Paterna, Luis Jaume, and La Peña. He begged them to think the matter over, and, all three, to celebrate a Mass for enlightenment from God the next day. He himself, on the morning of October 13, sang the Mass to the same purpose. After this he called his colleagues together and submitted for their approval the following lines, which were delivered to the Captain forthwith:

. . . My conscience bears me witness that in all circumstances I have preached to the soldiers the submission which they owe you. How many times, in addition, I have intervened to lead rebels back to the path of obedience! All my friars have followed the same rule of behavior toward them, I know. Have you yourself not often thanked me for the way they have all conducted themselves in this respect, and particularly for what Father Paterna did at the time of the desertions that took place here last year? I receive the orders of His Excellency with the respect due to this high representative of the King. My friars and myself will carry them out. But, without my casting any doubt upon the accuracy of your quotation, could you not show me the original of the passage which you have transcribed? The context will perhaps disclose to me by whom, and in what connection, the Report was drawn up which motivated the warning from His Excellency. If, as I fear, this Report makes false statements, because of malice, I shall thus be enabled to defend the honor of our holy Order by re-establishing the truth.

Fages would have named Barri, and would have been himself denounced, if he had acceded to Junípero's request. He refused.

Junípero then made up his mind, and in the afternoon of the same day he called his colleagues together for a final talk. In substance this is what he said to them:

"As civil and military head, it would be impossible to imagine anyone worse than the Captain. As an adversary of the missions, it would be impossible to dream of anyone better; for he keeps them from being born, and when they are born he works furiously and unceasingly to destroy them. Until day before yesterday evening, we felt reason to hope that he would be called to order or dismissed. There is no longer anything of that sort to be counted on, as the letter from the Viceroy proves. Instead of recall, he receives approval and encouragement; and it is we who are reprimanded and accused. With the allies he has found for himself, the measure of power is reversed in his favor; the battle joined against him has been lost here; lost thus, in consequence, is the hope of developing our missions and carrying out the ministry that has been entrusted to us. But of this our superiors are ignorant, as is evidenced by the only two letters I have received from them since June, 1769. As I am their representative, it is my duty to inform them; as I am your leader, it is my duty to assist you in following your vocation; it is my duty, finally, not to allow the sons of San Fernando to be ticketed in men's minds as mutineers and rebels. Cost what it may, our holy College must know the truth. When it knows, it will change this state of things and we shall pursue our task. If it does not succeed in this, it will send us to work elsewhere. In any case, we shall obey. . . . You know that letters, going and coming, take a year to arrive—when they arrive."

As a matter of fact, Fages and Barri were intercepting so many of them that Father Verger had to conceal his in boxes, and one of Francisco Palou's friars had to run back and forth like a shuttle between Loreto and Mexico City.

"We have struggled, prayed, suffered," Junípero concluded. "We may believe that God has condescended to enlighten us. . . . Is it your judgment, as it is mine, that divine will directs me to set out at once to visit our superiors?"

There was unanimous agreement. He named Father Paterna to act as his substitute while he was away.

Of the sailing ships, only the *San Carlos* was still in port, getting ready to weigh anchor. Fages forbade Miguel Pino and Canizares to let the Prefect come aboard. Both welcomed him with open arms. It was the second time Canizares had had the honor of offering him a refuge on his ship.

Fages forbade Junípero to leave the country. Junípero declared that he would not obey. Was the captain going to stop him by main force? He did not dare lay hands upon him, knowing that he would be excommunicated if he did.

Junípero devoted himself immediately to the preparation of a long report. If he were to die on the way, at least his report would reach Mexico. Not having time to write to Francisco Palou, he left it to his colleagues to inform him. And on October 20, 1772, growing more and more ill, he left San Diego with the young Juan Evangelista.

Twelve

The Fernandinos Leave Old California and Junípero Arrives in Mexico City
[1772-1773]

This time the winds were so favorable that the *San Carlos* made the trip in fifteen days. Junípero went ashore at San Blas on November 4, 1772; on the seventh he arrived at the Franciscan residency at Tepic; he dispatched his Report (which he had finished at sea) to Father Verger, wrote to Francisco Palou, rested three days, and then, still in pain, set out with Juan Evangelista for Mexico City.

Let us leave them on the way there, and, while waiting to meet them again at Guadalajara, let us see what was known and what was being done at the College of San Fernando.

Its head at that time was Fray Rafael Verger, who, before becoming Bishop of Linares (Nuevo León, Mexico), was twice Guardian of San Fernando: from 1771 to 1774 and from 1777 to 1780.[1] His recent recruiting trip in Spain had introduced him to the Court of Madrid, where he had formed especially close ties with the Fiscal (public prosecutor), Casafonda, confidant and advisor to Charles III. A great friend of Palou's, Verger was a little less the friend of Junípero, of whom perhaps he felt twinges of jealousy; in 1775, at all events, he joined with the other Discretos in signing the License that stripped him of his powers. He was wont to say, of Junípero, that "his zeal was rather to be bridled than spurred," which in itself shows that he had none of those sublime intuitions and that logical temerity that are possessed by heroes and saints. For the rest, he was a man of heart and a man of duty, and from the time he took office he fought valiantly for the missionaries and the missions of Upper California. Thanks to

[1] He was consecrated Bishop June 22, 1783, and died July 4, 1790.

Palou, he was much better informed than Junípero supposed: "I am completely in touch with what is going on," he wrote to Casafonda on August 3, 1771, "and I have lost sleep and suffered in health for the past year in knowing the hardships that have been endured, and the treatment that has been received, by my sons who are risking their lives at the ends of the world."

We must see how he castigates the parsimonious, the men who slander or misrepresent, and the advocates of the new methods of conquest. "Are you not ashamed of your niggardliness toward us?" he says to this same Casafonda. "I understand that you would wish to be thrifty with the King's money; yet you readily find four thousand pesos to establish a presidio and three thousand pesos as salary for the officer in command of it. How is it that you find only one thousand, when it is a matter of setting up a mission, and three hundred as *sinodo* for its ministers? A thousand pesos would perhaps be enough to establish a household of poor folk in the mountains of Andalusia; but it is absurd to pretend that one could found a missionary center of far-reaching activity and influence with such a beggarly sum.

"Will you count up with me what we spend in beginning such an establishment? We have to pay the costs of building, furnishing, the carpenter's saws, the mason's trowels, the food and clothing of the Indians who come to catechism class, the penknives and leaf tobacco that we give to those who remain in the background and whom we must attract. . . . After that, there are the animals—for you do not imagine, I hope, that we are going to create agricultural centers without horses, mules, and oxen. . . . You will tell me that every Mission has received nine cows. Do not expect me to thank you for them: first because they are not enough, and then, for the cows as for the *sinodos*, it is the Pious Funds and not the King's Treasury that you draw upon. Do you deserve thanks for the smaller livestock? Let us discuss the smaller livestock! For four missions, you have been so generous as to give us four pigs, two male and two female: that is, half a sow and half a boar for each mission. As for the farmyard, three missions have each received a hen and her brood; for one of them a rooster has been generously added; the fourth mission has got neither hens nor rooster! . . . Believe me," he added, in this letter of August 3, 1771, "it is a mere bit of stage scenery that the Visitor General has been setting up there. He is deluding himself if he counts on accomplishing durable work with such means."

In actual fact, it was not Galvez who had sent the *San José* to the bottom of the sea; nor was it Verger, but rather the *mal de Loanda*, that had decimated the supply of pigs aboard the *San Carlos*; and it was Fages who had eaten the fowl! But Verger was no less right in protesting against the men at Court who were keeping the King from opening his purse; and one must all the more admire the results Junípero obtained with the fifty cows that were given him.

"I watch over them like the apple of my eye," he wrote, during the famine of 1772. And these good animals responded so well to his care that there were a hundred thousand of them twenty years later. As for the rooster in question, what rooster here below had ever such an expanding progeny as this one which first saluted the sun of Upper California?

It was the reprimand from Bucareli that had determined Junípero to set out for Mexico City. But no sooner had it flowed from the Viceroy's pen than Verger seized his own pen and reprimanded this important personage in his turn. "You have believed what was told you by slanderers, Excellency," he wrote him, on December 23, 1771, "and you have allowed yourself to be deceived by them. I am now going to prove to you, by documents which I have at hand, that the man who is doing the slandering is the same man as is responsible for the desertions." He does prove it to him, paints Fages in his true colors, and adds, "In a letter from the Prefect of Monterey to the Prefect of Loreto I read the following sentence: 'It is impossible to imagine all that the Commandant has made me suffer in the past year; how many times I have thought that his persecutions would end by being the death of me!' I have the honor to tell you, Excellency, that the man who speaks so is Father Junípero Serra, an experienced missionary, a man virtuous and patient if anyone ever was. No one is ignorant of the services he has rendered to the Two Majesties in the Sierra Gorda and in California. For these words to have escaped the lips of this man who never complained, it must indeed be that the Commandant exceeded all limits. I therefore lodge a complaint against this officer, and ask that he be called to account."

Bucareli went thoroughly into the whole situation, and, on March 22, 1772, replied:

To the Reverend Father Verger and the Discretos of San Fernando:

As regards the desertion of the soldiers. . . . In consideration of your protest of December 23 last, and the letters attached to it. . . . In accordance with the Report of the Señor Fiscal who has examined them, I have given orders to Governor Barri and to Captain Fages to behave henceforth in such a manner that the missionaries may be able to devote themselves in entire freedom to their work of spiritual conquest. I am sternly commanding these officials to aid and support your friars, in the future, in every respect. Orders have also been given to Governor Barri to inform me of what has been done and what remains to be done, to assure the friars' satisfaction. I am bringing this to your knowledge so that you may induce them to persevere, according to His Majesty's desire, in their sacred mission.

Junípero knew nothing of any of this when he sent his own Report from Tepic to San Fernando. That Report arrived there weeks before its author. Verger transmitted it immediately to Bucareli, and added a Memorandum of his own which recapitulated the ideas of the Prefect of Monterey.

"It must be understood," we read here, "that this is less a matter of a military occupation than of a spiritual conquest. It is the friars' responsibility to direct the natives, since they alone have power to win their hearts and school their souls. They are succeeding in revealing the Gospel to them, in bettering the material conditions of their lives, in turning them into industrious people settled on the land, and in making them Christians. The soldiers, for their part, in shooting their blunderbusses at the Indian men and capturing the Indian women on their lassos, succeed only in sowing hatred. But what is it, now, that is brought to my knowledge? That, not content with allowing every license to their men, Fages and Barri are seeking to diminish our estate, in the eyes of the natives, by repeating over and over that we are there only to say Mass, to preach, and to hear confession. . . . If Your Excellency does not put an end to this, I assure you that the King will be squandering his money, that his Kingdom will never be increased in this part of the world, and that our Fathers will be wasting their time in Upper California." Finally there was this ultimatum: "Either you immediately take the steps which I suggest, Excellency, or my friars will return to the College."

The letter Junípero had written to Francisco Palou from Tepic had its motivation in the victory Father Verger had just allowed the Dominicans to win in Lower California. Although their numbers had always been smaller than the Franciscans', the Dominicans had never been willing to be of less avail for the glory of God, and we shall see them, until the end, trying to get Junípero's missions away from him. Junípero did not love them the less for that; he used to call them "angels," although he would have wished their zeal to be exercised elsewhere.

As early as March 9, 1769, when he was on the point of leaving Loreto, he had learned by hearsay that Father Juan Pedro de Iriarte was in possession of a royal Memorandum authorizing him to obtain a foothold in Lower California. He at once sent word to Galvez, who at once reassured him.

"My very dear friend," the Visitor General said, in a letter Junípero received while the muleteer Coronel was treating his bad leg, "I do not give credence to your information. In any case, you are to know that neither myself nor the Viceroy will permit the Dominicans to seize your missions."

While the Visitor General was fighting in Sonora, the Dominicans, in April, 1770, acquired a second Memorandum. It spoke of "the ideal of their holy Order which impelled them to convert the infidels": in it one read also that "it was intolerable to see so extensive a territory set apart for a single College." In the following November the second Memorandum was followed by a third. This last authorized Father Iriarte "to betake himself, with twenty-three friars, into California, there to occupy the posts which would be assigned to them by the Viceroy"; but it permitted the Viceroy "to send them elsewhere, if he thought best." This double-tongued "rider" was obviously the work of Galvez.

When Father Iriarte and his companions arrived in Mexico in November, 1771, the Marquis de Croix had just relinquished his office to Bucareli and was about to return to Spain with José Galvez. The new Viceroy would not have dared come to a decision without submitting the question to the future Minister of the Indies. He asked him what he ought to do with the newcomers. "Send them to Sonora or to the Island of Tiburon," Galvez answered, "but not into California. His Majesty will confirm your action as soon as I get back to Spain."

It was while Galvez and De Croix were on their way from Veracruz to Cadiz, an ocean crossing of five months, that Juan Pedro bore off the victory.

As he saw nothing coming from Madrid, and as he did not know any other way of getting rid of the Dominicans, who—armed with their three Memoranda—were besieging his doorstep, Bucareli besought Father Verger to come to an understanding with them. Verger realized at once that the new arrivals were in no way drawn toward the conversion of Sonora or the Island of Tiburon; that it was to Lower California and Lower California only that they were impelled to go. Since they knew it only through the enthusiastic recitals of the Jesuit Fathers, it was for them an Eldorado. Verger, better informed, was envisaging it as it actually was, and he was thinking that the Fernandinos would be spending their time to greater advantage in Upper California.

"I will gladly divide with you," he said to Juan Pedro de Iriarte. "You will take seven missions and we will keep six, to wit: Loreto, Comondu, San Ignacio, Santa Gertrudis, San Borja, and Velicata—that is to say, our line of communication with San Diego." Juan Pedro agreed at first to this arrangement. Then, changing his mind, he complained that the Franciscans were leaving him only the refuse. His three Memoranda deserved something better than that! He wanted more. Verger gave him everything.

By the *Concordat* concluded on April 7, 1772, "between Fray Rafael Verger, Guardian of the College of San Fernando, and Fray Juan Pedro de Iriarte, minister of the holy Order of Preaching Friars, commissioner of the mission sent by the King into California," it was decided that "the Dominican Fathers should take over the missions now held here by San Fernando, including Velicata, and that they should continue the work of converting the Indians as far north as the line drawn south of San Diego."

When this news reached Francisco Palou and his colleagues, in the course of the following August, they rang the bells and sang a Mass of thanksgiving. The fact is that they were ceding to their rivals only some stony mountains, some sandy deserts, and no more than a few handfuls of Indians to convert. Even to this day, to the traveler who traverses Lower California, nothing but the names of some ten villages and a few ruined walls indicate that the Dominicans expended their zeal for half a century in these countrysides. . . .

As soon as the *Concordat* reached Loreto, the first Fernandinos began to leave the Peninsula. We have met Father La Pena and his two companions at San Diego. Junípero encountered others at Tepic.

"They tell me," he wrote to Palou on November 10, 1772, "that of the twenty Fathers we have left, four have been assigned by the Father Guardian to Upper California, and that you would like to know whether I want any more. I ought to have from eight to ten if, as I like to believe, the College looks with a favorable eye upon the early establishment of San Buenaventura, San Francisco, and Santa Clara. I learn also that you are one of those whom the Reverend Father Guardian allows to choose the place where they are going. What a comfort it would be to me, if you should reach a decision which would permit us to live and die together! Yet you must follow God's inspiration only—I submit in advance to His will. . . . It is the same with the number of Fathers that are to be given me. If the instructions of the Reverend Father Guardian are so precise as not to permit more than four Fathers to come north, take it that I have said nothing. . . . Let us rely upon God to make provision for everything, and, on our part, let us merely obey. . . . I am leaving tomorrow, and by the grace of God I shall continue on my way."

Junípero and Juan Evangelista reached Guadalajara at the end of a march of two hundred miles. There they picked up a bad case of measles, complicated by a malignant fever, which brought them near to death. "The revered Father was resigned to dying," Palou writes. "His mind was at rest, since he had forwarded his final injunctions to the Guardian of San Fernando. Only one thing was troubling him, he spoke of it to me often: 'What would Juan Evangelista's parents say, if their child did not come back? They would think that the white men had killed him; and the other Indians would believe it, too; and the progress of evangelization would be retarded for this cause.' For that reason, while he himself was preparing to leave this world, Junípero was asking God to spare his young friend."

From his bed he dictated a letter to Francisco Palou. The letter itself has not been found, but Palou discloses the gist of it when, on November 26, 1773, he writes to his master, who is still in Mexico: "In compliance with what Your Reverence wrote me, I have come to Carmel. In the name of the Virgin Mary and our Seraphic Father St. Francis, you adjured me to come north to Monterey, adding that if God restored your health you would return there also, so that we might end our days together. I have done what you asked. I hope that you will keep your promise. If that were impossible for you, we should nevertheless soon meet again, as is my desire; for I should return to the sacred refuge of the College, where I should already be if it were not for your last letter." Having turned over their new fief to the Dominicans, Palou had left Loreto on the seventeenth of the preceding month to make his way to Upper California and, while awaiting the return of his friend, take over the direction of the missions there.

Junípero recovered, as did Juan Evangelista; and after a few days of convalescence they set out on the road again. Another journey of two hundred miles brought them to Santa Cruz de Querétaro. "There the revered Father had a relapse," Palou writes. "He was taken to the infirmary; and the Father Guardian told him that this time he was about to take his journey to the other world. This was, furthermore, the opinion of one of the three convent physicians, who ordered that he be given Extreme Unction. In the evening after compline, therefore, the last rites were about to be administered to him when one of the other two physicians came into his room: he was not on duty that week, but he wanted, none the less, to make the acquaintance of the famous Prefect of Monterey. He went up to the bed, looked at the dying man, took his pulse, and addressed the medical attendant.

" 'Is this,' he asked, 'really the Father to whom the last rites are to be given? . . . In that case, they should be given to me likewise, for I am just as sick as he!' And he turned to Junípero. 'You can get up,' he said. 'There is nothing more the matter with you.' "

A few days later, Junípero and Juan Evangelista were beginning to traverse the last hundred miles of their journey; and February 6, 1773, they arrived at San Fernando.

Thirteen

Junípero and Bucareli Save
New California
[1773]

Among the sixty-two Viceroys of Mexico, none has left a more lasting memory than the Chevalier Antonio Maria Bucareli, who governed this country from September, 1771, to April, 1779. He owes this to his moral worth and his benevolence. He administered the country according to the ideas of the King, which were themselves noble; he did all the good he could, without seeking any profit for himself. Except for a few restless-minded among the religious, whom he had to recall to their duty, no one ever brought any reproach against him. The Indians, the unfortunate, and the missionaries had especial cause to bless him. To his salary of sixty thousand pesos Charles III secretly added twenty thousand to help him carry on his charities, and at his death the King gave the wholly exceptional orders that his accounts should not be examined at all.

Bucareli realized, and readily acknowledged, that the saving of Northern California was due to Junípero. "He was half-dying when I saw him arrive here," he wrote. "The apostolic flame that burned in him made an extraordinary impression on me; it was his views and his desires which inspired my decisions."

This dying man brought about a rebirth in California. It needed almost a miracle, in fact, to save the situation in February, 1773. But who still believes this miracle to be possible? Is it Verger who considers that "the farce staged by Galvez has lasted long enough," and speaks of recalling his friars? In any case it is not Palou, who, arriving at Monterey in November, 1773, after making a tour of all the missions, deems the denouement of the drama to be not far away, and advises Junípero not to come back. Still less is it the Junta, which, for its part, has always repudiated the Utopias of the Visitor General. While he was there, the Junta was to all intents and purposes dead. But in the year since he went away it had raised its head again. If all its members did not yet declare aloud that there must be an end to the adventure, they were all doing what they could to keep the Viceroy from going on with it. Had they not just refused him the necessary credits for the completion of the frigate *Santiago?*

"The royal funds are being wasted," they said, "since our inability to navigate in this part of the Pacific puts Monterey out of reach. Has Russia ever succeeded, we ask, in making a landing there? And we who have done so, what a price we have paid! The *San José* is at the bottom of the sea, with its cargo; the *San Carlos* has only taken its cargo to its destination twice; we have had two famines in four years; dissension prevails between the military authority and the friars; as for the soldiers, all of them will soon have deserted. While we are waiting for the King to order the abandonment of the venture, let us close the port and the shipyards of San Blas and set fire to the frigate being built in the San Blas yards; let us confine our efforts to dispatching the indispensable minimum of aid, by way of Loreto, to the soldiers and the missionaries who are still in those regions."

Bucareli was so discouraged and disturbed that, in February, 1773, he wrote to Prime Minister Arriaga: "Although I have neglected nothing, the results I have obtained are disappointing. Everything, alas, augurs the ruin of this colony which will have cost so much in arduous labor and in money."

It was at this moment that Junípero appeared before him.

In the conversations between the two men from the sixth to the thirteenth of February, 1773, the Prefect of Monterey acknowledged that the new conquest was "in its death throes," but he added that it could be saved. The work had within it the possibility of life, he said, and the heaviest part of the task was done: "If you remove the obstacles which I point out to you, and grant the assistance for which I beg, we shall make of these pagan tribes a great Christian people, and of their land the most beautiful of all the colonies of the King."

Bucareli asked nothing but to believe him. "I knew," he writes, "that His Majesty was in persistent dread of the descent of the Russians; three maritime expeditions had just been sent out, disclosing their aims. All had failed; but might a fourth not have better fortune?"

He was immediately conquered and consoled by this apostle with a will of iron whom he had before him. At the same time realistic and imaginative, seeing what was and divining what would be, neither exaggerating nor undervaluing anything, envisaging both the whole and the parts, this astonishing friar appeared to him as a stupendous organizer and a veritable statesman. The plan of action that Junípero submitted to him was complete and practicable. "Judging it to be the best from every point of view," he writes, "I adopted it."

To Junípero, who had become his friend, he explained: "It only remains for us to convince the Junta. Draw up a Memorandum," he added, "which we will submit to it, and which we will stand up for together."

With his customary speed in working, Junípero drew up six, which, collected, would form a volume.

The first and most important, dated February 13, 1773, contains about nine thousand words, grouped under thirty-two headings. The general outline was as follows:

Article I: San Blas. The notion of abandoning this port is so absurd that I do not wish to dwell upon it.

Article II: The *Santiago*. This large frigate, which will replace the *San José* and put an end to our famines, should be finished as soon as possible.

Article III: Carmel. Since there should be three ministers there (the Prefect and two others), this Mission should receive three *sinodos*, and not merely two.

Articles IV, XXIII, XXIV, XXV: Concerning the Commissioner of San Blas, the Commandant of Monterey, and the Dominicans. "The Commissioner of the port of San Blas should be directed to ship to us the provisions, fabrics, corn, bells, alms, correspondence, in a word everything which has been sent to us by the King, the College, and our benefactors. Pedro Fages has instructed this Commissioner to send nothing more which is not addressed personally to him. When a ship puts into port, he takes possession of the entire cargo, divides it up according to his own intentions, and steals for his own benefit part of what belongs to the missions. It is equally urgent to put an end to the activity of the thieves at San Blas. A *fanega* (one and one-half bushels) ought to contain twelve *almudes*. Their *fanegas* contain only nine or ten when they measure out our corn and meal. Let there be an immediate checking and certification of the *fanegas, demi-fanegas, almudes, quartillos,* and other measures that are in use at San Blas. The Commissioner of this port should be severely called to account, for his lack of attention to the conservation and packing of our provisions. Because of his carelessness, missionaries have often had to eat meal and corn that was spoiled. Frequently, also, the bags he uses are so bad that they tear on the ship or on muleback, and are almost empty when they come to our hands. Be kind enough, too, to oblige the Dominicans to stop holding at Velicata the boxes and things that belong to us."

Article V: Anza's expedition. "What a great and rapid development would be in store for the new conquest if it should become accessible by land from Sonora! Since Captain Anza, Commandant of Tubac (Sonora) offers to attempt that expedition, I urge Your Excellency to authorize him to do so."

Articles VI and VII: Concerning Pedro Fages and his successor. "If I tried to tell of his conduct toward the missionaries I should never come to an end! As for the soldiers, all without exception are in rebellion against his brutality, and they will continue to desert if he is not recalled. Since Your Excellency authorizes me to propose a candidate, I nominate Sergeant Ortega to replace him."

Article VIII: Concerning the libertines and blackguards. "The future Commandant should immediately recall to the presidio, when the minister requests it, any soldier whose licentiousness or cruelty makes him unworthy to remain at the mission."

Article IX: On the government of the Indians. "In accordance with long-standing usage, the responsibility for educating and directing the Indians lies with the missionaries. Save for capital crimes, neither the Commandant nor the soldiery has the right to chastise and maltreat our poor neophytes without submitting the case to their spiritual fathers."

Article X: On the number of soldiers. "To protect the five existing missions and the three that are soon to be established, I consider a hundred cuirassiers to be necessary."

Article XI: Autonomy of Upper California. "The capital of the New Conquest, and the military headquarters, should henceforth be Monterey, and no longer Loreto."

Article XII: Concerning workmen. "Among the marines recruited in the San Blas countryside there is no dearth of agricultural laborers, cowherds, and muleteers. There should be at least four of these for each mission; but it must be understood that the Commandant cannot take them away from us."

Article XIII: Immigration. "When the cattle you have promised us comes from the Peninsula, I ask that some fifteen families of converted Indians be attached to the caravan. They will provide the missions with an extra supply of manual labor, and, above all, they will show that marriage exists among us. Christian women have never been seen in this countryside."

Article XIV: On the missionary soldier. "That is the term applied to the soldier who is relied upon, a kind of confidential agent, of whom there quite recently used to be one at each mission as a major-domo or steward. This practice should be brought in force again. We cannot be everywhere. We cannot, especially, look after the maintenance of the agricultural tools and machinery, since we did not learn mechanics in the convent."

Articles XVI, XVII, XVIII, and XIX: Regarding the skilled laborers. "To the smithy which you have sent to San Diego, I beg that you will add a blacksmith; this smithy will serve all the southern missions. We also need a smithy and a blacksmith at Carmel for the missions of the north. If an ax is broken at San Antonio and is sent to the Presidio of Monterey, the Commandant keeps us waiting a year for repairs that can be made in a quarter of an hour. Likewise, we need two carpenters, who will teach their trade to the Indians, as the blacksmiths will also do."

Articles XX and XXI: As for the King. "His Majesty is in the habit of giving to each mission two bells, one large and one small, along with the sacred vessels, altar linen, and other things necessary in worship. I shall send you as soon as possible the list of what is lacking in the present missions and in those that are shortly to be established. In addition it is my desire that the King should make us a present of a hundred mules."

Article XXII: Correspondence. "Please give the Commandant a strict order not to open our letters in future, or to mislay them. I ask the postal franchise for the missionaries that is granted to the soldiers."

Article XXVII: Regarding cows. "The cows meant for the Missions of Santa Clara and San Francisco are at the Presidio of Monterey. I ask that they be handed over to me along with their calves. We will take better care of them than the soldiers, not to mention the fact that their milk will be of benefit to our Christian children."

Article XXVIII: A doctor. "From emotion, it seems, Dr. Prat lost his mind at the time of the discovery of Monterey. The poor man stayed there for a year, then went to Guadalajara to die. His drugs and medicaments were distributed among all the missions; but no one among us knows the art of making use of them. Moreover, there are bleedings to be attended to. Therefore we need a new doctor."

Articles XXIX, XXX, and XXXI: Married soldiers. "To the soldiers who marry Indian women that have been baptized, I ask you to grant (in addition to a gift of money) two cows, a mule, and a plot of ground, and to authorize them to remain henceforth in the mission where they have taken a wife. I judge that with the arrival of the new Commandant a general amnesty will be proclaimed for the benefit of the deserters who are still running about among the pagans and doing a great deal of harm."

Article XXXII: Duplicates. "Before starting out again I wish to receive a duplicate of the decrees you will sign and the instructions you will give to the new Commandant."

Memorandum No. 2, under date of February 15, supplied the list promised in Articles XX and XXI of the preceding document.

The Junta would soon have to declare itself on the matter of the first Memorandum's thirty-two demands. The soundings Bucareli took showed him that a number of the Junta's members were not giving up their idea of closing the port of San Blas and burning the frigate. He passed this word on to Junípero, who drew up his *Memorandum No. 3*, dated April 22, 1773, with them in mind.

"You say," they were to read in it, "that it will be an advantage for the boats to be replaced by land convoys. In my opinion you are wrong—for three reasons: in the first place, you will never succeed in organizing these transports by pack mule [he proved this]; second, fifteen hundred mules will cost you more, on any hypothesis, than the boats [he proved this, also]; and finally, the third has to do with the hundred muleteers who for eight months of the twelve will be going back and forth on this three-hundred-league road [750 miles] between Loreto and Monterey. Rude and conscienceless folk as they are, these muleteers will have a good chance to do what they do everywhere—that is, to steal the Indians' pottery, violate their women, and kill anyone who resists them. The result will be that these Indians, who are as meek as sheep [!], will become raging tigers: they will refuse passage to the mail-carriers and the King's soldiers, they will hold white men in horror, and they will lose the good attitude they now have toward the reception of the Gospel."

The Junta met on the sixth of May under the presidency of the Viceroy. Bucareli had determined that Junípero should be at his side to defend the cause of the colony and the missions. It

was clear, from this day, that they were completely victorious.
Of the thirty-two articles only four raised any real question: the
third, which had to do with the third *sinodo* to be allotted to
Carmel; the tenth, concerning the replacement of Fages; and the
sixth and seventh, relating to the number of soldiers. As though
to allow the Junta to carry off one small victory, Bucareli yielded
on Article III. So as to show that eighty soldiers at the very least
would be necessary, if the King was too poor to hire a hundred,
Junípero drew up his *Memorandum No. 4,* dated May 21. He
prepared a fifth, under date of June 4, to demonstrate that the
recall of Fages was essential.

Bucareli soon informed him that the high Assembly had approved twenty-six of the thirty-two articles of *Memorandum No.
1.* It had decided that eighteen of them should be incorporated
in a code of rules (*Reglamento*), which the Viceroy was instructed to formulate; that eight others would be made the subject of as many decrees to be issued by the Junta; and that only
six would have to be submitted to new examination. On the sixth
of June, Junípero acknowledged the receipt of this communication in a sixth Memorandum, in which he thanked Bucareli and
called his attention to various details which he was afraid he might
forget.

The Junta assembled once more on July 8. It took cognizance
of the three last Memoranda from Junípero, settled the fate of
the six articles that had been held over, and approved—with slight
alterations—the projected *Reglamento.* Decrees and *Reglamento*
were to come into force January 1, 1774. The Viceroy cut down
the remaining formalities as much as he could, taking it upon
himself to sign the official documents before receiving the royal
approval. This was only to be given two years later—on July 6,
1775.

Junípero prolonged his stay in Mexico City by another two
months, following like a novice the conventual exercises at San
Fernando, exhausting himself in canvassing, making purchases, and
begging for the Indians. He was defending them against their de-
tractors: he never tired of expatiating on their intelligence and
their goodness of heart, attributing their thieveries to "curiosity,"
their taste for the shedding of blood to "a sort of natural uneasiness," and their most atrocious crimes to the "pagan darkness"
from which they were soon to emerge.

From that time on, several members of the Junta, such as the Fiscal Areche, considered him as a saint. Anxious that his physical features should be preserved for posterity, Father Verger made him pose for a painter, in an armchair. Of this man in his sixties whose bodily frailty had struck Bucareli—of the "indomitable old lion" of whom another eyewitness spoke—the incompetent artist made a placid Franciscan friar, some forty years of age, the healthiest and the most insignificant man in the world. The face is rosy and unwrinkled, the features are regular and characterless, the mouth is all honey, the eyes are expressionless and kind, the hands seem carved in wood. Except for the costume, a slight baldness, and an air of childlike purity, what is left of Junípero in this conventional portrait, the only one of him that exists? . . .

Bucareli arranged receptions in his honor. Junípero attended them in order to plead the cause of the Indians, proud of exhibiting Juan Evangelista, whose astonishment—and responses—used to entertain the company. Juan Evangelista continued to be surprised especially that there should be women among the Whites. Before long he would be going to report this news at Monterey, where in the end it would be no longer believed that the Spaniards had mules for mothers or were sprung from the earth after the same fashion as bushes and stalks of corn.

It was then that Junípero wrote—we think for the last time—to his family; his letter was addressed to Juanita's son, Miguel, who, as we know, had become a Capuchin friar. It reads:

My dear nephew:
Do not attribute to lack of affection the fact that I have made no reply to the letters I have received from you. I knew, when I left my dear fatherland, that this meant a total separation from the beloved beings whom I was leaving behind. . . . Your last letter came to me among the pagans, three hundred leagues from any Christian community. It is there that my life is; there also, I hope, that my death will be. When death overtakes me, some one will take the responsibility of informing our Province, so that my poor soul may be prayed for; thus you will learn that I have departed this life. . . . What more can you desire? You are living among saints; my poor advice is no longer necessary to you; my letters could not be of any use to you.

Let us employ our time, you and I, in moving forward on the good road; let each step we take mark a progress in the direction of our vocation; let us work for the salvation of our souls, with fear and trembling; let us devote ourselves to our brothers, with zeal and courage; in everything let us seek only the glory of God. In this connection, I have been so happy to learn that you were holding a mission on the island of Ivisa when our Commissioner, Father Verger, stopped there four years ago. It is, it seems to me, in devoting yourself to this ministry, in preaching by example and by word, in hearing confessions with patience and kindness, that you will best be able to make use of your time.

Although I am myself so faulty, so phlegmatic, and good for nothing, not a day goes by in which, at the holy sacrifice, I do not make mention of my only and beloved sister Juana, your mother, of her children, and particularly of my dear Capuchin friar. I like to believe that you do as much for me, who runs into so many dangers among the savages, among these naked folk who are my habitual associates. It is in this way that we shall continue to correspond; for the rest, God will take charge of it.

. . . This journey to Mexico has all but killed me. I have been close to death. At Guadalajara they gave me Extreme Unction; at Querétaro, again, they wanted to administer the last rites. Then the fever ceased to be continual and became intermittent, and in the end I arrived at the College. I remained for a long time without strength or appetite; but now my health is restored; my affairs have been attended to, and I am on the point of starting out again.

Where I am going back to, we scarcely get letters once a year; our Fathers in Mexico receive them no oftener from us. May our correspondents on other continents not be surprised if their portion is even worse! If God permits me to reach my destination I shall try, however, to let you know. I send my deepest affection to my beloved sister, your mother, and to all our relatives. My warm regards to my old pupils, friends, and acquaintances. Tell them to pray God to make me a worthy minister of the divine word, and to give me the grace of a holy death.

I kiss Your Fathership's hand, etc.

This letter was written on the fourth of August, 1773. Junípero left Mexico City early in September. Father Verger had given him Father Mugartegui as companion. If he should fall ill on the journey there would thus be someone to look after him, and if he should die there would be someone to take Juan Evangelista back to his parents. Junípero said farewell to his colleagues in the refectory of San Fernando. He knelt before them and asked their forgiveness for the bad example he had given them in the past seven months. And he added, "I beg you to commend me to God, for, this time, you will not see me again." He kissed the feet of each one.

"They were all sobbing," Palou writes, "for they felt convinced that he would succumb on the road. They saw him disappear in the distance, limping, and hardly able to stand upright."[1]

---

[1] From San Fernando on August 26, 1773, Father Pedro Font wrote a colleague in Catalonia: "We were both amazed and edified during Father Junípero Serra's stay here. He's a real lion, this old man of sixty and, like a lion, fever alone can vanquish him. Sick as he was, he followed every hour of the office with us, day and night. The Superior's order was needed to make him repair to the infirmary for a while. We saw him arrive half dead and then recover, a phenomenon which in his case was demonstrated many a time before. Despite his chest trouble, his shortness of breath, the sores on his legs and feet, he is preparing to depart for Monterey, a thousand leagues from here, as if it were nothing. In truth, from the austerity of his life, his humility, his charity, and his other virtues, one can say that in this man we have a real follower of the Apostles."

Fourteen

Junípero's Return to Monterey and Anza's First Expedition

[1773-1774]

Since the ships did not get under way until January, our three travelers had four months to put in before they could reach San Blas. "How many naked Indians are going to be clothed and little children fed by what I shall buy en route!" Junípero said as he started out. Had that admirable man Bucareli, for his part alone, not put 12,000 pesos in his pocket? And just at this time came the news that famine was once more raging in Upper California, since the disabled *San Carlos* had not been able to get beyond Loreto, and only the *San Antonio* had delivered its cargo at its destination. At Querétaro Junípero purchased hundreds of yards of blue cloth; at Guadalajara he recruited skilled workmen, and he bought more than two thousand bushels of corn and meal. The blue cloth cost one peso a yard; the meal, sent on to San Blas, five pesos a bushel.[1]

It was at Guadalajara, where he arrived October 10, that he received the duplicate copies of the decrees and the *Reglamento*. He noted that the hundred mules asked for in Article XX of his Memorandum had been forgotten, and that it was Rivera who was to be the successor to Pedro Fages. This last it was impossible to remedy; "but as for the mules," he wrote to Father Verger, "I beg you to give your attention to that matter; for I would have you know, in Mexico City, that although it might be raining mules in Monterey, not a single one would go to the missions without an official order. I learn also that Captain Rivera is in process of recruiting forty cuirassiers in the Compostella district, and it is said that, in this business of mules, every recruit is taking off three of

[1] The peso of that time would be worth from two to three dollars in present currency.

them, and he himself six or eight, with him. I do indeed hope that they are not going to embark with their animals on the frigate. How do you suppose that quarters are to be found for 40 soldiers and 130 mules, in addition to my provisions and my artisans and their families, on that boat? We should surely, in such a case, have a pestilence aboardship! I beg you that if you see fit, therefore, you will induce His Excellency to order them all to go by way of Loreto."

This letter was written on November 11, 1773; Verger stepped in and obtained satisfaction on both points.

When Junípero arrived at San Blas, in the early days of 1774, he found the frigate *Santiago* completed. A shipyard superintendent said to him, "You are a prophet, Father Prefect! In November, 1772, when we heard you announce that you would take the frigate for your return voyage, we, who had learned that things were soon going to be set fire to here, so as to salvage the scrap-iron—we laughed at you. And now here it is about to sail! Blessings upon you, Father Prefect; and forgive us!"

Palou, continuing this narrative, writes: "The revered Father smiled; and then, suddenly realizing that this man was speaking seriously, took pains at once to undeceive him. 'There is no question of prophecy,' he replied. 'I was thinking of the amount of foodstuffs that each boat would be able to carry to Monterey, and I simply meant to say that I hoped this one was not going to be destroyed. Now that God has fulfilled my desire, it only remains for me to give thanks to Him, and also to you, who have worked so well for the Indians.' "

The frigate, of which Juan Perez took command, had twice the tonnage of the *San Antonio* and the *San Carlos* together. Junípero embarked upon it on January 24, after packing most of his wealth of provisions in its hold; the rest was loaded on to the *San Antonio*, which, under command of Canizares, was to weigh anchor in February. The *Santiago's* orders, after putting into port at Monterey, were to proceed north, for the discovery of new lands. Galvez and Charles III dreamed of annexing the entire coast of North America, up to the Bering Strait. "Juan Perez is very well satisfied with this frigate that has been so slandered," Junípero wrote to Bucareli in a letter of January 27, 1774. "May God be pleased to fulfill the holy hopes you have placed in it, for the discovery of those unknown kingdoms where the light of the Gospel does not yet shine!"

On January 16 he had written to Father Verger's newly appointed successor as Guardian of the College, Father Pangua: "I do not want to set sail without expressing to you the homage of my most affectionate allegiance. I am discharging this duty in recognizing Your Reverence as my superior, my father, and my lord. Although I do not yet know your name, I send you a thousand congratulations; and although I am the most imperfect of your sons, there is none of them, believe me, who is more ready to carry out your slightest wish. Whether I am to continue, puny and inadequate as I am, to be your delegate in these distant missions, or whether it may please you to assign someone else to this work, I shall carry out your will to the utmost."

The *Santiago* took only seven weeks for the passage to San Diego. All the passengers were stricken with seasickness except Junípero, who never suffered from it. For an entire month he took care of Juan Evangelista and Father Mugartegui, who were quite seriously ill. As he wrote to a Franciscan at Tepic, on March 26, 1774, he had the sorrow of losing one of his workers from Guadalajara on this voyage, "poor Francisco Ramírez, engaged at a salary of ten pesos a month, plus food rations. Francisco died on the thirty-first of January," the letter continued, "after I had heard his confession and given him the last rites. It was the first time that I had seen a body cast into the sea. His poor rags of clothing were sold at auction; the proceeds served to pay off the debt to the King which he had incurred at San Blas; the few pesos that remained, as well as the things he left that nobody wanted, were sent back to his parents."

Junípero landed at San Diego on Laetare Sunday, March 13, 1774. "He came back in much better condition than when he went away," Palou writes. Was it happiness that was restoring his health? However that may be, the fact remains that the weeks that followed were to be beautiful weeks for him. Let us hasten to share his joy, for we shall soon have nothing to recount but suffering. . . .

The source of his joy was in returning to his "own country," the pagan earth that he loved and belonged to, and in finding himself once more among the Indians, his children; in seeing his fellow workers again, also, and especially Palou, who had come to "labor, live, and die with him." But he was happy above all in the thought that the total conversion of Upper California was imminent, since the future of the missions was assured. It was assured from the spiritual point of view by the decrees of the Junta and the *Reglamento*, by the friendliness of Bucareli, by the reinforcements of friars being supplied by Francisco Palou: three of them he had sent as early as 1772 (La Peña, Figuer, Uson), five he brought with him in 1773 (Lasuen, Murguia, Fuster, Amurrio, and Prestamero), and finally two (Sanchez and Cambon) who would arrive as soon as the Dominicans would let the coffers leave Velicata.[2]

From the material point of view the future of the missions appeared to be no less happy. Thanks to this frigate with rounded sides, from which the provisions brought by Junípero and those sent by the King were at this moment being unloaded, the present famine was practically over. "It was terrible, however, that famine," Junípero wrote to his Guardian. "At San Diego, missionaries and soldiers owed their escape from death entirely to the corn that had been harvested by San Gabriel; at Monterey, men were receiving only about a quart of it as their ration; at Carmel, our colleagues had only milk from their cows and grass from their fields to live on." But even if the ships might sometimes fail to arrive at the appointed time from now on, there would be no real famines in the future, "in view of the increasing prosperity of our missions and the recent exploit of the Tubac Commandant. On the one hand, our missions are almost self-sufficient; we have sown a great deal of wheat everywhere, and judging from the way the ears are forming, as I see them from my window, it is growing marvelously; our cows are multiplying, and we have the donkeys and mares needed for the breeding of mules. On the other hand—and it is great news that I am announcing to you—we shall shortly be connected with the Christian districts by land."

It had always been believed that no direct communication between Mexico and Upper California was possible. Vast deserts stretched between the two territories; the Jesuits had added the report of

[2] Escorted by fourteen soldiers under Ortega's command, Palou and his colleagues arrived at San Diego August 30, 1773. They brought six families of neophyte Indians with them. Palou reached Carmel the following November 14.

a great deal of water, also; and only recently Father Linck had located the impassable mouth of the Colorado River here as well. Yet a few explorers maintained that the Gulf of California did not extend so far north, and that one should be able to travel on dry land from Sonora to the "country of Monterey"; this opinion was held by, among others, the Franciscan Garces and Colonel Anza, father of the Commandant of Tubac, and himself killed by the Indians a short time before, as he was attempting to make his own investigation. How much mileage, time, and money would be saved, above all how many dangers and misfortunes would be avoided, when these men should have been proved right! For years Captain Anza had been consumed with the desire to take up his father's project again, undertaking to go from Tubac to Monterey without spanning either the gulf or the arm of the sea; and he had begged the Viceroys to authorize him to do this; but they had turned a deaf ear to his arguments. It was on the earnest entreaty of Junípero (in Article V of the Memorandum) that the Junta and Bucareli, hitherto recalcitrant, had granted the adventurous captain the means to set out on his expedition forthwith.

Now, it had just been successful. At what price? That is what Junípero recounted in the letters he wrote from San Diego on March 31 to his Guardian and on April 5 to the Viceroy:

"Great was my joy on learning that the captain from Tubac and Fathers Garces and Diaz had arrived at San Gabriel; but greater still was my pain when Father Garces told me the story of what they had gone through." Fathers Garces and Diaz, chaplains to the expedition, belonged to the College of Querétaro, whose Missions of Tubac, the Altar, and Caborca comprised the frontier of the Spanish conquests.

"There were first two unsuccessful efforts to make a start." Anza was about to set out, when the Apaches attacked his presidio and carried off all his horses. He got new mounts for his cavalry; the Apaches returned to the charge, killed his sergeant and his muleteers, and this time took the mules along with the horses. Finding a new supply of mules and horses, Anza was preparing for the third time to start on his way when he learned that an Indian named Sebastian Taraval had just arrived at the Altar Presidio from San Gabriel. "You remember Article XIII of my Memorandum, in which I asked that married Indians should be sent us from Lower California? Sebastian and his wife were one of five households of neophytes whom Francisco Palou had brought with him last October. Seized with homesickness, no doubt, they had run away from San Gabriel, persuading one of the bachelors to go with them. The bachelor and the woman had died of thirst in the desert; the aforesaid Sebastian had survived and had finally reached Sonora. Here, thought the captain, was the guide sent him by Providence! He had Sebastian brought along, and made up his mind to follow him wherever he might be pleased to lead. Father Garces pointed out to him that perhaps Sebastian had not taken the shortest route, and that it might be better to keep to an itinerary worked out in advance; but Anza would not listen to anything. . . ."

On the ninth of January, he set out from Tubac with his two chaplains, twenty soldiers, horses, a mule train, cattle, and provisions. On the twenty-second, he left the Mission of Caborca on the northwest frontier and plunged into the unknown. During the first part of the journey all went well: Sebastian was following a trail which, some sixty miles away, ran along the left shore of the Gulf of California. At the end of two weeks they reached the spot where the waters of the Gila River flow into the Colorado, about seventy miles north of the great river's mouth, not far from the present town of Yuma. "The animals were dropping in their tracks, dying of fatigue; Anza ought to have paused there for a few days to let them get their breath, and then go on with them for the 250 miles they had still to go. But, impetuous and bemused by Sebastian, who assured him that San Gabriel was close by, Anza left to the care of the Yuma Indians sixteen soldiers, his mules, his cattle, and his provisions; and with only six soldiers, the two Fathers, and almost no foodstuffs, he rode at top speed after his ill-chosen and incompetent guide. They made a zigzag journey that lasted six weeks, and were on the very edge of death until the end. On March 22 they just reached San Gabriel, pulling their dying horses by the bridle and having nothing to eat themselves; there had been nothing for the last twenty-four hours; not so much as a slab of chocolate was left to them."

The ministers of San Gabriel had at almost the same moment received a letter from Junípero urging them to send their mules to get their share of the wealth of provisions brought by the frigate. The mules went, and with them Father Garces and three of Anza's soldiers, who were transmitting to Juan Perez, to Junípero, and to Sergeant Ortega the commands and threats of their chief.

Anza, who had come in zigzags from Yuma to San Gabriel, now claimed that he had found a route which should connect San Gabriel with Monterey more directly than the one that had been used hitherto; and in the name of God and the King he called upon the authorities then present in San Diego to supply him with the necessary elements of a new exploring party. He demanded that Juan Perez give him his apprentice pilot to take the latitudes; from Ortega he expected soldiers; from Junípero, mules; from all three he counted upon receiving chocolate and other provisions. "And if you do not comply with my orders," he wrote to Ortega, "you will be responsible before the Two Majesties for the failure of my expedition!"

His adjurations were vain. The sergeant could not withdraw the garrison from his presidio; Junípero intended to keep his mules, and also what he was bringing back with him for the missions; Juan Perez needed his apprentice for the voyage toward Russia. "All he sent me," wrote Anza in his journal, "was six *fanegas* of wormy beans."

Junípero, for his part, sent congratulations and advice. He congratulated the captain on having proved that his father was right, and that Upper California was not a peninsula. All the same, Sebastian had shown him too much of the countryside! Junípero urged him then, instead of looking for a road that was known to everyone, to discover one that neither Sebastian nor himself nor anyone else yet knew. In other words, the best thing for Anza to do was go back and get his equipment of men and animals and provisions that he had left with the Yumas, and return with them, not in six weeks, but in two weeks this time, from the Colorado River to San Gabriel. These judicious counsels annoyed the captain, who paid no attention to them and slipped away from San Gabriel before Junípero could get there.

The Prefect, in fact, did not arrive until the eleventh of April. Still followed by Juan Evangelista, he had left San Diego on April 6, allowing the frigate to go on to Monterey without him. He wanted to return to Carmel by land so as to visit his confrères old and new and to deliver the good things he had bought for them. What he received from them in exchange was all good news. They told him, in particular, that Pedro Fages was completely transformed: he had inaugurated his conversion on the day Junípero had left for Mexico City and he had consummated it the day he had received Bucareli's "stern order" to put an end to his maliciousness and to assist the missionaries. Since then Fages had become their collaborator—which had made it possible for them to achieve progress everywhere.

In a letter written to Junípero on November 26, 1773, but never received, Palou said, "The captain overwhelms me with evidences of his affection. I respond to them with reserve, knowing how he has treated you. How many times has he acknowledged his ill-deeds, attributing them to his inexperience! But that is all over, he adds; he aspires to nothing more, as His Excellency has recommended, than to live in mutual good feeling with you. I answered that I would never stand in the way of that!"

Junípero's letter to his Guardian said: "I spent ten days at San Gabriel, and I left there the carpenter and his wife, whom I had brought from Guadalajara; from Guadalajara also came the blacksmith and his wife, whom I have left at San Diego." The first whites who were born, and founded families in Upper California all had people from Guadalajara, thus, as their ancestors.

Junípero started out next for San Luis Obispo, and reached there on April 30. But three days before, in a village on the Santa Barbara Channel, he had caught up with the fiery-natured Commandant from Tubac who was fleeing from him. A man like Anza could not but be moved on finding himself face to face with the humble and great missionary to whom he owed his realization of his father's dream and his own; he fell on his knees and asked Junípero for his blessing. They conferred all afternoon and part of the evening. "Anza acknowledged," wrote Junípero, "that it was not at the expense of our still feeble missions, but on funds from the King, that he should achieve his exploits. I lent him an *arroba* (twenty-five pounds) of chocolate, then we separated, after spending the afternoon and night together. Although in part abortive, what a success his expedition was on the whole! And what encouragement God gives us in having had him find this route by which His Excellency can send us, from Sonora, the cattle we are still in need of! And let it be known that once we have got that we shall never ask for anything else, even though these new conquests were to extend to the ends of the earth."

Anza reached Monterey by the Portola-Crespi trail which had been in use since 1769. He received from Fages six soldiers, who, added to his own, made it possible for him to get back to the Colorado River by following the zigzags he had taken in Sebastian's lead. It is only two years later that we shall see him finding the good road, the one that still today connects the cities of Yuma and El Centro with San Gabriel and Los Angeles, across the Anza Desert. . . .

From San Luis Obispo, Junípero made his way to San Antonio. He spent three days there, from the sixth to the ninth of May; and two days later he at last regained Carmel. "Fathers Palou, Crespi, Dumetz, and Uson were awaiting me there," he writes. "For me, and I believe for them likewise, my return after twenty and one-half months of absence was a source of happiness. After so many trials, theirs and mine, the missions had been saved, as much by the material resources which were reaching them as by the rule that would govern them henceforth."

For Juan Evangelista there was no less happiness in his reunion with his parents, and perhaps also with the little fiancée who was waiting for him. Junípero's gentle companion, who had become a member of the Third Order, was married the next year; but neither he nor his Indian bride lived very long. "My poor Juan died a week after his wife," Junípero wrote on August 19, 1778. "He had received the last sacraments, and I buried him in our habit."

The frigate had reached Monterey two days ahead of Junípero. Missionaries and soldiers unloaded it hurriedly, as much because they were hungry as because the boat had to continue its voyage as soon as possible. On June 7, Juan Perez and the *Santiago* were ready to "set out for Russia."

For certain beings it is no small matter to encounter a saint. "The noble and pious soul of the Viceroy," writes Palou, "had been profoundly impressed by the intimate and frequent conversations he had had with the revered Father Junípero." The apostle had communicated his flame to him, and had made him share his purposes. These were no longer bounded by the thirty-eighth parallel—that of San Francisco—but extended now "to the ends of the earth": at least to the sixtieth parallel, which was said to be the frontier of Russia.[3] For his part, Juan Perez was offering to go and reconnoiter these unexplored regions, pending the time when Junípero could come and convert them. Now, Junípero wrote to Bucareli and his secretary, Peramas, "I have assigned Fray Juan Crespi and Fray Thomas de La Peña to accompany Juan Perez." The letter continued: "On the Monday of Pentecost, I sang Mass aboard ship, all the officers of land and sea being present. In my sermon I avowed my deep regret at not being able to be one of them. This new enterprise is so holy, I told them, that everyone should consider it an honor to participate in it, even if only by swabbing the decks of the ship. Of those who in the first place were looking for excuses not to go, there is not one who did not change his mind: now all of them want to be in the first company to make its way among these unknown tribes."

On June 7, however, contrary winds forced the *Santiago* to put back into port. The *San Antonio* arrived the next day. "Juan Perez exchanged some of his sailors for more skillful ones whom Canizares transferred to him, and from the latter also he procured certain instruments of navigation which he lacked," Junípero goes on with the story. "This took three more days; after which we all assembled for a great banquet on the beach: we bade one another adieu and those who were leaving went aboard ship. The next day, a favorable wind bore the frigate away. We followed it with our eyes for a long time; then we could not see it any more. May God's blessing be upon it!" (*From letters of May 29 and June 14, 1774*)

The expedition disclosed the fact that Juan Perez was not so great an explorer as he was a seaman. When he returned to Monterey on August 27, it was learned with grief that he had not touched land anywhere, nor had he anywhere planted the cross. Juan Crespi's *Journal No. 7* told the whole story; but "all this was tantamount to saying," Junípero wrote to the Discretory, "that the frigate had reached the fifty-fifth parallel," off what we call Queen Charlotte Island; "that it had twice approached the coast but had not sighted any harbor. The rest of the voyage was a matter of latitude bearings, of storms, of fog." Perez and

---

[3] When these eighteenth-century explorers and missionaries in California spoke in this way of "Russia," it was of course Alaska to which they referred.

his sailors had seen nothing but fogs and glaciers on such land as they had glimpsed from afar; and when they were shown smoke rising from native huts they insisted that it was clouds! Juan Crespi had not once had occasion to make use of his astrolabe; he and his confrère had been obliged to let others talk, and refrain from interference themselves.

To return to Junípero's own narrative, as he continues in his letter of August 31, 1774: "If it had not been for two providential events, we should not even have come to know whether there were any living souls in those regions. . . . The first of these incidents took place at the fifty-fifth degree of latitude. Twenty-one rowboats, laden with people, came out to the frigate. The women were dancing and singing, to the sound of musical instruments. Some men, well set up, with white skins, fair hair and blue eyes, dressed in long robes like pilgrims, and wearing peaked hats of leather or fur, were coming to offer their goods, of wrought horn and wood, in exchange for iron rods and glass trinkets. They went back to shore when they saw that our men, to whom they were making signals of approach, were running away from them and heading for the open sea. The same scene was re-enacted as the frigate, going south again, was touching the parallel of 49° 5′; this time, in the fifteen rowboats that came out to meet it, there were from eighty to a hundred people, like the first, but more timid; and they, too, were eager to sell the little products of their industry."

But, for his own part, Junípero was not disheartened, and to keep Bucareli from being more discouraged than himself, he pointed out to him, "Obviously, for such a costly expedition, this is not much in the way of result! But it is far from being nothing. In impelling these poor folk to come to us—we who did not dare to go to them—it has been the will of Providence to reveal that they were there waiting for us, in great numbers, intelligent, industrious, and ready to love us. To know that—is it not already a first step toward conquest? For our beloved Redeemer, they have cost His life and His blood. To Your Excellency they will some day owe their salvation. Permit me to offer you a thousand congratulations already, dear and revered lord, and to hope for the duty of congratulating you still more in the future." This was in his letter of August 30, 1774. And he, who was sixty-one years old and had just returned from a journey of 2,500 miles in the course of which he had twice come close to dying—he regretted more than ever that he had not been able to accompany Juan Perez. There would indeed have been a landing, and a planting of the cross on those unknown shores, if he had been there!

"And whenever it may please His Excellency to make the attempt again," he sent word to Bucareli through Peramas, "let it be surely known that in spite of my worthlessness I shall always be ready to do my share."

Fifteen

Rivera Replaces Pedro Fages
at Monterey
[1774]

Instead of Sergeant Ortega it was the captain of cuirassiers, Rivera, upon whom fell the mantle of Pedro Fages. A rather shrewd man and one who created a good impression at first sight, he had made friends for himself in the Junta and at the College while he was standing around doing nothing in Mexico City. Bucareli accepted their recommendations of him, and thus put a nonentity at the head of the colony and gave Junípero a second persecutor.

A Creole born in Compostella, Mexico, a good husband and father, Fernando Rivera y Moncada had served for twenty-five years in Lower California and was well past the age of fifty. He was a colossus of a man, who knew how to command his cuirassiers and make them love him, who was happy and at home only with them, and who, as Junípero used to say, "would not have hurt or grieved a single one of them for anything in the world." He prided himself on being a man of duty. "Have I not always performed it, by mouth, by hands, and by feet?" he wrote, in a style of his own which was as bizarre as himself. "Has any one of the numerous Viceroys I have served ever had the least reproach to bring against me?"

It is true that no one had yet entrusted him with tasks beyond his abilities, which were most mediocre. When Galvez learned of his appointment, he wrote to Prime Minister Arriaga, on March 8, 1774, "With such a man, I am not much reassured as to the fate of those still pagan regions which the Russians would so much like to take from us!"

Unintelligent, given to whim, easily offended, quick-tempered, niggardly, intransigent in the face of any suggestion from without, he was an unbalanced man, the victim of his own inhibitions, and prey to the obsessive idea that the Indians were going to kill him. "How do you expect," he wrote to his friend Echeveste, President of the Junta, on June 13, 1774, "that with the twenty-five miserable soldiers I have at the Presidio I am going to punish the insurgents, if disturbances break out in one of the missions? They will have to summon reinforcements for me from the Peninsula; but I shall be reduced to ashes and my bones will have whitened in the sun before those reinforcements will have had time to arrive. That is indeed, alas, the fate that awaits me!" So he felt a mortal grudge against Junípero, not only for having supported the candidacy of Ortega, but still more for plotting against his safety and his life by daring to demand a few soldiers from him to found a mission!

Although he was very religious he loathed the Indians and took no interest whatever in their conversion. He seemed to have come to Upper California only to retire on a pension: God and the Viceroy had at last brought an end to his misfortunes and rewarded his virtues. Now that he had his revenge on Fages and was drawing pay of three thousand pesos a year, he hoped for nothing more than to be left in peace. Bucareli had supplied him with the subterfuge he would have dreamed of, moreover, by ordering him to keep a record of what he did.

To get a portrait of the individual, one must, in fact, have recourse to his *Journal*. Don Fernando had two loves: his peace-and-quiet and his cuirassiers; two phobias: Junípero and the Indians; and one occupation: his *Journal*. In it this sick man found a precarious equilibrium, a weapon against the people who were harrying him toward action, a means of concealing his impotence from himself and of drugging his remorse. He took notes, then, of what he did not do, set down by the sweat of his brow the daily record of his inaction. Junípero would ask him, "When shall we start out at last, dear Señor, to found a mission?" And he would answer, "You have already asked me that, and I have already replied that it was impossible on account of the lack of soldiers. Furthermore, I have put all that in my *Journal*, which has been sent to His Excellency. This business being settled, I am likewise entering your present demand and the present answer in my *Journal*, which, also, will be dispatched to His Excellency by the next mail." He believed, thus, that he had done enough. He had been directed to write; he was writing; they wanted to know his deeds and gestures; he was concealing nothing; and when he felt that they were not satisfied with him he offered his resignation, whimpering.

Appointed on August 17, 1773, Rivera left the City of Mexico to recruit cuirassiers in his native district. He enlisted twenty-two, with whom he arrived at Loreto on March 8, 1774. In accordance with Junípero's wish they were accompanied by a certain number of emigrant families. In all, fifty-one persons were concerned in the projected march to Monterey. As Barri was in no hurry to assist him in this work, Rivera, instead of taking up the matter orally, dashed for his pen and thus began his *Journal*. Barri sent him back his letters without opening them—which plunged him into despair. "If I must be subject to the orders of this Governor," he wrote on March 20 to Echeveste, "I beseech His Excellency to put me on the retired list. I really do not know how it happens that I have so little luck in life!" He calmed down when he learned that the authority of the Governor of Loreto no longer extended, in practice, to the new conquest.

He reached Monterey on May 23, and there found Pedro Fages greatly demoralized by his disgrace—which pleased him very much, and in process of giving the missionaries evidence of his repentance—which put him in a bad humor. It was in connection with cows that he entered upon the exercise of his functions.

On returning to Carmel, Junípero had written to Pedro Fages, "The four bells which you are holding at the Presidio are the property of the Missions. You have also, mixed in with your herd, the cattle intended for San Francisco and Santa Clara. Would you kindly—insomuch as the royal Junta has so directed—send me back these bells, as well as the cows and the cattle born of them in the course of four years?"

Fages had at once surrendered the bells. As for the cows that had numbered eighteen in 1770, they had multiplied, and it was quite an undertaking to recover eighty animals from among those that were at pasture in the Presidio fields! Fages was working away at it with zeal, aided by herdsmen and soldiers, when Rivera, dismounting from his horse, accosted him.

"You have no concern with any of this any more," he said. "I am the one who will find the cows and take them to the Father Prefect, when it seems good to me. What you are to do instead is make ready to leave."

Fages claimed that since he had begun this task it was his duty to finish it. Rivera, with his cuirassiers, kept him from doing so. For two months, the two officers quarreled like ragpickers.

"The *San Antonio* is sailing from Monterey at the beginning of July; after that date I do not want to see you around here any longer."

"I am going by land as far as San Diego, and I am going when I choose to."

"In the name of the Viceroy, I order you to leave here by sea. I need your mules and I order you to leave them for me."

"My mules are mine, and they will go with me as far as San Diego, where I shall take the boat. If, there, I think fit to make a present of them to the King, that is my business."

"I am the new Commandant, and you must obey me. You have been dismissed—now are you going to become an insurgent?"

"Your appointment is dated August 17, 1773; my dismissal is of the seventh of September following, and the letter that accompanies it leaves me free to travel at my own convenience."

There were twenty scenes of this kind. Quarters were cramped at the Monterey Presidio. The representative of the Crown had at his disposal only an office, a dining room, and a bedroom. This last had only one bed. For sixty days, the enemies ate at the same table, slept in the same room, shared the same bed. One can imagine the huge Rivera and the diminutive Fages, turning their backs and clenching their fists in silence, waiting for sleep to close their eyelids. For they soon ceased speaking. As was his habit, Rivera had not been slow in beginning to deal with the matter by letter. His bedfellow replied in the same fashion. Don Fernando inserted their letters in his *Journal,* and they have thus been preserved for us.

Fages is still there when, on July 10, Rivera writes to Bucareli, "I have had plenty of vexations, My Lord, and they are going to continue. I have a heavy burden to carry all alone, having no one who could assist me with my correspondence and papers. I have cramps in the arm and the hand; they will cease, I hope when it becomes possible for me to write more at my ease. I am sending you my *Journal;* it is rather long and diffuse; perhaps you will direct me to make it a little shorter as time goes on."

The dispatch of the *Journal* frightened Fages, who decided to bring an end to the combat and to leave Monterey on the twentieth of July.

He was sad, heavy-hearted, indeed utterly beaten. He was in a state of tremor over the future of his career. On many a night, no doubt, when with his skinny back so close against Rivera's powerful frame he had vainly sought for sleep, he had asked himself what could win him Bucareli's pardon when he reached Mexico. He would think of Junípero, then, as his only hope. "I have treated him ignominiously," he reflected, "but he is a saint, and the saints feel no resentment. He will have forgiven me."

On the eve of his departure he went to say good-bye to him. Junípero received him with boundless kindliness. The discredited Commandant had asked him for "a great favor, a little word of recommendation to His Excellency." Then and there, Junípero wrote the following letter, and, without reading it to him, sealed it and gave it to him to deliver to Bucareli:

Revered and Most Excellent Lord:
The ships have left the harbor. The provisions they have brought have been received and the inventory of them has been completed, as well as the other indispensable formalities. Likewise, the transfer of authority has taken place, and the new Commandant has been installed. The officer Don Pedro Fages is on the point of leaving this royal Presidio, to travel by land to San Diego and there take ship, in accordance with Your Excellency's orders.

Since my return here I have been struck by the courtesy and the wisdom displayed in his conduct, and the state of discouragement in which I see him causes me a great deal of distress.

Never, by the blessing of God, have I borne him the slightest ill will or wished him the least misfortune. Your Excellency may rest assured that when I have testified against his conduct in the past, it was because it was necessary in order to bring about his recall, which, to my mind, was required for the welfare of this colony and the pacification of its inhabitants. I have merely said, moreover, what my eyes have seen and what my ears have heard. These last witnesses have not, certainly, the same value as evidence as the first; perhaps some inaccuracy has slipped in, chargeable to my single sources of information. At all events, Don Pedro must be believed when he avers that his past mistakes were not at all due to malice but to thoughtlessness and slackness of mind.

Indeed, if I flattered myself that I had some little influence with you, there is nothing I would not do to move you to exercise your fatherly kindness toward him, and to grant him as many honors and favors as your sense of justice and your generosity could prompt you to bestow. Since I, alas, am nothing, this is what I shall permit myself to say to you:

It is solely for the love of God, and to obey, as I must, the Superiors of the holy apostolic College to which I belong, that I have established these missions. Circumstances have willed, however, that, through the small or large part which I took in these new conquests, I should also have been rendering service to the King our lord. Living among the soldiers, I have in fact shared their privations, I have been exposed to danger with them, I have done what I could. Very well! Most Excellent Lord, if all this has a value, and constitutes a thing of merit from the military point of view, I relinquish that merit, I renounce it in favor of Pedro Fages; I yield it to him, I give it to him, I apply it to him wholly. He does not know that I am offering this sacrifice for him, he has not asked anything of the sort from me; it is entirely of my own accord, in the complete freedom of my soul, that I am carrying it out.

The world must go in ignorance of the loyal services which the useless friar that I am has been able to render to the Crown; I want them all to be attributed to Pedro Fages, as if he alone were the author of them. And I also want, with the grace of God, to continue to add to the sum of such merit, in his favor. So long as I live, and so long as obedience does not require me to stop, I shall do everything I can to disseminate the holy Faith in these lands; and at the same time I shall labor to extend, by this means, the domains of our Catholic Sovereign—whom God preserve!

May God Our Lord grant Your Excellency many years of life and health!

In this Mission of San Carlos de Monterey on the Carmelo River, the nineteenth of July, 1774.

Kissing your hand, I am, et cetera,

Junípero Serra.

Even from two centuries away, these lines move us and set us pondering. What petitioner ever had the benefit of a "little word of recommendation" like this? What torturer was ever more ingeniously served by his victim? It makes us proud of our human species to realize that such noble inspirations can well from the heart of a man! *Dii estis. . . .*

The astonishing thing is not that Junípero should have forgiven him. The saints go beyond forgiveness; they love their persecutors all the more since these, by their ill nature and evil hostility, are more remote from God, and consequently more to be pitied; they are, in addition, grateful to them for being the instruments of the divine compassion by which they are chastened and purified.

What is strange is to see Junípero ingenuously transposing, from the supernatural to the temporal and military order, the idea of vicariousness in merit, and of the communion of saints. "Who should emulate the Divine Majesty, in all its magnanimity, more than the Royal Majesty?" he seemed to be saying to Bucareli. "And so, since God permits the merit of the Christ to be applied to our salvation, and allows even His followers to share their meager riches with one another, will you not permit me—you as the representative of the King—to dispose as I wish of the merit I have gained in the royal service?"

Bucareli espoused these sentiments and lent himself to the mystical transfer.

You have confided to me [he wrote Junípero on January 2, 1775] the grief you felt in seeing Don Pedro Fages so despondent. He arrived here in bad health. Your great kindness has impelled you to extol him to me, and to add all your merits to his own. You express the desire that I should promote his advancement. I promise you that I shall take care of your protégé in all circumstances, and he himself will be able to realize the worth to him of the deed—so noble, so generous, so highly religious—which you have performed in his favor.

On August 30 the Captain landed at San Blas with his Catalan volunteers. A few weeks later, sick and trembling, he went to call upon the Viceroy. He left his presence radiant and more than half cured. He had been received as a hero. As God sees our souls reclothed in the merit of His Son, as Junípero breathed the grace of Jesus Christ into the most ignoble Redskin, so Bucareli had seen in Fages only the saintly old man to whom the Crown owed in good part its new conquest. He never abandoned that attitude; his fear was always that he would not do enough for Pedro Fages, and he looked for every occasion to reward in him the merit which Junípero continued to acquire.

The dismissed Commandant thus received rapid promotion. He knew to whom he owed it, and was to show himself not personally ungrateful, as we shall see.

Sixteen

Rivera's Insubordination and Junípero's Patience

[1774-1777]

About two months after his return—on July 17, 1774—Junípero wrote to his Guardian, "If the new Commandant were not more cautious than I, we should already have founded two new missions."

There was nothing now lacking, indeed, for the establishment of San Buenaventura, San Francisco, and Santa Clara, the foundation of which had been authorized as early as 1771. Junípero had everything ready at hand: bells, vestments and liturgical equipment, agricultural implements, and cattle. Thanks to the reinforcements supplied by Francisco Palou, he had more ministers than he needed. As for soldiers, there were eighty of those, and enough, therefore, to furnish the essential bodyguards. All of them were cuirassiers, armed to the teeth; well paid, well fed, made much of by their old captain, they would never have dreamed of deserting. Every one of them had a horse and three mules; their ration included maize, meal, butter, bacon, and meat; as wages, the private soldiers received 365 pesos, corporals 400, and sergeants 450; Ortega and Moraga, recently promoted to be lieutenants, were paid 700 pesos, and Rivera 3,000. In regard to those 3,000 pesos, it may be said that Charles III never spent his money to worse effect, for Rivera drew his pay for doing nothing whatsoever, unless his blunders and general asininities can be called activity.

He had not been at Monterey two weeks before he made a point of showing Junípero that he came as an enemy.

The twenty-ninth of May was marked by the solemn celebration of the feast of St. Ferdinand (San Fernando), the patron saint of Spain. "As guests of honor," wrote Junípero, "we had all the officers of land and sea, Juan Perez and his apprentice pilot, Pedro Fages, Moraga, etc. Don Fernando was present at Mass, but refused to come to the table with us. On the second of June, we celebrated Corpus Christi Day; we are poor, but I may say that our wayside altars and our procession were worthy of a large city, and that our banquet itself was not to be disdained. Alone among the sailors and soldiers, Don Fernando did not see the festival at all: he excused himself by saying that he had to work over his *Journal;* as a matter of fact, he strolled along the beach all day."

It was not the wish to improve his health nor the aesthetic need to contemplate the ocean which impelled Rivera to pace up and down on the seashore. It was his way of saying to Junípero, "Aha, my little Father Prefect! It was Ortega whom you wanted to see here! Well, he is not here: I am; and while I am here, that will be your misfortune!"

Junípero understood, at once, what destiny had in store for him. "I went to ask him to hand over the cows that belonged to San Francisco and Santa Clara" (Article XXVII of the Memorandum), he wrote. "He replied that he had not time to attend to it and that I should come back later. I went back when the boats had sailed and he had nothing more to do. This time he said that he had put the inventory of the cattle in his *Journal,* and that it was now for the Viceroy to decide what animals should be returned to us. Rather than burden His Excellency with the task of sorting out cows, I suggested that the matter should be settled out of court. 'It is too late for that,' he retorted. 'The question is closed until further notice, since it is in my *Journal.'* "

He had been lying, however. The *Journal* did not mention the step the Prefect had taken, and when Junípero wrote to Bucareli a little later he did not know of this break in the record. "I am not going back to the non-delivery of the cows," he said, "inasmuch as the Captain, as he has assured me, is reporting the matter to you in his *Journal.*" What was the Viceroy going to say when he learned of this falsehood that was added to disobedience? Frightened, Rivera determined to parry the blow. Persuading the keeper of his stores, Juan Soler, who was a friend of the Father, to accompany him, he came on the Feast of the Assumption to ask Junípero if he might have luncheon with him.

"By the way," he said, at table, "there are those cattle that I never had time to attend to, and that I have at last found again: I am going to send them back to you tomorrow."

And, in fact, on August 16, 1774, the ninety-two horned beasts did make their entry into Carmel.

Although the best histories of fools are the shortest, a few more instances may nevertheless be cited, among a hundred or more that are set down in Junípero's letters to Bucareli and to his Guardian. . . .

"The Junta had granted us a soldier-missionary [Article XIV of the Memorandum]; he came; but Rivera compelled him, none the less, to take his turn on guard at the Presidio and to attend to the pasturing of the King's horses; and in this way, by imposing double duty upon him, he forced him to leave us."

"Every time that, with the authorization of the Junta's decrees, I have requested him to recall to the Presidio a soldier whose cruel or profligate behavior had become insupportable in the escort guard [Article VIII of the Memorandum], he took it amiss and I obtained no satisfaction. He loved his cuirassiers so dearly that to cast suspicion on the virtue of any one of them was enough to unleash his fury."

"The Viceroy's office demanded certificates of residence from me. I drew them up and asked the captain to sign them. I had had my letter taken to him by Father Dumetz, for whom he has less aversion than for me. He replied that since the case was not specified in the Regulations, he would not sign the certificates; and that, for the rest, he was mentioning my action in his *Journal*. To make a long story short, he kept me waiting ten months for those signatures which were an affair of five minutes."

"On Holy Thursday, the Blessed Sacrament was exposed in our church, and some soldiers from Monterey formed a guard of honor for it. As soon as he learned of this, he recalled them, under pretext of needing them for work. I am able to guarantee, however, that there is never enough work at the Presidio for the men who are crowded into the quarters there, and that they do not know what to do to kill time."

Let it not be thought that Rivera was irreligious; on the contrary, he was very devout, and had a terrible fear of the devil; so for a priest who would not have supported the candidacy of Ortega or been bent on founding missions, he would have been

the first to stand guard before the Blessed Sacrament, and would
have rushed to carry the canopy in the procession. It was only
to offer petty vexation to Junípero that he was guilty of irrever-
ence toward God. And the same attitude impelled this stout-bodied
man, who himself was so quick at whining, to let little children
go hungry or even die. To quote again from Junípero's recitals:

"To the carpenter and the blacksmith whom I brought from
Guadalajara, and their wives, the Regulations grant a full ration;
they have also the right to buy provisions for their children from
the Crown stores [Article XIV of the Memorandum]. Well, would
you believe that the Commandant had the ration of these unfortunate artisans made up of nothing but maize, without ever any
bacon, butter, or meat? That he reduced their wives' rations by
three-fourths? And that he forbade the storekeeper Juan Soler to
sell them an ounce of butter or ham for their poor children? Yet
he has so much maize on hand that he piles it up in the patio of
the Presidio for want of room in the storehouse; and he has packing cases full of ham that he will not allow to be opened—until
the day when it has to be thrown, spoiled, into the bay!"

It is easy to guess how Junípero's heart would be torn by such
actions. His worst grief, however, lay in being prevented from
founding the missions that had been planned. On July 17, 1774,
he wrote to his Guardian:

"I said to him, 'You have thirty-two men at San Diego: twenty-
six in the Presidio and six at the Mission. Since the Mission is so
closely attached to the Presidio, these last six are not needed there;
then make use of them to establish a new mission, as His Excellency wishes. Thus we shall have work for those unoccupied friars,
of whom three are about to go away (Uson, Prestamero, Juncosa),
with others to follow their example if no use is still found for
them.' His reply gave me to understand that, if he should be sent
a hundred extra cuirassiers, I should not get one of them. One
day, he said, the Indians might attack us. . . . I anticipate, in
short, that with him we shall never move forward one step. I
was not mistaken, alas, when, knowing his character, I foretold
to you in the presence of the Grand Inquisitor, of Señor Echeveste, and others, in the little summerhouse at San Fernando, just
what is happening today. . . ."

The next day Junípero wrote to Bucareli, "You may be sure,
Excellency, that the decrees signed by you will not be obeyed.

As for founding missions, the Commandant is absolutely opposed to that."

It will no doubt be asked how it was that Bucareli did not at once put a stop to this blockhead's schemings, and oblige him to carry out his orders. One must only consider the length of time it took for a letter to go from Monterey to Mexico City, and from Mexico City to Monterey. It was ordinarily the boats that took charge of the mail, and the boats made only one round trip a year. But suppose this mail was sent by dispatch-riders by way of Loreto? It would make its way more quickly, to be sure, but it would be quite an expedition to organize, with horses, mules, foodstuffs, and also with gunpowder and bullets, for it was a rare occurrence that in the passage through the Channel region and from San Diego to Velicata the couriers would not have to fight the Indians—and to kill some of them—in order to get through. Two examples will be enough to show the speed (!) at which the mails moved. Bucareli replied immediately to the letter of July 18, 1774, cited above, and he sent his answer "by special courier" via Loreto; yet it reached Monterey only on August 9, 1775—that is, almost thirteen months later. That is one example. For the second, when Pangua was elected to replace Verger, in 1773, the news was sent by "ordinary courier" to Junípero, with the result that its delay in reaching him kept him more than twenty months in ignorance of who his Guardian was. It was this slowness in the transmission of letters which made game of events as they happened, and assured Rivera's long impunity. It took six months for Bucareli to learn that the Commandant was insubordinate; another six months to let Rivera know that the Viceroy was dissatisfied with him; six months more for Bucareli to suspect that the man was mad; six months again for him to become convinced of it; and, finally, another six months to remove him from office and reduce him to the subaltern rank to which he naturally belonged.

"Paper work!" Junípero wrote to his Guardian. "That is my rudest ordeal, and the one that I most abominate. I who came here to convert the Indians, I spend half of my time putting black marks on white paper, realizing the while that I am still falling short of what was expected. . . . My bad luck has it that I should be not so much a missionary as a copying-clerk! But, after all, what do you expect? All this has to be done if we are not one day to find toads, snakes, and other venomous creatures under our feet."

Junípero meant to say, in these rather cryptic words, that Rivera's ridiculous and untruthful *Journal* must be balanced and opposed by a counter-journal, in which truth should once more have the upper hand. This counter-journal consisted of the letters he wrote to San Fernando and to the Viceroy, and with well thought-out purpose to the Commandant himself. Suppose it did often take ten pages to refute ten lines that were unintelligent or insincere? Some of Junípero's letters are as long as pamphlets. Being often no more than the chronicle of the fabrications of this Commandant who was suffering from an obsession, they would sometimes have become tedious, if the soul of the chronicler were not always seen to be so noble. What care for accuracy and right proportion, what rectitude and serenity we find on the part of this man of action whose activity is being paralyzed, this superior mind at grips with a lout, this heart so full of goodness being made to suffer so much! There is never any impatience, any irritation, any laborious effect of irony, never—above all—any personal or censorious complaint against anyone. He says what is, Yes when it is Yes, No when it is No, since it is his duty to speak; then, as the Gospel teaches, he proceeds without judgment. Or, rather, if he judges, his judgment is visited upon himself. He deems himself unworthy of better treatment, attributes the obstacles in his way to his "shortcomings and many sins," is convinced that someone else would be better in his place. Only, since God has willed that they two should be at Monterey—he as Prefect and Rivera as Commandant—he submits with joy to that sacred will, and the idea of giving up the struggle would never even graze the surface of his mind. Among the hundreds of thousands of words set down by this writer chained to his pen like a galley slave to his oar, there is not one that speaks of weariness or discouragement.

The letters change their tone as befits the correspondent to whom they are addressed. To his Superior, the Guardian of San Fernando, Junípero writes in a manner that is, so to speak, impersonal: as an obedient friar, an affectionate and trusting son, without fear, without circumlocution, and without flattery. As the Superior of San Fernando is the real head of the missions and must make his decisions with full knowledge of each case, he gives him detailed information, concealing nothing except the shortcomings of his colleagues, which he can cope with himself.

To Rivera, Junípero writes with a deep respect, the patience of an angel, and the most sincere friendliness. It may be wondered whether he ever considered him as a sick man. . . . One must read the letter he wrote him on October 24, 1775, to gain an idea of the attention and consideration he bestowed upon him. The Regulations said, "The frigate will try to bring to Monterey, on each voyage, married volunteers who wish to be employed in the missions. They will be entitled to wages and rations for two years." But now here is Rivera deciding that these rations and these wages shall be abolished as of January 1, 1776, "for the good reason that the two years here referred to are to be counted from January 1, 1774, the date when the Regulations came into effect."

"But this is unjust and cruel," Junípero told him.

"What? Don't you agree? . . . Write to me; I will put your letter in my *Journal*, and His Excellency will decide between us."

The letter that Junípero wrote on this occasion was no less than five thousand words long; sometimes he would appeal to the good sense and good heart of the Commandant, as if the latter were not seeking solely to annoy him; sometimes he would multiply legal reasons and the most closely thought-out syllogisms, as if the old cuirassier were the greatest jurist and logician of his time. Rivera, however, yielded not at all; he spent all the day and part of the night in transcribing the stirring dissertation in his *Journal*. When Bucareli read it he replied curtly, "The two years start from the day when the volunteers begin their service. Otherwise the Regulations would have been wasting words. I direct you to follow the advice of the Father Prefect, which is in conformity with the decisions of the Junta."

As might be expected, the letters to Bucareli are the most charming of them all. They breathe the same friendship and happy up-welling spontaneity as those that Galvez had earlier received. One realizes how fond they were of one another, the son of the Petra quarry worker and the Grandee of Spain, how they understood one another, respected one another, were happy to have been chosen to be fellow workers in such a great enterprise. Let us quote a few passages from the Report Junípero addressed to the Viceroy on December 31, 1774. He is finishing it in the evening, while in the neighboring cell his friend Palou is working on the

Noticias, that ten-volume history of the missions of Lower and Upper California. Obviously, we are once more about to count animals and measure seeds; but neither Bucareli, studying with his tutor in the feudal castle of his ancestors, nor Junípero, commenting on Aristotle and Duns Scotus in the Lullian University, would have guessed that mules, pigs, corn, and beans would have such place in their lives! The fact is none the less plain that it was through the instrumentality of corn and of mules that the natives of America became Christians. . . .

Since my return, Most Excellent Lord [the Prefect writes], I have baptized seventy-two children under eight years of age. At present, then, we have 245 little Christians at Carmel, without counting the many adults whom I shall baptize as soon as I know their language better. How happy you would be to see these hundreds of boys and girls, all of them now clothed, who pray, sing, give perfect answers to the catechism questions, and play and run about among us with as much friendliness and confidence as if they had known us all their lives! The five missions together have baptized 759 Indians and married 248 persons according to religious rites. As for livestock, we possess, in all, 304 cows, 170 ewes, 95 goats, 130 pigs, four donkeys, 100 horses, and 85 mules. We have harvested, this year, 475 fanegas of wheat, 540 fanegas of corn, 40 fanegas of barley, and 40 fanegas of beans, or a total of 1,095 fanegas [1,725 bushels].

Under instruction from the skilled laborers who came from Mexico with me, our adult Christians are learning to work. In particular, they harvested the wheat, and carried 430 sacks of it to the granary. They had scarcely begun on the wheat when schools of sardines appeared off shore. Then they would work in the fields in the morning and fish in the afternoon. It is really almost incredible, the number of sardines they caught—and the number they ate. And we filled twenty kegs with what they left. Two weeks later it was the hunt for little birds in the rocks which claimed their attention. These little birds, I must add, are as big as chickens. Their kind lives on fish. One Sunday afternoon I went with two of the Fathers to see our Indians roasting and eating their birds on the beach. They were divided into small groups around innumerable fires. I must say that, as recreation, we could not have found anything better.

And now, Excellency, I must indict myself for an offense, which, I hope, will not too greatly impoverish the King my lord. In our magnificent garden at Carmel we have planted a tobacco patch. There is no tobacco in the royal stores; and if there were it would not be given to us, even if we were to ask it for the love of God. Now we need it for the Indians. Halfway between Carmel and San Antonio there are villages inhabited by natives who are admirably disposed toward us. When one of the Fathers passes through the settlement, old and young run after him, crying, "Love God, Father!" That is the greeting they have learned from the folk around here. [Junípero had brought it from Majorca.] They always send friendly regards, also, to "the old Father." I am the one to whom they have given this name. On several occasions they have come to see us; they have admired our church, our fields covered with corn, and our neophytes covered with clothing; they have patted me on the shoulder, calling me "old Father," and urging me to "love God"; and again they have invited us to come and settle among them. As you can imagine, they also want presents. But it is no longer glass beads that they desire, as they once did; what they demand is tobacco. I hope therefore, Excellency, that you will not hold what we have done against me. If you should take exception to it, however, I shall carry out your will, in that as in everything.

In conclusion, Junípero thanks the Viceroy once more for having "banished famine and destitution for ever from these countrysides" by granting so much relief and assistance to the missions.

Sometimes the Viceroy also received presents. "As you already have articles in sculptured stone, I am sending you this time six little pieces of horn and some fabrics. The fabrics were woven by the natives of the Channel, who are as skillful as they are indiscreet." (Let us remember that "indiscreet" from Junípero's pen is another word for bloodthirsty.) "I have put these humble gifts in a redwood box," the letter continues, "and Don Francisco Hijosa will see to it that they reach you."

It goes without saying that Bucareli closed his eyes to the violation of the Crown monopoly, and allowed Junípero to go on planting his tobacco.

On the same occasion, Don Melchor de Peramas, secretary to the Viceroy, received a small keg of sardines. "This will give you a sample," Junípero wrote him, "of what may be found in the country of the little Indian to whom you have had the goodness to open your house. I hope you will accept this modest gift which Juan Evangelista offers you with all his heart, on behalf of himself and of his grateful parents."

There was also a little keg of sardines for a personage who

was, it seems, a hypocrite and a thief. That was the aforementioned Hijosa, Commissioner of the port of San Blas.

It was he who was responsible for embarking goods from his port to that of Monterey. So long as the Father Prefect, the friend of the Viceroy, was in Mexico, Hijosa had been all attention and devotion. Afterward he showed him nothing but hostility. "Some benefactors had given me four hundred fanegas of corn [seven hundred bushels] for our little Indians," Junípero wrote to his Guardian. "It is more than a year that this corn has remained at San Blas. Hijosa refuses to load it on the ships, on the pretext that there is no room for it. But the frigate had just arrived almost empty. . . . It contained exactly two rowboats of foodstuffs, and twenty-five rowboats of stones that were added as ballast; and that was in spite of the protests of the captain, who was in dismay over coming with so small a serviceable cargo on such a large ship. I have long liked Hijosa, and considered him an honest man. And here he is, no longer wanting to know me! It is Father Palou to whom he will send the provisions for the missions from now on! But, for the rest, if he wants to go on fighting with me, he will fight alone, for I am not going to fight with him. May God's blessing be upon him!"

What gadfly had stung Hijosa? Articles IV, XXIII, and those following, in Junípero's Memorandum, demanded that the corn for the missions should no longer be packed in bags with holes in them, and that false weights should no longer be used in measuring it. Had this request, granted by the Junta, upset Hijosa and interfered with his thieveries? The fact remains that for three years he placed a boycott on all the gifts in kind that were addressed to Junípero, and he sent him stones for the little Indians in exchange for his sardines.

Sebenteen

Fray Francisco Pangua and
Fray Firmin Lasuen
[1775]

Under Pedro Fages all the Franciscans rallied around their Prefect; it was to be the same under Felipe de Neve when, beginning with the year 1777, he commanded at Monterey. But there were certain friars who, under Rivera, became hostile to the Mission head; one of them, Lasuen, intrigued against him; and the pusillanimous Pangua, allowing himself to be deceived by these men, sacrificed Junípero to them.

Fray Francisco Pangua was Guardian of San Fernando from 1774 to 1777 and from 1780 to 1783, each time in succession to Father Verger. His first three-year term coincided with the rule of Rivera, whom he knew and respected. Verger would inform himself, intervene, fight, and, often, win. Pangua had no initiative, shrank from all difficulties, and was as much afraid of Bucareli as Rivera was of the Indians. So as not to have to confront him, he stayed in his cell and sent his directives to Junípero from there. What these amounted to was that the best thing to do was to do nothing. He developed this theme even in his first letter. As that took ten months to reach its destination, the Prefect was happily exempt from taking account of it in the interval.

"I have received five letters from you," Pangua wrote Junípero on November 8, 1774, "since which time, for the expiation of my sins, they have named me Guardian. Your great zeal delights me, and I thank you for sending me such detailed information. I hope that you will continue to do this, and that you will transmit to me, likewise, all your letters to the Viceroy. Thus, being fully informed, I shall be able to speak fearlessly when occasion arises." For Pangua, the occasion would rarely arise! In any case, it was not presenting itself at the moment. "Painful as it may be for you," his letter continued, "there is no basis for thinking of establishing new stations now between San Diego and Monterey. According to my information, the first missions to be set up will be those of the port of San Francisco."

He was mistaken: if he had gone to see Bucareli, the Viceroy would have told him that he wanted missions not only at the port of San Francisco but also in the Santa Barbara Channel. But Pangua's letter went on:

"This being the case, it is useless to argue about this matter with Captain Rivera. What is important above all is to preserve friendly relations, leaving to time itself the time for working things out. . . . His Excellency has been notified of the difficult situation of the Fathers whose boxes are held at Velicata; he has replied that they would receive satisfaction soon. As for the soldier-missionaries, the San Francisco livestock, and the cows of the Concordat, I have thought the best course was not to speak of them for the moment. For the rest, be assured that you will always find in me a servant of Your Reverence whose sincere affection will never be denied."

The "cows of the Concordat" were those which, by the treaty of April 7, 1772, the Dominicans pledged themselves to deliver to the Franciscans, who had just bought them. They numbered thirty, without counting the sixteen calves they had had. Junípero claimed them, and Barri and the Dominicans refused to give them to him: Barri to annoy him, and the Dominicans from attachment to the cows themselves, which they desired to keep. . . .

As for the boxes, there were forty of them, and they contained the books, notebooks, clothing, and other personal possessions of Palou and his companions. The Dominicans were holding them at Velicata. From time to time, in the presence of Fathers Cambon and Sanchez, who were watching over the boxes' fate, they would open them and go through them, making a new count of the pocket handkerchiefs of the Franciscans who took snuff, and assuring themselves that their underclothing was not altar linen, and that, in short, they were not carrying off anything that belonged to the missions. No more suspicious customs inspectors were ever seen. Junípero found it extremely trying. "Here are two letters, in the original," he wrote to Pangua. "One is from the Fathers at Velicata, the other from Father Hidalgo, their Prefect. Read them: you will see if there is anything in them that can be un-

derstood! Whose fault is it if our boxes are not sent? Governor
Barri's, declares the Prefect; the Father Prefect's, declares Governor Barri. . . . Meanwhile the Velicata Fathers, in order to justify themselves, have shown Father Cambon three letters in which
their Prefect officially forbade them to let anything leave the place.
And now here are these same Velicata Fathers writing me that
they have no recollection of any such prohibition! The fact is
that greater cruelty is being displayed toward us than toward the
Jesuits at the time of their banishment. It doesn't matter, after
all! I merely ask that the Dominicans let our boxes go, and hand
over to us the cattle which their Prefect acknowledges to be ours.
For the rest, may God bless them and give us also peace! Amen."

Father Hidalgo never did make it possible for the cows of the
Concordat to see their owners again. He did not keep them for
himself, however; for Felipe de Neve, immediately upon his arrival at Loreto, took them, to annex them to the Crown herds.
The new Governor, who detested the Dominicans, also considered
that the inquiry over the boxes had lasted long enough, and in
April, 1775, these were able to set out on their journey north.

We shall not follow them from Velicata to San Diego. They
traveled in the company of Father Cambon, who was returning
to the fold after three years of absence, and of Father Sanchez,
who was the last of the old ministers of the Peninsula to leave
that region, and who from then on until his death in 1804 devoted himself to the missions in the north. They made a stop at
San Diego and then at San Gabriel, where Lasuen joined them
and made his way with them toward Monterey.

There was the risk of death in crossing the Santa Barbara Channel. "On the twenty-fourth of May, in the village of San Pedro
and San Pablo," Junípero wrote, "an indiscreet native tried to
take possession of a soldier's gun, and the latter retorted with
shots. The Indians rushed to take up arms, and our men would
have perished under the rain of their arrows if they had not
joined battle with them. They killed at least six of their men."

At San Luis Obispo and then at San Antonio the caravan set
down the boxes whose owners were living at these missions, and
with what was left they reached Carmel in the early part of June.
There, Father Lasuen, after a year of intrigue, kept the appointment he had with Rivera.

A native of Vitoria in Biscaya, Fray Firmin Lasuen was approaching forty years of age. He was a man of good education, alert, zealous, and serious minded. So long as he was not appointed Prefect of the Missions he was apt to become disheartened, and on five occasions between 1774 and 1784 he made up his mind to leave Upper California. He had a great deal of ambition, the taste for diplomacy, real gifts as an administrator, and the talent for inducing his superiors to carry out his wishes—which, for a man dedicated to the religious life, constitutes the most opportune means of observing his vow of obedience. In Lower California Lasuen had tried to curry favor with Galvez and had formed ties of friendship with Rivera. Verger and Pangua admired him and recognized in him "a great maturity of judgment." Truth obliges us to say that from 1774 to 1776 Lasuen gave evidence of ingratitude and hypocrisy, and that his behavior during this period was not that of an honest man. He redeemed himself later, became a model of virtue once more, and from then on few missionaries did as much as he did for the Indians.

In 1769 Junípero wrote in his *Journal*, "April 28: After walking two days, I have reached San Borja, where I am staying with Father Lasuen. Although I am in a hurry to rejoin the caravan, the affection I bear this dear friend is keeping me for two days with him."

In April of 1774, returning from Mexico City, they met again at San Gabriel, where Francisco Palou had left Junípero seven months before. Lasuen was then begging to go back to the College. For wishing to leave a country to which he had so earnestly pleaded to be sent, and in which he had scarcely more than arrived, he explained, as his reason, that he had learned that his old father was dying of want in Biscaya, and that he would be better able to help him from Mexico City. "We will help him from here," Junípero replied. "I will share my *sinodo* with him, and I will ask the College to be responsible for the rest." He kept his word. "Fray Firmin was also wishing to withdraw, in order to assist his poor father," he wrote to his Guardian on July 19, 1774. "Not being willing to lose such a valuable collaborator and one of such a fine religious spirit, I insisted that he should remain, and he consented. I beseech you to permit the collection of alms for the unfortunate old man, and to have them sent to him as soon as possible. Attach to that, I beg you, a part of what the San Carlos Mission has on his account." Such were Junípero's sentiments toward Lasuen.

As for those of Lasuen toward his benefactor, they were expressed, by him, in a few words. "Some consider him a saint," he wrote, "but, myself, I do not like him." Did he like, as he said he did, Rivera, who went through San Gabriel two weeks later on the way to take over his command? He averred that he did. But what does the verb "like," or "love," signify for diplomats and those given over to ambition? However this may be, the fact is that the two friends sealed a secret alliance, at that time, against Junípero.

Lasuen wanted to get a mission as soon as possible, for he was languishing for want of something to do. He desired also to play an influential part. Perhaps his aspiration was to be Junípero's successor. Who knew whether Junípero might not soon be going to die, or whether his "excess of zeal" and Rivera's animosity might not induce the College to send him notice of dismissal? Whatever the future might bring, Lasuen would nowhere be better off for the realization of his hopes than at Monterey. That is why, man of resources as he was, he suggested to the Commandant that he should become his private chaplain.

The suggestion had features that Rivera liked. In Lasuen he would have an agreeable companion, an advisor, a support and stay against Junípero, a sort of guarantor in close touch with the College and the Viceroy. He was far from any suspicion that this good friend might be thinking only of making use of him, and would drop him at the first opportunity.

The conspirators lost no time. Pangua and his Discretos were fairly assailed by their letters all through the following months. They received similar letters from a few ministers, some regular occupants of posts like Cavaller and Paterna, others supernumeraries whose bad humor grew with their inaction. "We are bored to death and are not fulfilling our vocation," these latter said. "Why have we been brought here and why should we be kept here, if there is no desire to make use of us? The one responsible for this situation, moreover, is not the Commandant, but Father Junípero, who does not know how to get along with him." The two regularly assigned ministers above-mentioned also found Rivera a good husband, good father, good Christian, in a word very *simpático*, in which we shall not contradict them, except by adding that the disproportion between his difficult duties and his meager abilities for performing them was upsetting his precarious mental balance. . . .

What Rivera might write may be imagined. In substance, it would be as follows: "The Father Prefect's intentions are praiseworthy but his zeal is dangerous. If I listened to him the Indians would soon have massacred the Fathers and the soldiers as a result. His correspondence with the Viceroy is no less of a nature to unleash the catastrophes which I foresee; that is why it is advisable to put an end to it. Father Lasuen is as reasonable, however, as Father Junípero is Utopian. It is possible to get along with him. It is considered thought which impels me to beseech you to attach him to my person. His good sense and his adroitness, of themselves, could bring about an improvement in my relations with the missionaries, which are such, alas, that I think of sending in my resignation."

As for Lasuen, he forgot nothing, and played all his trump cards. He wanted to be the Commandant's "Grey Eminence," and at the same time to belong, like Palou, Crespi, and other friends of Junípero, to that Carmel community which was like a sort of Grand Council of the Missions.

"Let no one think it is faintheartedness that keeps Rivera from forging ahead! The Commandant," he writes in good round terms, "is a great Christian; in addition to that, he is a man of consummate wisdom, prudence, and courage." Unfortunately, he will never get along with Junípero, the argument continues. There is a state of war between the Presidio and Carmel; at San Luis, Father Cavaller is dissatisfied; the situation is growing worse everywhere. Who knows if Don Fernando's lively friendship for myself is not providential? And he not only likes me: he listens to me. Again it would be fitting that, to remain in his good graces, I should not seem to be merely Junípero's agent, and that, to preserve the confidence of my confrères, I should be accounted as of the same rank as themselves. That is why, if obedience sends me as chaplain to Monterey, I ask to be temporarily withdrawn from the authority of the Father Prefect, while holding the title of minister at Carmel. As the friend of both Rivera and Junípero, I could bring them together, if not reconcile them; enjoying some influence in both camps, I might perhaps succeed in restoring peace between the missionaries and the Presidio, and in finally obtaining the co-operation of the Commandant in founding the missions that are planned. . . .

Letters from Upper California never reached Mexico City so quickly! It is understandable that soldiers should have been lacking for escort guards: they were galloping over the Loreto road carrying the conspirators' mail and bringing back news! The news soon was seen to be of good omen for the two friends; and at last they learned that by a License and an official letter, both dated February 2, 1775, Pangua and his Discretory had granted their request.

Who was going outside his province, to send them the information so quickly? Was it Verger, who continued to be apprehensive about Junípero's ardor and to wish to curb it? He was a great friend of Lasuen's, and his regular correspondent. But he was not alone in the Discretory in liking and applauding Rivera, who had been a conspicuous frequenter of the College and knew how to be charming—when he was not mad. Moreover, San Fernando was not without its envious souls who would have welcomed the humiliation, if not the dismissal, of the Prefect of Monterey. What is certain is that Rivera and Lasuen got their information eight months at least before Junípero, who received the License only in March of 1776.

In June, 1775, therefore, Junípero understood nothing of the comedy that Lasuen had just played. On July 24 he reported ingenuously to Pangua: "Having to talk with me about important matters, Fray Firmin asked me to make it possible for him to come here; I authorized him to do so. When I urged him to go back again to San Gabriel, he assured me that he would consent to a return there as supernumerary, but that he would not go back, any longer, as a regular, or third, minister. In the midst of all this, Don Fernando intervened, with the object of having Fray Firmin with him at the Presidio. It was in vain that I brought forward my objections: they forced my hand; wholly reluctant, I had to give in. Fray Firmin, then, will reside at the Presidio, until a mission is given to him. May the good examples he gives them be edifying to the laymen in the midst of whom he is going to live!"

COMEDY IN FIVE ACTS

This comedy was the provisional outcome of the conspiracy. It may be summed up as follows:

Act I. The second week in June, 1775. Scene, Carmel Mission. Characters, Lasuen and Junípero.

Lasuen: When am I finally going to have that mission which I have been waiting for these last two years, and which you promised me last year?

Junípero: Rivera has not yet been willing to move an inch; but he will soon be forced to it. As soon as Anza's second expedition arrives, we shall found two missions near the port of San Francisco. They will be assigned to Fathers Palou and Murguia, who have a right to them, one in his rank as Vice Prefect, the other by virtue of his seniority. After that will come the stations of the Santa Barbara Channel. You will have the first of those, the Mission of San Buenaventura. Meanwhile, go back to San Gabriel.

Lasuen: As supernumerary?

Junípero: No! As a regular incumbent, since the supernumerary post has been abolished.

(Note. Virtuous men who follow the life of celibacy sometimes have need of earthly compensations. Vanity supplies them with these. Certain ecclesiastics attach an excessive importance to titles and questions of precedence. That is why, even before Pangua had thought of it, Junípero had appointed the supernumerary friars to be "titulary incumbents" of office. In this way they stepped from the rank of guests to that of ministers. Placed on an equal footing with their companions, they would become more patient, he believed, while waiting to be more fully occupied and better provided for. "Your idea of giving regular titles to the supernumeraries is one I had already had," Junípero wrote to Pangua in the letter quoted above, "and that is what I have done. The Fathers at San Antonio are delighted. Let us hope that the others will be, likewise." If Lasuen was not, it was because he was looking for a pretext to prolong the discussion and gain time; for he was well aware that, in demanding to be removed from the operation of the common law, he was asking for the moon.)

Act II. The third week in June. Scene, the Presidio. Characters, Rivera and Lasuen.

RIVERA: The *San Carlos* will not be long in getting here. According to the latest news, Father Pangua agreed to your appointment. Nothing more was needed but the approval of the Discretory.

LASUEN: If the Reverend Father Pangua agrees, the Venerable Discretory will agree also.

RIVERA: The *San Carlos* will let us know.

(NOTE. It may be that Lasuen and Rivera, at this moment, would already have known about the License in eight articles which had been on the way since February 2. In that case, our scenario omits the second act.)

Act III. End of the fourth week of June. Scene, the Presidio or Carmel. The *San Carlos* came into port on the twenty-ninth. Characters, Rivera, Junípero, Lasuen.

JUNÍPERO (*to Rivera*): What you ask is not in accord with any of our practices. I cannot agree to it. What would the other missionaries say? And what would the Superiors at the College say? Fray Firmin himself will never consent, I am sure, to—

LASUEN: I am the child of obedience. I shall obey the Reverend Father Prefect, as he himself and my colleagues are bound to obey the Reverend Father Pangua and the Venerable Discretory.

JUNÍPERO: Yes, the Reverend Father Pangua is Guardian of San Fernando. It is the *San Carlos* that has brought me the news. . . .

RIVERA: I, too, may have received letters by the *San Carlos*. . . . Be that as it may, I will not allow Father Lasuen to leave for San Gabriel again, for I know—you hear me, Reverend Father Prefect?—I know that the Reverend Father Pangua and the Discretos of the holy College will not refuse to assign him to me as chaplain.

JUNÍPERO: I call you both to witness that you have forced my hand.

Act IV. July, 1775. This act occupies an entire month. Scene, Carmel. Characters, Crespi, Palou, Dumetz, La Peña, Cambon, Santa María (chaplain of the *San Carlos*), Lasuen.

All are scandalized by Father Lasuen's revolt. What a hypocrite! For everyone knows that if he is at the Presidio it is because he wants to be there. And what a dastardly coward, to desert his brothers and his chief in time of trial, to side with the persecutor against the victim! "He is a traitor," they say, in so many words. They scorn him, and when he presents himself at Carmel they turn their backs on him. Only Junípero continues to treat him with respect and kindness. At the Presidio, on the contrary, there is a honeymoon of friendliness. It will soon be over; but meanwhile, "Fray Firmin and Don Fernando eat together, sleep in the same room, are never apart," Junípero writes.

Act V. This Act takes place during the month of August and will be recounted in the following chapter. It is the Act of the Separation. In it, Lasuen will be seen to deceive Rivera and Junípero at one and the same time, playing his game with such skill and lying so successfully that it is again on Junípero that Rivera takes revenge for having been deceived by his friend.

Eighteen

The Events at Monterey in August, 1775, and the "Great Sin" of Junípero

Without taking account of the memorable sin noted in the chapter heading, no month of all the 165 that Junípero spent in Upper California was so filled with events of every sort as this month of August, 1775. Here in chronological order are the chief among them. . . .

August 8. Rivera pardons Junípero for his "insults," and would kiss the walls of the holy College.

Once they had asked for and received Baptism, adult Indians had to settle at the mission which was their center, and were no longer permitted to live as nomads.

At the beginning of July, half a score of neophytes from Carmel ran away into the mountains. Junípero asked the Commandant by letter for a few soldiers from the Presidio to go in search of them. Rivera took eight days to send his answer—that he had no men available. The next day Junípero learned that one of the fugitives, a woman named Polvoa, was dying. He sent Father Dumetz to give her the last rites, and with him two cuirassiers from the escort guard.

"I realize, my very dear friend," he wrote at once to Rivera, "that the soldiers are forbidden to spend a night outside the Mission, and I have transgressed the regulations; but the Tribunal where I shall have to answer for the souls of my children is above those of Mexico City, and I was not willing that my poor Polvoa should die without a priest. Who would ever imagine, moreover, that a mission which is situated a league's distance from a presidio, and itself has six soldiers, should not be able to obtain four or five to overtake the Indians who are running away? One has to be at Monterey to see that! Forgive me for speaking to you in this way; but I cannot help it! My heart is bleeding at the thought of those new Christians who are in danger of being lost for all Eternity."

Rivera saw an insult in this letter written under stress of emotion, and he sent a copy of it to Father Pangua, along with the following lines:

What do you think, my very Reverend Father, of such liberties being taken with me! This letter appears in the rough draft of my *Journal;* the Viceroy will not read it there, however, for I shall not recopy it when I do my *Journal* in a fair copy. I shall not lodge a complaint, therefore, against this rebellious Prefect who is insulting me. Confess, nevertheless, that he would deserve it; but I shall spare him out of regard for you, to whom I am so beholden [i.e., *for having given him Fray Firmin as private chaplain*]. There is nothing in the world that I would not do to oblige you; I would kiss the walls of the holy College if I could. Write me, I beg, in all confidence, as to one of the men under your authority, and give me whatever orders you wish. We are at the eighth of August, 1775. Rivera.

August 10. Bucareli gives an order.

On August 9, letters arrived from the Viceroy "ordering the immediate establishment of, if possible, four missions on the Santa Barbara Channel, at sites selected by Father Junípero." [1] Rivera was crushed. In the afternoon of August 10, he presented himself at Carmel.

"We received him with transports of joy," Junípero wrote to Bucareli. "He himself seemed sad and uneasy. He asked me what I had at my disposal to get these projects under way. 'As for me,' he added, 'I consider them very difficult, if not impossible.'

" 'There is no objection,' I replied, 'to reducing the escort guards in the missions that are next-door to the Presidios. With two soldiers whom we withdraw from Carmel and two from San Diego, and with a few others whom you take out of your Presidio garrisons, it will be possible to found several stations.'

" 'I will not withdraw one man from Monterey,' he said at once.

" 'And from the Presidio of San Diego?'

" 'I will think about it.'

---

[1] These sites would correspond to the present cities of Ventura (San Buenaventura), Santa Barbara, and Concepción (La Purisima Concepción). San Juan Capistrano, the fourth mission that Bucareli had in prospect, is south of the Channel. Some of the letters from Junípero quoted in this chapter were addressed to Bucareli (July 2 and 3, August 17 and 21, October 12, 20, and 29, 1775); the others were to Pangua (July 24, August 22, October 10, 17, 29, and 30).

"It was in vain that we besought him to come to a decision then and there. To our best arguments he would merely reply that he was going to consider. . . ."

August 11. Rivera considers and Lasuen requests.

"So as to leave him time for reflection," Junípero wrote to Pangua, "I did not see the Commandant again that day. He was not yet able to make up his mind, I was told by Father Lasuen, who came to see me during the day to ask me for one of the missions that were about to be established. I promised to give him the first one there was."

August 12, Saturday. A stormy session at the Presidio.

Junípero arrived at the Presidio early in the afternoon. He had asked Palou to accompany him; but Palou, who had difficulty in getting along with people who were disturbed or abnormal, "modestly declared himself incompetent," Junípero wrote in the same letter, "and urged me to take Father Murguia—older and more composed—with me. We set out. On the way, we mutually exhorted one another to weigh our words and to listen patiently, so as not to do any harm. Fine resolutions that were scarcely kept to, alas! The captain received us amiably. He took us into his office, where we were joined by Father Lasuen. There were thus four of us. Rivera began by teasing us on the subject of San Buenaventura.

" 'There is an establishment that will have been for a long time in a stage of mere contemplation, thanks to your remissness,' said Rivera. 'When I think that you were already trying to get it under way at the time of the first expedition, in 1769!'

"I replied in the same tone:

" 'Yes, but it is a little your fault too, for you helped at that time to use up its reserves. You remember how one night, unbeknown to Portola, you came to ask for provisions for yourself and your soldiers? I ceded you several almudes of maize, in exchange for a bit of textile stuff and some glass beads. It was the maize of San Buenaventura that got you out of your difficulty that time.'

" 'Yes, yes, I remember,' he said.

"For a moment we went on recalling old memories—and so agreeably, my word!, that I had no more misgivings. This time, I was thinking, San Buenaventura is founded. . . . Then, all of a sudden, Rivera lowered his head and demanded, sternly,

" 'How many soldiers do you need for one mission? I say, for one mission?'

"He was giving me to understand that I had to speak to him of only one station, although His Excellency mentioned several. I replied—just as I had said two days before—that I was offering four men, taken from the escort guards, and that it was for him to see how many he could withdraw from the presidios.

" 'You see, I am not fixing a figure for you,' I said.

" 'Yes, Señor, you see that,' my companions put in, in chorus. 'The Father Prefect is not fixing any figure. One really cannot speak better than that.'

"He became thoughtful once more, and lowering his head again, was lost anew in muteness. This long silence, which showed no signs of ending, was becoming embarrassing. To restore the more or less playful tone of the first minutes, I said,

" 'Confess, Señor, that you are afraid of seeing me ask for a dozen men! But I am asking nothing. I shall be satisfied with the figure you set.'

"Father Lasuen came to my aid.

" 'After all, a dozen men is not very many,' he observed. 'I was thinking that the Father Prefect would be harder to please.'

"I let it be understood that I would even be satisfied with a smaller number, and that in any case we could come to an agreement. Father Murguia was entirely of the same opinion. After a long silence, Rivera let fall these words:

" 'We should be able to consult His Excellency on this matter.'

"I still succeeded in keeping calm. 'His Excellency,' I observed gently, 'knows the number of soldiers we have, and orders us to go ahead. It is for us, therefore, to make the best use of the means we have. So long as we do something, and do our best, His Excellency will be satisfied.'

" 'In this case,' he said, 'there can be no more than six men.'

"I was not too much disappointed. Six men that he would give, and four to be given by us, I was thinking, that would be ten. . . . With that number, we could create a Mission. . . . As I was always desirous that this should be San Buenaventura, and in view of the conciliatory tone he had taken, I thought I could press the point.

" 'Well done, dear Señor, our friend!' I said. 'Here we are almost agreed. With what you offer, we arrive at the sum of ten

men. Just a little more effort and we get up to twelve—and San
Buenaventura is established! Let us procure this testimony to God's
glory, and may the name of Jesus resound through the Channel
region! Let us give His Excellency, also, this joy of—' My companions continued to support me, but what they said and what I
said had no effect beyond making him repeat, in a glacial tone,

   " 'We cannot go beyond six men! We cannot go beyond six
men!'

   "As we kept on trying to make him say something else, he
brought out,

   " 'The existent missions have each six men, and I cannot give
any more to the new ones without a new order from His Excellency.'

   " 'Then we are not in agreement on ten?' I replied.

   " 'No, no, and again no! I said six in all.'

   " 'Then the presidios are giving only two men?'

   " 'Exactly, Father! They will supply only two!'

   "I confess that, this time, my spirit faltered. How was this!
After His Excellency's official orders, after three days of reflection on Rivera's part and so much urgent entreaty on mine, when
I was thinking the question was settled, was this what it had come
to? I was close to tears. But I was still able to control myself.

   " 'Never,' I said, 'has a mission been established with six men;
and in the Channel it is more impossible than anywhere else to
be satisfied with that number.'

   "It was at this moment that the incident occurred which set
off the powder keg.

   " 'You will have to be satisfied with that number for the Missions of San Francisco,' the Commandant said, 'for His Excellency
has decided that none of them shall have any more.'

   " 'I beg your pardon,' I put in. 'His Excellency does not say
that.'

   " 'Yes, he does say that!'

   " 'No!' I retorted.

   " 'No!' said Father Murguia also.

   "I saw then that all was lost. Rivera leapt from his seat.

   "It must be understood that, in his letter of December 14, 1774,
His Excellency had written me, with his own hand, 'The chief
object of Anza's second expedition is to bring up the soldiers that
are necessary for the two Missions of San Francisco.' From then

on I had supposed that the thirty-or-so men Anza was bringing were for those Missions. And as confirmation of my mistaken assumption, I read in the letter's postscript, 'The escort guard of each of these Missions will be thirteen men.' Yes, it is indeed 'thirteen,' I say it to my shame, that I had read—I who am called 'lector'! And I was as sure of that as if I had seen it in large letters in the lectern antiphonary.[2] Fathers Palou, La Pena, and the others had read it the same way. Now one day at Carmel, when we were talking of these thirteen men, Don Fernando had smiled his little smile, and asked, 'Is it written in figures or in letters?' And we had all replied, in chorus, 'In letters, and in His Excellency's own hand.'

"And he had kept silent, with the air of a man particularly pleased. Twenty times, in the last few weeks, those thirteen men had been spoken of in his presence, and he had never corrected the figure. . . . And now here he was, standing up, ranting till he was out of breath about the long and loyal services he had rendered His Majesty. His career was without blemish. He had always comported himself in an exemplary manner. Among so many Viceroys who had followed one another in the City of Mexico, not one had ever had to complain of him, or had directed toward him the slightest reproach. And it was I, a man vowed to the religious life, a Father Prefect, a scholar, a mystic, who dared to come and steal away his honor by this contradiction of his word! . . . While I, with head down, was letting the storm pass over me, Father Murguia, by an unfortunate interruption, put his finger on the sore spot.

" 'But, Señor, you yourself have admitted that His Excellency spoke of thirteen men,' he said.

"Had he not admitted it in neglecting to correct it? He was flabbergasted by this.

" 'When was that?' he demanded. 'I do not recall . . .'

" 'That proves that you are beside yourself,' Father Murguia shot back, 'since you no longer recall what you said.'

" 'Señor,' I broke in then, 'I have never had any wish to attack your honor. The fact that I am here as a petitioner should be enough to prove that, for it is not the custom to insult people from whom one is asking a service. I had not come here,

[2] The mistake is more easily understood in Spanish than in English: *trece* is closer to *seis* than "thirteen" is to "six."

Petra, the island of Majorca *(Foto Balear)*

The house in which
Junípero Serra was born,
Petra *(Foto Rul-lán)*

Mexico City in the eighteenth century, looking toward the Cathedral with the Viceroy's palace to the right (La Illustración Mexicana)

The Church of San Fernando, Mexico City *(Foto Arte)*

The Mission of San Carlos at Carmel

(Drawing by William Rich Hutton, reproduced by permission of The Huntington Library, San Marino, California)

The Mission of San Antonio

(Drawing by William Rich Hutton

The Mission of San Gabriel

(Drawing by William Rich Hutton, reproduced by permission of The Huntington Library, San Marino, California)

The Mission of San Luis Obispo

(Drawing by William Rich Hutton, reproduced by permission from *The A...*

The Mission of San Francisco

(Drawing by William Rich Hutton, reproduced by permission of The Huntington Library, San Marino, California)

The Mission of Santa Clara

The Mission of San Buenaventura

(Drawing by William Rich Hutton, reproduced by permission of The Huntington Library, San Marino, California)

The only authentic portrait of Junípero Serra, painted in 1773. The original painting is in the Dispensary of the Church of San Fernando in Mexico City. *(Photograph taken by the author with the kind permission of R. P. Domingo Diaz, superintendent of the Franciscans of Mexico.)*

Francisco Palou *(From* The Missions and Missionaries of California *by* P. *Zeph-yrin Engelhardt)*

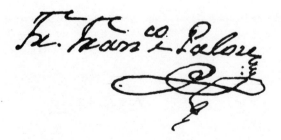

José de Galvez *(From* The Missions and Missionaries of California *by P. Zeph-yrin Engelhardt)*

Antonio María Bucareli *(From* The Missions and Missionaries of California *by*
P. *Zephyrin Engelhardt)*

Juan Bautista de Anza (*From Bolton*, The Spanish Borderlands)

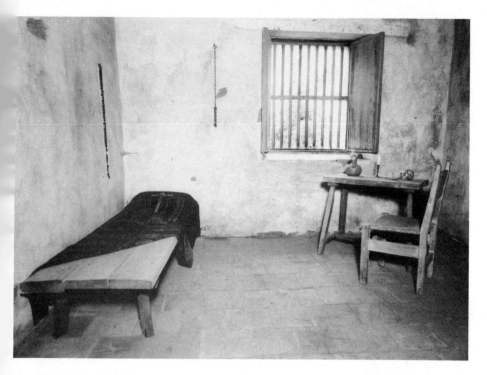

The cell at the Mission of San Carlos where Junípero Serra died *(Photograph by Lewis Josselyn, Carmel, California)*

The statue of Junípero Serra in the Capitol, Washington, D.C.
(Religious News Service)

moreover, to discuss the Missions of San Francisco, about which there can be nothing to discuss at this moment, but those of the Santa Barbara Channel, the foundation of which His Excellency ordains. There would have been no talk of San Francisco if you yourself had not started it, flinging the figure of six men at us in this connection, without telling us where you got it. You have no ground for surprise at our protests, since you have always avoided undeceiving us. . . . Dear Señor, let us forget all that, I beg! Calm yourself, forgive us, and let us remain good friends. You know very well that we have only the best of sentiments toward you.'

"Then he placed before us two letters from His Excellency, in which we could read *six* men and not *thirteen*.

"Father Murguia and I spent the night at the Presidio."

August 13, Sunday. The foundation of San Capistrano is decided upon.

The night did Rivera good; and even more, perhaps, did Junípero's sermon at Mass on Sunday. "I commented on the Gospel teaching that centered on brotherly love, insisting upon the forgiveness of trespasses and the union of hearts," Junípero wrote. Did he also evoke the hell of which Rivera went in almost as much fear as he did of the Indians? However that may be, "the interview that followed was cordial." The same persons took part in it as in the conversation of the day before.

Rivera still held stubbornly to the figure of six soldiers; but, this time, he ceded four from his presidios and authorized the missions to withdraw two from their escort guards. Since these six men were not enough to permit establishments in the Channel, as the Viceroy ordered, Junípero suggested that all foundation of missions be postponed. It was the Commandant who insisted that, anyway, something should be done. They compromised on San Capistrano, which was in a less dangerous situation, between San Gabriel and San Diego. "The agreement was concluded rapidly," Junípero reported, "and by eleven o'clock everything was finished. As soon as the decision had been reached I turned to Fray Firmin and said, 'Well, now, Father Lasuen, you see you are provided for. You should have had San Buenaventura if it had depended on me. Now you have San Capistrano, and it is to the Commandant that you owe it.'"

August 17. A letter from Junípero to Bucareli.

. . . The twelve men necessary to the establishment of San Buenaventura having been refused me, I decided upon San Capistrano.[3]
Imagine, the Commandant claimed that he could not give me more
than six soldiers, without referring the matter to you! He even lost
his temper completely at one moment. Peace has been restored, but
I earnestly urge that in future your orders shall be so precise that
he cannot cavil or wrangle over them.

The same day. A letter from Lasuen to Pangua.
Lasuen first recounted the turbulent scene at the Presidio.

My Reverend Father Prefect and Father Murguia averred that they
considered it possible to found San Buenaventura [he wrote]. The
Señor Captain objected that this would need more than six men, and
that his orders did not authorize him to go beyond that figure.

"I have, however, a letter in which the Viceroy assigns thirteen
men to the future missions (of San Francisco)," my Reverend Father
Prefect replied.

This was a misunderstanding, due to the bad writing of the letter
in question. The Fathers had read "thirteen," and indeed one could
just as well read "thirteen" as "six," as I have been able to ascertain.

"I have an order that says six men," the Señor Commandant kept
repeating. "I have an order that says six men!"

He seemed unwilling ever to stop. A part of the session went by
like this. Finally, my Reverend Father Prefect exploded, and, striking the table a great blow with his fist, cried out,

"No such order exists!"

"And I tell you that it does exist," Don Fernando repeated in a
grave voice.

"No!"

"Yes!"

"No!"

"Yes! . . ."

The Father did not back down. The Yes's and No's went back and
forth for a long moment. "In any case, we are not going to continue
this litany all night," my Reverend Father Prefect ended by saying.
After a pause, the Señor Commandant got up, in rage. He showed
us two letters from the Señor Viceroy, in which the word "six" does
indeed appear. Then, with extraordinary violence, he expressed his indignation that his word should not be believed. The next day, the

---

[3] A native of Capistrano (Naples, Italy), the Franciscan John Capistrano (1386-
1456), one of the greatest preachers of all time, spoke throughout Italy, France,
Germany, Austria, Hungary, and Poland. The victory over the Turks at Bel-
grade is attributed to the Crusade he preached.

foundation of San Capistrano was decided upon. My Reverend Father Prefect named me minister then and there. To tell the truth, I have always had a horror of that locality; but, by God's grace, nothing more would be needed to make me go there all the more willingly.

. . . Yes, I am like that, very Reverend Father Guardian, the tenor of the letter made plain. Not only do I not pound on the table, like my Reverend Father Prefect, but grace has truly triumphed, in me, over nature, and, like our Father St. Francis, I find in vexation and mortification the perfect joy. . . . After these boastings comes a shocking untruth:

Shall I tell you how troubled I am in seeing the Commandant so annoyed? He is annoyed because of what I have just related to you. He is also annoyed because, in appointing me to San Capistrano, *they* are taking me away from him, without regard to the request he had made and the granting of it. He feels this so acutely that he has sent in his resignation, strongly insisting that it be accepted.

Let us bear in mind this dishonest "they," which refers to Junípero. Following this, the wily and tortuous-minded Lasuen mingles his repentance with his hopes of advancement:

From what I have seen in these past few days, and from what the Fathers have told me, I am forced to recognize the fact that it is not their fault if cordial relations do not prevail here, and that it would be unjust to hold them responsible. Today I would not write my letter of the third of this month, and I would not now send that letter. Take account of the present correction, then, as you read it. The suspicion and hostility which I have told you my colleagues were showing me came, I now know, from their seeing me attached to the man who gives them so much cause for complaint and causes them so much suffering. It is not that the tender and deep affection which I have for the Commandant is dependent upon the offices and benefits which I expect from him. I remain nevertheless convinced that he is, for me, a very powerful friend whom I cannot dispense with. Convinced likewise that something should be done to give him satisfaction. . . .

Yes, but what kind of satisfaction should Rivera be given? Should it be the satisfaction of recalling Junípero and appointing Lasuen in his place? . . . All that is complicated, contradictory, and scarcely edifying! One always has some sense of disgust in seeing those who preach Gospel humility to others seeking honors for themselves, and in hearing lying and intrigue take on the tone of devoutness.

Yet how fortunate we are that this letter should not have been lost, and that we may see that "fist pounding on the table" brought into it! From it we glean at last one of those "great and many sins" of which Junípero used constantly to speak! In truth, it is the only one we encounter in the course of his life. And again, is it indeed a sin? . . . Let those decide who have had to treat of important affairs with hysterics! Utter madmen arouse no irritation at all, but only pity. It is the half-mad who, on the contrary, are both exasperating and dangerous.

August 18. Lasuen leaves Monterey and sets out for San Luis.
There he will meet Father Amurrio, and together they will go on to San Capistrano.

August 19, Sunday. Rivera's two incurable wounds.
Having learned during the week that the Captain was set against him, Junípero took it upon himself to perform the services on this Sunday at the Presidio. "When Mass had been said, I besought the Commandant to grant me a private interview," he wrote, "and I questioned him about the reasons for his resentment.

" 'There are a great many,' he replied.

"I begged him to let me know them all, without exception.

" 'St. Bonaventura,' I said to him, 'observes that our outer acts do not always express our real intentions; that is why it has been possible for me to offend you, by my words or my deeds, without meaning to.'

"After refusing for a long time to explain himself, he assured me that certain of his wounds were old. They came from two or three letters I had written him not so very long ago. He would agree, nevertheless, to forget them, seeing that I had already explained myself in regard to them in such a way as to make amends.

" 'But there is something else,' he continued. 'There is what has happened in these past few days. You have offered me two affronts which have wounded me so much that I shall not set foot in Carmel again and I have resolved to resign my position.'

"The first of these was the incident I have reported above. I apologized for having seemed to accuse him of untruthfulness, for the same reasons that I had given during the conversation in question: we had not correctly deciphered the Viceroy's handwriting; we were honestly mistaken, and his—Rivera's—silence had confirmed us in our error. I pleaded, in addition, the heat of the discussion, our disappointment, etc. Above all, I entreated him to be so kind as to forgive us.

"I was ignorant of what the second offense could be, for which he was holding a grudge against me. It was, he said, that I had taken Father Lasuen away from him, by appointing him to San Capistrano. And here indeed was something I was farthest from expecting—I who had made this appointment only to please the two of them! I informed him that Father Lasuen, fearing that his title of chaplain might debar him from being made minister, had come, on the ninth of this month, to entreat me to give him a post. 'Everything,' I said to him, 'bore me out in supposing that you knew his wishes and the step he was taking, since you ate, slept, and spent all your time together! Ah, how sorry I am that he should already have gone!'

"He listened to me without uttering a word; but I have since learned that my explanations did not satisfy him, and that he went away reiterating that I was very much mistaken if I believed that sophisms (*razoncitas*) like mine would convince him. The result of all this is that he has a greater grudge against me than ever, and is going to try to get himself transferred. I should be sorry if he succeeded in this; for since, to my way of thinking, we shall always have our difficulties, we must bear our lot patiently; and, when all is said and done, it is better to keep this Commandant who perhaps will some day leave off persecuting us, than to see another come who might be even worse."

Once again, this is a worthy response; and could one better carry out the Gospel teaching? Lasuen was dishonest in letting Rivera believe that he was leaving him against his will; he was guilty of cowardice in shouldering Junípero with the responsibility of his leaving; and Junípero not only omits any characterization of these procedures, but even accepts without any complaint their undeserved consequences for himself.

August 22. A letter from Rivera to Bucareli.

I received Your Excellency's two letters, on the ninth of this month, with joy. In one of them, Your Excellency sets a high value on the information I gathered in the course of my San Francisco expedition. In the other, Your Excellency notifies me of his desires [*they were orders*] to see the missions established in the Channel.

On the afternoon of the tenth I made my way to Carmel. After debating for a long time with the Father Prefect, I withdrew without coming to any conclusion. On the twelfth, His Reverence came to see me, accompanied by Father Murguia. His wish was that action should be taken toward the foundation of San Buenaventura, for which fourteen soldiers seemed to him necessary. [*Junípero was asking twelve.*] He offered to withdraw two from Carmel and two from San Diego, but I, for my part, had by no means ten men to give him. We spent the whole night [!] without coming to an understanding. Next day, the thirteenth, the conversation was resumed. His Reverence then proposed the establishment of a mission station between San Diego and San Gabriel. [*Junípero wanted to delay founding any mission; it was Rivera who suggested San Capistrano.*] I agreed. This will be done with the number of soldiers customarily fixed upon for the escort guards [six].

Permit me to tell you, Excellency, that your observations on the urgency that exists for the establishment of the missions have plunged me into profound thought. I have only twenty-two soldiers here; I have no more than that at San Diego. Have you reflected, Most Excellent Lord, that in case there were a revolt of the Indians, we should not be able to meet it? Without going so far as that extremity, I can show you that there are not too many of us here. Oh, I sometimes feel that I am terribly badly off! And there are the mails, Excellency. It must not be forgotten that when the dispatch riders are not in full force, the natives are emboldened to attack them. It is a fact that when they have taken that risk, up to now, it has cost them dearly; but, in a word, if the odds should turn against us, the victorious Indians would do us great harm, Excellency.

Fortunately it is to me, and not the Father Prefect, to whom the settling of these questions belongs; otherwise our forces would be scattered all over the country, and there would be no longer any corner of the land that did not have a Mission. I may say that he does not surpass me in noble desires, but if I allowed myself to be guided solely by them, Excellency, I should be forgetting the responsibilities of my office. Merely to establish one Mission in the Channel, he needs at least twenty-five men. [*In Fages' time, Junípero insisted upon fifteen; now, twelve were enough for him.*]

Most Excellent Lord, I am at the feet of Your Excellency.

                                   Fernando de Rivera y Moncada.

The same day. A letter from Junípero to Father Pangua.

. . . The great news is the foundation of San Capistrano, while we await those of San Francisco. These last establishments will only take place when Señor Anza arrives. I am not giving my attention to their patron saints in the meantime; but as regards St. John Capistrano, I beg you not to commission his portrait from Alcayseria: he would put him in a blue habit, as he has done to other Franciscan saints whom we have here. Find a good engraving; turn it over to Paez, and let him give his subject the air of piety and the energetic features that are proper to him.

What shall I say to you in conclusion, except to tell you again of the happiness I always feel at being a member of the holy College, to which God has set aside the care of evangelizing these pagan regions. . . . I do not deserve it at all. My faults of judgment, my imperfections, and my sins are without doubt many. At least, it will always be my will to allow myself to be corrected by my superiors. I accept in advance all the decisions of Your Reverence and those of the Venerable Discretory. Once more, be fully assured that I place the disposal of my person and my ministry in your hands.

August 29. The frigate returns from Alaska.

A few more leaps forward, Galvez thinks, and all the western coastal region on the Pacific Ocean, ten thousand leagues from Tierra del Fuego to Alaska, will be subject to the Spanish Crown. Velicata, San Diego, Monterey are only the first relays in this northward march. The time has come to clear a further passage, while awaiting those that are to come. This was in Bucareli's mind when he wrote to Junípero: "I have decided upon the early occupation of the port of San Francisco: first, to establish an advance post in view of further ventures; second, to show that this place belongs definitely and finally to the King; and, third, to spread the Faith into other pagan regions."

Junípero was exultant. "I am impatiently awaiting the arrival of Lieutenant-Colonel Anza," he wrote in answer to the Viceroy, "and, if it please God, I will accompany him to San Francisco; for my great desire is to see the standard of the Cross and the flag of His Majesty set up there. The weight of years robs me of the hope of ever journeying northward toward the upper latitudes; but the younger and more robust will go. I shall at least have had the happiness of helping to establish that advance post."

All efforts at this moment, then, were directed toward the occupation of San Francisco. Anza, in charge of bringing the company of soldiers and the necessary settlers from Sonora, was on the way. Meanwhile the boats would go to reconnoiter the fa-

mous bay once more. There were four of them now: to the three
we already know, a schooner had been added. All had sailed from
San Blas in February: the *San Antonio* with San Diego as its destination; the *San Carlos* for Monterey—where, as we have seen,
it weighed anchor on June 27; the frigate and the schooner bound
for Alaskan latitudes.

Now, today, the frigate is back again, having reached the forty-
ninth parallel. This time that distant coast has been taken possession of in the name of the King by Ezeta who commanded the
ship, Juan Perez who piloted it, and Father Campa, former minister of Velicata, their chaplain; and the cross has been planted
in two localities.

"We saluted their return by the pealing of the bells of Carmel," Junípero writes. "We sang the *Te Deum*, and Father Campa
celebrated the Mass of solemn thanksgiving." It was, alas, the last
time he was to pray with Juan Perez, his beloved Mallorcan com-
patriot, the friend of so many good and evil days: on October 11
following, the great navigator died of the pestilence on his ship
between Monterey and San Diego, and his body was committed
to the sea.

The activity at Carmel, through all the next month, was tre-
mendous; there was a constant coming and going of missionaries,
chaplains, and naval officers; everyone was getting ready for the
approaching mission foundations. The *San Carlos* returned on September 19 with its chaplain Father Santa María from a forty-day
tour of exploration in the bay of San Francisco. Five days before
that, Palou and Campa had set out with Ezeta to explore it from
the land side. They came back enchanted; what a vast estuary!
what an excellent harbor! what beautiful countryside! From this
time on there was nothing more that was unknown: it was quite
clear where the fort was to be set up and where the two mission
posts were to be established. One of the missions would have
Francisco Palou and Benito Cambon as ministers, the other Murguia and La Peña. Rejoicing prevailed everywhere. "Our community now comprises eleven men," Junípero wrote to his Guardian.
"The Fathers have become seamen; I hear no talk at table of anything but latitudes, bearings to the northeast and southwest, and
so on. It is true that I understand this as much as I understand
the making of pottery; but my happiness is no less great in seeing them all so happy."

On October 9 the appearance of the schooner set the bells a-peal again. "We have sung the *Te Deum* anew and celebrated a Mass of thanksgiving," Junípero wrote to Bucareli. "And there is a little boat that is wonderful! Parting company from the frigate at the forty-ninth parallel, it went as far north as the fifty-eighth parallel, in sight of Alaska. Six times its crew was at death's door. The pagans carried away its long-boat and killed seven of its men. That did not prevent its taking possession of two provinces in the King's name, and planting the cross there. Your name will live, Excellency, in these new lands, for the names of *Bucareli Alta* and *Bucareli Baja* have been given to them. No one can be happier than I in congratulating you. . . . Meanwhile, the crosses are planted there. . . . May God bring it about that as time passes apostles will go to tell the poor folk who see them what it is that they represent! . . ."

Nineteen

The Destruction of San Diego and the Martyrdom of Fray Luis Jaume
[1775]

Founded by Junípero in 1769, the Mission of San Diego had since 1771 had as its head minister Fray Luis Jaume, a Mallorcan now in 1775 thirty-five years old.[1] In 1773 Father Vicente Fuster, just arrived from the Peninsula, had been assigned to him as associate.

A man of excellent education whose piety had won him the sobriquet of *Rezador* (the one who prays), Father Jaume had exerted himself mightily among these Indians who were reputed difficult to get on with. At the time of his arrival only sixteen had been baptized; by 1775 the number had reached 470. He had translated the entire catechism into their idiom; and in every *ranchería* (Indian village) he had schooled young people who knew it entirely by heart and were teaching it to the others; to say nothing of the choir boys who gave the responses perfectly at Mass, and the little musicians who executed the liturgical chants in a manner nothing short of remarkable.

As long as it remained close to the sea, and cheek-by-jowl, so to speak, with the Presidio, the lack of streams and irrigation canals had made it impossible for the Mission to develop its agriculture. Every year the weather renewed the same beautiful promises, and then came a drought in which all the crops, half-grown though they might be, perished. "There are a great many pagans who wish to embrace the Faith," Fray Jaume was writing to Junípero in 1773. "Recently again," his letter went on, "all the children of the Rincon appeared in a group at catechism; as

[1] Born at San Juan (Majorca) on October 18, 1740, Fray Luis Jaume or Jayme entered the Order in 1760. After his ordination as a priest, he taught theology at the monastery of Jesus-outside-the-Walls until his departure for Mexico in 1770.

we had only a little maize left, we could not give it to them every time they came; and now they are not to be seen any longer. If our next harvest is good, they will come back. I am obliged to confess, however, that so long as we stay here we shall not make real progress, because of the lack of water."

The transfer of San Diego Mission took place in August, 1774. Followed by their neophytes, Fathers Jaume and Fuster moved to a site five miles from the Presidio on the hill of the Cosoy.[2] From that time on, the crops throve and conversions were multiplied. On the single day of October 3, 1775, sixty baptisms were performed. "Such success," writes Palou, "infuriated the devil, who drove certain neophytes to destroy their Christian community themselves." Eight were later arrested, and were convicted of having provoked the uprising: Carlos, Bernardino, Diego, Dismas, Nicolas, Joaquín, Francesco, and one other. Carlos and Francesco were Christians. All had gone about everywhere repeating that what had happened at the Cosoy on the third of October was a prelude to what would soon happen elsewhere: all the natives would be baptized by force and deprived of their liberty if the Spaniards were not massacred first.

The attack took place on the night of November 5-6, 1775. The warriors from some forty *rancherias* took part in it. They were divided into two armies of about six hundred men each, one of which marched on the Presidio, the other on the Mission.

There were eleven persons at the Cosoy that night: Fathers Jaume and Fuster; two children, Lieutenant Ortega's son and nephew; the two blacksmiths Romero and Arroyo; the carpenter Urselino, Corporal Rocha, and three soldiers. Father Jaume was in bed at the Mission residence, Father Fuster and the Ortega children were at the storehouse, the three artisans at the smithy, the soldiers at the guardhouse. The escort should have numbered six men, but one soldier had been withdrawn for the establishment of San Capistrano, and another was on sick leave at the Presidio. The garrison of the Presidio itself, moreover, was reduced by half at this moment, inasmuch as ten of the men, under command of Ortega, were installing Father Lasuen's mission, sixty-

[2] The Cosoy was the name of the hill; in the Indian language the place was called Nipaguay; the old documents name the Mission, San Diego d'Alcala de Nipaguay.

five miles away. The enemy was aware of this, and took advantage of it to carry out his plan of attack.

In a letter to Junípero, two weeks later, Father Fuster told the story of that terrible night.

"I was awakened with a start by the sound of gunshot and yelling, at about one A.M., and rushed to the guardhouse, where the soldiers were shooting. The darkness was pierced only by the fires that had broken out here and there. The Mission was surrounded by Indians, shrieking like death itself; some were shooting arrows, others were throwing stones, still others were scattering burning embers and firebrands. The stockade had been forced on this side, and the residence and smithy were already aflame, while the roof of the guardhouse was catching fire also.

" 'It's better to get under the shed!' I cried to the soldiers.

"Falling back step by step, and continuing to shoot, the soldiers reached the lean-to shed at the storehouse. I went into the house again, to reassure the little Ortegas, and we prayed together. Then, all of a sudden, I thought of Father Luis. I shot like an arrow through the fire, holding my breath. I reached the residence; I called; I ran to Father Luis' bed and felt all over it, in the darkness. The Father had disappeared. I escaped from the house just as the roof collapsed in flames.

"The storehouse had caught fire by the time I got back to it. The children and I pushed three huge chests full of cloth out in front of the door, and then joined the soldiers in the lean-to. At this moment the sound of a gunshot came from the direction of the smithy; and almost immediately afterward Romero came running up, with his gun in his hand.

" 'May God receive the soul of José Arroyo!' he said. 'He has just died, pierced through with arrows, as he was charging the Indians with his sword. I killed one of them with a bullet. The others fled—which is how I was able to escape.'

"The carpenter Urselino had been mortally wounded, also, in the smithy.

"But now the roof of the shed, in turn, had caught fire. Nothing was still intact except the kitchen, a small isolated building with three walls of unbaked brick, no front wall at all, and no roof.

" 'Let us take refuge in the kitchen,' I cried. 'The fire will not get a hold there.'

"The soldiers dragged some bags of bullets and a box of powder out of the storehouse. Two of them helped Romero and me carry the three big chests to the kitchen. We set them up, one against the other, and they filled half the space where the front wall should have been; it was behind this rampart that the four soldiers, the two children, Romero and myself passed the rest of the night, showered upon with bricks, stones, and incendiary firebrands, peppered with arrows, exposed every instant to death.

"Three of the soldiers had been wounded in making their way as far as the kitchen: two of them had their arms paralyzed, and the third was so severely injured that he, too, was no longer able to fire his gun. Only the corporal could still shoot. For five hours he kept on shooting, without pause, like a madman, directing a running fire against the assailants, and continuing to yell at them, as his comrades did also; Romero and the soldier who was least seriously wounded loaded the guns and passed them to him. The Ortega children had lain down flat on their stomachs. As for myself, I held the keg of powder on my knees, one hand protecting it with my cloak, the other hand protecting my head with a pillow. Arrows were flying in a swarm around us. One of them landed in my pillow. We thrust back the burning firebrands as they came. Several of them fell on the powder chest just as it was being opened, but God ordained that none of them should reach the powder. The corporal received a wound, of which he breathed not a word lest we should be frightened. He only became the more furious because of it. . . . But, revered Father, this night of horror is something impossible to recount in words. This is what Purgatory must be. What prayers and promises we made to Heaven! And how we yearned for the light of day, to bring us out of this darkness full of deadly shrieks and conflagrations!

"A period of quiet intervened toward dawn. The archers interrupted their shooting, though the others did not stop yelling and throwing stones. The warriors were regrouping, in company with those who were coming back from the Presidio. With daylight the combat was resumed. I believed, then, that we were lost for good and all. Our attackers now numbered more than a thousand. And I had the anguish just at that time of recognizing some of our neophytes, my beloved children, who were running through the ranks transmitting orders and urging the fighters on to make an end of us. The corporal was firing faster and faster, yelling louder and louder, and, now that he could see what he was doing, hitting his man every time. The enemy were hard put to it to take away their dead and wounded. This went on until God brought it about that a last burst of gunfire unleashed panic and provoked a general retreat.

"The neophytes from the nearby *rancherias* then began to put in an appearance with their weapons, in little groups. If they had not come to our aid during the night it was, they confessed, because they were too afraid. . . . Next, the Indians of the Mission came out of their huts. I asked myself at first whether this was not an ambuscade; then I took the risk of going toward them. They flung themselves upon me with fervent embraces. I swooned in their arms. . . . When I came to myself my first thought was for Father Luis.

" 'Go and look for him!' I cried to the ones who were standing around me. I sent others to warn the Presidio, still others to look to the horses, others, finally, to go for water to put out the fire which had now reached the grain in the storehouse. It was one of these last who found Father Luis half a mile from the Mission.

" 'The Father is in the brook,' he cried, as he came running back.

" 'Is he alive or dead?' I asked.

" 'Dead.'

" 'Bring him here!' I still had enough strength to say.

"They carried him up the hill. I did not recognize my colleague in the corpse that was set down before me. The chest, the abdomen, the entire body was as if studded over with knife thrusts; the head had been beaten flat with stones. There was no bone left unbroken in this bloody pulp. Except for the white color of his skin and his tonsure, this was no more Father Luis than any other man. The consecrated hands of the young priest had remained intact. . . . We learned later that, wakened at the beginning of the onslaught, the Father had gone to meet the Indians, greeting them with his usual salutation of 'Love God, my children,' and that, seized by them and dragged into the wood toward the stream that flowed at the foot of the hill, he had allowed himself to be taken without uttering a word, without making one movement of resistance.

". . . I had fainted once more, over these mortal remains of my comrade, whom I had revered and so greatly loved.

"When I recovered consciousness, the soldiers from the Presidio had arrived. Five stretchers were constructed: two for the dead, the Father and Arroyo; the other three for the severely wounded soldiers and Urselino. Neophytes took them on their shoulders, and the procession set out toward the Presidio. In spite of their wounds the valiant corporal and his stouthearted companions covered the distance on horseback. I had strength enough to go on foot, walking by the side of the dead. All the wounded are now recovered except Urselino, who died five days later."

This Urselino, a carpenter whom Junípero had brought with him from Guadalajara, had been ill and unable to get up when the Indians broke into the smithy. They shot him through with arrows. Feeling himself to be mortally wounded, he cried out, "Indians, you have killed me. May God forgive you, as I ask Him to!" He had no relatives left, and he still possessed, in the royal storehouse, the little he had earned since entering the King's service. He wished that all this should belong to the Indians, and in his will he made his murderers his heirs.

"It is a miracle, my revered Father," the letter from Father Fuster continues, "that the Presidio should not also have been destroyed. The impatience of our assailants saved it. According to the plan as conceived, the Mission should have been attacked only when the Presidio was burning. Our aggressors at the Mission did not wait for this signal to commence their onslaught. Seeing that, the second group, which was arriving before the Presidio just at this moment, thought that the sentinels had raised the alarm, and, believing that the surprise action had thus gone wrong, retraced their steps to the Cosoy.

"Father Luis was buried the next day, November 7, in the Presidio chapel. And that same day the corporal and some soldiers went back to the Cosoy. Except for a few consecrated vessels, buckled by the fire, the two bells, and about fifty fanegas of wheat, everything had been destroyed. Few animals had been killed, although the pagans had tried to slaughter them.

"On the evening of the sixth, three soldiers had already set out for San Capistrano. Lieutenant Ortega abandoned the new establishment on the spot and arrived back here on the eighth with several of his men. The others returned on the eleventh with

Fathers Lasuen and Amurrio. Although the lieutenant has taken all sorts of security measures, and a mounted guard patrols the post, we are living in a continual state of watchfulness; we are always on the qui-vive. . . . One night we heard war cries sounding back and forth from one wood to another in the mountains. Our enemies are fondly hoping to return soon in greater numbers to make the final assault, the first attack having been, as they say, only a trial stroke intended to feel out our forces. . . . I am awaiting instructions from Your Reverence to reconstruct the Mission. . . . May I say to you in the meantime that I have lost confidence in my own neophytes? And it is this, alas, that is causing me the greatest grief and disheartenment." [3]

The soldiers charged with delivering this letter to Junípero left San Diego on November 28 and arrived on December 13 at Monterey. "God be praised!" he said when he had read it. "On the earth watered by the blood of this young missionary, conversions will bourgeon ever increasingly from this time forth!"

There is no irremediable disaster for him who believes in eternal life and who has no other will than the will of God. Not for one moment did Junípero allow himself to be crippled or confused. He had no impulse of aversion for these parricide sons; far from calling down curses upon these Indians who had behaved so wickedly, he loved them even more. Making no concession to grief, he thought only of immediately repairing the damage that had been done, and of sparing the guilty men the punishment that would have made impossible the good he wished to do them. No other preoccupation is to be found in his letter of December 15 to Bucareli:

"The news cannot always be good, for we are in a vale of tears. What I have to tell you today is dreadful, Excellency: the Mission of San Diego has been destroyed and its head minister has been killed. The Commandant announces that he is leaving this

---

[3] As the disinterested American citizen reads this account of Fray Luis Jaume's murder, it is impossible to keep from wishing that the place where California's first Christian martyr was tortured and died might receive greater honor than is now accorded it. A cross of coarse and crumbling cement is left to mark that site. It has no fence to protect it, so that the dogs and donkeys of the neighborhood rub themselves against it and go to sleep there, while Sunday strollers feel free, it seems, to leave their empty bottles and cigarette packages lying about on the ground. May those who are interested in their country's past some day assure this humble monument greater respect.—TRANSLATOR.

evening, and he refuses to take me with him, on the pretext that he will be traveling too fast and does not count on stopping at any mission. When I asked him for an escort to take me to San Diego later, he refused that, too, alleging the lack of soldiers. So here am I, kept from going to set those two missions on their feet again as I was counting on doing. I am not even left the time to send my instructions in writing to the three Fathers who are down there waiting for them. . . . All that is left to me is God; I put my trust in Him; for from men I expect nothing more."

That is the only cry of grief, to our knowledge, that ever fell from Junípero's lips.

"There is you, however, Excellency, in whom I have faith," he went on. "And that is why I entreat you to order officially the immediate re-establishment of the missions that have been closed, in the same places where they were. Each had promise of such a flourishing future! That of San Capistrano was founded on the thirtieth of October; the natives had given the missionaries the best of welcomes; on the evening of November 7, the lieutenant decided to withdraw all the soldiers, and San Capistrano was suppressed. May God's very holy will be accomplished! But, once more, it is Your Excellency upon whom it rests to put everything right, and I beseech you to do so for the love of God.

"These sad events have, naturally, moved me to much meditation; but I shall keep that to myself, since it is futile to moan over the past. As for the future, you will permit me to insist anew upon one general observation which I have made to you before. In a conquest such as this, I said to you, the place of the soldiers is in the missions, and not in the presidios. That elsewhere they may be needed in the fortress-barracks, I do not deny; but, with full knowledge of the circumstances, I affirm that that is not the case here."

The basis of this argument is that Junípero no longer believed in the likelihood of a foreign invasion, since the shadow of a Russian or English ship had not been glimpsed on the horizon for six years. Why then should so many soldiers be left idling in the presidios? It was not to defend an unthreatened coast but to convert and subdue a new people that the King was keeping them in his pay. Since you are poor, the Prefect would say to the Sovereign, practice economy with these garrisons, which are a luxury; organize seven or eight escort guards from among these fifty men who are reposing at San Diego and Monterey; they will make it possible to found as many missions, which, themselves, will rapidly advance the work of the conquest.

"The complete futility of these garrisons has been substantiated in the present instance," he writes. "See how well they sleep, Excellency, although they can scarcely be said to be tired, in the King's presidios! From the Presidio of San Diego, which is on a height of two little leagues from the Cosoy hill, the Mission is to be seen clearly. And every morning the Mission clearly hears the shot that marks, at the Presidio, the relinquishment of the night's countersign. But, although the atmospheric conditions were good, no one at the Presidio saw the soaring flames that, from one o'clock in the morning, were rising from the Mission, and no one heard the firing that went on there all night. . . ."

Junípero wishes, next, to prevent the massacres that Rivera is getting ready for. . . . The Indians being homicidal by nature, and in consequence incapable of understanding that murder is justly punishable by death; we ourselves being crusaders whose presence here has nothing to justify it if we do not preach the Gospel by example and by word; what is the right thing to do, not for the purpose of avenging the dead who refuse vengeance, or of satisfying the pride of soldiers who are often libertines and murderers, but in order that the work of the Christian conquest may go on? . . . "Do not," he begs, "authorize the reprisals that are being heralded. At the beginning of these conquests I asked as a favor of the Most Illustrious Visitor General that if the Indians, pagan or Christian, were to kill me they should be pardoned. It is through an oversight that I have not sooner made the same request of you. I present it to you today, in my own name and that of the present and future friars of this Mission. If you will condescend to sign a decree to this effect you will give great comfort to the old man I am, for the time God grants him still to live. So long as he lives, may the soldiers guard the missionary as the apple of God's eye! So be it! But once the Indians have killed him, why attack them?—Because they have deserved such punishment, and to destroy their desire to do the same thing again? So it will be said. What I say to you is that the real way of keeping the others from being killed is to give them a better escort guard than to the one who is gone. As for the murderers, let them live, so as to make it possible for them to save their souls. It is for this that we have come here; this is the only reason that justifies our presence in these localities. After inflicting upon the guilty man a moderate punishment which he will understand, send him home forgiven. He will know that you do it in order to carry out the word of the Gospel, which obliges you to forget injuries, and he will only be the more drawn toward that religion of goodness and kindness which we have come to bring him."

Rivera took this letter south with him. But he was lying when he said that he was leaving that same evening; he did not start out until the next day. He was lying, also, in saying that he would travel by forced marches; he actually journeyed in tourist fashion, taking a month to cover a distance that required twelve days, stopping and lingering a long time at every Mission. But as he intended to "make the Indians pay dearly for their revolt," and to prevent the reopening of the missions that had been closed, he did not want the Prefect at his side, and he had to all effects made him a prisoner.

The months that followed were among the most painful in Junípero's life. Rivera had him at his mercy in refusing him any escort guard; Lasuen and his fellow plotters contended against him; a number of the supernumeraries were preparing to desert. And now, as an additional blow, came Anza with the news that Bucareli had been recalled to Spain, and with a Patent or License that humiliated Prefect Junípero and stripped him of his authority. Yes, it was truly as he had said: all that was left to him was God. . . .

Twenty

Anza's Second Expedition, the Affair of the License, and Junípero's Humiliation
[1775-1776]

When Junípero was writing the above letter to Bucareli, Anza was no more than a few days' march from San Gabriel.

He had scarcely returned to Tubac after his first expedition when the Viceroy summoned him to his presence and, after promoting him to the rank of Lieutenant Colonel in recognition of his achievement, called him to another exploit. This consisted in directing, on the march to San Francisco, the settlers whom the royal authorities wished to establish there. Anza left Mexico City about the middle of February, 1775. At the last minute Pangua handed over to him, to give to Junípero, the envelope containing the License we have already mentioned.

The expedition set out this time from the Mission of San Miguel (Arizona), twenty miles from Tubac. The date was September 29, 1775. The long caravan was made up—in addition to the ten veteran campaigners who formed the head guard—of three chaplains, the geodetic expert Vidal, the lieutenant Moraga, the sergeant Grijalva, 28 private soldiers, 20 muleteers, four agricultural laborers, with interpreters, cowherds, manservants, and with 29 women and 110 children: 240 persons in all, to which number must be added 530 horses, 165 mules, and 350 head of cattle.

On November 30 the caravan reached the confluence of the Colorado and Gila rivers. When Anza saw that none of the children confided to his care had been drowned in the river crossing, he fell on his knees to thank God. The next day he presented the chief Palma, on the part of the Viceroy, with a bespangled uniform and a long staff with a silver point, creating him Captain in the service of His Majesty Charles III. Four leagues farther on he did the same for the Indian named Pablo, another Yuma chief, who also had won merit by allowing him to pass through alive the year before.

These episodes are reported to us by Pedro Font, one of the chaplains of the expedition. The other chaplains were the celebrated Father Garces whom we know, and Father Eizarch, like the first two a friar of the College of Querétaro. To his talents as explorer and writer of memoirs, Pedro Font added gifts as a musician; he took his psaltery with him wherever he went. Every morning before the caravan set out and every evening before they all retired for the night, he would intone the *Alabado* to the accompaniment of this instrument, and the crowd would take it up in chorus. This was a canticle to the Holy Family sung in all the missions of the Apostolic Colleges. High Mass was celebrated on Sunday, with the enhancement of a sermon and the music of Pedro Font.

Four days after crossing the Colorado River, Anza bore to the northwest, and on December 5 he plunged into the desert where Sebastian had led him about over so wide a territory. This time he went straight through, and emerged from it on Christmas Eve. The next night the wife of one of the soldiers gave birth to a baby, and Pedro Font baptized it under the name of Salvador Ignacio. And on January 4, 1776, at eleven in the morning the immigrants made their entry into the Mission of San Gabriel. A large number of animals had been sacrificed to the rigors of the journey, but not one person had been lost. On the contrary, with the little Salvador Ignacio, there was one future colonist the more, to develop the country of San Francisco Bay. . . .

For two days Rivera had been resting at San Gabriel with all the serenity in the world, having completely forgotten his plan of going on to San Diego "by forced marches."

The instructions Bucareli had sent Rivera were as follows:

The Commandant of Tubac is about to conduct to Monterey soldiers who have been recruited in Sonora; they will be accompanied by their families, and will serve to form the escort guards of the two missions which Fray Junípero is to establish without delay at the port of San Francisco. I direct you to assist him in this, in every way. Between these two missions a fort is to be constructed to defend them in case of need. Once the soldiers and settlers have reached Monterey the matter is your concern; but it is understood that Anza will take part in the reconnaissance and occupation of the various localities.

Rivera might have continued on his road and left the new arrivals to follow theirs. Since Anza, Moraga, Junípero, and Palou were all on the spot, he was not needed at all in the building of a fort and the foundation of two missions. But this did not fall in with his intention. Nothing could be done unless he were present; and his presence was first required at San Diego, where the rebels, he said, were about to exterminate all the Spaniards. So that he might more quickly get through with his business, Anza suggested giving him his help, which Rivera gratefully accepted. The Lieutenant Colonel took seventeen soldiers with him, and the two leaders set out, accompanied by Pedro Font. When they arrived at San Diego on January 12, the assailants of November 6 had been back in their distant *rancherías* for the past two months.

Rivera had seldom been happier than he was during the weeks that followed. He had never felt so well guarded; the enemy— that is to say, Junípero and the Indians—was far away; he had recovered his chaplain, Lasuen; finally, he was getting his food free, for he had the impudence to invite himself three times a day to Father Fuster's table, devouring the slight store of provisions that the Fathers of San Gabriel and San Luis had sent to their now completely impoverished colleague. Thus he installed himself at San Diego as if for the rest of his life. Between meals he spent his time questioning the soldiers who had been asleep and a few Indians who had been arrested; he described the punitive expeditions he was going to undertake, and he put all this down in his *Journal*. He and Lasuen talked a great deal about Junípero, deploring his responsibility in the attack on the Cosoy. Fathers Amurrio and Fuster echoed their words. Pedro Font would shake his head, asking himself whether all the Fernandinos were not doomed to an imminent martyrdom.

As for Anza, he was boiling with rage, fell ill, and vomited. "To distract him I would make him music on my instrument," writes Pedro Font (who, incidentally, was the first person to whom it occurred that Rivera was unbalanced). "But, Señor," Fray Pedro said to his friend Anza, "have we come to San Diego to help this Commandant despoil poor Father Fuster, who, as you can well see, has no longer either chocolate or candle to give us? Since you are not campaigning, let us go away from here."

On the ninth of February they left. "I shall catch up with you soon!" Rivera promised. On the twelfth they were at San Gabriel. On the fourteenth, Father Paterna brought his neophytes together to hear a concert by Pedro Font. On the twenty-first, Anza set out on the road to Monterey, leaving twelve soldiers and their families at San Gabriel in custody of Sergeant Grijalva. "It was Ash Wednesday," Pedro Font writes. "I celebrated Mass, and I dissolved in tears in the midst of my sermon to see the grief of those we were abandoning."

The caravan made a halt at San Luis Obispo, then at San Antonio, and on March 10 reached Monterey. With the excuse that this was the rainy season, Rivera had refrained from joining it again. But orders from Rivera had been received meanwhile at the Presidio, inasmuch as "his apartment was locked," writes Junípero, "and Anza could not get himself supplied with a mouthful of bread or a piece of chocolate or a bed to sleep on. So then he came to ask the hospitality of Carmel," the Prefect adds, "accompanied by more than two hundred persons."

On March 11 Anza handed over to Junípero the envelope that Pangua had entrusted to him thirteen months before. On the thirteenth he sent Gongora, the sergeant at Carmel, to deliver to Rivera the following ultimatum: "Either you come or you do not come. If you come, be here by April 12 at the latest. If you do not come, tell me, by return of courier, whether I may build the fort on the site that I judge to be suitable. If I have no news from you by the end of this allotted time, I shall leave the country, placing upon you the responsibility for the non-execution of the Viceroy's orders. In the meantime I am about to reconnoiter the bay, as is my duty to do."

He set out on March 20 for San Francisco, accompanied by Moraga, the geodesist Vidal, and Fray Pedro Font. Meanwhile Fray Pedro was recording in his *Journal* what he had observed in the missions. . . .

"Nowhere are adults admitted to a baptism which they have not freely and expressly asked for. The Fathers' corn contributes in large measure to making them want it. The reception of the rite is preceded by a preparation that lasts for at least three months. The catechism in use everywhere is that of Father Catani, which they must all know in Castilian to meet the King's decree. The explanations are given to them by interpreters, for none of the ministers except Father Sitjar, at San Antonio, speaks the Indian language fluently. This acquirement, moreover, is not necessary, since the children learn Spanish quickly; and in any case it would be impossible, since in the same Mission the Indians sometimes belong to tribes that do not understand one another's speech.

"In all the missions the regime which is followed is that of the communal life. The Fathers take it upon themselves to feed and clothe their neophytes, and these eat as much as they want. The 'order of the day,' regulated by the bell, is as follows: In the morning, all are present at Mass which is followed by the catechism and the distribution of the *atole*.[1] After which they all betake themselves to work. The chief meal is at noon: it consists of *pozole*, with the addition of seed kernels, vegetables, and even meat. After this, each one goes back to his occupation. In the evening, the bell assembles the community once more at the church, for the catechism and for prayer. After a final meal—at which, as at those preceding, there is no dearth of *tortillas*—the men, women, and little girls disperse to their cabins. The little boys lodge in the school building, and so do the young girls, who, during the day, learn to sew and to weave, and, at night, are locked in to protect their virtue."

It was in the region of San Gabriel and Los Angeles that Pedro Font saw the ugliest women ("They are all short and plump, like pots") and the filthiest men. Of these and other details about the Indians, he continues: "They would serve us our meals on an old cow-shed door covered with dirt a finger thick; they themselves had hardly less of it on their skins, so that poor Anza would vomit worse than ever. Apart from that, the place is an earthly paradise, where everything grows luxuriantly of itself, and where the animals are all as fat as pigs. I have also noticed almost everywhere that the Indians adore their children, whom they allow to do as they please. On the other hand, they have little respect for their wives, and apparently scarcely any love for them, for they chastise them at every turn, and even when they are pregnant they kick them in the stomach."

---

[1] The *atole* is corn porridge, a very substantial dish; the *pozole* is a thick corn soup; *tortillas* are corn pancakes. To this day, all the Mexicans eat tortillas.

While Pedro Font and his companions are on the shores of San Francisco Bay (where we ourselves shall soon be about to see something other than explorations), let us give our attention to the envelope which Anza had delivered to Junípero, and which, in the form of two documents dated February 7, 1775, contained one of the most remarkable pieces of stupidity and injustice that the mind can conceive. These two documents, the contents of which had been known to Lasuen and Rivera for eight months past, were, first, a License bearing the signatures of all the Discretos of the College of San Fernando, and, second, a letter which only Pangua had signed but which had likewise received the approval of the Discretory. The tenor of this License and this letter will be made sufficiently plain if we look at the two replies that Junípero made to them.

The first of these answers is dated April 13, 1776, the day before Anza, returning now from San Francisco, set out again from Carmel on the way to Mexico. It is addressed to "the Very Reverend Father Guardian and the Venerable Discretory of San Fernando," and it reads as follows:

I have received, on the eleventh of March, last, the License and the letter which accompanied it.

Although I might have been somewhat shamed in doing so, I had the License read then and there to the friars at Carmel,[2] and by a courier who was at that moment leaving for San Diego [Gongora, the bearer of Anza's ultimatum to Rivera], I sent it to those of the other missions, asking them to send it back to me as soon as they had read and signed it. I have also had delivered to Captain Rivera and Father Lasuen the letters that were destined for them, informing them that this Father, attached henceforth to the personal service of the Commandant, would no longer be obliged to obey me in anything incompatible with his new duties. You see what promptness I have brought to the carrying-out of your orders; it will be the same in the future; God grant that I may never lack an iota of holy obedience!

The License started off with praise of the apostolic life. "The missionaries," one reads, "are angels that God sends to men, to

---

[2] Palou, Crespi, Murguia, La Peña, Dumetz, and Cambon, who were part of the household, and Pieras, from San Antonio, who was ill and had been resting there for the last three months.

manifest His will to them." Junípero, who knew this, thanks the Discretory no less for recalling it to him.

How far I am from what I ought to be! [he adds]. So far, that at first I wanted to beg you to retire me, so unworthy am I of them, from those angelic duties which you have entrusted to me. If I do not do that, it is because, after reflection, I have deemed it better, with the help of God, to labor for my improvement until the day when Providence and my superiors shall wish to make some other use of me. I shall promptly carry out your decisions, and shall see to it that the other friars do the same.

The humiliation which I felt at first, moreover, was only an initial impulse; I got hold of myself at once, and I realized that it was my own bad behavior which had provoked the measures of restriction placed upon the exercise of the Prefect's function. I must confess that they are unheard-of, for such measures have never been taken either at San Fernando or at Santa Cruz de Querétaro, to confine myself to the two Apostolic Colleges that I know. If they have seemed necessary, it is evidently because there are abuses to correct. As for the existence of these abuses and the reasons for their being brought to your notice, may I ask you to hear my testimony?

Article I: Injunction against transfer of ministers by the Prefect, unless the ministers themselves should ask for it.

I could confine myself to the transfers made since my return from Mexico City, inasmuch as there was never any complaint before that; but I shall review them all since the beginning. . . . [He shows that all these transfers from 1769 to 1774 were due either to departures which he could not prevent (Parron, Gomez, Viscaíno, Juncosa, Cambon), or to grave reasons "which he will reveal if it is demanded of him" (Somera and Dumetz).] As for transfers that took place after I returned from Mexico City, that is very simple: I have not shifted or moved anyone.

Article II: Injunction against the Prefect's interfering in the temporal affairs of the missions and obliging the missions to help one another.

One day, one of the Fathers at San Luis [it was Cavaller, but the name is charitably passed over in silence] spoke to me of the abundance of his harvest. I replied by urging him to give a little of his corn to the Missions of San Francisco which we thought were about to be founded; he refused. Learning after this that he had promised Rivera to supply provisions for his escort in the future, I reproved him, but without inviting him any longer to come to the aid of his colleagues. This is the only case in which I remember intervening in the temporal administration of the Missions.

Article III: The Prefect's obligation to deliver to each mission what is due it.

This article, also, is no doubt motivated by something that happened at San Luis. In case the story may have been distorted, I will tell it again. At the time of my sojourn in Mexico City, I had portraits of their patron saints painted for the Missions of San Gabriel, San Luis, and San Antonio, which did not yet have them, and charged each of their accounts eighteen pesos to pay the artist. The Fathers of San Luis, alone among the missions, refused the portrait I brought them; I kept it for myself, and promised to reimburse them. Here, Venerable Discretory, is where my sin lies. In the letter I wrote you by the following mail, I neglected to tell you to transfer eighteen pesos from the account of Carmel to that of San Luis. Your Fatherships are free to believe that I wanted to appropriate them, but I assure you that it was forgetfulness on my part. I made amends the next year by mentioning the matter twice in my correspondence. My conscience does not reproach me with any transgression of the Seventh Commandment.

Article IV: The Prefect's obligation to make an equitable division of the common resources, so that no mission shall have cause for complaint.

This has to do with provisions which I brought in and mules which were sent by the Viceroy. In regard to the provisions, if I was not fair, I nevertheless tried to be. I thought I had sent you the list of the distributions I had made. I still possess all the receipts but I have no time to look for them again today. As for the mules, they were allotted in accordance with the attached statement in such a way as to satisfy the most urgent needs. All of them, moreover, have not yet reached here, which is why certain missions have been put at a temporary disadvantage. As soon as the rest arrive, I shall arrange that each mission has its allotment.

In addition to this inventory, the Reverend Father Guardian asks me to indicate the number of mules, cows, and horses just left by Señor Anza in each mission. Once more, this is very simple: he left absolutely nothing anywhere. He even forgot to speak to me again about the *arrobe* of chocolate which cost me fifty pesos and which I ceded to him to get him out of a difficulty in 1774. And if I speak of it again to you, it is that there may be no more talk about my having kept for myself everything Anza brought us!

Article V: Injunction against the Prefect's informing the Viceroy of mission transactions.

In this, obviously, I am as guilty as can be, although I have always sent you copies of the letters His Excellency wrote me and of my answers to them. I purpose to mend my ways, come what may. I regret, however, that you do not lay down with precision the line of conduct which I shall have to follow in the future.

Article VI: I am forbidden to urge the establishment of new missions upon His Excellency, since the College cannot undertake to carry any more.

In asking so urgently for the establishment of San Buenaventura, Santa Clara, and San Francisco, I was doing no more than second the projects which the holy College had adopted long since. Was that not why it sent all these supernumerary friars here? I have always been of the opinion, nevertheless, and I still am, that the apostolic field set aside for us will not be truly cleared for cultivation so long as a few stations have not been founded in the Channel. I shall carry out the orders that are given me, again, leaving it to the Divine Will to take care of the rest.

Article VII: Father Lasuen is assigned as companion to Don Fernando, being named at the same time chaplain at the Presidio and minister of Carmel.

I shall refrain from opposing this in any way. Let us hope that, in recompense, Don Fernando will occasionally do us some little favor. One favor, in any case, which he will always be ready to do the holy College is that of not obliging it to maintain too many missions. . . .

Shall I tell you that I am a little saddened by what is said, here and there, about my imprudences? At San Diego, Father Font heard such stories about me that he wrote to Querétaro in the following terms: "These Fernandinos are on the road to ruin in adding more and more missions in a haphazard fashion, without soldiers, without provisions, without any prudence, forgetting that the Indians always remain Indians, after all." He changed his opinion when he came here; made his apologies; told us, without being asked to, who his informers had been; read us the letter to his Guardian, of which he had kept a copy, and added that he was going to correct it. Whether he did that or not, *per infamiam et bonam famam*, whether we are slandered or extolled, we shall continue, for our part, to do the best we can.

And there, Reverend Fathers, is what I had to point out on the subject of the License. I do not attack it one iota; I accept it with veneration and shall obey it wholly; but it seemed to me that you ought to know how I had behaved in the exercise of my trust, in case things might have been presented otherwise.

Junípero turned this letter of reply over to Anza to take with him when he set out again for Mexico on April 13. It had scarcely gone when he repented having written it. "Since I had learned

that the License owed its existence to reports which had originated here, I believed that I ought to correct it on every point.
On thinking it over I realized that my corrections had turned
into my defense; that is why I did my utmost to get them back
again; but as I had no escort to go and join Anza, my letter continued on its way with him. Although I said nothing but what
was true, I regretted no less that I had justified myself."

These lines were written on October 7, 1776. The License, of
which all the ministers had been able to take cognizance and to
which they had all appended their signatures, was about to go
back to the College. During the seven months that it had been
in force, meanwhile, Junípero had been greatly troubled. "Three
articles especially perplex me," he wrote to Pangua on the above
date. "I beg you, come to my assistance, and enlighten me."

*I: It is forbidden me to give His Excellency information about the
missions.*

You know how our correspondence originated—a correspondence
which was obviously advantageous for the missions and which no
less obviously provoked envy. . . . What puts me in a dilemma is,
on the one hand, this injunction laid upon me by the License, and,
on the other hand, the complete lack of any rule of conduct in which
I am left by you. You do not say to me, "If His Excellency asks you
for information, answer him in such-and-such a way," or else, "Do
not answer him at all," or, again, "Open his letters, send them on to
us with your comments, and we will answer them ourselves." I had
six of these letters by the last boat; three more arrived today by
courier from the Peninsula. I enclose herewith copies of these letters
and my replies. If you consider that they should not be transmitted
to His Excellency, have patience! I shall have done nothing whatever
about it.

A few months ago Señor Anza, exasperated by the obstructions
Rivera was placing in the way of current undertakings, said to the
ministers at San Luis, "But, then, why does the Father Prefect not
inform His Excellency?" "If His Excellency wishes news, let him apply to the College," answered one of the Fathers, "for the Prefect
has been forbidden to write to him. There is to be no more of that
correspondence." I have no alternative, for the future, but to let such
words pass. They have written me from the College that it is to please
Captain Rivera that I have been forbidden to correspond with the
Viceroy. Personally, I lose nothing in not writing. I should lose a

great deal, on the contrary, in not obeying; and therefore I shall take pain to obey, with the grace of God.

II: The Prefect may not transfer a minister in future, unless the minister has requested it.

This article puts me in a worse dilemma than the others, as you may judge from the instances that follow:

First. In a mission which I do not name, I have two ministers whose altercations are a scandal. I have tried to reconcile them: one is willing, the other is not—he even promises his colleague a beating. . . . If he passes from words to deeds, may God help them both! For my hands are tied by the License. Neither of them, you see, is asking me for a transfer. One of them, indeed, the irreconcilable, has for a long time been begging me to move the other; but since the latter is not asking me anything, the scandal goes on. I have quite a file on the matter, and I have marked it "Private documents." I had thought at first that if the License forbade me to make transfers it would at least authorize me to send the incorrigible minister back to the College. But that also is forbidden me: all the friars hold their posts, so to speak, for life. Look at the text: "The Prefect may not oblige a minister to *leave* his Mission. . . ." Tell me, I beseech you, how I ought to set about meeting this situation. . . .

Second. In another mission, one of the ministers is making life unbearable for his colleague, in order to make him ask to be moved. He is succeeding; for his scapegoat is begging me to put him somewhere else. But then it is the humble and good friar whom I am punishing, and the bad one whom I reward! And is it not unjust to inflict upon the victim the necessity for leaving the mission he loves, while his persecutor is enabled to stay on with a companion of his own choice? This, moreover, is what has impelled such a man, and the others like him, to maneuver for the restraint of my authority. I have seen a letter in which they congratulated one another on having succeeded in that.

Third. It is absolutely essential that you should settle the following questions:

A.—When two ministers are in conflict, is the Prefect authorized to move one of them, though neither has made such a request?

B.—When a minister persecutes his colleague and the latter, driven beyond endurance, asks for a transfer, is it the victim or the aggressor whom the Prefect should move?

C.—When two ministers get along perfectly together but behave in such a way as to scandalize the Indians and the soldiers, what ought the Prefect to do if remonstrances continue futile and neither of the offenders asks for a transfer?

D.—When a friar is the object of ill-treatment from his associate but, being resolved to suffer for the love of God, expresses no desire at all, may the Prefect nevertheless move him to another station if he considers him to be needed elsewhere? This case is presenting itself at this moment. [This friar was Juan Figuer.]

III: Missions in need.

I have four of those on hand at present: two to be established (San Francisco and Santa Clara), and two to be restored (San Diego and San Capistrano). The first question put to me by the men I send there is, "What are we going to eat at the beginning?" To answer that, I think of the missions that have a surplus, and ask them to help me. One of them (San Luis) is going to refuse, the only one, I know, which will reply that it prefers to sell its surplus to others. May I oblige it, all the same, to let me have its supplementary foodstuffs if I pay for them from the Carmel cash-box?

. . . So far as I myself am concerned, I tell you once more: I am in accord beforehand with everything the superiors would have me do. I do not offer you my resignation; but if I am a bad servant, may you impose it upon me without waiting for me to offer it.

Junípero remained in this dilemma and virtual impasse until he learned eighteen months later that, Rivera having been dismissed and Pangua himself being at the end of his term, the Guardian had canceled the License.

It will no doubt be wondered what the reasons were that had induced Pangua, and with him Verger and the other Discretos, to listen to Lasuen and Rivera and to make the rulings they did. It seems that there were at least three. The first was pusillanimity. A little while before his death, when he was saying his last Farewell to his beloved College, Junípero was to feel that he must remind it of its vocation: "This demands that we know how to expose ourselves to danger," he was to say then. "This was forgotten; we were afraid of going ahead when opportunity offered; and that is why, perhaps, God is about to punish us by taking away all our missions."

The second reason was cowardice. Faced by a problem to be solved, the Discretos took the easy way: "Rivera, Lasuen, and their fellow plotters are screaming? Let us sacrifice Junípero, who is keeping still. Then they will be quiet, and so shall we!" It was the solution of Pontius Pilate: "Do with this Man what you like, so long as my wife may sleep again and I once more be left in peace." The third reason was envy. The envious suffer from the proximity of greatness, and nothing upsets them like the sight of a neighbor or friend who becomes a "prophet in his own country." The envious in California—Lasuen, whose old father was begging in Biscaya, and who himself, in such a hurry to succeed, was not succeeding; Cavaller, who jumped for joy when he learned that his Prefect had been forbidden to write to the Viceroy in future—these envious men had their counterparts in the Discretory, and their support, added to that of the pusillanimous and the cowardly turned the scale of effectiveness.

Pangua and his Discretos were not mistaken in expecting Junípero to offer no resistance. Any other Prefect, meeting with such treatment, would obviously have sent in his letter of resignation. It would, one may guess, have contained the following passages:

Your decisions, very reverend Fathers, seem to me regrettable, and cannot be complied with. The men who have inspired you to make them are ill informed, and have an interest in deceiving you. Why have you listened only to these men, and made your decisions without preliminary inquiry? . . . I call your attention merely to the following points:

I. Irremovability of the ministers.

Nothing is more reasonable than to avoid separating ministers who are well paired with one another; the life here is so hard that one needs the succor of friendship; so I have always tried to bring together friars from the same country and the same Province. Knowing, on the other hand, that they are naturally attached to the mission they have founded and the Indians they have converted, I have likewise been careful not to tear them away from a task which others might not accomplish so well. But the error lies in setting up a *de facto* situation as a situation *de jure.* Your decree, which abolishes no abuses, is going to create them; it puts a premium on bad conduct. As soon as they know that they hold permanent tenure as a legal right, the two or three disturbed and disturbing elements in my flock escape my control; they will let me go on talking, when I try to correct them, and will do only what they please.

II. Autonomy of the missions in the management of their property.

Here again you have brought legislation to the category of the absolute. The principle of granting the missions economic and financial autonomy is excellent; it is still fitting that the consequences should not be carried to the point of absurdity. Certain ministers need to be checked on. Who is going to do the checking? Will it be you, whose decisions take a year to reach us? Something irreparable could happen in the course of a year. There ought to be somebody on the spot to forestall abuses: somebody, that is, the Prefect. And when a mission is poor, the Prefect should also be able to oblige those that are rich to assist it.

III. My correspondence with the Viceroy.

Have my letters to His Excellency not contributed to the conversion of the Indians to Christianity, and have they ever injured anyone? Let the jealous be reassured! I shall not take advantage of His Excellency's friendship to become a bishop or anything else of the sort. So long as we have the good fortune to have a Viceroy like Señor Bucareli, you should authorize your Prefect to reply to his communications, on condition of obliging him to transmit those replies to you, and leave to you the responsibility of destroying the ones that do not deserve a better fate. I know that Rivera is vigorously opposed to this correspondence. But your acquaintance with Rivera is only with an officer on vacation, assiduous in attendance at the San Fernando novenas. As a Commandant, it is impossible to imagine anyone more lazy, cowardly, stupid, etc. May God bless him! I am far from passing judgment on his conscience; and perhaps he will have a finer place than all of us in Paradise. But meanwhile the Viceroy should be informed of his behavior. Except for Father Lasuen, who reckons on making use of him, and two or three others who like him for himself or against me, all my colleagues are of this opinion. And Father Font, Señor Anza, and the naval officers who see him at work think the same.

IV. In conclusion, I come to Father Lasuen, whom you have given to the Commandant as chaplain without consulting me. This innovation may have far-reaching effects. Were there not enough Fathers here to hear Rivera's confession? Are their Masses not as good as those of Father Lasuen? Does Rivera need—like the King St. Louis— a friar reciting the breviary and discoursing on theology with him? Ah, if these two friends could only confine themselves to dogmatizing and praying together! . . . But it is I who will be the principal subject of their dissertations, and whose authority they will conspire together to destroy. By the same stroke, Father Lasuen escapes from my jurisdiction to whatever extent he may be pleased to determine. . . . In addition, he becomes titular minister at Carmel! . . . No, this time it is too much! That would truly make too many dignitaries at Carmel! Already, at this Mission, there is a Prefect—or, since the License, a quarter-of-a-Prefect—which is myself. There is also a Vice Prefect, my eventual successor, who is Francisco Palou. There is no need for an Anti-Prefect besides, to reinforce my adversaries and make it impossible for me to carry out the duties of my office. That would be anarchy. Would you accept an Anti-Guardian and an Anti-Discretory at San Fernando?

I have transmitted the License to the ministers, informing them that I was offering you my resignation. I now offer it to you in fact, as also does Father Palou, if you do not restore the prerogatives of our office. Neither he nor myself can exercise the authority without having the means to do so. You might as well set us to ploughing the fields with our fingers or reciting our office without the breviary. We hope to find you welcoming our request and at the same time we reserve to ourselves, in the opposite case, the right of appeal to the Commissioner for the Indies, who will decide the question in the last resort. For the rest, whatever decision you may reach and whatever use you may make of my person, you will always find in me, with the help of God, a good Franciscan ready to serve no-matter-where, and respectfully submissive to his superiors. . . .

This imaginary letter would have been good sense itself, for whoever receives improper and excessive orders is justified in arguing that they should be revoked, and any man unjustly maltreated may try to escape from persecution. Yet since the first preaching of the Gospel there have always been those who, following the example of the Christ who was "obedient unto death," knew how to renounce their rights and the wisdom of the world in order to embrace the "madness" of the Cross. Such a one was Junípero, who, far from sulking, protesting, appealing, resigning, bowed his head, accepted humiliation and repudiation, and continued the task set before him with the diminished means that remained to his hand. Will someone say that he was running the risk of seeing his work imperiled, and even wrecked? But a true follower of the Gospel never courts disaster in abiding by the example of Him whose ignominious torture assured the eternal triumph of good and won us our redemption. Perhaps for Junípero, likewise, the final success was due to the heroic and mystical renunciation of those unhappy days.

Twenty-one

*Rivera's Excommunication, the Occupation of
San Francisco, and the Re-establishment
of the Missions of San Diego
and San Capistrano*
[1776]

Protected now by more than thirty soldiers, Rivera was no longer
thinking of leaving San Diego.

He devoted the latter part of January, 1776, to the "administration of justice," acquitting the cuirassiers who had been asleep
on the night of November 5, and degrading Lieutenant Ortega.
Some fifteen natives who had taken part in the attack on the
Cosoy were brought before him. Since there were not enough
jail cells for them all, he had the least guilty flogged and sent
them home; the soldiers struck so hard that one of the Indians
died under their blows. The other natives were held prisoner.
Among them was the neophyte Carlos, who had heard talk of
the right of asylum and cherished a dream of profiting by it.[1]

Rivera consecrated the month of February and almost all of
March to repose. Toward the end of March he decided to make
his first excursion, so to speak, and betook himself to the *rancheria* where one of the leaders of the insurrection was said to
be hiding. The Indians rushed to take up arms. Rivera made haste
to parley with them: he was not coming to make war on the
village, he said, but merely to arrest one guilty man. He was told
in reply that the chief had disappeared, and he hurried briskly

---

[1] The right of asylum was not abolished in Spain until the nineteenth century. It assured at least a temporary inviolability and impunity to the guilty
who sought sanctuary in a holy place. The letters from Junípero to Bucareli
which are quoted in this chapter are dated July 3 and 27, October 8, and November 1, 1776, and March 1, 1777; those to Pangua are dated April 17, July
30, and October 7, 1776, and February 26, 1777.

back to the Presidio at the head of his troop. When he got there, he was informed that during his absence several *rancherias* implicated in the Cosoy attack had sent men under a flag of truce to negotiate peace. "Let them come back," he said, "and I will welcome them with gunshot!"

He also learned that Carlos had escaped from his cell and sought sanctuary in the Presidio chapel; and this news threw him into a state of utter fury. "These things only happen when I am not here!" he cried. "That is proof enough that I should never stir from this spot! Moreover, the chapel, which used to be a shed, does not offer the right of asylum."

He shut himself up in his office and, by letter, called upon Fathers Fuster, Lasuen, and Amurrio to hand Carlos over to him. "And if you will not bring yourself to do this," he added, "I will go and seize him where he is."

The Fathers replied in writing that Carlos could not be handed over unconditionally, and that if the Commandant should go and seize him where he was he would incur excommunication.

That could not stop Rivera. He summoned the troop, restored Ortega to his rank of lieutenant, and, followed by the soldiers, marched toward the chapel with sword unsheathed.

The Fathers were on the threshold, and among them his private chaplain, who adjured him to stop before he committed sacrilege. The frenzied man pushed them aside and defied them.

"Don Fernando," called out Father Fuster, titular minister of the Mission, "if you are so unfortunate as to touch the Christian Carlos I remove you from the communion of the Holy Catholic Church."

"Excommunicate me as much as you please, Fray Vicente! It is not you who will keep me from going to get this brigand," replied the Commandant; and he strode into the chapel and seized the unhappy Carlos, while the Fathers, crushed, went back weeping to the Mission.

From that time, they refused all dealing with him, as canon law demands. The "great Christian" had made himself an outcast from the Christian community. Excluded from the rites of worship and from the sacraments, accursed, exuding the odor of damnation, he took his meals in his bedroom from this moment on, more isolated than a leper. He touched the threshold of madness then, and remained in this state through all the month of April.

It was then that Sergeant Gongora arrived, with Anza's ulti-matum.

Up to this time Rivera had pleaded the rain as an excuse for doing or undertaking nothing. As it was not raining, he fell back on the lack of soldiers. But he soon repented of having written that excuse, which Bucareli would read, and he rushed off on the heels of Gongora. He joined him south of San Gabriel, retrieved his letter and tore it up, demanded in addition the three letters addressed to Junípero by his confrères, was refused them, reduced the sergeant to the ranks, snatched the coveted envelope from him, broke the seals, and read its contents; then he climbed back into the saddle and, with his nine cuirassiers, went on his way north. Which way was he headed? At San Diego it was believed that he had set out on a campaign against the Indians, as he al-leged; in reality he was going to ask Junípero to annul the cen-sure passed upon him and restore him to the communion of the Church.

On April 15, north of San Antonio, he met up with Anza, who, having had no reply to his ultimatum, had left Carmel the day before. Anza called him to account on the subject of San Fran-cisco. Rivera fled from him without listening. He arrived at Mon-terey the next night. "Along with Fathers Murguia, Cambon, and La Peña, I went to see him in the morning," Junípero wrote Pan-gua on April 17. "He handed over to me, opened, the letters from Fathers Lasuen, Fuster, and Amurrio, affirming under oath that the seals had been broken by accident and that he had read noth-ing of what was in them. Then he told me about his excommu-nication, adding that all the soldiers considered it invalid. 'At first sight, I am not of their opinion,' I replied. 'But I will give you mine as soon as I have studied the papers you are bringing me.' All of us agreed, at Carmel, that our colleagues at San Diego were right, and that he was indeed excommunicated; Father La Peña was assigned to inform him of this. He—the Commandant—is about to set out again. The business in the south, according to him, is only beginning; no one but he can settle it. He is going to re-voke his resignation—which was irrevocable—offering to end his days here. The plans for San Francisco, he says, must be given up for a long time. . . . Will the idea the College has of this

'great Christian' not be changed a little, when all this is learned
there? . . ."

More excommunicated and deranged than ever, Rivera dispatched
a courier to Anza on April 17. "It is absolutely necessary that I
speak with you!" he demanded.

"I am continuing on my way without any hurry," the Commandant of Tubac replied from San Antonio. "Join me if you
wish; but I shall no longer negotiate with you except by correspondence, so that His Excellency may form his opinions on
documents at hand."

Rivera had announced that he was leaving again on the nineteenth. Junípero was preparing to accompany him; the Prefect's
presence was pressingly needed at San Diego, where the three
Fathers, disheartened, were talking of nothing but going back to
the College. That was all that was needed to make the Captain
set off stealthily twenty-four hours earlier. Before this he had
found a way of affronting Moraga, the lieutenant at the Presidio.
Above all, he had enjoined him to refuse any escort guard to
Fray Junípero in the future.

Anza arrived at San Gabriel on April 29. Still on the chase,
Rivera joined him there almost at once. Captain Anza settled down
at the Mission; Lieutenant Colonel Rivera set up his tent in the
forest; this precaution, along with the intervention of Father Paterna, who was Rivera's close friend, kept the two officers from
coming to blows. Don Fernando had another demand made to
Don Juan for an envelope he had given him to be delivered to
Bucareli. Don Juan sent it back to him. Fernando begged him
to take along another addressed to Father Pangua, whom he besought to annul the censure against him. Anza sent that back to
him also. Then, accompanied by his guard, the geodesist Vidal,
Pedro Font, half a score of muleteers and some hundred animals,
the Commandant of Tubac set out again for Sonora on May 2,
having accomplished his mission.

At the last moment he had written to Moraga to indicate what
measures should be taken in the not improbable eventuality of
Rivera's soon going completely mad. This prognostication was not
fulfilled. The month of May was, on the contrary, beneficial to
Don Fernando. When he arrived at San Diego he humbly led the
Christian Carlos back to the chapel, and his excommunication was

lifted, in consequence, by his private chaplain. Thus reconciled with the Church, he returned to sit at table with the friars and to be fed at their expense. His next thought was of forestalling Bucareli's anger, which was certain to burst out against him as soon as Anza's report reached the City of Mexico.

He sent off two couriers in succession, one to Loreto and the other to the north. To the Viceroy he announced that, in view of the gravity of the situation and the impossibility that anyone else could stave off the complete ruin of the colony, he would withdraw his resignation; he also informed him of the steps he had just taken for the occupation of San Francisco. These measures formed the substance of the orders which Gongora—now restored to his former rank—was carrying to Grijalva and Moraga. Grijalva was directed to set out at once for San Francisco with the twelve families from Sonora still billeted at San Gabriel; Moraga was to do the same with the two hundred settlers billeted at Carmel; once there, both officers were to begin work on the construction of the fort. But only of the fort! "For as to the missions, I forbid their establishment, and I beg you to inform the Father Prefect Junípero to that effect," he added.

This time his prohibition was inoperative, and his attempt at obstruction was frustrated.

Junípero had friends among the officers and noncommissioned officers who were at Carmel at the beginning of June, 1776: notably, Fernando Quiros and the beloved Canizares, whose *San Carlos* had come into the harbor on June 3; also Diego Choquet, whose *San Antonio* had dropped anchor eight days earlier; not to mention Lieutenant Moraga, Sergeant Grijalva, and especially Gongora, the sergeant at Carmel.

Now all of them except Diego Choquet had orders to go and build the Presidio of San Francisco. Junípero asked them to take Francisco Palou and Benito Cambon with them; they agreed, with joy. "I do not know," he wrote to the Viceroy on June 27, "when we shall be able to start San Francisco and Santa Clara, for the Commandant is still refusing to come to any decision; but I have a piece of good news for you all the same. When I learned that Moraga was about to leave for San Francisco with the Sonora settlers I had the idea of attaching the ministers of one of the projected missions to their party; and that is what has been done. They left on the seventeenth of June, taking their ninety head of livestock with them; Lieutenant Moraga has pledged himself to look out for them. Fernando Quiros and Canizares have taken the bells and the farm implements on their boat. The mission will be two short leagues from the fort; Don Fernando Quiros has generously promised to build it as soon as the authorization comes from the Commandant. The lively enthusiasm they all felt as they set out is a good omen for the future! As for Santa Clara, its ministers are only awaiting the captain's good pleasure and their escort guard to betake themselves to their post. One thing which I dare not ask of you, Excellency, but which I do ask just the same, is a monstrance for the San Francisco Mission, which has none at all." We may assure ourselves that Bucareli sent it.

It is time once more to sing the praises of the Spanish sailors. . . . While the Commander of the *San Carlos*, together with Canizares, was building the church and residence for Palou, the Commander of the *San Antonio* was liberating Junípero, who had been a prisoner for seven months. "As Don Diego Choquet was about to sail," the escaped captive wrote to Pangua, "I begged him to take me with him. This delightful chevalier consented then and there, adding that it was a pleasure and an honor for him to have me on his boat. Along with Father Santa María, one of the naval chaplains who has decided to serve in these missions, I embarked on the twenty-ninth of June, and after a marvelous voyage we arrived on July 11 at San Diego."

Junípero's unheralded appearance plunged Rivera into a complete spasm of mysticism.

"We had scarcely dropped anchor when the Commandant came aboard, accompanied by Fathers Lasuen and Amurrio. He was horror-stricken at the sight of me, as everyone on the boat remarked. And he had no sooner got back to the Presidio when he took to his bed, suddenly ill. To Father Lasuen, who hurried to his bedside, he disclosed a state of profound upheaval in his soul and said that he wanted to begin a new life without any possible delay, that he was anxious to enter the Third Order of St. Francis, etc. Fray Firmin encouraged him eagerly in these holy resolutions.

"It must be understood," Junípero continues, "that a letter he had received from the Viceroy had brought about a mood of extraordinary jubilation a little while before. His Excellency was at last deciding in his favor, acknowledging that the soldiers of

his troop were few in number, etc.—in short, the same old story.
. . . He was in such a state of elation that the Fathers were beginning to wonder uneasily whether by chance the Viceroy was
not disapproving of our enterprises. And they continued to be
worried until Fray Firmin succeeded—I do not know how—in
reading this famous letter. He made one bound, then, from the
Presidio to the Mission residence. 'Set your minds at rest,' he said
to his comrades. 'Señor Bucareli approves so fully of what the
Father Prefect thinks, does, and proposes, and he loves him so
deeply, that he would send poor Rivera to penal servitude if Fray
Junípero asked him to!' Father Lasuen was exaggerating a little,
it seems to me! But the fact is that Don Fernando had read the
letter wrong. His Excellency was indeed willing to acknowledge
that the soldiers were few in number; but he reproached the Commandant no less for having given no aid toward founding San
Buenaventura; and, for the rest, he gave him stern orders, as Fray
Firmin pointed out to him, to follow my advice in everything.
And that is how the poor creature came to be seized with such
terror at the sight of me! He had assumed that the Viceroy was
sending me with terrible instructions from which there could be
no appeal, or else—remembering the fate of Pedro Fages—that I
was again on my way to Mexico City. As soon as he knew that
his fears had no foundation his illness disappeared, and his good
resolutions with it."

The personnel of the *San Antonio* was unwilling to do any less
for the San Diego Mission than that of the *San Carlos* was doing for San Francisco. "As we do not sail until October," Diego
Choquet said to the Father Prefect, "we have time to rebuild the
mission that was destroyed."

The same letter to Pangua tells the story. "As soon as I saw
Rivera again," Junípero wrote, "I made him admit that the region had been pacified, and obtained permission to undertake the
work. We set out for the Cosoy on the twenty-second of July:
Captain Choquet, myself, his pilot, his first mate, a carpenter, and
twenty seamen. They carried their guns and took with them tools,
foodstuffs, and tents. The six soldiers of the escort were attached
to our party, but you know that they no longer work but merely
stand guard. As for the seamen, they fell to wholeheartedly, mixing the mortar and banking up the earth like the Indians. The
Commandant, meanwhile, was grieved to see how well everything

was going. At the end of two weeks he came up to announce that there would not be time to finish the work. Captain Choquet brought up reinforcements of sailors who manufactured seven thousand bricks in three days. On the morning of August 8 the foundations, the stones, the bricks, the wood for the framework, were all ready, and the construction was about to begin when Rivera turned up at the yard. He was smiling.

" 'You have no message to send the Presidio?' he said as he was leaving.

" 'Give my regards to the Fathers and to Captain Choquet,' I replied, 'and tell them I am coming to see them tomorrow.'

"He had scarcely disappeared from sight when a word from the captain informed me of the stoppage of the work. The Commandant had ordered this on the pretext of a possible attack from the Indians. 'Have you warned the Father Prefect?' the Captain and the Fathers had asked him. 'No,' he replied. 'I have not dared.'

"I hurried to the Presidio but I could not make him open his mouth; he listened to me with bowed head in silence. Don Diego Choquet had said to him,

" 'But if you are so afraid of what the Indians may do to us, give me an extra supply of powder, and add three men to the escort guard!'

" 'I will not give up one grain of powder,' he retorted, 'and, as opposed to your demand, I am recalling the escort guard for my own defense.'

"And that evening we were presented with the spectacle of forty armed Spaniards, interrupting a work of this importance and rushing back precipitately into the Presidio-fortress, because a neophyte was saying that an unconverted native had said to him that perhaps the Indians were going to attack! This piece of dubious information had been welcomed without the slightest investigation! The men of the King's navy could not find words for their execration of this officer who was forcing them to behave like cowards. . . . Where do these untoward happenings come from? I do not know. In any case, I do know that for several days past Don Fernando has been going about repeating, with deep sighs, 'Here is the Devil once more, driving me to harass the Fathers!'

" 'But then, Señor,' Father Santa María said to him, hearing him groaning in this fashion, 'you should thrust aside this temptation, since that is what it is!'

"If he would take himself away, Captain Choquet would soon have everything finished. But he will not do that; his presence, he claims, is needed here to pacify the Indians, as it is at San Francisco to begin the Mission. So that here it is his presence, and at San Francisco it is his absence, which make it impossible for us to sow any seed this year. . . . Have I told you that I had to write to him for months to get him to give each of the Fathers his food ration? He was intending to allow us two rations for six Fathers! . . . And after sending me a letter of refusal, here he was coming back to the table to eat our share of farina as if nothing had happened. . . . We have endured all this, however, with perfect serenity."

At the end of the month, there arrived at San Diego a neophyte from the Peninsula, who, having fallen out with the Dominicans, had run away from his mission twenty days before. He told of having seen Sergeant Carrillo at Velicata, waiting there for soldiers who were coming from Loreto and with whom he was to go to Upper California. "These must be the twenty men that the Junta refused me earlier, and that Bucareli is giving us now," Junípero said.

He urged Rivera to send for news. "That is unnecessary," the Commandant replied, curtly. "This Indian has got things wrong."

It *was* those soldiers, however. There were even twenty-five of them! They arrived at San Diego a month later, headed by Carrillo, who brought a voluminous mail. Junípero found three letters from the Viceroy.

"What a joy this is!" he wrote back, on October 8. "Your letter of March 1st informs me that the Audit Office has decided to send at the Royal expense everything intended for the San Francisco Missions. That of March 26 tells me of the soldiers' coming: they have arrived, in their fine uniforms, and completely armed. But it is your letter of April 3, which grants pardon to the guilty men and orders the re-establishment of the Missions of San Diego and San Capistrano, which fills the measure of our happiness. Nothing more was needed to persuade these few unoccupied friars who wanted to return to the College to give up their plan. . . . I cannot find words to express my satisfaction and to tell you again of the gratitude aroused in me by the kindly feelings you show toward me. . . ."

On the subject of the murderous Indians, Bucareli wrote him: "Your arguments have convinced me: I, too, find that we shall gain more from kindness than from severity; I have directed the Commandant, therefore, to abide by what you suggest." And forthwith Junípero had taken with him as companion the Indian named Bernardino, one of the three neophytes who had killed Luis Jaume with their own hands.

"I hope that, thanks to His Excellency's kindness, I have saved his life," he wrote to his Guardian, "and I am certain that Fray Luis, from Heaven where he now is, approves my having acted so." And, always suspicious of Rivera, he added, "If by chance some danger were still to threaten my Bernardino, may I beg you to intervene, to keep him from being killed on me?"

But Rivera was no longer concerned with being disagreeable to Junípero. What the Viceroy was writing him robbed him of any such desire. Bucareli had already reproached him for the non-establishment of San Buenaventura. At present he was referring to the Missions of San Francisco as if they had been in existence for a long time. What wrath he would feel when he learned the truth! So this Commandant had done nothing in three years except refuse to do as he was told and squander the King's money the while? Was this preposterous jumping-jack a traitor? . . . Lasuen was doing no harm this time in giving his "powerful friend" to understand that punishment was near.

Thus, in a few hours, Rivera was entirely transformed. Far from lending his ear to the incitements of the devil, he was moved by great fervor and a devouring zeal. One may imagine a conversation between him and Junípero, on September 29 or 30, while Carrillo and his men were resting after their long journey:

"His Excellency, therefore, forbids the deportation of the guilty men. . . ."

"But of course! How else could it be, Reverend Father Prefect! Your arguments are convincing in every detail. I know well that these Indians are born murderers, and would not expect to be deported for such petty offenses as that. Not for anything in the world, believe me, would I send Father Jaume's poor assassins off to San Blas."

"The Cosoy Mission—"

"It must indeed be rebuilt immediately, Reverend Father Prefect; and since the missionaries ought to be protected like the apple of God's eye, I have determined to double the escort guard: therefore, you will have twelve soldiers at the Cosoy instead of six."

"San Capistrano—"

"It, too, must be re-established at once; I am putting eleven cuirassiers there."

"As for the two San Francisco stations—"

"But, excuse me! Your Reverence is forgetting San Gabriel, where I am adding two soldiers to the escort guard. . . ."

"Thank you. As for the two San Francisco stations—"

"I was coming to that, Reverend Father Prefect; I think of nothing else. How well inspired Your Reverence was, to send Fathers Palou and Cambon to the spot as early as last June! I hope that dear Father Murguia and dear Father La Peña, too, will be setting out without delay for Santa Clara. In any case I am going there in one bound myself."

And on October 11 he was off at a gallop toward the north with twelve soldiers. We shall let him hurry on his way, for from now on he will do neither good nor evil to anyone.

The work at the Cosoy had been resumed on the first of October. The sailors from the *San Antonio* had worked so hard and accomplished so much that by October 25 the work was finished. On that date Junípero signed the title-pages of the registers of baptisms, marriages, and burials which Father Fuster had put in order once more, and on that same day set out for San Capistrano.

His leg had become infected again, and he was suffering from the angina pectoris that was later to cause his death. The caravan was made up of the eleven soldiers of the escort guard, some cuirassiers lent temporarily by the Presidio, servants, muleteers, and a large mule train. Father Amurrio, one of the original founders of the Mission, was attached to the party. The other founder, it is recalled, was Lasuen, who persisted in running at Rivera's heels instead of going back to his post. Father Mugartegui, supernumerary at San Luis, had been named to replace him. The Mission, founded and abandoned a year earlier, was re-established and re-inaugurated by Junípero on November 1, 1776.

Two days later Junípero set out for San Gabriel to recruit an extra supply of manual labor and to levy on the San Buenaventura livestock what might be needed to put the reborn Mission on its feet. On the way back he came near to being killed.

In a hurry to reach his destination he had gone on ahead, and was riding with a neophyte on one side and a soldier on the other in the van of his herd of cattle, when, some twenty-five miles from San Capistrano, they fell upon a band of Indians who had smelled out loot. The natives were already voicing their war cries and drawing their bows.

"Woe betide you if you kill the Father!" cried the neophyte. "For there are many soldiers coming on behind us who will massacre you to the last man!"

It needed no more than that to stop the Redskins. Junípero signaled them to draw near, and handed out to them those multi-colored glass beads which he always took with him on a journey. He made the Sign of the Cross on each one's forehead, and invited them to come to see him at San Capistrano; and they parted good friends.

He left San Capistrano on December 6 and reached San Gabriel four days later. There he met Father Mugartegui, who was going to join his Mission, and Father Lasuen, who had been planted here by Rivera: since his conversion he no longer wanted a private chaplain. . . . The Captain had kept Lasuen until they got to San Gabriel; then he had run off without him, dashing on impetuously toward Monterey. The reign of the "powerful friend" was drawing to a close, and Fray Firmin had just asked Pangua to let him return to the College.

Junípero had the sense of a general rout. Lasuen and Santa María were in revolt. Paterna had rushed off to San Diego to sail on the *San Antonio*, which was about to leave. Amurrio was wondering up to the last moment whether he would take the ship himself. Fuster wanted to hear no more of his former neophytes. The poor Prefect, whose hands were tied now by the License, wrote to Father Guardian Pangua:

The letters from His Excellency have decided Father Amurrio to stay on. But Father Fuster is absolutely determined on a transfer: he has taken a horror of these Indian parricides who killed his fellow minister; only to think of them fills him with nausea. We shall need another man than he at San Diego. It is the portico of the missions. There is a presidio there; the ships make it a port of call; there must be a friar there who is well brought up, endowed with maturity of mind and with adroitness. It is Father Lasuen who would be suitable for this post; he would do so much good there! How much I have besought him to take this mission in hand! He answered that he had no taste for it; that he would only accept if he were given orders to that effect, and that those orders must come from you. [Why not from the Pope? Did the Prefect of the Missions, then, no longer have any authority?] I am at an impasse. Must I myself take over San Diego and desert Carmel? I shall resign myself to doing that if it is necessary, although my chest is beginning to trouble me a good deal. Fortunately, however, it is still bearable. . . . What do they have against this ill-starred mission? When I saw Father Lasuen leaving with the Commandant, I went to call on Father Santa María in his room and suggest that he become associate to Father Fuster, who was with me. How I was received! He flew into a rage, reproaching me with the affront I was putting upon him by offering him, at the last minute, a post that nobody wanted. I did not succeed in calming him down. Since then he has sulked and has refused to speak to me. Before I left for San Capistrano I went to take leave of him. "Well, what news, Father Santa María?" I said, by way of addressing him. He did not reply. "Then good-bye! I leave you with God!" I said. He came with all the others to see the caravan off; but no more then than before did he consent to say farewell to me.

Father Paterna was there; happily for me, he had missed the boat by one day. Since the License forbids me to command, I implored; I besought him to go with Father Fuster to officiate at the Cosoy while waiting. . . . He agreed, on condition that it should be, as I said, "while waiting." That is as far as we have got. While I was at San Capistrano and San Gabriel, Father Santa María never stirred from San Diego for fear of encountering me; but no sooner had I left San Gabriel than he was seen arriving there. Will he stay there, or will he take the boat? I have no knowledge as to that. Perhaps, after all, he has no more need of my permission in one case than in the other.

Such were the effects of the License. Following Lasuen's example, the restless souls went running where they would. Instead of commanding, the Prefect entreated, and saw his entreaties thrust aside. So greatly had his authority been curtailed that he himself no longer knew how much was left to him; and with a plethora of ministers he could no longer find one to replace a martyr. Diego Choquet had said to Rivera as he left the Cosoy, "You are dishonoring the Spanish sailors in forcing them to flee well armed before the Indians!" So too Pangua and his Discretos, with their License, were in process of turning Luis Jaume's fellow workers into cowards.

Temporarily reassured as to San Diego and San Capistrano, Junípero was burning to know what was going on in the north. Had Palou founded the Mission of San Francisco? What progress had been made with Santa Clara? Was Rivera still sufficiently converted not to ruin everything?

He left San Gabriel toward the fourteenth of December and arrived at the site set aside for San Buenaventura. The Santa Barbara Channel began there. The trail ran along the sea for a distance of about seventy-five miles. "It was the third time that I had traveled through this region," Junípero wrote Bucareli. "The storm, the raging sea, the wind, and the torrential rains kept us from following the beach, and forced us to clamber up perilous paths where we sank up to our knees in mud. When shall I be able to pay those dear Indians the debt of gratitude I contracted then? I, who am so little susceptible to emotion, I would feel my eyes brimming with tears when, taking me around the waist, they would pull me out of the bogs and help me scramble up the slippery slopes which I should not have been able to climb either afoot or on horseback. Some of them went along with us in groups for days. When I was seized with the desire to sing, they would sing with me. I blessed them as they went away. And when others saw that, they came up to me and besought me to make the sign of the cross on their foreheads, too. I have loved them, and they have been waiting for the Gospel, for a long time, Excellency— these dear Indians—but now they have won a further claim on my affection and devotion."

When he reached San Luis Obispo on December 27, our traveler found half the mission buildings in ruins, his "dear Indians" having deliberately burned them a month before. He spent New Year's Day in the midst of these ruins in company with Fathers Cavaller and Figuer, the ministers, and the former chaplain Lasuen, who was continuing to follow his own inclinations, and had come from San Gabriel with Junípero. "He was counting on resting at San Luis while awaiting events." It was understood that events would be forthcoming; for a high personage, soon to become known, had made his appearance in the country.

The fact remains that Lasuen did not quite know what was go-

ing to become of him. It had done him no good to put all his
irons in the fire. The thread of his intrigues had got terribly
tangled. His private chaplaincy had yielded nothing. He had just
refused to return to San Capistrano; he had likewise refused the
San Diego Mission. He was earnestly requesting to be sent back
to the College; but was there a succession open at San Fernando?
He would have been agreeable to the exchange of his situation
as Anti-Prefect for that of Prefect, but Junípero had not resigned,
he did not seem to be near death, and Bucareli liked him more
than ever. So then? . . .

At the last moment Lasuen made up his mind to ask Junípero
for the explanations he had had three weeks to try to get. "At
the very moment when I was leaving San Luis," Junípero wrote,
"he came to me, begging me to tell him whether, in a word—and
contrary to what he was able to believe—I still loved him." Meanwhile, the order for departure had been given. The little Prefect
had just been hoisted into the saddle. The soldiers had mounted
their horses. It would take four days to reach San Antonio. Among
the lowing of cows, the pawing of mules, the cries of the cowherds, the heavy caravan was getting under way. "Two mules,
often changed, had been carrying the Santa Clara bells since we
left San Diego; I had taken on another part of the Mission's equipment at San Gabriel; the rest of the way from San Luis I led its
cattle along with me—eight hundred animals in all, of which only
one small calf strayed away. . . ."

What, then, was driving Lasuen to this last minute step? Cal-
culation? Remorse? Confusion? . . . In the absence of documents,
we do not flatter ourselves that we can make out the Lasuen of
January, 1777. Whatever his idea, he had chosen his time badly.
This was not the hour for "the frank and cordial explanations he
desired," Junípero wrote, "but I promised to give them to him in
writing. I have done that. A copy of my letter is attached herewith."

Regrettably, neither this copy nor the original has been rediscovered. It must have been admirable, that letter, to have accomplished—or at least to have permitted—the miracle that took place
shortly afterward. It transformed the behavior and—why not admit it?—the very heart of Lasuen, who returned to the fold of
dutiful obedience and from that time on was Junípero's friend in
perfect rectitude and loyalty until the day when he became his
successor and the continuer of his work.

Twenty-two

The Founding of San Francisco and Santa Clara
[1776-1777]

When Junípero returned to Carmel on the fifteenth of January, 1777, after six and one-half months of absence, he had the joy of learning that the Missions of San Francisco and Santa Clara had at last been founded. Palou recounts the course of events.

"On orders from the revered Father," he writes, "Father Cambon and I had left Carmel on the seventeenth of June, 1776. We traveled with the land expedition, commanded by Lieutenant Moraga; in addition to twenty-five families of settlers and the soldiers, it was taking along with it the future Presidio's cattle and our own. The agricultural implements and the rest were coming on the *San Carlos*, commanded by Quiros and piloted by Canizares. Having the idea that the idiom of San Francisco was similar to that of Monterey, we had taken two interpreters from Carmel with us; but our idea was mistaken, so that in fact our interpreters were of use for nothing but looking after the cows.

"We reached the Bay of San Francisco, forty leagues [100 miles] north of Monterey, on the twenty-seventh of June. The royal encampment was set up on the shore of a vast arm of the sea which extended fifteen leagues inland: it was there that the Mission was to rise. Fifteen tents were put up, and we waited for the *San Carlos*. At the end of a month it had not yet arrived, and there was no sign of life from Rivera; so the Lieutenant took it upon himself to begin work on the Mission. When the boat appeared on the horizon he interrupted this labor; leaving us six cuirassiers and two settlers, he started for the harbor with the rest of the column. Delayed by adverse winds, the *San Carlos* did not make land until the eighteenth of August. As soon as it did, the sailors joined the soldiers in building the fort and the Presidio, which were opened on the seventeenth of September. Then the men turned to the completion of the Mission, which was situated two leagues from the harbor, and we inaugurated it without Rivera's authorization on the ninth of October. No native was present at the ceremony: in the face of an attack by their hereditary enemies, the Salsonas, they had all fled in their reed canoes. They returned six months later from the distant island where they had taken refuge, and frequented the Mission from that time on."

Palou goes on to describe the men and the customs of this period along the California coast from San Diego to San Francisco. His information is of unparalleled value, as no historian had penetrated that region before him since the beginning of the world. . . .

"At San Francisco and in the country roundabout," he writes, "the Indians are of medium height and with swarthy skin, as if they were sunburned; elsewhere there are those who are taller and whose skin is white. In the north, men and women often cut their hair, especially when they are in mourning for a relative or friend. In such a case they cover head and body with ashes, as is also done by the Indians of the south. But the latter are too proud of their magnificent hair ever to cut it. The women let it fall down their backs in carefully combed tresses; the men coil it turban-fashion, and make use of it so, as a purse in which they put small articles and tidbits that are given them.

"The food of the natives in Upper California is what the sea and the forest offer them. The women gather certain herbs and wild berries, strawberries and ripe fruits, as well as bulbous roots of which some are edible and others serve to make soap. They also collect acorns and various other seeds, which they reduce to a meal from which they make pies, porridges, and cakes. The men go fishing and hunting. They catch songbirds, quail, duck, rabbits, and all kinds of fish, not to mention the shellfish that swarm hereabouts. When it so happens that they catch a whale, there is a general celebration throughout the tribe. They cover the huge beast with earth and make a great fire around it; once it is cooked and smoked, they carve it up and hang the pieces on the trees as reserve stock.

"Nowhere between San Diego and San Francisco have we encountered any trace of religion or idol-worship. My colleagues and myself found there a clear slate, and we had no opposition in winning an opening for the mysteries of our Faith. The people who were ill, however, always attribute their maladies to some personal enemy who has the evil eye and has cast a spell upon them. There are also old sorcerers, some of whom make a specialty of bringing rain, others of attracting whales to shore; nothing was easier for us than to unmask the imposture of these exploiters of public credulity! In the north they burn the dead; in the south they bury them here and there; in the Channel region, they maintain cemeteries.

"The men go as naked as Adam before the Fall, without being any more embarrassed than he was. For protection against cold they smear themselves with a thick hide of mud; when the sun begins to shine, they wash themselves and get rid of this mortar. The women and girls, more modest, wear two aprons made of rushes, one which falls from the waist to the knees, the other, of equal length, behind; when it is cold they put a third apron over their back.

"Marriage is not subject to any ceremony. People live together until such time as they no longer agree. In case of separation the children ordinarily go with their mother. In speaking of her former mate the woman will say, 'I am no longer with him'; in speaking of his former companion the man will say, in the most natural way in the world, 'I have left her.' One sees old households, nevertheless, where parents and children continue to live in agreement and to love one another. Custom wills that a married man should consider his sisters-in-law and his mother-in-law as so many wives also. No jealousy results from this among the women, moreover, each one regarding the children of the others as her own, and all living in cordial relations under the same roof. Polygamy diminishes, it must be added, in measure as our Faith spreads. May God bring an end to infamous vice also! We encountered one example of it at Santa Clara and another at San Antonio. In the Channel region relations between men are, alas, more numerous, for there one counts two or three per village."

It was a great comfort to Rivera when, returning to his long-deserted Presidio in November, 1776, he learned that Francisco Palou had founded the Mission of San Francisco. What were Fathers Murguia and La Peña waiting for, then, to do as much at Santa Clara?

They were waiting, Palou replied, for "the authorization we did without and especially for their escort which the Commandant has been using as his guard for the past year."

The zeal of Don Fernando was just now a consuming passion. It became even more so when he learned that the Governor of Loreto had made his appearance in Upper California. As a matter of fact, Felipe de Neve, who had arrived at San Diego toward the end of November, was proceeding slowly on the road to Monterey. Rivera, who felt that this journey augured no good, picked up Father La Peña and dashed north with him to found the Mission of Santa Clara.[1] They established themselves at the extremity of the arm of the sea mentioned above, thirty-seven miles from the harbor of San Francisco, on the banks of the Guadalupe River. There Father La Peña celebrated Mass for the first time on January 12, 1777; some ten days later Father Murguia joined him, with the bells and the cattle that Junípero had brought from San Luis.

On the eleventh of February Governor Neve made his entry into Monterey. He delivered to Junípero several letters from the Viceroy.

"I see how you have suffered from the interruption of the work at San Diego," Bucareli wrote, "inasmuch as the reasons adduced were absurd. Through Don Diego Choquet I am acquainted with them, and I have been greatly displeased. I have been no less displeased to learn that my orders concerning the foundations of San Francisco were not carried out. . . . I assume at least that the San Capistrano Mission has been re-established. If it has not been, may Your Reverence not grieve! The new Governor will make amends for the remissnesses of the old one, and, knowing him, I am sure that he will act in conformity with your desires. . . . This very day I shall see to it that Rivera receives the order to leave the country at once."

Rivera's punishment was not such as might have been feared. In 1774 Galvez, learning that Rivera was succeeding Fages, had written to the King, "The place of this mediocrity is not at Monterey. Let him be stationed at Loreto as deputy to the Governor of the Two Californias, whose own residence will be at Monterey." This was the solution that Bucareli himself might have

[1] St. Clara of Assisi (1194-1252), the spiritual daughter of St. Francis, founded with him the Order of Poor Ladies, or Clarisses (Poor Clares), in 1212.

suggested. For his part Junípero did not want the men who drew up the License to imagine that the Commandant's dismissal emanated from any action of his. "I have nothing to do with Don Fernando's departure," he wrote to Pangua, on February 26, 1777. "His friends are at liberty to go on ascribing to him all the virtues in the world; I shall be henceforth exempt from contradicting them when they extol his wisdom, his prudence, and his other fine qualities. What remains for me to do—and what I shall by no means fail in doing—is to ask God in my poor prayers to bless him and make him happy."

Rivera left immediately, taking with him his savings and his *Journal*. Passing through San Gabriel, he handed to his friend Paterna a promissory note for two bulls stolen by deserters and a receipt for two mules which he took away, and which perished "in the King's service." Then he went on his way toward the Peninsula.

As far as Velicata the road was still not without danger. When he reached that point he breathed freely again. He was re-entering a countryside that had been pacified: the Indians had not killed anyone there for more than a century. He himself had spent twenty-five happy years in this bit of the world. Those were the good days: people would say to him "Go!" and he went; they would say "Come!" and he came. Then the period of responsibilities and misfortunes had begun for him. After having charged him with taking away the missionaries' cattle, and having made him march in the vanguard of Portola's expedition, the Visitor General had deprived him of his job because of that old story of missions' being pillaged. Finally there had been this hand-to-hand tussle with Junípero, which lasted three and one-half years and from which he emerged bruised and vanquished. At San Borja he again saw the former Mission of Lasuen, his private chaplain. There was a fellow, he thought, whom one could trust! To think that I, Father Pangua's friend, who have always said my prayers so faithfully, that I have been excommunicated by this Lasuen! He arrived at Loreto. Was he going to have a little luck from now on? This was a quiet place, protected from the arrows of the Redskins; his duties here, for which he would continue to draw three thousand pesos, would be safe and simple. Above all, Junípero would no longer be around, with his mania for "founding missions in every corner" and wanting to get Rivera killed by the Indians. . . .

Yet destiny had it that these Indians should get the better of him. He was an incomparable man for recruiting soldiers, was Rivera; applicants for enlistment as cuirassiers used to come running to his call. After leaving him in peace for three years at Loreto, his chiefs sent him to raise troops in Sonora. His orders were to lead them then into Upper California by Anza's road. It was on this occasion, as we shall see, that the Yumas of the Rio Colorado murdered him, leaving his body abandoned for three months on the sand.

Junípero continued to commend him to God "in his poor prayers," and when Rivera was spoken of in his presence he would avoid making the least criticism of him. "He was as strong as an oak tree; I have never seen such perfect health!" was all he would say of this sick man.[2]

[2] He left a widow and three children, who had a hard time getting possession of the property he left, as is shown by the files relating to this matter which are preserved in the Archives of Mexico.

Twenty-three

Neve Succeeds Rivera
[1777]

Rivera's departure was followed by a few months of calm. If he had not been the man who had chosen to suffer for his work, Junípero might have been able to look forward to a period of tranquillity.

The respite of the moment was due, however, to the slowness of the mails and the fact that Neve, ignorant of the changes that had unexpectedly taken place in Mexico City, believed that it was Bucareli who was still to be his chief. As for Bucareli, he wrote about Neve to Junípero on December 25, 1776: "I have liked that officer since I first knew him in Spain. He will earn your affection by establishing the missions you want, as I have instructed him to do. I have a guarantee of this in his fine qualities and the zeal that distinguishes him in the King's service."

Everywhere he went, Neve would leave a few mules, a few horses, and a great many promises. "You are too poorly off," he would say to the ministers, "and not enough is done for you. The King must loosen his purse-strings. You can count on me to induce him to do so."

To the Prefect of the Missions he promised the moon and the stars: livestock *en masse*, fruit trees, aid for immigrant families, and especially the early establishment of the three Missions of the Channel: San Buenaventura in the south, Santa Barbara in the center, and La Purisima Concepción in the north.

Junípero could scarcely believe his ears. He was taken in, and continued to be so for some time. "God be praised," he wrote Bucareli on March 1, 1777, "for having sent us at Monterey—which has been promoted to being the capital of the two Californias—a Governor who has made up his mind to embrace your ideas and carry out your orders!" And on the sixth of June he wrote to his Guardian: "What you have said about the capacities of the Lieutenant Colonel seems to me quite exact. He makes an excellent impression on me so far."

At the moment when these lines were being sent out from Monterey, Verger was again becoming Guardian of San Fernando for a term of three years. As soon as Pangua had learned of Rivera's dismissal, he had recovered his senses and repealed his fantastic License. But Junípero knew, before he had even been informed of this, that the office of "Anti-Prefect" had been abolished and its incumbent requested to return to the ranks.

"I thank you," he wrote to the Superior of the College in this same letter of June 6, 1777, "for having induced Father Lasuen not to leave. On the receipt of your letter he bowed his head beneath the yoke and accepted San Diego, where, as I was saying to you, his consent alone was needed for filling the post. I have given him all the encouragement I could and have assigned Father Figuer, whom he wanted, to be his associate."

Lasuen had come to make his submission a week before. Another former friend of Rivera—who had traveled 400 miles to reach Carmel—accompanied the leader of the conspirators. Junípero's report continued: "Father Paterna has also come in all humility to ask again to be allowed to serve, even as a supernumerary if I should have nothing better for him." Paterna replaced Figuer at San Luis.

"I still have no news of Father Santa María," Junípero added. This Santa María, described as "so difficult to handle," made an equal submission a little later, and Palou accepted him as supernumerary at San Francisco.

Let us note, finally, the "conversion" of a man who, however crabbed he might be, was most excellent, otherwise, in his management of the Mission farm. Father Cavaller, even while engaged in the restoration of his burned-out Mission, was himself becoming his Prefect's good angel with the corn he grew. "Not only has he given eleven fanegas [17 bushels] to Father Mugartegui for San Capistrano," Junípero wrote, "but he has let me have twelve fanegas [18 bushels], which my mules have carried away for Santa Clara."

As a result of all this, there was no one left who sulked or was jealous. When they saw how Junípero behaved under test they all gave in. They had never obeyed him so well as after the period when he could no longer command them. Such is the strange power of saintliness over naturally religious souls. After the actual Person of Christ, and His Word, it is the saints who most attract us to God. Their kindliness touches us; their humility disarms us; their purity of heart and their self-denial awakes our compunction; what is best in us is encouraged by their example. How many souls that would otherwise have remained empty and sterile have come to fruition through having encountered a saint!

Junípero's influence over his ministers attained enormous strength and scope. It extended as far as San Fernando, where the envious ceased to envy, and where from this time on the Discretos were guided by his judgment and advice. From 1777 on, the fact is, he imposed his wishes upon them.

Perhaps his greatest success was to have made his fellow workers heroes in spite of themselves. It was as if he carried them along with him by his own strength. Tired, disgusted, surfeited with effort and discouragement, they had many times of wanting to give up and go away; among others, Lasuen, Sanchez, Amurrio, Mugartegui, Santa María, Paterna, Figuer, and Palou were more than once on the point of taking ship again. He would say to them:

"I know very well that your ten-year enlistment period is at an end, but that is not a reason for leaving me alone. Since no one is being sent to help me here, put off your departure for a little while."

From the eighteen men who were left to him, Amurrio was the only one he lost in eight years.[1]

What letters he had to write them! The following was addressed to Juan Figuer, a friar of great virtue, and one to whose prayers he attached much value. In addition to the reasons already indicated, the fear of being killed—cut to pieces like Luis Jaume —sometimes moved Juan Figuer to the urgent wish to go back and seek sanctification at the College. Junípero wrote to him, on March 30, 1779:

[1] Amurrio reached Mexico in 1779. Lasuen, Sanchez, Paterna, Figuer, and Santa María died at their posts, as did Crespi, Murguia, Cruzado, Sitjar, Fuster, Cavaller, and Dumetz. The other missionaries of Junípero's band did not leave California until after his death: Riobo in 1786, Noriega in 1787, Mugartegui in 1789, Cambon in 1791, Pieras, La Peña and Noboa in 1794.

Very dear friend, my Señor:

Your letter reminds me of a story I read in an old book. As matins were beginning in one of our convents, a Brother went to find the Father Guardian and whispered in his ear, "My Father, I ask your permission to go back to my cell, for I really am not feeling well." "My Brother," replied the Father Guardian, "go quickly to your place, for the love of God, and sing matins with us; for if those here who do not feel well could go back to bed we should all leave the choir, with myself the first to go; and matins would not be celebrated at all."

Is it these elections of the alcalde and the magistrates that impel you to go back to your cell? But wait, then, until they have taken place! How do you know—as I am writing to dear Father Lasuen— if the thing will be as terrible as you imagine? In any case it will be no more serious than what we are going through on that account at Carmel.

What is pulling you down, over and above that, is the trouble the Presidio is giving you, the fear of a revolt, the poverty of your Mission.

You know, as for the distresses that the Presidio visits upon you, I guarantee that they are nothing beside what we are suffering here and what is being endured by the Fathers of San Fernando. There are vexations everywhere, my dear friend, and there always will be. . . .

If I did not know that one is wasting one's time, as the proverb says, in preaching to a preacher, what a fine sermon on the benefits of suffering I could treat you to! But I prefer to send you to that library from which St. Bonaventura used to say that he had drawn all his knowledge, that is, to the foot of the Cross.

My dear friend, when you are engaged in winning souls to God, and when no one can do this at San Francisco as well as yourself, are you going to look backward and refuse to keep your hand to the plough? When an ox refuses to do his work in the fields, what does he deserve but to be driven off to the butcher? Who knows if several of the men who have gone away are not now regretting that action? . . . I think, at all events, that they would have done better not to desert.

This is the third time, and for the same reasons, that you have asked me to let you leave the Mission. Obviously, I authorize your departure, for, in justice, you have the right to such authorization. But justice is not everything; there is charity. What St. Paul was speaking of when he said, "Love urges me on. . . ." Can you testify, in your behalf, that it is this charity and this love which are urging you on to return to Mexico? . . . No, my dear friend, you are not going to abandon us, are you? You are going to continue to sing matins with us all the way through? . . . God, who permits suffering, will grant you grace to bear it. . . . However you decide, write to me soon. You know that you are speaking to someone who respects you, who desires your happiness and your good, who is truly your friend. . . .

And on reading this letter, Father Figuer, like all the others, decided to seek sanctification where he was and to wait a little while longer before deserting.

Neve, for his part, waited only six months before revealing himself as the missions' implacable enemy.

Master of perfidious tactics, he at once attacked Junípero's correspondence. On the eighth of August, 1777, Lasuen, who had only just arrived at the Cosoy, wrote to inform his Prefect that twelve neophytes had been carried off by the Presidio. He wrote him again on October 30 and 31, November 2 and 24, and finally on March 24, 1778. Now Junípero acknowledged receipt of these six messages only on July 10, 1778. Instead of one month, letters would henceforth take seven or eight to reach their destination.

Neve was violating the Law of the Indies in taking over and making use of the newly converted Christians against the will of the missionaries. "As soon as I received your letter," Junípero wrote to Lasuen on July 10, "I went to protest. Señor Neve responded that the question of the laborers was no longer at issue, inasmuch as the Presidio, not having enough food for them, had been obliged to send them home. Some weeks later he came up to me as I was riding away after Mass, and said to me casually, with his spiteful little smile, 'By the way, I have ordered the Lieutenant at San Diego to take back those laborers we were discussing and feed them, upon my word, as best he can!' I went on my way without replying. . . . If the order is carried out, try to persuade the Lieutenant to choose those men among the Indians who are least assiduous in church attendance. Since the Law is no longer respected, we have no other recourse than to discuss and negotiate."

To the other items of news Lasuen sent him, Junípero replied:

"My thanks to your Reverence and to Fray Juan Figuer for having transferred the bones of my beloved Luis Jaume from the

Presidio to the place where he yielded his saintly soul to God. While awaiting the resurrection he will rest, thus, among those Indians whom he loved and who showed him so little gratitude. . . . You tell me that four of his murderers have been condemned to death," in spite of Bucareli's ruling which granted them pardon. "This," the letter continues, "grieves me greatly. If the sentence is not revoked, stay with them through the night before their execution. Baptize them in the prison. Pray with them, and do not leave them until the tragic end. Try to procure for each of them a white tunic, reaching to their feet, in which they may be clothed at the moment of the *Accipe vestem candidam* ["Put on this robe of innocence"]; and may they keep it in death and in the tomb.

"In regard to the reduction in your escort, when you were asking to be more effectively guarded," the letter went on, "the Governor, to whom I protested immediately, exclaimed,

" 'But what have they to worry about, like that, at San Diego? It is like the ministers at San Capistrano being alarmed because the Indian Clement had been struck down and the prisoners who were arrested had avowed that they wanted to kill them. . . . If the soldiers struck down the Indian Clement, it was because he was running away and there was reason to suspect that he was about to injure us. As for the prisoners, don't the Fathers know that the Indians answer Yes to every question, and if they were asked whether they wanted to kill the Pope they would reply that this was precisely what they meant to do?'

" 'But when all is said and done,' I replied, 'those two Fathers at San Diego are not children: they are sensible men who have shown their mettle; if they ask for additional soldiers it is because they need them. I have confidence in their judgment, and if you refuse to protect them there is nothing for me to do but direct them to withdraw to the Presidio.'

" 'Well, my word, that is all the same to me!' he retorted. 'If you think that I shall be sorry to see this mission suppressed—' "

This rejoinder, which had burst from the Governor and disclosed his true sentiments, both enlightened Junípero and filled him with consternation.

"I recommend," he continued, writing to Lasuen on April 22 and July 10, 1778, "that you keep the rooms you have at the

Presidio ready for use, and everyone is able to understand why. Do not leave the Mission, however, except in case of extreme peril; do not allow yourselves to be alarmed too soon. May it be sweet to you to reflect that if you are killed it will be because you belong to Christ. As I should gladly accept the same fate! . . . Yet, if the devil is to be driven to still further fury, we must do our best to keep you, so as to go on increasing the number of Christians; and no precaution, therefore, is superfluous."

He himself believed it was his duty not to expose himself unnecessarily to peril; but how he would have loved to be a martyr, if that had been God's will!

"In the days that followed the burning of the Cosoy, an evil wind blew over all the coast," Francisco Palou records. "The fear of revolt was everywhere. There were six of us Fathers then at Carmel: Junípero, Fray Crespi, and we four ministers who were to be sent to the San Francisco and Santa Clara Missions. The rumor was going about that the Sanjones, evilly disposed Redskins who lived six leagues [15 miles] away, were getting ready to attack the Mission; and one evening one of our Indian women came running to us in terrified dismay.

" 'It is to be this coming night!' she cried. She had seen the Sanjones, armed to the teeth, assembling *en masse* in the forest.

"It was too late to confirm the report. The Presidio was put on the alert, and the Commandant took horse with the troop. Junípero was a man transfigured.

" 'Courage, my dear colleagues!' he said to us. 'Perhaps the moment has come to yield God the witness that he expects of us.'

"We made our confession one to the other. As we were lodged, as usual, in timber huts covered with rushes, which caught fire like kindling, we decided to spend the night together in the smithy, which had mud walls and a palisade around it. A soldier went in there with us. It was quiet; rain was falling; we were tired; we should have liked to get a little sleep. But Junípero would not let us. Habitually so given to silent reflection, he never closed his mouth for one instant until morning, so exuberantly did he continue to rejoice over the approach of danger. As a matter of fact, nothing happened. Was it that the rain had held the enemy back from attacking, or had the Indian woman, with her terror of the Sanjones, cried out in premature alarm? However that may be, we were all of us very much frightened, with the one exception, as I have said, of God's servant Junípero."

Neve changed his attitude in July, 1777, at the precise moment of learning that Bucareli had ceased to be his chief. Since the beginning of the year, in fact, the two Californias had been no longer under control of the government of Mexico. They had been detached from it to form, with New Biscaya, Coahuila, Texas, New Mexico, Sinaloa, and Sonora, a General Commandery called that of the "Interior Provinces," of which Arispe became the capital and Teodoro de Croix the first Commandant. Today these territories correspond to a half-score of states, of which some belong to Mexico and some to the United States.[2]

The Knight Teodoro de Croix, who was born at Lille-en-Flandre in 1730, was the nephew of the Viceroy, the Marquis Charles de Croix, with whom we became acquainted at the time of the conquest.

He was a boorish sort of man, a domineering martinet, who seemed to have received his education from his aristocratic father's stablemen. Did he love the Indians? His *Memoirs* would give us to understand that he did. He loved them as one may love animals who will one day become men, whereas Junípero and his fellow workers loved them as their equals and treated them as their brothers in Christ. De Croix was anticlerical like his uncle; he was an advocate of the secularization of the missions; he held the missionaries in little favor. Yet of all the friars it was the Franciscans whom he found least intolerable. An upright and just ruler, he was possessed of administrative and military talents and a deep devotion to the Crown, and Charles III had chosen him to pacify those northern territories which continued to be disturbed by the Apaches and other still unconquered tribes. He served as Commandant General of the Interior Provinces from 1777 to 1782, Generalissimo of the Armies from 1782 to 1784, and Viceroy of Peru from 1784 to 1790; he died in Madrid the year after that.

We shall have little association with him. His jurisdiction extended over territories six times the size of California. California constituted only a small part of that domain, and he never came

[2] The village of Arispe became a "city," and the seat of a bishop, on July 6, 1780.

there. There was a lieutenant to do duty for him in that region, a man who enjoyed his entire confidence and who was, moreover, destined to succeed him.

Junípero was informed of the accession of the Commandant General by the following letter, which reached him on June 19, 1778:

To the Reverend Father Prefect Fray Junípero Serra.

From the information which His Excellency has given me in regard to you, and the letters from you which he has transmitted to me, I am acquainted with the fervor of your zeal, your fine religious spirit, the discretion you bring to the administration of the Missions and to your relations with the Indians, as well as your intention of working for their happiness.

I am communicating to the Governor the reasons which at this moment prevent my occupying myself with giving you the assistance you crave. I hope to be able to afford you satisfaction later on, desiring as I do to contribute with all my power to the welfare of these new settlements and counting upon the counsel of your experience to enlighten me.

I direct all the Reverend Fathers to treat the neophytes well, and Your Fathership to inspire your subjects [sic] with the proper spirit, so that a false zeal on their part may not, in an instant, destroy the fruit of so much effort.

Your Fathership will always find in me a zealous propagator of the Faith and a man devoted to the interests of religion. I beseech your prayers and those of your friars, in order that I may acquit myself with success of my high and important duties. I ask God to keep you in good health for many years.

Querétaro, August 15, 1777.

Knight de Croix.

In the five years during which he was at the head of the Commandery General of Arispe, De Croix addressed hardly ten notes to Junípero. Some stupid blunder or egregious characteristic was always stuck into them somewhere. The Petra quarryman's son, who had been so well brought up, was amazed that this Knight should continue to be so boorish. "Except when he was asking me for prayers on behalf of Spain at war, he has never written to me without giving utterance to some piece of ill nature," he wrote to Lasuen on January 8, 1781. "Is that to be attributed to his stomach acidity," he asked, "or to some other malignant humor? . . ." De Croix was in fact often ill; but his prejudices were due more to the perfidious statements made to him by Señor Neve than to his discomforts and infirmities.

The Father Prefect replied to the Commandant, at length, two months later. "We shall all pray for you," he said to him, "and you may rest assured that we shall follow your very prudent recommendations on behalf of the Indians. Believe me, Excellency, we love and respect them as our own children, begotten of ourselves in Christ. We have obtained a pardon for those of them who killed our fellow worker Luis Jaume. . . . I venture to hope, therefore, that Your Lordship will not be obliged to complain of us on that score."

Junípero always had a slight reaction of impatience when a De Croix, a Neve, or a satyr like De Troos took it upon himself to bid him treat the Indians kindly!

"The Knight orders me," he wrote to San Fernando on October 29, 1783, "to support Señor Neve's measures against the Indians who have been stealing livestock. I am ignorant of the measures with which his order has to do, and I do not yet know what answer I shall make to him. But I have a great mind to ask him whether, among the punishments provided as atonement for some mare that has strayed among their huts and been eaten by them, there is an order to castrate them, rip them open, hang them, and slaughter them *en masse*, as his soldiers have done many times over."

De Croix was asking for counsel. Junípero gave him two pieces of advice to begin with: one had to do with the "Spanish villages," which we shall take up farther on; the other was concerned with the occupation of the Channel. Under date of August 22, 1778, he wrote to the Knight: "May I point out to you, Excellency, that the Mission of San Buenaventura, the imminent establishment of which was announced to the world in the Manifesto of 1770, has not been established yet? That the Channel, of which your Most Excellent uncle announced the approaching occupation in a letter in 1770, has not yet been occupied? I have gone three times by sea and three times by land into this very thickly populated region. You cannot imagine how friendly and courteous the people are. When we were traveling by boat the islanders would come out in their canoes to greet us, but the Indians of the mainland coast were in no way behind them in kindliness. I realized this again last year, when they pulled me out of the bogs in which I was foundering, and did not leave me until they had accompanied me for a long distance and set me on the good road again."

The mail that delivered the surly announcement to which he was responding in this way brought him also a letter from Bucareli. In it, the Viceroy took official leave of the Prefect of the Missions and notified him that he would no longer, since the King had so willed, be able to do anything for them or for him. Junípero's grief was boundless. In future he would be alone, facing the enemies of his work without recourse to any support or assistance. And besides there was the tie of a deep affection broken. Bucareli's heart, too, was torn.

Friendship speaks a beautiful language in the letter of farewell that Junípero wrote him on June 30, 1778. In sum, he said:

This child, which is yours, since you have saved it, and from which you are being separated—take comfort, it has grown up, it is out of danger; and God will eternally bless you for having made its life possible. As for me, who am also being separated from you, the only consolation left to me is that I have never betrayed your trust in me, and that for these five years I have always done what you directed me to do.

The frigate, which has just arrived at San Francisco, has brought me your letter of the fourteenth of January last, along with a copy of the one you wrote to the Father Guardian on the twenty-fourth of February, 1777, to notify him of the orders from the King.

. . . Here am I, then, unable from this time on to take my problems and difficulties to the man who, in spite of my unworthiness, never turned a deaf ear to the least of my prayers. I am too sad to find words for the expression of my grief, and it is better to hold back my tears in my bosom.

. . . When you took office, Excellency, all that was here was a presidio and five missions. My Memorandum of 1773 reveals the embryonic state of these establishments. The number of neophytes did not reach a hundred; not one ear of grain had been harvested; the missionaries themselves had gone hungry many times; the soldiers, a very small band, could assure them only a precarious protection. Your Excellency stepped in, and the results of your intervention are before our eyes: three presidios which lack for nothing; eight missions which succeed in feeding their three thousand newly converted Christians. Last year two of these missions were even able to send supplies to the royal storehouses, without detriment to the assistance they were giving their less well-to-do neighbors. . . . In short, the condition in which you are leaving this colony differs from that in which you found it as greatly as a living person differs from a poor and spiteful portrait.

. . . I have at least the consolation of telling myself that I did not deceive you in my Memorandum when I assured you that your intervention would speedily transform those puny and undeveloped establishments on behalf of which I was appealing to you.

. . . I have waited, before writing to you, to read over again all the letters that you have addressed to me. I wished to examine my conscience, and see if there was a single one of your orders against which I might unwittingly have transgressed—so that, if so, I might ask your pardon. In rereading those letters, what expressions of your kindness to me I have discovered again! I have, above all, been able to follow that long series of generous and efficient decisions which you have handed down in favor of our poor Indians. How is my anguish not to be increased by this rereading, as I reflect that this collaboration, which was so fruitful, is henceforth at an end? I can at least bear witness that I have seconded your views as well as I could. If—as is surely the case—I have been guilty of some failures, may your kindness forgive me for them! . . . May it please God to reward Your Excellency, in this life and in eternity!

After a six weeks' call at San Francisco, the *Santiago* came to anchor at Monterey. In its cargo it carried a chest containing a magnificent monstrance, on the base of which was engraved the following inscription: "The Gift of His Excellency, the Knight Commander Antonio Bucareli y Ursua, Viceroy of New Spain, to the Mission of Carmel in New California." It was the Viceroy's farewell gift to his friend.

"We used it on Sunday for the first time," Junípero wrote on August 19, 1778, "in a High Mass at which all the crew of the frigate were present. In my sermon I mentioned the name of the man to whom Our Lord owed this sumptuous gift; the cannons roared; all our Indians had a serving of meat in addition to their customary menu. . . . May God bless Your Excellency even more than my grateful heart entreats Him to!"

Junípero's last letter to Bucareli was written on the fourth of the next October:

It is from San Diego that I am writing to you this time; I came here by the frigate, on the sixteenth of September, to encourage the friars who are working at the rebuilding of this Mission, and to make it the start of my first tour of confirmations. I count upon continuing that tour in a journey as far north as San Francisco, 210 leagues [525 miles] from here.

. . . Among those three hundred neophytes whom I have just confirmed were Bernardino, the Macamo captain, Dismas Chichicup, and Nicolas Supelpex, who killed Father Luis Jaume with their own hands. Also in this number was my dear Diego, with whom I wished to begin, taking him ahead of everyone else, including the sons of Lieutenant Ortega and the storekeeper. I had baptized him in the early period of the conquest. Then he, too, went wrong, took part in the revolt, was made prisoner and condemned to death. But now he was so ill that he had to be carried to the church on a stretcher; and he died three days later, giving expression to sentiments so beautiful that I wept with emotion. . . . The two brothers who had been the actual leaders of the revolt were also confirmed. . . . Such are the results of the measures of clemency taken by Your Excellency in granting pardon to these poor souls. . . .

These letters were bound to console Bucareli and rejoice his heart. He sent them on at once to Madrid. This was one last service he was rendering to his friend Junípero before his own death, which he may have felt to be near. His covering letter repeats what we already know; nevertheless, we reproduce it here because it presents in one final association the names of the three men who were the veritable founders of California:

To His Excellency Señor José de Galvez.
My dear Lord:
The Father Prefect, Fray Junípero Serra, has just replied to the letter in which I notified him of the creation of the new Commandery General, to which he is to address himself henceforth.

He informs me of the progress of evangelization and the development of agriculture in his missions. Not only are they now feeding their neophytes, but last year two of them exchanged their surplus produce for fabrics which the royal storehouses sent them to make clothing for the Indians. . . .

By the ship *Santiago*, Fray Junípero received the authority to administer the sacrament of Confirmation. Already, on October 4, he had confirmed three hundred persons, among them four of the murderers of Father Luis Jaume.

All this is set forth at length in the three letters which I have the honor to send you, begging you to impart them to His Majesty, who, I hope, will read them with satisfaction.

To the protection of God. . . .

Knight Antonio Bucareli y Ursua.
Mexico, November 26, 1778.

Galvez did transmit the file to Charles III, as is proved by the existence of two notations on the margin of this letter's text. The first one says: "The King has taken cognizance of these documents with pleasure. He renews to the Viceroy and the Commandant the order to treat these establishments with all the solicitude which their importance merits. March 1, 1779." The other adds: "His Majesty's commands have been carried out, March 6, 1779."

Junípero never knew that the King, "his lord," was pleased with him. Bucareli would have been happy to tell him, if he himself had been still alive when the evidence of the royal satisfaction reached Mexico. But he died on April 6, 1779, and was buried in the church of the Guadalupe. He had wished for neither a mausoleum nor a statue, nor even a preferential site for his tomb. He had wanted to be buried in some inconspicuous and ordinary place on one of the side aisles.

A simple stone slab in the lateral nave on the left marks the spot where he rests. One must hunt to find it, and must lean down to read the inscription it bears. This states that "the Excellentissimo Señor Bailli Fray Don Antonio-Maria Bucareli y Ursua, Henestrasa, Laso de la Vega, Villacis y Cordova," was "humble and loved the poor." Among those, he especially loved "the poor Indians," whom he was wont to regard as brothers and equals. And that is why, fearing lest he humiliate them in his grave, he had chosen that it be placed where their feet might tread above his body when they came to pray to their dark-hued Virgin.

Twenty-four

Neve Persecutes in the Name of the State
[1777-1784]

In Neve, Junípero found a "foeman worthy of his steel," an adversary against whom he had to deploy all his forces.

Spanish in origin, a former sergeant major of cavalry at Querétaro, Felipe de Neve was personally esteemed by the King, and, like De Croix, enjoyed the confidence of Masonic circles at Court. He had given proof of his talents in many a campaign and difficult situation, and could well aspire to greater responsibilities. The temporal power of the Church and the wealth of the higher clergy irritated him beyond measure; and for his part he counted upon doing something toward reducing both. Secretive, courteous, persistent, an honest man in his private life, he brought to the exercise of his official functions the special morality of the soldier who, obliged to conquer, feels that the end justifies the means. In religion he was, like the majority of the governing class at that time, a Febronian, recognizing in the "god-state" all rights, including that of regulating the spiritual activity of the Church's ministers.[1] Such were the sentiments and ideas that inspired his policy.

To insure its triumph, he had at his disposition the "Royal Patronate" and the *Reglamento*. The Royal Patronate had existed since the time of Popes Innocent VIII and Alexander VI: in giving to the King of Spain the title of "Patron of the Church" in his overseas possessions, it had granted him the right to appoint the bishops and parish priests there, and thus placed the ma-

---

[1] It was in 1767 that Febronius, Canon of Trêves, published his famous work reviving and promulgating the doctrine that places the Pope below Councils, and charges the civil power with keeping him there. Charlemagne, long before, had written to Pope Hadrian, "Confine yourself to praying and raising your arms to Heaven, Very Holy Father, while I defend the Faith by the means which seem best to me." (Mon. Ger. Hist., *Epistolae*, IV, 137)

chinery, and the life, of the Church in Mexico in his hands. The *Reglamento*, with the preparation of which Neve found himself entrusted in 1774, was intended to replace the earlier rules, among them Bucareli's. It was destined to be completed in 1779, approved by the King in 1781, and printed in Mexico, as a thirty-seven-page booklet, in 1784.[2]

As this new rule seemed to him to hold a baleful portent for the missions, and as, moreover, he was never to receive notification of it in the King's name, Junípero resisted it stubbornly. He likewise opposed all extension of the prerogatives of the Royal Patronate. This was the principle and practice at issue in the uncompromising and unremitting fight in which he was to engage during the last seven years of his life.

The Febronians of Madrid, who had persuaded Charles III to put Neve in charge of drawing up the *Reglamento* and to appoint him Governor, were aiming at bringing the missions under government and lay control by making the missionary a functionary of the State; his work would be limited to the saying of Mass and he would have no further authority over the Indians. The *Reglamento* did not proclaim this design, but made it possible to carry it out; and Neve had every intention of rendering it effective and durable. For success in this he wanted to detach the Franciscans from the College, transform them into parish priests, and substitute native alcaldes for them as heads of the mission settlements.

PARISHES OR MISSIONS, MISSIONARIES OR PRIESTS

No doubt considering that things are sometimes changed by changing their names, he decided to call the missionaries "priests" and the missions "parishes." And as De Croix had ceded to him his title of Vice Patron of the Church in California, he took upon himself the right of appointing the officiating priests of these so-called parishes. Moreover, he would not appoint more than one for each station, in order that each incumbent should be overburdened with duties and have no time left for mixing in temporal affairs.

[2] *Reglamento para el Gobierno de la Provincia de California Approbado par Su Majestad en Real Orden del 24 Octubre de 1781*. Mexico, 1784.

"I thought I was dreaming," Junípero wrote to the Discretory on August 13, 1778, "when [in July of that year] he first spoke to me of this. As soon as I could be sure that I was actually wide awake, I told him in reply that for the past thirty years I believed I had known the difference between a mission in a heathen country and a parish in a Christian land, and that if our missions were not missions, then there was none and there never would be one upon the earth."

"Nevertheless," Neve added, "I do not intend to make any appointments at the moment, since all the stations are provided for."

"You are right in that, Señor," Junípero responded.

"None the less I am going to write to the Discretory, so as to have an understanding with them on the subject."

"In that you are wasting your time, Señor, for the Discretory will answer that the King and his Vice Patrons cannot dispose of rights that don't exist."

It must be understood, on this point, that the Fernandinos, subject to the College and the Roman Propaganda Congregation alone, did not belong to any diocese and were not under the governance of any bishop. The Royal Patronate, therefore, did not affect them. But Neve wanted to bring them absolutely under episcopal authority, so as to put them effectively under his own.

"In temporal matters, that is in regard to your appointment," he persisted in saying, "you come under the Vice Patron, that is myself. In the spiritual realm, that is in the 'power' of administering the sacraments, you are under the bishop of this place, who is the Bishop of Guadalajara."

"In temporal matters," Junípero, on his part, insisted, "neither in the Sierra nor on the Peninsula nor here has either Señor Galvez or Señor Bucareli ever availed himself of the prerogatives of the Royal Patronate. If these Vice Patrons have not made use of their rights as they should, it is because where we are concerned those rights do not exist. As for the spiritual realm, it is obvious that this territory will be attached to some bishopric when we give it up. Will that be Guadalajara, as you say? I know nothing about that, nor, Señor, do you. There has been no ruling on that point as yet. What I can tell you is that the Bishop of Guadalajara has never made any sign to us. The Bishop of Durango was on the spot sooner: when he learned that you were establishing the village of San José, near Santa Clara, he wrote me that this parish was subject to his mitre, and asked me to take account of that. I thought he merely wanted to commend himself to our prayers. Since then, he has not lacked mine. Every day, in the order of the Mass, I pray for the Pope and *pro antistite nostro Antonio* [". . . and for our Bishop Anthony"]. His name is Anthony; and since Anthony is also the name of the Bishop of Guadalajara I am so fortunate as to be able, without knowing for which Anthony I am praying, to acquit myself of all my duties toward the bishop of this place—if there is one. I say, 'of all my duties,' advisedly, for, in my opinion, we have no others. To repeat once more, we are—my colleagues and myself—subject to the College."

"We are not in agreement" was Neve's rejoinder. And in the letter of August 15, 1778, in which he was making this report to the Discretory, Junípero summed up: "We never were, and we argued for years over this matter."

In the beginning, when the friars uttered the word "Mission" in his presence, Neve would rebuke them at once. When Bucareli's parting gift arrived, Junípero showed it to him.

"And this marvelous monstrance is for Carmel?" the Governor said.

"Yes, Señor: the inscription makes that plain: 'The gift of His Excellency . . . to the Mission of Carmel.' "

"There is an error in that text."

"What?"

"Carmel is not a mission."

"Then His Excellency is less well informed than you?"

"He is not conversant with the situation, that is all!"

"Nevertheless, this belongs among the matters which His Excellency has been obliged to study," Junípero replied.

Officers and soldiers received orders to change their vocabulary. But they kept making slips of the tongue, and continued to speak of the "Missions." De Croix himself made use of that term in a letter to Junípero, and the Prefect lost no time in taking advantage of the lapse.

"Permit me to tell you how I have rejoiced," he wrote, on April 26, 1782, "to find the word 'Mission' set down by your pen. Following the example of the Fathers and the soldiers, the Señor Governor has, moreover, ended by speaking like everyone."

We shall see that Neve, who had been forced to give up in the matter of terminology, ran aground also in actual practice: the only appointment he attempted to make was rejected by his appointee.

REDSKINS TRANSFORMED INTO ALCALDES AND JUNÍPERO INTO A SERPENT

The affair of the alcaldes was, from the start, more eventful.

The *Reglamento* which had de-baptized the missions in order to re-baptize them as "parishes" had transformed them by the same stroke into "communes." Each of these had at its head a native council made up of an alcalde and two aldermen (*regidores*), elected for a year and subject only to the Governor. The alcalde was charged with the maintenance of order; the aldermen were his advisers and lieutenants; all were independent of the missionaries, who could no longer direct or chastise them. On taking office the alcalde received a large scepter and a certificate; before retiring at the end of his term he and his aldermen were to name the "municipal council" for the following year.

Junípero frowned upon this innovation, deeming it to be both illegal and dangerous: illegal, because not in conformity with the Law of the Indies, which gave the missionaries "the same rights over the Indians as a father possesses over his children, including the right to correct them"; dangerous, and of a nature to stir up revolts, because these alcaldes, still veritable savages, would do nothing but follow their own inclinations once they were freed from the authority and the sanctions of the ministers of religion.

The two antagonists had been in dispute on this subject for months when, on Palm Sunday of 1779, the Prefect arrived at the Presidio to say the Mass. That morning the Governor, furious when the man whom he needed to carry out his reform showed him anew that the reform was leading to disaster, burst out at Junípero in rage. On March 29 Junípero wrote to Lasuen: "When I once more implored him to postpone the election of the alcaldes he insulted me so that I could not restrain my indignation. 'Never has anyone permitted himself to address such lying abuse to me!' I cried.

" 'The fact is that I also know logic,' he retorted, with his ironical smile, indicating by this that his accusation was no less well deduced for not being obvious.

" 'Then you are a bad logician, and you ought to go back to school,' I answered, 'for your conclusion is a hundred leagues away from the truth.'

"More sarcastic than ever, he enjoined me not to take what he had said too seriously, inasmuch as all that was to remain between us two.

" 'If there were only one person in the world to think like that, it would still be too many,' I added, to close the discussion.

"Such was, alas, on such a solemn day, my preparation for the holy Mass. Prostrate for a long time at the foot of the altar, I tried to calm the tempest that was rumbling within me. When the Mass was finished, I went back to Carmel to sing the Passion with my companions.

"But all day it was impossible for me to think of anything but this miserable incident. I was unhappy, completely upset. What was I to do? . . . It seemed to me that I must write to this gentleman, and add to my letter those in which Father Figuer and yourself ask permission to go back to the College if these famous elections are held.

"That evening, when I began to write my letter, an objection would present itself at every sentence and keep me from going on. I would begin again to think, then once more to write, then would return anew to reflection. It was the agitation of my soul that was reducing me to impotence. Toward midnight, when I was getting nowhere, I took a fresh sheet of paper and straight off wrote a long letter to Father Sanchez [of San Gabriel]. When this was finished I tried to begin the first one over again; but it was no use; the inner debate, and my confusion, had once more taken hold of me. The night was already far advanced. I thought: If I do not lie down for a little, even though I have no desire whatever for sleep, I shall be good for nothing tomorrow. I went into my cell, determined to throw myself down, without undressing at all, on my bed. I was trying to reason with myself, calling upon considerations beyond this world. It was effort wasted. My distress remained so great that I ended by crying out, 'But, Lord, what does this mean?'

"It was at this moment that I heard an inner voice speaking

to me, clearly enunciating the following words: 'Be as wise as the serpent and as simple as the dove.'

" 'Yes, Lord,' I responded at once. 'That is what I shall do, with the aid of Thy grace.'

"I slept well. At dawn I got up, to recite my office and to sing the Mass of thanksgiving for the daughter born to the Prince of the Asturias. She is called Maria Luisa, as no doubt you already know."

What was that slanderous imputation that made him so furiously indignant and threw him into such confusion? We do not know; but there is no doubt that it was directed beyond him personally, to the Prefect as Prefect, making it plain to him that a mortal blow was aimed at his work. Moreover, this is the only time in his life that we see him lose his poise for more than an instant. It is also the only time when he is found making note of a revelation from on high. Reticent soul that he was, he would never speak of what God said to him as he prayed. So we know nothing of his inner life. "He carried its secret to the grave," Palou wrote.

If he broke his silence today, it was because he owed it to his ministers to justify his future pattern of action and to give them the reasons he had, at the age of sixty-six years, for transforming himself into a serpent.

"I send you forth as sheep in the midst of wolves," Jesus said. "Be ye therefore wise as serpents and simple as doves."

The dove, with its white wings, shows its flight and exposes itself to the arrows of the hunter, while the serpent, gray as the rock or green as the grass, conceals itself, advancing only with deliberation, never willingly confronting the enemy.

Junípero had always been the dove. "We hide nothing," he wrote to Verger, in his letter of August 15, 1779. "The people in the Presidio can know what it is that we do and what it is that we say. Thank God, our life has no fear of the light."

"You are right on one side and wrong on the other, Junípero," God seems to have said to him that night. "If you are no longer able to compose a sentence, and cannot 'think of anything else,' it is because you are disturbed and driven to the wall, my friend. Therefore follow the Gospel, which always makes it possible to find peace again; obey Him whom I have sent to rescue mankind from every impasse. You must be a dove with your Superiors, your confrères, with Bucareli and other honest men here below; but with that wicked wolf of a Governor, who will eat you if you are not prudent, you must be a serpent. Since I have not sent you here, with your fellow workers, to be eaten but to convert the Indians, do not write any more explanatory letters to give information to the enemy; do not confess to the devil; do not reveal your plans to the man who wishes to thwart them; and if three roads are barred to you, take a fourth which may still be free. And if any imagination is left to you after that, use it to circumvent the designs of the wicked wolf. Do you understand, Junípero?"

"Yes, Lord. That is what I shall do."

"Good! Now you have made enough 'first drafts,' have thought enough, suffered enough, for today. And there is that Mass you must sing tomorrow for the little princess. Go to bed, Junípero. You know that I am your Father, and that I shall always be there to help you find that fourth road. Come now. Good night! Sleep well, Junípero!"

And it was plain to be seen, next day, that Junípero had slept as well on his two rough boards as the little Maria Luisa in her royal cradle; and that after this he had sung the Mass for her without any distraction of mind. Entering upon his prescribed role he sent, that very day, a new directive memorandum to his associates.

"Henceforth," he said to them in substance, "we shall comply as little as possible with the Governor's measures that are in violation of the Law of the Indies, and we shall try to thwart his plans. As alcalde, for example, let us put forward our bell-ringer, our sacristan, or some other inoffensive neophyte. We shall take advantage of his elevation to office to enjoin him to ring the bells at the right time, not to drink the wine from the altar cruets, and to be more obedient than he has been heretofore. We shall not breathe a word, obviously, of the immunities and lofty prerogatives which these Indians will henceforth possess."

To Lasuen, in letters of March 29 and August 16, 1779, and January 12, 1780, he wrote: "As you have a choice, take Francisco; add an iron knob surmounted by a cross to his great staff of office; dress him in his festival-day uniform. As for his certificate, let it be as grand as anyone would desire, since neither he nor any of the others will be able to read a word of it. The essential thing is that they should not think of any change, and that the respect in which you are held should not suffer. Beg our good brother Lieutenant Ortega, from me, to watch his words at the ceremony of installation. . . . Here, I have taken care to leave my alcalde in his cotton shirt and his ordinary short breeches. Even though he should go complain to the Presidio, he will have nothing else, and will remain as he was. . . . Thus the Governor's innovations will not, I hope, have untoward results. He prides himself on being a clever man. But who knows whether, with the help of God, the evangelical wiliness of the serpent will not get the better of his?"

If the reign of Francisco at San Diego was without incident, this was not the case in other mission settlements, where Balthasar, Nicolas, and others like them compelled the Governor to call for help. As the first of January—date for the re-election of the municipal councils—drew nearer, Neve was saying, "You will see how well these Indians are going to choose their successors, and you will realize that they are as capable as the Spaniards of organizing themselves as a society!" Had he read the homilies of Jean-Jacques Rousseau on the natural goodness of man, or the dissertations of the Abbé Raynal, who, without having gone to see them, stood sponsor for the virtue of the "good savages"?

The fact remains, Junípero wrote to Lasuen, in a letter of April 25-26, 1780, "that he was all on fire to see the new dignitaries get on to the elections. He wasn't able to keep still. He wrote me that he was surprised that nothing should yet have been done. I replied that we should take good care not to interfere in the matter, inasmuch as he had decided against it. He returned to the charge by beseeching me to intervene, declaring that it was our wisdom in which he had always put his hope, and adding that everything we did would be done well. For once he covered us with praises."

The tone of Junípero's response was that in which the Prefect was henceforth to write to the Governor: "I regret that we do not agree in general, and on the question that occupies us in particular. It is not possible for me to change my opinion, and it is not the results of your policy which could bring such a change about. You will always find me ready to meet your wishes, nevertheless, when that is not contrary to the spiritual interests entrusted to my care."

On January 7, 1780, he wrote plainly to Neve:

I have received your letter of day before yesterday, dear Señor, my friend. . . . You ask that the missionaries, everywhere, shall henceforth take charge of the elections. This is to acknowledge that the officials you chose last year are incapable of giving themselves proper successors. There you recognize an initial mistake, and wish to correct it. I strongly urge you to recognize a second error, more gross than the first, and to correct it likewise: it is the error which consists in withdrawing these functionaries from our jurisdiction.

How many times you have told me that they would mount guard at night around the Mission, that they would take the people to work and to worship, that they would render us all sorts of good services! You are acquainted with what they did, from the time they learned that you had taken from us the right to punish them. Balthasar, our first alcalde, gave his chief attention to leading the Indian women astray; he even had a child by a close relative; he applied the bastinado to one of our Indians from the Peninsula to punish him for having carried out our orders, et cetera. He is now at the head of a band of brigands in the mountains; and after enticing away our blacksmith, our carpenters, and several neophytes, he is inviting the others to go and join him. Nicolas, the alcalde at San Gabriel, had made it his specialty to procure Indian women for the soldiers who asked for them. His colleague at San Luis confined himself to kidnapping the wife of a neophyte and running away with her.

They have shown themselves to be detestable creatures, these chosen men of yours, dear Señor. To be sure, the functions with which you decked them out were not easy to fulfill. But in any case they were less easy than what you are demanding of them today, in charging them with the naming of their successors. That is why, if they need us in order to be good electors, they had greater reason to need us in order to be good administrators. And that, again, is why the excellent logician you pride yourself on being ought to restore to us the right to school, supervise, and if necessary correct the alcaldes.

Neve judged that "the Fathers would dishonor him in punishing his representatives."

"But what can there be that is ignominious in a practice customary throughout the kingdom?" Junípero demanded, in reply. "If the rod is bad for the alcaldes, then may it be bad also for the soldiers and the other subjects of the King!" He was clearly unable to comprehend that since the alcalde represented the State his back was sacred, that only the State could make it ache, and that the Church was committing a sacrilege in bruising it a little.

Powerless to inculcate this Febronian idea upon him, Neve fell back on some excess of severity on the missionaries' part.

"Alas, we are fallible, and some abuses there will always be," Junípero replied. "You will not deny, however, that it is neither the taste for adventure, nor money, nor ambition, that has made us come here, but love of the Indians. You will agree also that we are like fathers in our treatment of them and that we truly seek their good. Can you say as much, you who allow your soldiers to behave like savage brutes, violating the women, castrating the men, et cetera? . . . Perhaps you will not admit that I am right," the letter concluded. "In that case, since you are two steps away from Carmel, it is you whose duty it will be to keep watch on, and correct, our alcaldes. But who will be responsible for those of San Gabriel and San Luis, who are forty or fifty leagues [one hundred or 125 miles] from the presidios? I await your kindness in telling me this, so that I may inform the ministers concerned."

This letter solved the problem. Four months later, Junípero notified Lasuen that the Governor had capitulated. "He has swallowed the pill," he wrote, on April 26, 1780. "Not that he has digested it; but everything indicates that from now on he will leave us in peace on this matter. As he has never answered me, and as for him *qui tacet consentire videtur* ["silence gives consent"], I have written to the Fathers at San Gabriel and San Luis to inflict upon Nicolas and his colleague the punishment that is their due. In consequence I do not look forward to any important trouble from having the alcaldes, since we are left free to deal with them as seems best to us."

All that came out of it, then, was the enrichment of the thirty-seven-page Book of Regulations by an article that was not enforced, and the Spanish vocabulary of the Redskins by a new word.

INDEPENDENT FRIARS, INJUSTICE
AND MALICE

Neve met with similar defeat in his attempt to break the tie of the Fernandinos' dependence upon the College.

"The first time he brought up that subject," Junípero wrote, "I answered that on the day this happened he would see me vanish from this place and return posthaste to Mexico."

What would the Governor not have given to stop the interposition of the College between himself and the friars! But the slightest victory on this terrain would have opened the breach for the loss of his other reforms.

He wanted to have the originals of the annual balance sheets which the ministers drew up for their Prefect, which the Prefect would then send on to the College, and which would finally reach the King by way of the Viceroy. "I will only deliver them to him on an order from you," Junípero wrote to the Discretory. Neve claimed to reserve for himself the right of authorizing the friars to return to the College. "I am quite willing to inform him in advance of departures," Junípero continued. "As for recognizing him as our superior and asking his permission, I shall do that only if you expressly order it."

The College ordered nothing. In fact it supported its Prefect from that time on. So long as the *Reglamento* had not been officially approved, it either turned a deaf ear to the Governor's complaints or else would say to him, "These measures being contrary to the Law of the Indies, we cannot take them into consideration." After the *Reglamento* received the royal approval, in 1781, the response of the College was, "These measures being contrary to our holy Rule, we are appealing to His Majesty, who has surely not thought of this, and who will not fail to repeal the said measures as soon as he reflects on the subject." The King was notified, among other things, that the Fernandinos would leave California rather than submit to a regulation that would not suffer more than one minister for each mission.

It was the conception he had formed of his duty, and the love he bore the Indians, which inspired Junípero's intransigence. He knew too well how the Redskins would be ill-treated and exploited from the moment Neve and his soldiers became their masters. As for concessions that had no importance, Junípero made as many of those as the Governor wished. It was thus that he gave Neve the gratification of judging, if not condemning, him for theft. The inquiry was held on the demand of the Dominicans of Lower California.

These friars were vainly seeking liturgical ornaments for a new mission they were about to establish. What, then, they asked, had become of those the Jesuits had left behind in 1768? It was not Palou who had taken them away: his boxes had been too carefully rummaged through in the course of eighteen months to leave any doubt on that score. But could not Junípero, by chance, have been the thief? They called upon the Governor to shed light on this obscure affair.

"You are pleased to interrogate me, dear Señor," the supposed culprit replied in a communication of June, 1780, "as to whether I carried off some chandeliers and sacred ornaments when we left Loreto in 1769 for Monterey. . . . When Señor Galvez had the good idea of abolishing the Missions of San Luis and La Pasión, he had their liturgical furnishings and their bells transported to La Paz. It was there that in his presence I took out enough material to fill three large chests: one for San Diego, another for San Carlos de Monterey, the third for San Buenaventura. The Visitor General had authorized me to take in addition, there and elsewhere, anything I might wish. I profited by this at La Paz to take a green chasuble, some ribbons, several acolytes' cassocks and surplices, and several baptismal bonnets for children; from Santa María I carried away a complete liturgical equipment, which would make it possible for me to say Mass when traveling; this served me during the entire expedition, and it is Your Lordship's Royal Presidio that is now in possession of the chalice and altar-cruets which I made use of at that time. . . . I do not recall anything else. Obviously, if I had known that you would one day interrogate me on this matter, it would have been easy for me to make out a complete inventory of what I took; but the idea did not enter my head; and this is why I regret that I am unable to inform you more fully. . . . You ask also who gave me the orders and how they were drawn up. The person who gave me the authorization was, I repeat, the Most Illustrious Señor Don José de Galvez, Visitor General. As for knowing by virtue of

what authority he was acting, it is better that you should ask
him that yourself, for it is a question which does not concern
me in any way."

These last lines show that even his little victories did not all work
out so as to satisfy the Governor wholly. As for the large tri-
umphs, he never won any; in essential matters, he met only with
defeat. After years of struggle, he was just where he was when
he began. His adversary had not allowed him to move forward
one step. No bishop was exercising jurisdiction over the Franciscan missions; the ministers were still recognizing the authority of
their Prefect alone, and the Prefect recognized the authority only
of the "holy College"; as for the alcalde of the "commune," in
his short working breeches, he left other men's wives in peace,
no longer acted as procurer for the Spaniards, and kept quiet,
since he knew that in spite of his big rod with its iron knob the
rod would fall on his own back if he did not behave himself.

Really good humor is not to be expected from a general who
is always beaten, from a reformer who in spite of plenary powers
succeeds in reforming nothing, from a man of great arrogance
who scores only failures and humiliations. Neve admitted that he
had suffered terribly in California. Was it suffering and resentment that made him like a man beside himself, and moved him
to such extraordinary malice against Junípero?

He stopped at nothing to put affronts and injustices upon him.
Although held responsible for facilitating his correspondence, he
deliberately deceived him as to the arrivals and departures of the
mail carriers; he refused him escorts in cases where they were
most indispensable; he lied to him, caviled over little things, held
him up to ridicule, forbade his soldiers to render him any service. One could fill a hundred pages with his cruel operations. As
many would be needed to enumerate his thefts. The growing prosperity of the missions exasperated him. He tried to ruin San Francisco, Santa Clara, and San Capistrano by forcing them to give
back thousands of ration allotments lawfully collected. This went
so far that their discouraged ministers, Palou, La Peña, Mugartegui,
and Amurrio, asked to return to the College. Only the old Father
Murguia, of Santa Clara, unwaveringly stood fast.

As for Junípero, he kept watch on the robber with an angelic
patience; politely placed obstacles in the way of his removing his

stolen goods; harried him with the most ingenuous marks of respect, pressing him unremittingly to settle outstanding accounts and demanding as many as 23,738 ration allotments that had not been delivered. Seven years after their death, "the two mules from San Diego, dead in the King's service," were still the subject of remark from Junípero to Neve, as were "the two bulls stolen and eaten by military deserters."

"When will you restore them to me, dear Señor?" he would say.

"Did you remind him, at the time of his visit, that he owes it to us to make good their loss?" he wrote to Father Lasuen. He carried out this strategy so well that in sheer weariness Neve ended by becoming almost honest.

The following incident, which had to do specifically with Lasuen, was one of those that were constantly setting the Prefect and the Governor at loggerheads with each other. One may see, from it, whether there were any limits to Neve's capacity for hostile acts.

FATHER LASUEN'S WHEAT

During the year 1779 Junípero borrowed twenty-one fanegas (thirty-three bushels) of wheat from the Presidio of Monterey, and Father Lasuen lent sixteen fanegas (twenty-five bushels) to the Presidio of San Diego. When the Carmel had harvested its grain, Junípero informed Neve that he was now about to pay his debt.

"As I need corn," the Governor replied, "send me eight fanegas of that, as fair exchange; add thirteen fanegas of wheat, and we shall be quits."

So it was done. Almost at once, however, Neve changed his mind. "Corn is not worth so much as wheat," he said. "The King has therefore suffered a loss in accepting it as fair exchange for the wheat that was lent you. As I have to have corn, I will keep it and pay you for it. But pay me back the eight fanegas of wheat that you still owe me."

So, again, it was done. Neve paid for the corn in fabrics, plainly reckoning it as cheaper than the wheat; and at Monterey the matter was closed.

At San Diego, on the contrary, it was only beginning. Ortega, on orders from Neve, announced that he was going to send corn in repayment for the wheat he had borrowed. The boat had just brought a shipment that had worms in it. This, Father Lasuen refused. "I do not want your wormy corn to give my children," he said. "Moreover, corn is not worth so much as wheat."

Ortega transmitted this refusal to the Governor.

"I have just now issued a decree," Neve replied, "which fixes the value of corn and wheat at the same figure: ten pesos a fanega. I am sending it on to you. The Father, therefore, must accept your corn."

"Very well," Father Lasuen said to the lieutenant, "but in his decree he refers to corn in good condition. Bring me sixteen fanegas of good corn or else pay me for my wheat at ten pesos a fanega, as this same decree provides."

Except at San Diego, where the new decree had gained access, there were outcries of indignation in all the soldiers' headquarters and presidios when it was learned that Father Lasuen was selling his wheat at double its value; for it was known everywhere that Pedro Fages had fixed the price at five pesos the fanega.

"It is obviously highly regrettable that people should be able to bring such a charge against Father Lasuen," Neve said to Junípero, with his sanctimonious air. "How could such a thing have come about?"

"And you say, Señor, that he demanded this exorbitant price of ten pesos?"

"I declare to you that he did."

"I shall never believe that of Father Lasuen. There is something about this business which I do not understand."

"Alas, Father, what I am telling you is only too accurate. The soldiers would not repeat it if it were not true."

"No, no! I shall never believe that!"

Because of the habitual remissness in the mail deliveries, Junípero was ignorant of what had happened at San Diego. Neve also continued to leave him in ignorance of the decree fixing the new prices. As soon as he had got at the clear facts of the affair, he wrote at length to the Governor.

May we be permitted, for once, to depart from his manner of expressing himself and, making free use of the basic elements of his letter of April 18, 1780, word it in the way Neve would have deserved?

Dear Señor and friend:

Obviously, we shall never understand each other. In us, Franciscans, you see agents of the temporal power of the Church and enemies of the civil authority, although in my opinion we are the State's best auxiliaries and the only faithful interpreters of the intentions of the King. Knowing that the Redskins can be changed into Spaniards only by first making them Christians, His Majesty has entrusted to us, experienced missionaries, this task which neither you, nor your soldiers, nor the State can bring to a successful issue. To succeed in it, we need time and freedom. Now you have not yet come to understand that this fifteen-year period, in which the State must be satisfied to watch us at our work and help us in it, is a necessary stage; the mere idea of this interregnum causes you sorrow and a boundless disturbance of mind.

It is not, however, because we have different opinions on the best way to civilize the Indians that you are absolved from the observance, towards us, of the laws of common morality. As to that, you have committed so many offenses against us in the course of a few days that I can hardly count them; will you do that with me?

You certainly have the right to decree that corn is worth as much as wheat and that the price of each shall be ten pesos a fanega. Only, decrees of this kind should be issued in the morning before anyone is out of bed, and not at midday, so that you can receive wheat in the forenoon when you are a creditor and refuse to give it up in the afternoon when you are a debtor. That is a dishonest sleight-of-hand trick. So there is one!

You directed Ortega to pay in wormy and unusable corn for the good wheat you had eaten; that is theft. So there are two!

You communicated to him, confidentially, your decree that should have been made public everywhere at the same time; that is again a fraudulent maneuver. And that makes three!

When, believing that the price of wheat was still five pesos and learning that Father Lasuen was demanding ten for it, the soldiers cried Shame, they were uttering a literal slander; but the true slanderer is yourself, who are alone responsible for the error. And that makes four!

You aggravate your misdemeanor in allowing the slander to spread toward the north, although all you would have had to do to stop it was to post your decree in the presidios. So there we have five!

You aggravate it again in yourself disseminating these defamatory remarks. And that makes six!

You aggravate it, finally, in perfidiously repeating these remarks to

me, in order to diminish the esteem in which I hold Father Lasuen.
And there are seven!

You would rejoice, besides, in the harm that this infamous rumor
could do the missionaries. And that makes eight!

I pause, dear Señor, so as not to go on counting until tomorrow.
Confess that you have acted in defiance of all morality. If you doubt
it, ask your conscience, your relatives, your friends, your soldiers, I
was going to say your horse, and find out what they think. . . . But
this is enough to say about you. Let us speak for a moment of myself, since that also is of a nature to facilitate the intercourse which
there must be between us.

I will tell you in the first place that, old as I am, my head is still
good. I am therefore still capable of understanding what you say,
observing what you do, and divining what you are planning. I will
tell you, next, that, "miser" that I am, I will never allow you to steal
as much as a fistful of corn or one old hen from the missions. I will
shout so loud that they will hear me all the way to Madrid, if you
take the risk of doing that. This "cupidity and stinginess" which I
share with my colleagues is not inspired by the desire to pile up riches
or to eat six meals a day; it comes from the fact that the Indians are
poor, and that His Majesty, the King, our debtor, is solvent. Finally,
I will tell you that I shall always love you, and were you to put me
in prison or hang me I should bear you no grudge. Moreover, I should
be ashamed at my age to have any fear of death, when my beloved
Luis Jaume, at the age of thirty-four, allowed himself to be slaughtered without offering any resistance. For this reason I fear nothing;
no one can make me keep silent when I ought to speak; I shall do
my duty at all costs. . . .

Junípero's actual letter, which in substance was as severe as
what we have just set down, was, as always, irreproachable in
form. It recounted, at length, the inquiry he had carried on,
cleared Father Lasuen of all blame, and besought the Governor
to impose silence upon the soldiers and to cease imputing mo-
tives of avarice to what was nothing but charity. "Charitable we
are and must be," he said in conclusion, "in demanding equitable
remuneration for the work and the sweat of these Indians whose
condition is so miserable. Are we to be accused of cupidity because we defend their right to be clothed and to eat enough to
satisfy their hunger? . . . May I beg you, finally, always to com-
municate first to me the measures you are taking in regard to the
missions and the ministers? Much vexation will be avoided by that

means. The Most Illustrious Señor Galvez used constantly to deal so."

None of the Governor's contrivances and frauds, for the rest, were able to accomplish anything more of consequence against the missions.

"In the matter of livestock," Junípero wrote in his annual balance-sheet for 1778, "we possess at the Carmel one donkey, five male and thirty-five female mules, one stallion, nineteen geldings, eighteen mares, ten fillies, ten colts, forty-eight sheep, sixty goats, and 248 head of cattle. Not to mention the peas, barley, and beans which have given a good yield, we have just harvested more than one thousand fanegas [160 bushels] of wheat."

During the following years the figures rose rapidly everywhere. Conversions of the heathen continued, families of new Christians increased, the children in the schools grew tall and sturdy. In 1781 there was an average of no less than five hundred neophytes and two hundred catechumens per mission.

And what shall we say of the increases in the harvests and the flocks? In 1780, at San Diego, there were 250 head of cattle, 630 sheep, 300 goats, 26 swine, and 135 horses; in 1782, at San Gabriel, there were 600 head of cattle, 968 sheep, and 610 goats. Two years later, Fathers Lasuen and Figuer had a herd of 500 cows; Father Palou had 614, and Father Cavaller nine hundred.

What could Febronius, Neve, and the *Reglamento* do against fields that were so fertile and good animals that made it their business to multiply like this?

Twenty-five

The Affair of the Confirmations and the Death of Father Crespi
[1779-1781]

The cruelest episode among the persecutions Junípero endured at the hands of Governor Neve is what we have called the "affair of the confirmations." In that, the Governor employed every means within his grasp. But Junípero had more at his disposal than his adversary had: more, in fact, than any of the men, save Galvez, with whom he had to do in the course of his life.

The sacrament of Confirmation is, as is known, "the complement to Baptism, and the second phase in the Christian initiation." It bestows the Holy Spirit upon the person thus confirmed, and "obtains for the Christian regenerated by Baptism the energies and faculties which will permit him henceforth to live in Christ." [1] The right to administer confirmation belongs in principle to the bishops, but in the absence of bishops the authorization is sometimes given to simple priests.

This authorization had been requested for Junípero by Father García, Prefect General of the Missions of Mexico. It was procured from Pope Clement XIV on July 10, 1774; the Papal brief granting it reached Mexico City in 1776; but it was only on June 19, 1778, that Junípero received his powers. That day the boat brought him a "Certificate," and "Instruction," and a letter from the Guardian Father Verger. The Certificate was a "true copy" of the pontifical brief, bearing the signature and seal of Father García. The Instruction, or "Directions for Use," was one of those printed documents which the Roman Court annexes to the favors it grants; the beneficiary was directed, among other things, to "inform those present, before administering confirmation, that he

---

[1] Cabasilas, *De Vita Christi*, Migne, *P. G.*, Vol. CL, cols. 560, 569.

was qualified to do so." The letter from Father Verger read, "The present Certificate permits you to administer confirmation; as for the original brief, it is deposited in Father García's strong-box at San Fernando."

Junípero commenced to make use of his powers forthwith. On June 29 he confirmed ninety children at the Carmel. On August 24 he sailed on the *Santiago* for a tour of confirmations in the southern missions. After San Diego, whence he sent his farewell to Bucareli, he visited San Capistrano, San Gabriel, San Luis Obispo, and San Antonio; when he returned to Carmel on Christmas Eve he had performed 1,897 confirmations.

The first eight months of the year 1779 were filled, for him, with the cares and distresses of which we know. An aggravation of his chronic ailment reached the point of keeping him from going to the Presidio for ten weeks, and even, on certain days, from ascending to the altar; he was suffering so much that he could not sleep. "It is true," he wrote to Lasuen, however, "that my attacks of insomnia come from the head of the Presidio rather than from my bad leg."

At the beginning of September, still in pain but in a hurry to conclude his circuit of confirmations, he applied to Neve for an escort guard, so as to go to the missions in the north, Santa Clara and San Francisco. It was refused him. From that day the conflict between the two men entered upon its acute phase. It had begun a year before. Not only had the Governor abstained from attendance at the confirmations at the Carmel, but, encountering Father Crespi, he had demanded, "By what right does the Father Prefect administer confirmation? Have his powers been viséd by the Bishop of Guadalajara?"

"You had better ask him about that," Juan Crespi replied.

Junípero showed his papers, which carried the visa neither of the Bishop of Guadalajara nor of the Bishop of Durango. Pronouncing them to be irregular, Neve tried to take them from him under pretext of having them regularized. But Junípero refused to give them up.

Certainly Neve, as Vice Patron to the Vice Patron of Arispe, had the right to visé the Prefect's powers before supplying him with an escort to go and exercise them, the same right as a customs officer verifying a passport or a policeman checking a driver's license today. But in this case the customs officer had decided in advance not to accept the passport, the policeman was determined to issue a summons at all costs. Neve had to get his victim, and if he could not catch him on the wrong road he would put him there. What was his compulsion? Vengeance? The desire to make Junípero suffer, to condemn and even to expel him? Solicitude or anxiety for his own career, his Febronian zeal, the hope of assuring the observance of the disregarded *Reglamento* by means of a signal victory? Without doubt, all this had place in the fierce animosity, the treachery and lack of equity, which marked his dealings with Junípero.

The fact remains that in September of 1779 he again demanded Junípero's papers and formally requested him to put off all further confirmations. This time it was no longer the prerogatives of the Bishop of Guadalajara that he was invoking but those of His Majesty himself. He entrenched himself now behind the Royal Edict issued at San Lorenzo (Spain) on November 13, 1777, on the occasion of a Papal brief concerning the Holy Year, which reminded the bishops overseas of a prerogative of the Royal Patronate.

"Every brief *of a general bearing*, like that of the Holy Year," Charles III stated, "must, before being *made public* and coming into force, receive the visas of my Council of the Indies (Madrid) and of my Viceroys or Vice Patrons."

"I will not give you my papers this year any more than last," Junípero replied to Neve, "inasmuch as I do not wish to give the appearance of allowing their validity to be suspected nor to run the risk of never seeing them again." He continued, under date of September 17 and 24, 1779:

As for the Edict of San Lorenzo, permit me to say, dear Señor, that you have no understanding of it whatever. It has no application to my case. Alluding to the briefs *of general bearing, which must be made public*, it does not concern briefs such as mine, of which the bearing and the public notification are limited to a few hundred neophytes to whom I announce that I am about to confirm them, being supplied with the necessary powers. Moreover, not having a retroactive effect, since it does not so specify, this Edict of 1777 has nothing to do with my brief, which dates from 1774.

But if it were to apply to the present case, my brief would still be in order. I possess only the copy, it is true, and in consequence cannot show you the visas of Madrid (Council of the Indies) and of

Mexico (Vice Patron), but I am certain that they are on the original. As guarantors of that, I have Father García, Father Verger, and the Vice Patron himself. The first two are too intelligent and conscientious to force me, by negligence in fulfilling in the first place the formalities that are incumbent upon them, into disobedience to the King. As for Señor Bucareli, he, too, would by no means have congratulated me on my confirmations if, through his fault and mine, they had been performed at the cost of a trangression of the royal orders. I am then entitled to administer confirmation.

You tell me that you are under order to report to the Señor Commandant General as to how I comport myself in this affair. If your powers are limited to drawing up official reports on my conduct, I no longer ask you for an escort; but if they go beyond that I again request that you give me one. Finally, you praise me for my resignation. Let us understand one another, dear Señor. Resigned I am, as every Christian must be when the divine will permits him to be the victim of human injustice. But Your Lordship has deceived himself, if you have seen in my preceding letter any assent whatever to your interdict. And on the day when you show me any such enormity escaping from my pen, I shall agree that I am commencing to become indeed distracted; for that is precisely the opposite of what I have meant to say.

This letter had scarcely been dispatched when Junípero received one from his friend Palou, announcing the arrival of two ships. "The *Princess* and the *Favorite* have just come in here," he wrote, "and their officers want by all means to see you again. Hurry, for the two frigates are leaving again soon." They were returning from the third northern expedition, having this time planted the cross in the vicinity of the Arctic Circle.

Junípero pleaded his bad leg as his reason for not taking to the road.

"If the Father Prefect cannot come to us, we will go to him," said Captain Quiros and his comrades. And they announced their imminent arrival, in company with a physician charged by the commander of the expedition to go and give treatment to Junípero.

Neve knit his brows over this news. He had little relish for this pilgrimage from the Spanish fleet to the founder of New California, and no desire that the pilgrims should go about telling everybody that he, like Rivera before him, was holding the revered Prefect a prisoner. The way to avoid that? . . . He reflected; he searched; he found it.

"Because my duty obliges me to refuse you an escort for a tour of confirmations," he said to Junípero, "it does not follow that I shall not be doing myself a favor in giving you one to go to see your friends. Indeed, it is quite the contrary! I do not wish to be accused of a lack of affection for you. Go! I want you to, wholeheartedly."

"Look twice, Señor," Junípero answered. "For if—as is certain—I am asked to perform confirmations—"

"You will reply that the Edict of San Lorenzo prevents you from doing so."

"The probability is that I shall be able to reply only by confirming those who seek it."

Junípero writes that on hearing these words "the Governor smiled and said nothing more." Neve was smiling because Junípero's file would thus be enriched by an act of formal disobedience to the King.

Meanwhile the ships' officers had started on their way, accompanied by Francisco Palou. Junípero met them at Santa Clara, and performed confirmations there during the course of three days. "What a joy it was for us all to see him again!" Palou wrote. "But, alas, what a sorrow to find him so ill!" His leg was swollen and covered with ulcers.

"What miracle has brought you these twenty-five leagues?" the doctor exclaimed. He wanted to give him treatment then and there, but Junípero begged him to wait until they reached San Francisco. They arrived there on the fifteenth of October, and the physician returned to the charge.

"I am very grateful to you," Junípero responded, "but I shall never have time to follow out your treatment. Let us leave it to God, if it is His will, to cure this ailment which has already accompanied me through thirty years of my life."

On October 21 Junípero began to administer confirmation. In addition to the Indians, members of the crew received it, with the officers serving as godfathers.

On October 24 a courier arrived from Lower California, bringing two items of news: that Spain had gone to war with England on the side of the United States; and that Bucareli was dead.

"How can one describe the revered Father's grief," wrote Palou, "on learning that his beloved benefactor, upon whom he was still counting in these cruel hours, was no more! As was his custom, he resigned himself to the will of God. . . . The sailors were sad also, at the thought that from now on it was all over with the great expeditions and the occupation of the North."

The frigates left San Francisco for San Blas on October 31. Father Palou had made preparations to go back with them: he was ill, discouraged, and in dread of having to replace Junípero when he should die. On Junípero's insistence, however, he consented to postpone his departure for one year; and so it was always to be. He was always to put off going away, so, until the following year; and he was not to leave his master until he had closed the old man's eyes in death. Benito Cambon, on the contrary, who some time ago had ceased to travel, made an urgent plea of his bad state of health and the necessity he was under of returning to the College. The Father Prefect was obliged to let him go. It was learned a little later that when he reached San Blas Fray Benito had embarked as a ship's chaplain for the Philippines. We shall not see him reappearing for two years. The missionary team was not reduced by one, however, for Father Matthias Noriega, chaplain of one of the boats, asked to be allowed to join it. He was assigned to Carmel, where Juan Crespi's physical strength was failing from one day to the next.

It was from San Francisco, where he stayed for three weeks, that Junípero sent two letters on October 29: one to the Commandant of Arispe and the other to his Guardian. To De Croix he wrote:

Because I administered confirmation at Santa Clara and San Francisco without the visa of the Señor Governor, I am probably about to be accused by him of having violated the royal Edict of 1777. I mention only those two missions, for at the six others the confirmations took place before the Edict of San Lorenzo arrived in our midst. In order to submit to this decree, I had resolved to interrupt my tour and not to come here at all, although I had long since been announced and long expected. It was Señor Neve's own entreaty that induced me to come. I shall plead in my defense the further fact that no sooner had I arrived at Santa Clara than the Indians, the settlers, the soldiers, and the friars pressed me to perform the confirmations. What was I to answer? Should I disclose to everyone, when they were all ignorant of it, the fact that the Governor had forbidden me to administer this sacrament? Or that it was the King, through the Edict of San Lorenzo, who was placing an interdict upon me? Whatever my reply might have been, it would have created a scandal in subjecting to contempt both the holy sacrament of Confirmation and the person of the King himself. . . . Not being able to escape from this dilemma, I therefore performed the confirmations. When I had warned the Governor that this was how the matter would turn out, he had confined his response to smiling, and had only urged me the more strongly to set out on my journey.

I am asking the Father Guardian to reassure you as to the regularity of my powers, by addressing to you an Attestation proving that the Papal brief does indeed bear the visas of the Council of the Indies and the Viceroy. I venture to hope that your very pious Lordship will excuse me for having acted as I was bound to do.

To his Superior, Junípero transmitted the entire file of the affair, begging him to send the aforesaid Attestation to the Knight de Croix at once. More openly than in the other letter, he spoke of the scandal that would have been caused among Spaniards and Indians by the interruption of the confirmations. How he hoped that neither group had any cognizance of the Interdict! "The soldiers and the settlers," he wrote, "would cry out that since the Governor had intervened it followed that his authority extended also to the sacraments, and that he knew more on this subject than all the missionaries together, among them their Prefect, whose powers were not in order and to whom he was bound in duty to prohibit their use. As for the Indians, most of them would say that if the Governor did not like the confirmations it was because they were a bad thing and it was right for him to put an end to them; the others would impute to our pious Sovereign the impiety which consists in depriving Christians of such an indispensable sacrament. . . . And now," he said in conclusion, "I am wondering how I am going to be welcomed on my return! . . ."

Neve's welcome was wholly affable. How could he have desired anything better than what had happened? The Prefect had fallen into the trap, had put himself in the wrong. All that need be done now was await the consequences—obviously disastrous for Junípero—which the Commandant of Arispe was about to visit upon his disobedience to the royal command.

In view of the almost incredible distances to be covered and the irregularity of the mails, there was a time lapse of twenty-

two months before the conclusion of this affair, which in our
day would have been disposed of in twenty-four hours.[2] It took
four months—from October, 1779, to February, 1780—for Junípero's letter from San Francisco to reach the College; ten months
—from February to December, 1780—for the Attestation to cover
the ground from Mexico to Arispe; nine months again—from December, 1780, to August, 1781—for the final decision from Arispe
to arrive at Carmel.

To his letter of October 29, 1779, to the Commandant General,
Junípero received a reply on July 19, 1780. De Croix upheld Neve
all along the line. "I call upon you and enjoin you," he wrote under date of April 20, 1780, "to cease your confirmations, and to
turn over your documents (Certificate and Instruction) to the
Señor Governor, who is receiving orders accordingly."

Junípero first made up his mind to comply, as is proved by two
drafts of letters in response—written to the Commandant General
that very day—which have come down to us but which were
never sent on their way to Arispe; for the next day, after a night
spent in prayer and renewed reflection, he changed his mind, and,
on July 20, wrote to the Knight:

However deeply it may pain me, and although it is very prejudi-
cial to the spiritual welfare of the poor Indians, I shall submit, revered
Señor, to the prohibition you have put upon my administering confirmation. In the matter of handing over the two documents in question, I will tell you that the boat that is to bring me the Attestation
from the College, which I asked for eight months ago, has never kept
us waiting so long. Since my papers, as they are, would not receive
Señor Neve's visa, and since all that could be done with them would
be to destroy them, lose them, or send them to Madrid, they are better left in my own hands. They will therefore remain there—unuti-
lized—until such time as, completed by the Attestation of visas which
is to be brought by the boat, they can receive that of the Señor Governor, which will definitely close the affair.

Fortified by the "orders received accordingly," Neve tried to
take possession of the documents in the case. They were refused
him. "I have just asked Arispe," Junípero answered, "not to oblige
me to give up the papers before the arrival of the boat. So let us
be patient and wait for a little while longer!"

[2] From Monterey to Mexico was 3,000 miles; from Arispe to Mexico, 1,300
miles; from Arispe to Monterey by the Anza road (Yuma), 1,050 miles; from
Arispe to Monterey by the Gulf of California and Loreto, 2,200 miles.

"It is no longer a question of waiting," the Governor replied. "The matter is too serious. Do you want to make me commit a mortal sin by forcing me to humor you further?"

"God forbid that I should drive Your Lordship to mortal sin!" Junípero responded, in a letter of July 22, 1780. "In reiterating the order to hand the Certificate and the Instruction over to you, you tell me you would be failing in your duty in a grave matter if, through friendship for me, you should allow yourself to be satisfied with my reply to the Knight de Croix. To that I will reply that I do not want you to commit even the slightest venial sin for love of me. Do your duty, therefore, as God inspires you, without 'humoring' me. I may add that, since our disagreement has been submitted to the higher authority for action from now on, I do not see what can trouble your conscience in the thought of awaiting its decision. You add that the Attestation I am expecting from the College will probably never come, and that if it does it will not conclude the affair. Neither of us knows what will come from the College. What I do know, in any case, is that at the College there are men who are intelligent enough to bring to an immediate conclusion an affair which is as uncomplicated as this. But, seeing that it has to do with the future, let us stop prophesying and arguing, and let us wait!"

Two weeks later, the Governor was obliged to depart for Lower California. As he did not have the mules for the journey, Junípero lent him the six best among the forty in the stables of Carmel.

Neve had been gone for five weeks when, on the seventh of October, the long-awaited ship arrived, bringing the Attestation that had been so earnestly wished for.

On receipt of Junípero's letter of October 29 of the preceding year, the Guardian Father Verger had hurried, with the Pope's brief in his hand, to Viceroy Mayorga, asking him to attest the fact that it bore the visas of the Council of the Indies and of the late Señor Bucareli. Mayorga had given him two affidavits. Verger had at once dispatched one to the Commandant at Arispe; the other was the one Junípero found in the mail from San Fernando. He kept it most carefully. But he sent his Certificate and his Instruction back to the College by the boat's return trip.

"I am forwarding these two documents again to you," he wrote to Father Pangua by the same mail (October 24, 1780). It was, indeed, Pangua who had become once more his Superior, that timid sheep of a Pangua of whom we have spoken so much ill, and of whom we shall now speak nothing but good, inasmuch as he was henceforth to show himself as very courageous. "I shall abstain, for the time being, from administering confirmation in public," Junípero continued, "but I shall continue to confirm, in private, neophytes in danger of death. As for delivering to these Lordships the documents they demand, I shall by no means do that. If the battle is to be decided on the score of justice and legality, I shall have power to win it; but I am confronted by arbitrary action. My most convincing arguments are answered with injunctions. The arms are not equal. Since the College has the best weapons and since it is to it that the King has entrusted these missions, I am asking it to enter the lists. After all, I am only its delegate. Following consultation with Fathers Palou and Murguia, therefore, I am sending back these papers, of which I was only the depositary for their owner. If these Lordships want them, let them go and look for them at the College! Need I add that the days will be centuries long for me, while I am obliged to administer such a necessary sacrament clandestinely? . . . My other grief arises from the humiliation which redounds from this state of things upon the missionaries, and even to some extent upon God Himself."

Junípero's stratagem of war was inspired, as is seen, by the refusal to admit that the descent of the Holy Spirit in Upper California could be dependent upon the good pleasure of a former cavalry sergeant from Querétaro, and the repugnance of his filial heart to approve a maneuver that smirched the honor of the College. To take his powers from him was to judge them to be excessive or improper and to arraign those who had stood security for them. "Ah, the guarantee of my superiors means nothing to you?" he seemed to say. "In view of the fact that it means everything to me, and that in handing over to you documents guaranteed by them I should look as if I were associating myself with your insulting judgment, you shall not receive those papers from my hand!"

Neve returned to Monterey on December 6. After returning Junípero's mules, and bestowing a remnant of cloth on him as an expression of thanks, he pressed him to make a final submission. "I am obliged by higher order," he wrote to Junípero on December 29, "to include your papers of authority in the mail now being sent to Arispe; you no longer have any reason for postponing the delivery of them, since the boat you were waiting for has now arrived."

"The precise fact is," the Prefect replied the next day, "that the Attestation which the boat brought, and which I have shown you, proves that I am in order. The Father Guardian, *to whose hands I have entrusted everything,* has sent the same to the Commandant General, who, therefore, is now satisfied, and in consequence expects nothing more from here. Let us both hold our peace until the imminent moment when we shall receive his decision. As it will certainly be favorable, you too will be satisfied, and I shall rejoice the more in view of my affection for you."

Fury over being again put off no doubt kept Neve from noticing that incidental, *"to whose hands I have entrusted everything";* for three months went by without his suspecting that the documents he had been pursuing for three years had left California. He learned it on March 23, 1781, when an order arrived from Arispe to wrest them from their holder by force if he still persisted in refusing to give them up voluntarily. This order had gone out from Arispe on November 29, 1780, when the Attestation from Mexico had not yet arrived.

"I no longer possess the documents which you command me to deliver," Junípero, on March 23, replied to De Croix. "I sent them back to the College by the boat that sailed on the twenty-fourth of October last. Since it is to Your Lordship that they should go, and since the Señor Governor would continue to be absent for some time, there was no quicker means by which they could reach you. I am notifying the Father Guardian that you are again demanding them from me. Moreover, they are perfectly in order, as will have been proved to you by the Attestation dispatched to you from Mexico on February 16 of last year."

He also advised Neve, who had been getting ready to institute actual search, not to disturb himself. "My letter of December 30 last," he wrote to the Governor on March 24, "told you that I had 'entrusted everything to the hands of the Father Guardian.' That referred, among other things, to my Certificate and my Instruction; I swear to you that they are no longer in this province. Everyone is free to think what he will about my mode of action. You are free to seize my person, if you consider that it can take the place of my papers. What this affair will have made me suffer is the secret of my soul; but there is nothing that it would not be one's duty to endure with patience, aided by divine grace." A few months earlier—on the eighth of January—he had written to Lasuen, "I am ready to go to prison and to death, but they will not do me that honor." Who would have dared to imprison the friend of Galvez and the founder of California?

Neve's fury reached the point of an almost insane rage. He ventured to accuse Junípero of perjury, to claim that he was hiding his papers. In making so loud an outcry, he was only serving to aggravate the humiliation his friend De Croix inflicted upon him in the following words addressed to Junípero:

"Having received from His Excellency the Señor Viceroy the official proof that the brief authorizing you to administer confirmation has been viséd by the Supreme Council of the Indies and the Captaincy General of Mexico, I am today enjoining the Governor, Don Felipe Neve, no longer to oppose the exercise of your powers, but to aid you in them when you so request. The Knight de Croix, Arispe, December 24, 1780."

This decision verified the juridical interpretation that Junípero had given to the Edict of San Lorenzo. "This Edict has no retroactive effect," he used to say over and over again. "Otherwise all the briefs that antedated the establishment of the Commandery of Arispe would have to go back to Madrid to be viséd anew, and in that case the existence of this Kingdom would date only from today."

Neve was at San Gabriel, where he had just settled himself in order to be closer to Arispe, when this letter came to him on May 18, 1781, together with his chief's instructions to transmit it to the Father Prefect. He took three months, if not to digest his defeat, at least to acquit himself of his commission. This was just so much more extra suspense inflicted upon Junípero. It was only on the sixteenth of August that he learned that the affair had been closed. The Governor informed him of it in six lines, which were assuredly the lines that, in all his life, cost him the most to write: "The Señor Commandant General addresses to you the following communication. . . . I, in turn, inform Your Reverence that you may henceforth make use of your authority at your convenience."

Almost seventy years old and limping more and more, Junípero started out again on his travels. On October 9, 1781, he was at San Antonio, where he confirmed 165 persons. On the twenty-third he was at Monterey, where he accompanied the soldier Juan Labra, condemned to be hanged for theft, to the place of his execution. On the twenty-fifth he set out toward the north with Father Crespi, who had asked to go with him.

"What a joy it was to me," writes Palou, "to see my dear co-disciple Fray Juan Crespi arriving with my beloved master! We had studied together from our A-B-C's to our final theses in theology. I knew, alas, that he was coming to bid me a last farewell. My grief and his own were great when, on November 9, we took leave of each other. Meanwhile the Father Prefect had confirmed the sixty-nine neophytes whom we had baptized since his last visit."

With his companion Junípero passed again through Santa Clara, where he administered 151 confirmations; and on November 19 he blessed the first stone of Father Murguia's church. In haste to get back to Carmel before the streams were in flood, the two men took to the road again that same day. They had been traveling no more than a few hours when, as Junípero wrote, "the mule that was carrying me as its burden took fright, swerved violently, and precipitated me rudely into empty space. I was kept motionless and well covered up until the bone-setter arrived. In spite of my contusions and my pains, it was ascertained by this specialist in the reduction of fractures that all my bones were in place. The next day I continued painfully on my journey. We reached Carmel on the twenty-second of November, and the effects of the accident gradually disappeared."

Seeing his poor master tossed into the air and lying inert in the ravine, Fray Juan had thought that he was dead. Did this shock to his heart hasten his own end? He had been a cardiac case for several years. "He sank rapidly," Junípero wrote to Pangua on July 17, 1782. "From before Christmas he was confined to his bed, his feet swelled, his legs were affected by dropsy, the oppression in his chest became constantly greater. We took care of him according to the *Book of Remedies*."

The great traveler who had wielded the astrolabe and accompanied Juan Perez to the waters off Alaska was about to arrive in port. The disciple was leaving before the master. Junípero, at his bedside with the *Book of Remedies* in his hand, would try to assuage the spasms of suffocation. During the sick man's attacks of self-doubt he would hearten him by reminding him of the fine church he had built at Tilaco, in the Sierra, and of all the children he had baptized who were awaiting him in Heaven. What trials they two had endured together! . . . He thanked him for his companionship and his friendship of many years, and promised that he would never forget him and would soon come to find him again in the Life Everlasting.

Fray Juan was reaping the harvest of his fidelity. The man he had refused to abandon on the beach of San Diego was at his side now. Tender and always pure in heart, a mystical and silent soul, he had been given twelve years of living with a saint, and now that saint was helping him to die. He slipped away in peace, at the end of a long winter night, a little before the children were awakened in the school. Junípero closed his eyes, washed his body, dressed him in his Franciscan homespun, embraced him for the last time, and pulled the cowl down over his face. The next day, after the funeral, he dedicated to him the following lines in the Carmel's *Register of the Dead:*

No. 247. The second of January, 1782, after having sung the vigils and the Mass for the dead, I have buried Fray Juan Crespi, at the corner of the high altar, on the north side. He had been minister of this Mission since its establishment. Son of the holy province of Majorca, he left it in 1749 and became a member of the San Fernando College in Mexico. He died yesterday, the first of January, toward six o'clock in the morning, fortified with all the sacraments, assisted by his companions—sons of the same province—in the sentiments of one truly dedicated to the vows of the religious life. He lived sixty years and ten months, spent forty-four years less three days in the religious life, and, in a period of thirty years, was a missionary successively in the Sierra Gorda, in California, and in the region of Monterey. In faith of which I, who was formerly his teacher, and after that through many years his companion, have signed this: Fray Junípero Serra.

Twenty-six

The Founding of Los Angeles and
San Buenaventura and
the American War of Independence
[1780-1782]

Immediately upon taking office, the Knight de Croix had made up his mind that the occupation of the Santa Barbara Channel must be promptly carried through. As he and Neve envisaged the enterprise, it called for the establishment of five settlements: Los Angeles and San Buenaventura in the south, Santa Barbara with its Presidio and barracks in the center, and Purisima Concepción in the north.[1] In its major outlines, this was the plan originally conceived by Bucareli and Junípero. But an essential alteration was secretly introduced: for our Febronians the question was no longer one of founding missions but of applying their "new method of conquest" in the establishment of "parishes," or "Spanish villages," instead.

The nucleus of each of these settlements was to be composed of families recruited in Mexico among the *gente de razón*. If the Indians saw these "people endowed with reason" living and working beside them, the promoters of the plan believed, this in itself would be enough to move them to emulation; from these superior beings the Redskins would learn agricultural and mechanical arts, domestic economy, and good habits, and through their contact with them they would become civilized creatures and good subjects of the King. As for their conversion to Christianity, the

---

[1] It was at the Portiuncula (*Porciuncula*), near Assisi, in the chapel of Our Lady of the Angels (*Nuestra Señora de Los Angeles*), that the Franciscan Order was founded. St. Bonaventura (1221-74), called the Seraphic Doctor, was Minister General of the Franciscan Order, and died a Cardinal. The Missions of San Buenaventura and Purisima Concepción became the towns of Ventura and Concepcion.

conquerors would provide sufficiently for that by placing a priest or two in each parish to say Mass.

As early as 1778 three settlements of this kind had been established: two among the Yumas, at the confluence of the Colorado and Gila rivers, which were served by four Fathers from Querétaro; and the third at San José, near Santa Clara, which had remained without a priest. Junípero rose in immediate revolt against this new method of conquest. "There will be one of two things," he wrote to the Commandant of Arispe, on August 22, 1778, "either you place the education of the Indians in the hands of laymen, in which case we go away, or you make us responsible for it, in which case we ask to be left to perform our task without being choked by this scum of adventurers who elude our authority and frustrate our efforts. I protest, therefore, against an innovation which is hateful, untimely, and contrary to the interests of the Two Majesties; and I beg you to transmit this protest to my eminent friend, Don José de Galvez."

Once more he was standing out against the injustice that would deprive the natives of their goods without giving them, in exchange, the benefits of the Christian faith and the improvement of their lot. De Croix made no reply at all.

He likewise omitted to inform the Prefect when in 1779 he notified Neve that the occupation of the Channel was to be put through in that same year. Seeing himself thus set aside, Junípero at once reminded the Knight of his existence. "May God be praised, and may you be congratulated," he wrote, "that you are crowning my hopes by hastening the conversion of these heathen folk whom I find so sympathetic. I am at present writing to the Father Guardian about the six friars upon whom the enterprise must rest. You may rely on me to see to it that they are men who exercise wisdom, prudence, and all the virtues which you have commended to us. May I also rely on you to prevent the soldiers—the indispensable auxiliaries to the missionaries—from destroying, by their behavior, the work that they should supplement and complete? I hope that, thanks to you, the missionaries will lack for nothing, and that the new missions will enjoy the same treatment as the old. Probably I shall have to give new consideration to the guarantees which we should like to have in this matter."

This letter was dated March 30, 1779, two days after the mys-

terious Voice had incited Junípero to the "wisdom of the serpent." There could be no better warning to the Commandant
General and the Governor that their designs had been guessed
and would be circumvented. Must they still underestimate Junípero by neglecting—as they did—this clearly-given notice?

In this year, furthermore, De Croix fell ill. It was even announced that he was dead. Then he recovered, had a relapse, got
better again—as a result of which succession of ups and downs
he was unable to take his projects in hand until the following
year. We have seen that Neve and the six best mules from Carmel had set out for Lower California on September 6, 1780. The
Governor was going to give his final orders to Rivera. In substance, Neve said to him:

"For Los Angeles the fifteen families you recruited last summer, on the Sinaloa coast, will be enough. When the time comes
they will take ship at Guaymas for Loreto, whence they will
proceed through Lower California to San Gabriel. But for the
settlements on the Channel we should have four times as many
colonists and soldiers, not to mention livestock. You are to go
and recruit them in Sonora, and it is you who will bring them
to me, by the Anza road, in Upper California. I shall soon be
establishing myself in San Gabriel, and from July on, next year,
I shall await you there."

For the rest, Neve had urged Rivera to collect parishioners of
the highest quality for his parishes.

Let us now leave Neve to return to Monterey, and Rivera to
make his way to Sonora, and let us betake ourselves in spirit to
the College of San Fernando, where the following order, transmitted by the Viceroy Mayorga (successor of Bucareli), arrived
on December 9, 1780: "The Commandant General of the Interior
Provinces having informed me that six friars from your College
would be needed for New California, I call upon and direct Your
Reverence to designate those whom you consider the best qualified for this ministry."

The Reverence in question was Pangua, who had come to put
his whole confidence in Junípero. He was acquainted—he and
his Discretos—with the interdict laid upon the confirmations, the
thirty-seven-page *Reglamento*, the project for an independent Custody of which we shall soon speak, the way the Fernandinos were

being treated in Upper California. Six friars nevertheless volunteered to go and join them.

"Here are their names," Pangua replied to the Viceroy in a letter of December 16, 1780, "and here are our requirements for them. . . . We ask, first, that their stipends (*sinodos*) for the first year—three hundred pesos each—shall be paid them in advance, so as to cover the expense they will be put to before leaving. We ask, next, that in addition to the thousand pesos customarily allotted, each new mission shall receive, for its church, sacristy, residence, and farm, all that may be necessary to the success of the enterprise. We insist particularly that the supply of livestock shall be as large as possible. And do not, as sometimes happens, forget the hens, if you please! The list of what we require is attached hereto. We hope that all we need will be granted to us. If it is not, we shall not hesitate to make public the fact that it is the fault of the Commandant General, and not ours, if the new conquest does not progress in accordance with the pious desires of His Majesty, whom God preserve!"

Mayorga referred this letter to De Croix, whose answer arrived four months later. The advance payment of the *sinodos* was allowed, and traveling expenses would be paid as far as San Blas. "For the rest—liturgical equipment, agricultural implements, and livestock—all that," Mayorga himself wrote in his letter of April 5, 1781, "comes under the jurisdiction of the Commandant General and the Governor. If your Reverend Fathers have any complaint to make, they can put in a claim once they are on the spot. In the meantime, I call upon and direct them to set out on their way without losing a moment."

Since it was not to found farms that men were enlisting, it was indeed with "parishes" and "villages" that the whole matter had to do. But our missionary-candidates were not at all interested in becoming parish priests, with Neve instead of Junípero as their chief. As for "putting in a claim once they were on the spot," the affair of the confirmations had enlightened them quite sufficiently as to the fate that would be awaiting their eventual "claims." They changed their minds, therefore, and those who were about to leave declared that they were no longer willing to go.

"They respectfully beg the King's representatives not to count upon them any more," Pangua sent word to Mayorga on April

7, 1781, in reply to his pronouncement. He added that the missionaries had his approval, and that the Discretory would soon be acquainted with the incident; "but not until after Easter," he explained, "since the Discretos are too busy, in these last days of Lent, to come together and deliberate."

After Easter, then, the Discretos took counsel and drew up a long Memorandum. "We give our approval to our friars who have withdrawn," was what was to be read under date of April 19, 1781, "for the methods introduced on the Rio Colorado, which have been visualized as methods to be applied to the Channel district—those methods are not ours. We are convinced, furthermore, that His Majesty will condemn them as soon as he is fully informed." The document concluded with an indignant indictment of Señor Neve: "It is he who is responsible. He is the real culprit whom we accuse of destroying our friars' work. Not content with evidencing a total hostility toward them, he eggs on his soldiers to treat them as enemies and to make them ridiculous in the eyes of the Indians. In addition to this, he does what he can to lead the soldiers astray, thus making them agents in the corruption and apostasy of the neophytes."

The Discretos' Memorandum, signed by Pangua, García, Sancho, Parron, and others, was taken to Mayorga that same day, and a copy of it was dispatched to Junípero. So the recruitment of the "parish priests" destined for future parishes proved an abortive effort.

The recruitment of parishioners met with less difficulty. It was impossible to look at Don Fernando de Rivera without feeling the desire to become a cuirassier, and no one understood better than he how to requisition livestock. He proved this once more in Sonora, and it was a huge caravan which, in June, 1781, set out under his leadership from Alamos, south of Arispe, on the way to Upper California. Along with the seven soldiers who formed his guard, the column was made up of seventy-five cuirassier-settlers and their families, with a thousand head of cattle, as well as ten soldiers from Sonora, familiar with Anza's road, under command of Second Lieutenant Limon.

When the party arrived in the country of the Yumas, Rivera thought that the animals needed rest before continuing on the 280 miles still to be covered. He decided to stay where he was for several days, with his guard and his livestock, while the rest of the caravan should go on with Limon and his soldiers. He set up his camp on the left bank of the Colorado, opposite the two villages on the right bank.

On July 14 Neve noted the arrival of the Sonora emigrants at San Gabriel. The very next day Limon and his ten men set out again, to meet and join Rivera. On August 18 the Sinaloa emigrants, coming from the Peninsula, arrived in their turn. In regard to them, what Rivera offered was none too happy. Neve did not restrain a grimace when he saw these parishioners "of the highest quality" whom Don Fernando had sent him to found Los Angeles. Since some of them had deserted en route, only forty-four put in an appearance: eleven men, eleven women, and twenty-two children. Among the eleven fathers of families, there were two Spaniards married to Indian women, a half-breed married to a mulatto, four Indians of whom one was married to a mulatto and the other three to women of their own race, finally two Negroes and two mulattoes with mulatto wives. It was upon this mixture, in preference to former university professors and other men of distinction among the followers of the religious life, that our Febronians were depending for the education and development of the Redskins.

Neve signed the charter that founded Los Angeles on August 26, 1781. The future village was situated on the stream called Portiuncula, ten miles northwest of San Gabriel. The Governor was just on the point of installing the recruits from Sinaloa when Limon reappeared—with only seven soldiers; of the three that were missing two had been killed and the third seriously wounded.

The news the junior lieutenant brought was frightful: the two parishes on the Colorado with their parishioners, Rivera with his bodyguard and his animals—all were gone. The survivors had had to fight like lions to escape the Yumas, whose chief, clad in Rivera's uniform, was leading the assault.

Neve sent Limon and his men back to Arispe to warn the Commandant General. They set out again by way of the Peninsula, and he himself, fearing that the revolt would spread in this direction, gave up for the time being all plans of settlement. At the end of four months, when he saw that nothing untoward was happening, he returned to the execution of his project, though on a reduced scale on account of the Yumas' seizure of the live-stock.

At the end of December he assigned a corporal to conduct the Sinaloa families to their destination; and it was this corporal who laid out the central square of Los Angeles, 300 feet in length and 200 feet wide. Home sites were drawn by lot, in his presence; each consisted of a large piece of arable land and a building plot 120 by 60 feet in size. Every head of a family also received four horses, two pair of oxen, two cows and a calf, two sheep, two pigs, a mule, a plough, an ax, a spade, a sickle, a gun, and a large buckler.

The settlers from Sinaloa had been consoled, on starting out with no priest, by the assurance that one would come to them soon and that meanwhile they could have recourse to the ministers of San Gabriel. It was not possible to promise as much to the future inhabitants of San Buenaventura and Santa Barbara, who were going to live about a hundred miles from any mission: poor folk who, after all, were not professed atheists and whose children did not deserve to be brought up like animals! What was to be done until the six Fernandinos mobilized by the Viceroy might be expected to arrive?

Determined not to recognize the Prefect and to act himself as Vice Patron, Neve fixed his choice upon Benito Cambon, who had returned from the Philippines and was taking a rest at San Diego as supernumerary. At the beginning of January the Governor appointed him officiating priest at San Buenaventura and summoned him to San Gabriel. "I am waiting for you there," he told him, "and we shall set out together for the Channel."

But Fray Benito, who was so fond of moving about, refused this time to move. He replied to the Governor with a letter that ran somewhat as follows: "My vow of obedience does not permit me to accept honors and charges unless they come from my canonical superiors. As you are not one of those, I regret that I am unable to respond to your call. The only way of arranging the matter would be by addressing yourself to my superior, Fray Junípero Serra, Prefect of the Missions, at Carmel, near Monterey."

Assured of receiving the same reply from the Father whom he was planning to send to Santa Barbara, Neve resigned himself to the dispatch of a courier to "Carmel, near Monterey."

"I received his letter in January, a few weeks after the death of Father Crespi," Junípero wrote to Father Guardian Pangua. "He asked me for two friars. My response consisted in going to impose my presence upon him."

With the escort to which he again had a right, the Prefect left Carmel on the second of March. On the fifth he was at San Antonio, where he administered several confirmations; on the ninth, at San Luis Obispo, where he confirmed 148 persons; on the eighteenth, at Los Angeles, whose parishioners, in the three months they had been there, had done nothing but pursue the Indian women and play the guitar. On the nineteenth he arrived at San Gabriel, where he sent for Benito Cambon and began confirming. He administered 271 confirmations in six days—administering, by this fact, 271 reminders to Neve of the latter's fresh and smarting defeat.

The men, women, and children from Sonora came to kiss the hand of the little old lame man whom they knew to be spitefully persecuted. The Fathers of San Gabriel and Fray Benito, running to his call, radiated satisfaction and pride. The noncommissioned officers and soldiers rejoiced in the humiliation of the Governor even more than in the freedom of action restored to the Holy Spirit.

It had taken Junípero two years to get the better of Neve in the affair of the confirmations. To settle that of the San Buenaventura parish it was enough for him merely to appear on the scene. In an instant San Buenaventura became once more the Mission of that name. Neve did not utter one word about the projects worked out at such length and in such minute detail. If he had ventured to do so, Junípero, we know, would have answered, "Where there are no missions, the missionaries have no concern. We who are missionaries and nothing else do not go with you if it is not missions you are setting out to establish." In that case, many colonists would have refused to go in the first place or would have followed the example of those of their companions who had deserted on the way, and the rout would have been general. So Neve left the Prefect to assemble the livestock for San Buenaventura and get everything ready for that mission, biding his time, as we shall see, to take his revenge once he reached Santa Barbara.

The column setting out in the direction of the Channel on Tuesday of Holy Week—March 26—numbered no less than two hundred and fifty persons: the Governor and the ten men of his bodyguard, Fray Junípero and Fray Benito, Lieutenant Ortega (who had been appointed Commandant of the Santa Barbara Presidio), a second lieutenant, three sergeants, three corporals, seventy private soldiers, almost all of whom were accompanied by their families. Behind them, in a pious march, went the mules bearing the bells, vases, and sacred ornaments that Galvez had set aside at an earlier date for the mission that was to have St. Bonaventure as its patron. And following these were plough horses, mules, goats, sheep, and about two hundred head of cattle—descendants, for the most part, of the sixteen cows left by Pedro Fages at San Gabriel in 1771.

They traveled along by the sea for four days. "On the first night the Governor was awakened by the arrival of horsemen," Junípero wrote Pangua in a letter of July 17, 1782. "They came from Pedro Fages, who had reached San Gabriel with news from Arispe and the Yuma country. This was of such a nature that Señor Neve first wanted to make us turn back on our tracks; but he changed his mind, and turned back alone with his bodyguard. The soldiers got up in the middle of the night to dance for joy, not so much from devotion to the patron saint of the mission we were about to establish as from lack of affection for the less congenial patron they were seeing depart. . . . After a march of thirty-two leagues [eighty miles] we reached San Buenaventura. It was on Easter Sunday, March 31, 1782, that the Mission was founded. Everyone took part in the ceremony, which was magnificent. We had asked authorization in due form from the Indians of the neighboring *rancheria* to establish ourselves among them; they gave it to us with joy. The good cheer was general. The soldiers and the settlers ate a small bull; for the officers, Father Cambon, and myself, a sheep was sacrificed. As these victims belonged to the Governor's herd, he was irritated when he learned about it; but the blame was put on me, and he did not dare wreak punishment on me for it."

This was the last mission that Junípero founded, and the last great joy of his life. "San Buenaventura is born!" he wrote to Lasuen. "God has granted me the happiness for which I have been sighing since so many years ago. . . . And, you know—

considering that I am what I am, it is not at all bad, my Mission! Oh, forgive me, forgive me! Once more, forgive me for having said 'my Mission' in speaking of the Mission of my beloved doctor St. Bonaventure! The truth is that there is nothing good that belongs to me, in this world, but, when all is said and done, I love this Mission, first among them all." (*From letters of March 31 and July 22, 1782.*)

The Governor's nocturnal departure was justified by the order given him by the Commandant General, to go, with Fages, to pacify the Yumas. It was Fages whom De Croix, on receiving Limon's report in the preceding autumn, had first placed in charge of the operation; betaking himself from Arispe to the Rio Colorado, he had found only calcined ruins on the site of the two villages on the river's right bank. The entire male population, including the four Fathers from Querétaro, had been exterminated, the animals stolen, some twenty women and forty children taken into captivity. A mass of corpses, half-devoured by jackals and vultures, lay rotting here and there. Fages was able to identify those of the missionaries, especially Fathers Diaz and Garces, Anza's former companions. On the left bank, too, the same spectacle awaited him. Rivera's livestock had been carried away, he himself and the soldiers of his bodyguard had been massacred. Since the preceding July 17, when the insurrection took place, poor Rivera's bones were whitening in the sun. As for the Yumas, Fages found them so numerous and so well entrenched that he avoided starting an armed fight with them. He had to negotiate within gun range, and give up a great many fabrics and knives, to buy back the women who for months had been the prey of their lusts. With them and the children he set out again for Arispe, taking with him also the martyred Fathers' mortal remains.

Such was the result of the "new method of conquest," of which Father Garces had never stopped writing to De Croix: "You will see what it costs you to provoke the Indians and to keep us from converting them, while you confine yourselves to stealing their lands, sending your animals to ravage their little harvests, taking everything from them and giving them nothing in return!"

But Neve was not yet of Father Garces' opinion when he returned to San Buenaventura on April 11. "Why did he have to come back?" Junípero wrote to Pangua on July 17, 1782. "I had called Father Fuster from San Capistrano, where he was super-numerary, as companion to Father Cambon. Father Cambon, with his customary skill and the aid of his good sergeant, had begun the construction of a dam; he was going to plant corn; it would shoot up under irrigation; this very year there would be a harvest. They had already been hard at work for eleven days when the Governor reappeared."

He was reappearing because he and Fages had decided to await the abatement of the spring freshets before undertaking the expedition to the Rio Colorado. The fact remains that he was furious over what had been done in his absence, and the thought that the mission just established should know prosperity so soon. He kept the soldiers from continuing their help to the Fathers, had the preparations for departure speeded up, and four days later set off for Santa Barbara, followed by the rest of the column and leaving the two ministers with their few neophytes, their many farm animals, and a guard of fifteen soldiers. Junípero arrived at Santa Barbara with Governor Neve's party on the evening of April 15.

Here, Neve took the revenge he had promised himself. "He began by stripping me of my powers," Junípero wrote to his Guardian. "After that—but I neither can nor wish to recount to you what I saw and heard during those three weeks." Was the Governor's rage transformed into a demoniac seizure? He had just learned that he was soon to leave California: did he wish, before he left, to make the man who had triumphed over him pay for his recent humiliations and four years of defeats? Knowing that the real way to torture the saints is to attack God and offend Him in their presence, he committed profanations and allowed the satyrs among the soldiers to attack the Indian women without restraint. "No! I beg you to excuse me," Junípero replied to questions from Lasuen. "No more to you than to anyone else in the world will I report the things to which I was a witness. When I tried, as was my duty, to inform the College, the pen fell from my hand." (*From letters of July 17 and 20, 1782.*)

Junípero had withdrawn to a hut made of branches, on the edge of the forest. He emerged from it every day, to go and ask the Governor when the Mission was to be begun.

"When the Presidio is finished!" Neve would answer, with a sneer.

The old padre would then go back and shut himself up in his cabin. There he would pray, weep, and suffer from his leg, where the sores had reopened; and there he would work on the voluminous and difficult correspondence that his responsibilities forced upon him. Lacking a table, he wrote on his knees. And it was thus that he drew up, on April 26 and 28, a four-thousand-word reply to the Knight de Croix, who had just enjoined him, first, to transfer no more ministers in future, "except under urgent necessity," and, second, to send him, De Croix, "immediately and without delay," the annual balance sheets of all the missions since their establishment.

To the first injunction Junípero answered, "While waiting for the King to decide the question of the appointments and transfers of the ministers, I report with pleasure, Very Revered Señor, that I am already carrying out your orders. To be sure, I have been obliged to replace Father Luis Jaume, who was murdered by the Indians, and Father Crespi, who has recently died. But, seeing that of the nine missions entrusted to me no two speak the same language, it has never occurred to me, nor will it, to move, 'except under urgent necessity,' a minister who is habituated to the language and the customs of his own Indians."

On the second point, Junípero wrote:

You assure me that a decree of the Junta, under date of March 30, 1772, obliges me to send the Governor the annual inventory of each mission. You have not read correctly, Revered Señor: this decree says merely that the balance sheets must reach the Viceroy, without specifying how. Up to now they have reached him by way of the College. While waiting for the College to draw up a new line of procedure for me, I may observe that we have no more paper, having given all our reserves to the war-tax collectors and no boat having arrived here in the past twenty-two months to replace them; not to mention, Revered Señor, that this is an exorbitant punishment you are inflicting upon such an old man as I am, for a fault he did not commit. Instead of obliging me to do over those hundreds of annual reports, the originals of which are at the College, what would you say to this: that we shall speak no more of the past, and the inventories of people and goods will be sent, beginning with this year, to you? . . . Ah, Señor, how great is the power of him who commands, and how hard the fate of the weak, whose rights are incessantly violated!

Since you have them there at hand, read the Junta's other decrees of that same date; they are entirely clear, those decrees! They direct the Governor to assign a guard of six men to each mission, to remove soldiers who are dissolute and immoral the moment the minister so requests, to notify us of the departure of the mail couriers, to interpose no obstacle whatever in the way of our correspondence. . . . Would you like to know how these decrees have been observed? . . .

Was De Croix convinced by the dialectic and the wisdom of these replies? Did he dread the counteroffensive vaguely envisaged there? Was he afraid that the King, to whom the College was appealing, would decide against him? He must have been impressed, also, by the reminder of Luis Jaume's martyrdom—he who had four martyrdoms on his conscience now, since the massacres on the Colorado River. He was coarse and crude, but fair-minded and upright. His *Memoirs* bear witness that he loved the Indians, whose interests only Junípero and his missionaries really cared about and worked for. Perhaps it was this feeling that prevailed over his Febronian ardor and his desire to gratify the Governor. Be that as it may, he dropped all insistence, and things remained as they were.

Junípero continued to gain time, and never to take one backward step. It was by this means that he succeeded to maintaining intact, and in leaving intact to those who came after him, the communal rule he had established. It is true that the "men of reason" who coveted the Indians' wealth put an end to it after fifty years. But for beings who up to that time had known no God, who had been dying of hunger, and who had spent their time in killing one another, these were nevertheless fifty years of Christian life, of material well-being, and of peace.

When he realized that the Presidio was never going to be finished, Junípero abandoned his hut for good and all, took leave of the Governor—whom he was never to see again—and, on the fifth of May, set out once more for Monterey.

Neve did not glory long in this victory of Santa Barbara—the only victory he ever won in Upper California. No Indian came near his village-barrack-fort: the King was wasting his money, since, far from the Redskins' becoming Spaniards, it was the Spaniards from Sonora and their children who, without a priest, were reverting to a state of barbarism. The moment he replaced De Croix as Commandant General, therefore, the former Governor ordered the construction of the Mission of Santa Barbara, and also that of Purisima Concepción.

While Junípero was on his way back to the Carmel the American War of Independence came to its victorious end. He had taken his humble part in it and he showed himself proud of having contributed, with his Indians, to England's defeat. As soon as Charles III took Spain into the war, the Prefect had sent a circular letter to his ministers. "Whereas gratitude obliges us, poor Franciscans that we are, to pray for the Sovereign whose alms keep us alive; whereas the success of his arms is of a nature to promote the spiritual conquest which we have so much at heart. . . . I direct you all," he wrote, on June 15, 1780, "to beseech God to give His Majesty the victory. To this end, every Sunday you will sing the Litany of the Blessed Virgin or the Litany of the Saints after High Mass. They are to be followed by three Credos which the Indians, young and old, will recite in common. For your own part, you will add to the orisons of the private Masses that which is found in the missal, *Contra Hereticos* [Against the Heretics]."

Charles III had imposed a tax of two pesos on the "reasonable men" more than eighteen years of age, and of one peso on the Indians of the same age bracket. In notifying the Prefect of this ordinance, De Croix authorized the missions to pay in kind, and the poorest to give nothing. All of them except San Diego and San Capistrano, which were in debt, were bent upon making their contribution in money.

"Yet our Indians, who have never seen any pesos," Junípero wrote to Father Pangua, "were astonished that the King should ask of them, and should need, those things to fight the war, inasmuch as they themselves had such good and such frequent success in killing one another without any pesos."

Actually the friars were being bled white. "We have paid by making use of our honoraria for Mass and of the provisions we sold to the royal stores," Junípero wrote further, on July 17, 1782. They had also given their precious paper. "The collectors had none. We supplied them with it; some of the ministers are writing me at this moment on pages torn out of the *Baptismal Register;* others sent me their inventories on quarter-pages. . . . The holy College has therefore no reason to blush for its missions; they have fought by all the means they possessed. We have not only prayed, the neophytes and ourselves, from the beginning, but, along with our poor Indians, we have solved the apparently insoluble problem of giving what we do not have—that is to say, about two thousand pesos—to aid in the victory."

Twenty-seven

The Second Administration of Pedro Fages
and the San Gabriel Custody
[1782-1784]

Junípero returned to Carmel on the nineteenth of May. He would soon be seventy years old. The sores on his leg were much more inflamed. "They prescribed a lot of remedies for me," he wrote to Pangua on July 17, 1782. "I took none of them, and I have got well again."

During the month of August, Neve and Fages attempted to bring the Yumas to a state of reason; but these tribes did not cease to be dangerous, and the Anza road became practicable again only when Missions replaced the Rio Colorado villages that had been wiped out. Having brought their campaign to an end, the two officers separated: Neve, appointed Inspector General of the Interior Provinces, set out for Arispe; Fages, appointed Governor ad interim of the two Californias, made his way toward Monterey. A year later, when De Croix had been promoted to be Viceroy of Peru, Neve succeeded him in his office and Fages was confirmed in his. It was Neve and Fages, therefore, with whom Junípero would henceforth have to deal.

"Before leaving the country, the former Governor dictated his instructions on current and unfinished business to his lieutenant," Junípero wrote to Father Pangua on December 8, 1782. Neve demanded from Fages the strict enforcement of the *Reglamento*, and the continued harassment of the missionaries. "I expect nothing but vexatious measures from them," the Prefect wrote to Lasuen on the same date. And to his Guardian, some months later (October 29, 1783), he wrote, "When Señor Neve announced his promotion to me, I was on the point of replying that I would never ask anything from him for the missions, since that would be to invite him to take sides against himself. In the end, I confined myself to expressing the hope that he would become as acceptable to God as he was to the King, making himself worthy, by his conduct, of being one day promoted to eternal glory."

Was this a prophecy? Be that as it may, the fact is that Neve was as close to death as was his correspondent.

On October 12, 1782, Lieutenant Colonel Pedro Fages made his entry into Monterey. The next day, he was received at Carmel to the sound of bells, with full honors, according to the ceremonial that was customary when a strange Father arrived at a mission. What changes had taken place there since the day when he came to beg Junípero to recommend him to Bucareli! It was the same, too, elsewhere. In 1774 there had existed in Upper California only two insignificant and miserable presidios, whose soldiers, lacking bread, were becoming eaters of grass like their horses; and five moribund missions that were hardly able to supply the needs of a dozen children. Today there were four presidios manned by well-fed soldiers, and nine missions where, with the single exception of San Buenaventura, the granaries were full, the animals were numbered by thousands, and five hundred neophytes ate three meals a day.

The presidios were San Diego, commanded by Zuñiga; Santa Barbara, commanded by Ortega; San Francisco, commanded by Moraga; and finally Monterey, where Fages himself would have his residence. Lieutenant Zuñiga exerted himself for the conversion not only of the Indians, through his devotion to the ministering friars, but even the "men of reason," by means of edifying brochures which he wrote himself. Lieutenant Ortega trembled before Fages as fearfully as Fages trembled before Neve. Lieutenant Moraga kept up an unceasing argument and dispute with Francisco Palou.

As for the missions, let us pass them in review for one last time, inasmuch as Junípero was never to have the happiness of founding others. Proceeding from south to north, they were San Diego, with Lasuen and Figuer as ministers; San Capistrano, with Mugartegui and Fuster; San Gabriel, with Sanchez and Cruzado; San Buenaventura, with Cambon and Dumetz; San Luis Obispo, with Cavaller and Juncosa as heads and Paterna as supernumerary; Carmel, with Junípero and Noriega; Santa Clara, with Murguia and La Peña; and San Francisco, with Palou and Santa María. If Fuster is to be seen going back already to San Capistrano, it is because he had been sent there to replace Amurrio, who had returned to the College, at the same time that Dumetz had left Carmel to serve as associate to Cambon.

To these missions and presidios let us not forget to add the tiny village of Los Angeles, whose contribution to the American War of Independence had reached the figure of fifteen pesos, and that of San José, where an "overt act" was about to renew the war between the civil authority and the missions. For with the establishment of that community it was again war in which Pedro Fages was engaged.

Fages himself, nevertheless, had changed a great deal. Without counting the gratitude he seemed to have sworn to Junípero, age and the trials of life had improved him. "He does nothing but speak of his friendship for me," Junípero wrote Pangua in his letter of December 8, 1782. But he added that "he will only be able to show me this friendship when Señor Neve is no longer there. Meanwhile, if he does not carry out his orders punctually, he will be hopelessly lost. Unhappy man, I understand him only too well!"

An unhappy man—how could he be anything else? Behind him, Fages had Neve, commanding and threatening. Before him was Junípero, with resistance and counterattack. As a crowning misfortune he had at his side Señora Eulalia, his wife. Bored to death at Monterey, she was trying with all her might to get back to Mexico City; and, while awaiting the action for legal separation which she intended to bring against her husband, she accused him all day long of adultery and at night locked her bedroom door. One time she did not open her door to him for three months on end. Was Fages attracted to Indian women, as his wife claimed that he was? However that may be, it was Junípero whom he begged to appease Señora Eulalia, at the very moment when he was calling upon him to deliver the originals of the old Mission balance sheets and forbidding him to move the missionaries from one place to another without previous authorization.

With a compassionate feeling toward the disdained husband, and willing to help him—in spite of everything, Fages was to become the father, in 1784, of a little girl who would be named Carmen—Junípero did not yield an inch to the Governor when the latter presented himself in the role of the promulgator of excessive demands as a henchman doing as he was told.

When Fages came back, a letter from Arispe in his hand, to talk about the parishes and the appointment of the priests who would officiate in them, Junípero's answer was prompt and unequivocal. "There will never be any question of that while I am alive," he said. "I will listen to you when you come with some proposition that is more sensible."

And when Fages, constantly driven by pressure from Neve, demanded possession of the past, present, and future inventories of the missions, Junípero had again a clear and straightforward reply.

"So far as the old balance sheets are concerned," the Prefect wrote, on February 25, 1783, "Señor de Croix has wiped the slate clear. Your orders, therefore, have to do only with the present year and the years to come. You will not have the originals, since they go to the College, but I will gladly send you copies of them. There are, however, two conditions: the first is that you direct your presidios to supply us with paper at a reasonable price; the second is that you will grant the missions a postal franchise, in conformity with the Junta's decree. If these conditions are not met, you will have only yourself to blame if I am late in executing your orders, or if I do not execute them at all."

Fages waited "until Neve was no longer there" to grant the postal franchise to the missionaries; also to pay for "the two mules dead in the King's service, and the two bulls eaten by deserters seven years before," whose memory Lasuen and the Prefect never ceased to recall. As an obedient policeman, the Governor was at present carrying out his orders. He sent back to Mexico, for example, the valuable artisans whom Junípero had brought from there in 1774.

He had not been two weeks at Monterey when he dashed off to San José, his angle-gauge and surveyor's rods in his hand. On the last Sunday of October, 1782, Fathers Murguia and La Peña saw boundary marks being set up, under his direction, to separate that adjoining village from their Mission. This land-surveying operation was the last straw. Nothing could be a greater vexation and handicap to the ministers of Santa Clara than the proximity of these "reasonable men" who would spend their time in incessant invasion of the property, theft of the livestock, and pillaging of the harvests of the Mission, to say nothing of their pursuit of the Indian women, and the scandal their way of practicing Christianity would arouse among the neophytes!

"What does this mean, Señor? You know very well that this village must be moved away from here. There is no lack of space for you to move it to! The Law of the Indies obliges you to take it somewhere else, moreover, and Señor Neve has officially promised me that this would be done."

"My orders are to keep it here."

"Here is our protest against it. We beg you to put the Commandery General in possession of this at the earliest possible moment."

"My orders are not to accept it at all."

"Yet you know that it is through you, henceforth, that we must approach the Commandery General."

This time it was too much! On the one hand, by the terms of the *Reglamento,* appeals to the Commandant General had to reach him through the Governor. On the other hand, Neve was ordering the Governor not to receive them. In future, these Lordships would permit themselves to do anything they liked, and the only recourse against them would be Madrid. . . . Junípero made up his mind, then, to strike back, by making the position of the presidios untenable. On October 29, 1783, he announced to the College that his counteroffensive was fully under way.

Before quoting his letter, however, we must mention an interview he had with the Governor during the last weeks of the year 1782.

"This refusal to accept our protests is, you will admit, inconceivable and intolerable."

"I had my orders. Your Reverence knows that you have a friend in me."

"Likewise, it is not against you personally that I have taken a step from which you will all suffer."

A wordless gasp of inquiry. . . .

"Beginning with this coming year, you will no longer have Mass celebrated in the presidios."

"Your Reverence is not unaware, however, that when the *Reglamento* provided that there should be two priests in every mission adjoining a presidio, it was precisely in order that one of them would officiate at the presidio itself."

"I have told you that I neither recognize nor acknowledge this ruling, since the College is appealing from it to the King."

"You always have officiated at the presidios."

"We did it so long as there was an attitude of friendliness toward us. That is not the case any more. When we ask the soldiers to take our mail, or to bring us half a bushel of seeds, they haven't the time, or else they haven't the mules. Each of them has a horse and three mules, however. And as for time, they always have enough of that to give offense to God and scandal to our neophytes."

"We can't prevent everything."

"What I blame your leaders for is that they prevent nothing. Among other things, they do not 'prevent' it when our priestly character is held up to ridicule. This scandal will cease when we no longer come to you, and when it is you who come to us."

"It is ten leagues from Santa Barbara to San Buenaventura."

"And it is ten leagues [twenty-five miles] from San Buenaventura to Santa Barbara, which makes twenty, coming and going. Father Cambon found that a long way, too. The journey gave him an appetite, and you made him pay for the luncheon he had after Mass."

"Those were my orders, very Reverend Father." [1]

"In coming to pray with the *gente sin razón*, your soldiers will see how these Indians 'without reason' understand the Mass, and respect those who have journeyed so far to say it for them."

"Aren't you supposed to officiate at the presidio chapels?"

"There is nothing in writing, anywhere, to that effect."

"But custom, here, makes law."

"We will change our customs, since you have changed yours. Was it the custom to go plant a village a stone's throw from a mission? Or to refuse to transmit the protest of a friar like Father Murguia to the higher authorities?"

"This will be the first time, in this Kingdom, that Mass will not be celebrated in the King's presidios."

[1] It was apparently on orders that José Francisco Ortega acted in this way. This brave soldier, the only one of the early group who never left California, died in 1798 with the rank of captain and is buried in the Old Mission cemetery at Santa Barbara.

"It is also the first time in this Kingdom, where murderers may present appeals for mercy, that an old servant of the King like Father Murguia should not be able to have his appeal delivered to its destination."

"I have come as a friend—Your Reverence knows that."

"Certainly! But after taking away the two artisans from San Gabriel, you are now depriving me of the blacksmith Chamillo, whom I need so much at Carmel."

"Those are my orders. Arispe wants to economize, I believe."

"When the time comes that the holy College again provides you with chaplains, it will require you to pay them; and they will cost you more than Carmel's blacksmith and Father Cambon's luncheons."

"What am I going to say, for my part, to the gentlemen of Arispe?"

"What God inspires you to. They know very well that they have to come to an understanding with San Fernando, since they cannot do so with its delegate. And as a last resort there remains the King. However that may be, when the ministers appeal to their old Prefect against those who cause them suffering and obstruct their work, it is his duty to defend and assist them."

Junípero's letter to Father Sancho, who had succeeded Pangua as Guardian, written under date of October 29-31, 1783, shows that the reprisals against Monterey began in March of that year.

Without being obliged to do so, or receiving remuneration for it [he wrote], we used to go to say Mass in the presidios. I have put an end to this custom. At San Francisco, the Fathers have not been since the first of January. At San Diego they still make their appearance at long intervals, in view of the friendly attitude of Lieutenant Zuñiga. At Monterey I suspended the service of the Mass in March. At Santa Barbara Señor Neve made a new attempt to usurp my functions, by having Ortega order the San Buenaventura ministers to officiate at the presidio, taking turns, every Sunday. Needless to say, Fathers Cambon and Dumetz did not obey. There, as elsewhere, we no longer go to the presidio except to administer the sacraments to the sick. It is not necessary for me to expatiate on the reasons for my determination. The principal one is the attitude of the soldiers and their chiefs. On their part there was nothing but ridicule, malicious behavior, and the refusal to assist us. They claimed the right to dictate to us, saying, "You are under the obligation of serving

us as chaplains; therefore we owe you nothing for your trouble."
Imagine—at Santa Barbara they made Father Cambon pay for his food;
at Monterey they made us bring the wine for the Mass in our sleeves,
rather than give us a few drops of theirs! To me that seemed rather
harsh! Moreover, it is the case that, now that there are only two
Fathers at each mission, if one of them is absent on Sunday to go
to the presidio, some of our neophytes find themselves deprived, by
the failure to have a second Mass, of the benefit of that Mass and
of instruction.

You see that we shall not lack weapons if so be that we are attacked. For my part, even if Señor Neve were to give me orders in
person on this matter, I shall refuse to carry them out so long as I
have not received yours.

As in the affair of the confirmations, Junípero was sending Neve
to pit his strength against the College on a terrain where he was
beaten in advance. For when one thinks of those officers, store-
keepers, soldiers, settlers, men, women, and children—all those
Spaniards and Mexicans who carried scapulars and medals—can
one possibly imagine them forced to forego their religious duties,
or else to travel five, ten, or, in the case of Santa Barbara, more
than twenty-five miles, every Sunday and festival day, to perform
them? Neve would be obliged, it can be seen, to obtain the re-establishment of the suppressed chaplaincies as soon as possible. But
before the College granted that re-establishment, would it not have
something more to say about the *Memorandum* to Mayorga?
Would it not demand the revision, if not the abrogation, of the
Reglamento?

Meanwhile, the Fathers, instead of betaking themselves to the
Presidios, carrying the wine for the Mass with them, to be treated
to impertinences, would see their new congregations arriving every
Sunday at the Missions. There was a great hustle and bustle that
day at the Presidios: all the King's stable had to be mobilized. The
men would set forth on horseback; the women and their young-
sters would be hoisted on to mules; Señora Eulalia was borne in
a litter drawn by two he-mules. The caravan would arrive wet in
winter, burned by the sun in summer, sweating and panting at all
seasons. Everyone took part in the service of the Mass, praying
and singing with the Indians. The Fathers would preach noble
sermons to which even the soldiers had to listen in silence. Then
the missionaries would go back to luncheon in their own houses,

after wishing a happy return to the *gente de razón*, and making an appointment to see them again the next Sunday.

Neve, meanwhile, was counting upon finding a solution to this problem and all the others in the forthcoming establishment of the San Gabriel Custody. Although it never came into existence, we must speak of this project, for it haunted Junípero's mind during the last two years of his life, and was, we believe, the cause of the greatest suffering he had to endure upon this earth.

In the language of the Franciscans, the word "Custody" designates a small group of houses and of friars, responsible only to the Minister General of the Order, and enjoying a practical independence.

The man who originated the plan of establishing Custodies in the Interior Provinces was Father Antonio de Los Reyes, bursar of Santa Cruz College at Querétaro. He was a zealous friar, ambitious, gifted with social resourcefulness and skill, meagerly endowed with common sense, and quite in the habit of lying for the greater glory of God. As early as the year 1772, when it was proposed to withdraw the four Provinces called Interior (New Biscaya, Sinaloa, Sonora, the Californias) from the jurisdiction of the Viceroy, Father Reyes had declared that the missions established in these Provinces must be detached, likewise, from the Apostolic Colleges and grouped into Custodies. The colleges concerned were Guadalupe in Zacatecas, Santa Cruz in Querétaro, and San Fernando in Mexico. His scheme, after the necessary rearrangements, provided for four Custodies—one for each Province. Each of them would include a large convent housing the Custos, the students, the old men, and the sick, together with as many small residences as there were missions. The plan also called for a bishop at Arispe, who would exercise jurisdiction over all the Interior Provinces.

If the initiator of the project was to be believed, the new organization would offer as many advantages as the old one possessed inconveniences. Reyes averred, among other things, that thanks to the philanthropic zest of the neophytes and the settlers every Custody would find all its needed resources at hand, without recourse to the royal treasury. Another advantage would be the elimination of the distances separating the missionaries from their superiors, vast and paralyzing distances which, he used to say, were hindering the development of the missions.

One can guess at the enthusiasm with which the Febronians welcomed this project! No more all-powerful Colleges or invulnerable Discretories to interpose themselves between the missionaries and the agents of the State! The friars subject to their Custos, and he to the local Governor; the Bishop of Arispe keeping watch over the Custos and himself obedient to the Commandant General, his neighbor—what admirable centralization! what well-geared machinery! This system would work to the advantage of the Vice Patron and of the *Reglamento*, then in course of preparation, as of the State. One might think that Neve himself had breathed the idea in Father Reyes' ear!

Father Reyes had presented it, in 1772, to Bucareli, who could not be said to have shown himself favorably inclined. Returning to the charge two years later, he had just as little success. He then determined to lay his project before the King, and accordingly set sail for Madrid. Charles III gave a cordial reception to the Franciscan who was ready to propose the cessation of payments of *sinodos*, rations, transport, and initial expenses in the establishment of the missions. After four years of solicitations and maneuvers, and a great many falsehoods, Father Reyes departed from Madrid with an episcopal mitre, a pontifical brief, and all the royal decrees he could have wished for. The mitre was for himself: he became Bishop of Arispe. One of the royal decrees created the four Custodies in question; another charged the new Bishop with their establishment; still another enjoined the Viceroy, Commandant General, and Superiors of the Colleges to assist him in his task. The brief of Pius VI, under date of November 19, 1779, gave supreme official sanction to the new institution.

After his consecration, which took place in Mexico City on September 15, 1781, Bishop Reyes went off to occupy his episcopal seat and to set about establishing his four Custodies. At almost the same time, a Memorandum of protest addressed to the King by the three Apostolic Colleges was dispatched to Madrid. These Custodies were simply Utopias, they said in effect. The date of this document was February 15, 1782, and in October of the following year Junípero, on his part, drew up a Memorandum establishing the same point of view. "To rely for the basic sustenance of these Custodies upon savages of whom the majority are still running about without clothing," he said, "is to ask one naked man to clothe another. I foresee, therefore, that these 'large con-

vents' and the missions will die a natural death unless the City of
Mexico is picked up and planted among the Indians, and His
Majesty assumes all the expense."

Forcing the hand of the College of Querétaro, to which the
Sonora Missions were subject, Reyes and Felipe de Neve set up
their first Custody, San Carlos-en-Sonora, on October 25, 1782.
It was when they tried to found the second, that of San Gabriel,
that they came to grips with a difficulty of real consequence. Inasmuch as the territory allotted to this Custody—Lower and Upper
California—was in fact divided between Dominicans and Franciscans, it followed that one of the Orders would have to give place
to the other. But which of the two should be sacrificed? The King
was postponing his decision until Neve and Reyes should have
taken counsel together and reported to him. Once more, to whom
would our reporters give the preference?

The Franciscan Reyes, who held a continuing grudge against
San Fernando for its hostility to the project, fixed his choice upon
the Dominicans. He sent for Father Hidalgo, Prefect of the Dominicans in Lower California, who hurried to Sonora with a
Memorandum of one hundred articles, and the Bishop was equally
charmed by the Prefect and by his document. On taking leave of
him, he warned him not to divulge any plans, so long as the King
had not yet pronounced himself on the subject at issue. But how
could the Dominicans of the Peninsula keep silent over such a
happy event? How could they refrain from caroling their victory
already? Their songs of rejoicing reached Junípero, who thus
learned that the former Father Reyes was planning to banish him,
him and the Fernandinos, from California.

In this, God was visiting upon him his crowning trial. As he
wrote his last letters he found himself shedding tears, even breaking into sobs. On October 31, 1783, a letter shows him still hoping
that "the danger is not imminent." It quickly became so, as is seen
by what he wrote to Lasuen on April 4, 1784:

"Judging the Dominican Fathers to be more capable than ourselves, the Commandant General is about to put an end to our
apostolate in this region where we were the first to bring news
of the true God and to plant the cross. . . . What evil things must
have been said of us at the court of Madrid, that Señor Galvez
would permit us to be expelled! All this must be the result of my
sins. What else does it mean, if not that the hour has struck for

me to improve! Ask God to grant me grace to do so; and may dear Father Juan Figuer also pray for me! . . ."

Two months later, on June 18, he wrote to his Guardian: "Our dishonorable explusion has become everybody's secret. The soldiers speak of it openly. The Dominican Fathers themselves announce that it will not be long before they go northward. God's will be done! . . . If those who are coming to supplant us do better than we, we must not regret it, since all we have to wish for is the advancement of God's kingdom. Without doubt we should have preferred that those friars would exercise their zeal elsewhere, leaving us to do a little good here; but the judgments of God are inscrutable, and it is not for us to find fault with what He disposes and what He allows."

And three weeks before his death—on August 6, 1784—he wrote: "The College no longer has many missions, and it did everything (in Rivera's time) not to have any more. Who knows if it is not a just punishment from on high, if we are now on the point of not having any?"

It might be wondered where the Dominicans, so few in number, would find the necessary ministers to officiate in the northern missions; but the hundred-article Memorandum stated that quality would make up for the deficiency in numbers, and that the Dominican methods would make up for everything.

"I am sending it to you," Bishop Reyes wrote Neve (in reference to this document) on December 13, 1783. "Read it, and you will be convinced that these friars have found the only good way of converting and dealing with the Indians. They have applied it, moreover, in Lower California, where they have restored the missions which had been handed over to them [by Palou] in such a bad state. They will certainly do as much in that northern California which the Franciscans are in process of dragging down to ruin! It is therefore my conclusion that the Dominicans should have Upper as well as Lower California. I am waiting for word of what you think about this."

"What do I think about it, Your Excellency?" Neve replied ten days later (December 23, 1783). "I acquiesce completely in your conclusion, provided that it is reached by taking precisely the opposite point of view. After maturely weighing the serious interests at stake, I am of the opinion that the Franciscans should be given the Peninsula, where the Dominicans have accomplished

nothing in all the time they have been there. I know their methods, and I know them personally, having been Governor there
for four years: they would no sooner have taken possession of
these missions—all of which would be handed over to them in
good condition—than they would throw everything into confusion and do one thing after another to bring them into disrepute.
Do you want names, dates, and facts, Your Lordship?"

Neve cited some of these facts, which would have seemed hard
to believe if other documents had not proved them to be true. "I
tell you again," he continued, "they are all restless souls; most of
them have changed their posts three times in ten years. Fortunately
it is in a district long since pacified that the arrogance and despotism of these friars has had free rein. But we should have to fear the
worst if they should come to exercise their activity in a region
where uncounted pagan populations do not yet recognize the authority of the King. Not for anything in the world, therefore,
would I be willing to see the Dominicans in Upper California.

"As for the Fathers of San Fernando," Neve went on, "what
they have accomplished in this region is, strictly speaking, unbe-
lievable; and the annoyances they have caused me in the course of
six years do not prevent my recognizing the fact that, in a very
short time, they have obtained results that are literally marvelous
(*monstruosos*). Their success in stockbreeding is magnificent, in
spite of the small number of animals brought into the country;
their harvests produce more than the natives can eat; the roll of
their neophytes increases day by day, and although they manage
them with a certain rudeness they have succeeded in making themselves masters through their understanding of the character and
customs of these savages, as well as the manner of dealing with
their chiefs. They have neophytes at a radius of as many as eight
and ten leagues [20 and 25 miles] from the Missions. . . . Would
you like me to cite a few examples of their methods? When an
Indian woman gives birth to a child it is taken to the mission
where the friars baptise it and give it a shirt and other clothes.
From time to time the child's relations come to make a present
of food to the missionaries, always bringing corn and other supplies, until the day when the child is definitely taken into the
sanctuary to be instructed in the mysteries of our holy religion.
It is by these ingenious and affecting methods that these friars
have succeeded in bringing vast populations into submission to His

Majesty's authority, accomplishing a work which has no equivalent in the Interior Provinces. . . . Of all that, no doubt, Your Lordship has been ignorant. But now that you know it I feel sure you will agree with me that the missions of Upper California should be left to the Fernandinos and that, at the same time, they should be given back those which they lately possessed on the Peninsula."

This is certainly the greatest—and, when we think who it was that signed it—the most just eulogy that could have been pronounced upon the work Junípero had performed. Not that Neve had reached a reconciliation with him. Although his expedition among the Yumas had taught him much, his letters show that he still cherished resentment against the old man who had held him in check. But Neve was one of those statesmen in whom the service of the prince and the good of the country take precedence over every other passion. Since his travels and his government service had convinced him that no missionaries were as valuable as those whom Junípero had trained and directed, it was less than ever the moment, now that he bore the supreme responsibility, for giving up a team that was capable of such "miracles" (*monstruosos*). He therefore showed the door, so to speak, to the bishop who suggested it.

It was in vain that Bishop Reyes returned a month later (January 21, 1784) with a new report ringing the changes on the boastings of the hundred-article Memorandum and the rancors of his own heart. Neve stuck to his letter of December 23; and on January 26, 1784, he sent it to the Minister of the Indies, along with the other documents in the case. Only too happy to avenge his old friend Junípero at last, and to expel from the Peninsula the Dominicans who in 1772 had insinuated themselves there against his will, Galvez sent the King a report urging him to adopt the Commandant General's solution.

Charles III allowed himself to be persuaded. But when San Fernando refused the gift of the Peninsula when the King offered it, the Sovereign decided in the end to leave things as they were, and on March 23, 1787, he issued an edict forbidding his subjects to make further mention of the Custody of San Gabriel. It died, thus, before it was born. And Bishop Reyes, who had never been able to establish the other two, died in his turn a few months later.

Junípero had then departed from this world. He did not see the service of the chaplains re-established in the Presidios, the *Reglamento* shorn of its objectionable and harmful provisions, his own methods finally recognized as most beneficial to the welfare of the "poor Indians"; he did not know that the cause on which he had expended so much intelligence, courage, and labor had won a victory that was to endure for the next fifty years in Upper California.

Twenty-eight

Junípero's Last Labors
[1783-1784]

Reaching the College at the same time as the news of Señor Neve's access of authority, Junípero's appeal for missionaries had slight repercussions. The only active response to it came from Fathers Riobo and Noboa, who disembarked at San Francisco on June 2, 1783, and traveled thence to Carmel by land.

The old padre, who had been confined to his bed, got up to welcome them, and embraced them with exuberant warmth. Yet what sadness, and what disappointment, he must have felt in seeing that they were only two! It was four new fellow workers, at least, that he had been expecting. So he would not be able to establish the Missions of Santa Barbara and Purisima Concepción before he died, as he had so longed to do? . . . "As always," writes Palou, "he thanked God for this unforeseen challenge to endurance, and only prayed the more that He would send additional workers to the harvest."

It might have been said that he felt the last year of his life had come. He had seldom been in such bad health. "His asthma, an ailment which had first come upon him twenty years ago and to which he had always refused to pay any attention, had laid hold of him again. The scars of the burns he had inflicted upon himself in the pulpit, when preaching on Hell, had reopened. He was only just recovering from a serious attack of pneumonia. He would have seizures of choking. . . ." In this condition, and in spite of the protests of his colleagues, he made up his mind to undertake a general tour of confirmation at the various missions. His ten-year Indult would expire on July 16, 1784. Fearing that it might not be renewed, he wished at any cost to assure its benefits to the two thousand neophytes who, in one place and another, had not been confirmed.

313

At the beginning of August, Fages' appointment as Governor was ratified, while Neve became Commandant General in succession to De Croix, who had been named Viceroy of Peru. About the tenth of the month, Junípero announced his intention of taking the boat that was about to sail back to San Blas. A few days later, his confrères helped him to climb on to a mule, and he rode off toward Monterey.

As they embraced their aging Prefect, Fathers Noriega, Riobo, and Noboa might well believe that they were clasping him in their arms for the last time. As for himself, he had set his affairs in order. In making an appointment for a meeting with Father Riobo at the end of October, he added, "If no notice is received to the contrary"—that is, if no notice was received of his death. On the day of his sailing, as he gave his instructions to Vice Prefect Palou—his eventual successor—he concluded his letter, "And I am telling you all this because my illness has become so aggravated that perhaps we shall not see each other again. Commend your friend to God!"

He disembarked at San Diego about the sixth of September. "I arrived in good health," he wrote to his Guardian on October 27, 1783. And God, who had again healed him, gave him the consolation, in the months that followed, of seeing that his fourteen years of faith and effort had borne fruit.

To begin with San Diego, which had dealt him so many blows of disappointment in the course of eight years. . . . In 1769 he had found only naked savages there. Now solidly constructed buildings rose on the Cosoy hill, with a fine church where seven hundred Indians, decently clothed, assembled every Sunday. The harvests were becoming better and better. Fathers Lasuen and Figuer now possessed a thousand sheep, five hundred goats, more than two hundred horses, and a proportionate number of cows. On September 13 Junípero made a note, in the Register for that purpose, of the Mission's 606th confirmation. Two days later, the boat weighed anchor, bearing his Memorandum against the Custody of San Gabriel on its way to Mexico City.

Junípero lingered two weeks longer in these spots that brought back so many memories. Here, his dear Juan Crespi had declared that he was willing to eat grass with him. There, his servant José María, spitting blood, had died in his arms. A little farther on, the tombs of the sixty victims of the pestilence stood in rows. Good

Dr. Prat, who had taken care of them, had died insane. Dead, also, and committed to the sea not far from here, was the great seaman Juan Perez, whose boat—when they caught sight of it on the evening of March 19—had prevented the withdrawal from these lands. And what old friends among the Indians he was finding again! There were, for example, those who had tried to kill him in August, 1769; those also who had murdered Father Luis Jaume, and whom he had saved from the supreme punishment.

The command of the Presidio of San Diego was now in the hands of Lieutenant Zuñiga. An admirable man, a friend to the Fathers, author of a brochure entitled *The School of Truth* which Junípero (to whom it was given in personal homage) had declared to be "full of excellent matters," José Zuñiga aspired to the title of "Associate Brother of the Holy College." His mother, who shared his aspiration and left no stone unturned to help him achieve it, had failed in her efforts at San Fernando. She failed also with Father Lasuen, who answered her appeal with the statement that such a favor was reserved for "the greatest benefactors of the Order." But with Junípero she succeeded: "Let us not be so strict," he wrote to Lasuen on April 17, 1784. "For whom have titles been invented if not for those who attach importance to them? 'Great benefactors of the Order'? Here is just the case for the application of the adage, 'There is an exception to every rule.'" Was it his fault if Zuñiga was not one of the greatest benefactors of the Order, as he was not one of the greatest writers of Spain? "I beg you," Junípero wrote to his Guardian on August 6, 1784, "let us support his request; let us do all the good we can, and as much as we are able."

And the final lines of his last letter to the College asked that the diploma of "Associate Brother" be given to the dear Lieutenant.

On the second of October, the eve of his departure, Junípero solemnly baptized José Setemerp, a six-year-old Redskin, whose godfather was José Zuñiga. It was the 984th baptism celebrated at San Diego, where, thirteen years earlier, he himself in nine months had not been able to achieve a single one.

Making his way northward, Junípero reached San Capistrano, a mission in which there were to date only four hundred Christians. He probably found this number meager, for he increased it upon his arrival in Paradise. "We baptized more people in the four months after his death than in the three years that preceded it," wrote Father Mugartegui in 1785.

He left San Capistrano on October 15, passed once more through the place where the Indians had tried to kill him in 1776, and came to San Gabriel. There he administered 237 confirmations, which brought to 866 the number of neophytes confirmed at this mission.

Father Riobo, faithful to the appointment made with Junípero, arrived on the twenty-seventh of October. He brought a letter from Father Sancho, who had succeeded Father Pangua the previous May. Sancho was an old friend of Junípero, and had been his fellow worker on the Peninsula. "Thank you, my Superior and my friend," Junípero wrote him on that same day, "for having thought again of naming me Prefect. But I shall not finish my present term; I shall leave office before you do—for, although I do not know the date of my death, I know that it is near. The twenty leagues [50 miles] I have traversed just now have rather fatigued me, and I tremble a little at the idea of the hundred more that I have still to go. May God be my help! If He wills that I am to reach Carmel, I shall risk my destiny anew by setting out for the north as soon as possible, to complete the circuit of my tour. It will soon fall to you—unless you should do it now—to choose the man who is to replace me. Remember that this must be a Prefect who will have more of health and of judgment than is possessed by the sinner that I am."

Without naming him, he seemed to be urging the candidacy of Lasuen: "Father Palou has long cherished the hope of going back to the College; your two predecessors have given their authorization to this. It is on my insistence that he still delays his departure, but I have qualms about continuing to hold him here any longer. His health, which is completely shattered, is incapable of supporting the long journeys that a Prefect is compelled to take, and his presence would be more useful in Mexico City than here. It is a fact that he has a right to a good rest. As for myself, I am not counting on that in this life."

This letter was hardly written when Junípero fell ill again. One morning during Mass the young Indians who were assisting went running out with cries that he was dying. Father Sanchez, the chief minister, at once warned Francisco Palou that a fatal outcome was to be feared. Then the dying man came back to life, and on the ninth of November he himself informed Lasuen that he was "quite recovered. The oppression in the chest has almost disappeared," he added. "I am counting on leaving tomorrow. But who knows what will happen to my poor carcass on the roads over which I am going to drag it? Old statues run a greater risk of falling to pieces when they go in a procession than when they remain in their niches. . . . I received your two letters yesterday: the one that dealt with the King's service; the other—how shall I say it better?—that related to our friendship. . . ."

On November 10 he bade a last farewell to Fathers Sanchez and Cruzado, and set out with Father Riobo toward San Buenaventura. It was there that, on November 24, he spent his seventieth birthday. He administered only a few confirmations in his "dear Mission," which, although it had been in existence for eighteen months, still counted few baptized Christians. Benito Cambon and Francisco Dumetz were not of the first rank, actually, as converters of the heathen; and he proposed that Father Riobo should replace one of them; but they both cried out against it.

"Whatever would become of Father Dumetz if I were sent elsewhere?" Benito Cambon demanded.

"For Father Cambon's sake, do not take me away from here!" cried Francisco Dumetz.

Junípero had not the heart to order the separation of companions who were, for the time being, so united. Taking Father Riobo with him, he made his way toward Santa Barbara.

When he was on these confirmation circuits, each mission he left supplied him with an escort as far as the next mission. From Santa Barbara to San Luis, it was a detachment from the presidio that accompanied our travelers. They all slept under a tent, even in the cold of winter. Did the old padre wake Father Riobo as he often used to wake Francisco Palou? On these occasions Father Palou would ask, "What is the matter? Do you need anything, Reverend Father?"

"*Gloria Patri et Filio et Spiritui Sancto,*" Junípero would reply, without stirring from his sleep.

"And that is how I learned," writes Palou, "that he prayed and worshipped even when he was sleeping."

Junípero "wept without ceasing," Palou continues, while he was going along by the sea, on that part of the coast known as the Channel, where some twenty heathen tribes lived in their sugarloaf huts. "It was to his own sins that he attributed this manifest failure in his apostolic career. Indeed the two Missions of Santa Barbara and La Purisima Concepción should have been founded a long time ago. They had not been established in Rivera's time, on the pretext that there were not enough soldiers; they could not be, now, because the missionaries themselves were lacking. With a Prefect endowed with greater righteousness, he argued, matters would have taken another course. . . . He continued to be inconsolable on this point, and, in my opinion, this grief hastened his death."

At San Luis Obispo he met up again with two former members of the opposition who had long since become his friends: Father Cavaller, whose Mission now counted riches to the extent of nine hundred cows, five hundred goats, sixty pigs, and 106 horses; and Father Paterna, who now looked upon Junípero as a saint.

The Prefect arrived at San Antonio about the twentieth of December, and spent the end of the year with his compatriots Fathers Pieras and Sitjar. No men had worked better, or had caused him less vexation or grief. They had baptized 1,127 Indians since that day when only one had come running to the sound of the bell Junípero had set pealing in the forest wilderness. "He who could not hear a religious chant without weeping," writes Palou, "what tears of gratitude he must have shed in singing the Christmas canticles with this throng of neophytes before the crêche!"

As soon as he returned to Carmel in January, 1784, he set to work once more, refusing to take any rest. He celebrated all the long and fatiguing rites of Lent and Holy Week. On the eve of Easter, April 10, he administered the Mission's one-thousandth baptism. A fortnight later, when the Indians' Easter confessions and communions were finished, he set out in a litter on his last confirmation tour.

One is happy to think that he should have made this tour, thus, in a certain amount of comfort, and grateful to Pedro Fages and his wife for having done this for him.[1] Fages consented to officiate, as sponsor, at the dedication and inauguration of the new church at Santa Clara. They set out with the escort. The Governor rode

---

[1] The name of Señora Fages was Eulalia Calliz. The birth of a little girl in August, 1784, brought about a reconciliation between her and her husband, but this can hardly have lasted long, since as early as 1785 Eulalia sued Pedro on a charge of adultery. See *Provincia Internas, Archivo Nacional* (Mexico), Vol. CXX, for her complaints and the inquiry to which they gave rise.

by the door of the litter. "Señora Fages occupied the center part of this handsome contrivance," Junípero wrote, "enclosed in her little cabin, sheltered from sun and wind. Myself, I was in the open air," behind the head mule.

They reached Santa Clara on April 29. On Sunday, May 2, Junípero said Mass and confirmed 140 children. "This was a beautiful day for us all," he wrote to Father Sancho on June 16, 1784, "especially for the Governor and his wife, whose extreme satisfaction was plain to be seen. The next day, Father Murguia fell ill. We thought it would be a matter of no consequence, and, the day after, we went on our way toward San Francisco, putting off until our return the confirmation of adults and the consecration of the church."

On the Thursday evening, in San Francisco, Junípero learned that Father Murguia was worse. He sent Francisco Palou to him immediately. On Tuesday, the eleventh, at 4 o'clock, he received word of his death. He announced it to his colleagues in the following letter:

Dear colleagues, my lords,
The peace of Our Lord be with you!
I have to break some news to you which will grieve you all very deeply: this morning, at a quarter past nine, it pleased God to call to Himself the soul of the Reverend Father Fray José Antonio de Murguia. He died as a true friar and a good son of our Seraphic Father St. Francis, at Santa Clara, fortified with the sacraments of Penance, the Eucharist, and Extreme Unction, solaced by the presence of Fray Thomas de La Peña and Fray Francisco Palou. I had left his Mission on the fourth of May to come here. He had taken to his bed the evening before. We thought at first that it would be no more than an attack of indigestion; but soon the symptoms of brain fever appeared, and the Father succumbed. May God receive him in His glory!
That he may as soon as possible enter into the enjoyment of eternal repose, I bid each one of you to celebrate twenty low Masses and one high Mass in his behalf. I also direct that each mission, on the receipt of this circular letter, will make all haste to deliver it to the mission next on the way. God keep Your Reverences in His grace through long years to come!
In this Mission of San Francisco, the eleventh of May, 1784, I kiss your hands, and remain your servant and affectionate colleague,
Fray Junípero Serra.

Father Murguia's funeral took place the next day, May 12. Francisco Palou officiated, as well as Father La Peña. "Things do not ordinarily happen like this," Palou wrote. "We are all separated from one another by such distances that when one missionary dies the one who survives is left alone to bury the one who is gone, without any other presence than that of the neophytes and the six soldiers of the escort guard."

After completing the San Francisco confirmations, Junípero set out again for Santa Clara, with Pedro Fages and his wife, on Thursday the thirteenth. In the afternoon of Saturday the fifteenth, the church was dedicated. At the head of the procession, with Lieutenant Moraga at his left, marched the Governor, holding an enormous key in his hand. He opened the door of the new temple, which was consecrated forthwith. In his sermon, Junípero paid homage to the man who had just built this great church, and who for the last four days had been reposing in his tomb before the altar. In the following month he spoke again of the dead friar to Father Sancho: "I do not cease to regret the loss of this outstanding worker, whom none of us, perhaps, could equal as a missionary. Although his Mission was so recently established, it was, in every respect, the most advanced of them all. And to think, too, that because of Father La Peña's illness all the burden of the work has fallen on his shoulders for several years back! I am sending herewith the little list of books he was accustomed to using; Your Reverence will dispose of them as you see fit."

Junípero let Governor Fages and his wife go back to Monterey without him. As Francisco Palou was preparing to return to his Mission, he stopped him. "He told me," Palou writes, "that this might be the last time we could be together, and he wished to take advantage of it in preparing for death. He went into retreat for several days, then he again made his general confession, shedding abundant tears as he did so. I wept as profusely as he, for there was little likelihood that we should see each other again. We had always hoped that, if we could not die together, the one who went first would be helped and comforted in his last hours by the presence of his friend. But with all the leagues that lay between how could we expect God to bring about that favor for us? . . . The revered Father baptized several more catechumens, and confirmed several sick people in their distant huts; then we parted."

Early in June, Junípero went back to Carmel. He assigned

Father Noboa to succeed Father Murguia, sent Father Riobo to replace Father Cambon (who, already tired of San Buenaventura, wanted to return to San Francisco), and remained alone with Father Noriega as sole companion. In spite of his increasing weakness and the oppression in his chest, he returned to his customary routine of activity. He taught the Indians, prayed and sang with them, regulated their affairs for them, and superintended their work. In addition to a half-hour spent in saying his Mass and an hour in reciting his breviary, he gave two long periods daily to meditation. And he continued to write to his superiors and his colleagues those immeasurably long letters that had always cost him so much labor.

He kept the fullness of his faculties to the end: his magnificent intelligence, his prodigious memory, and that acute sensitiveness through which so much of human suffering pierced his own heart. And we know, too, that God constrained him to drink his cup then, to the lees. At any moment the Dominicans might appear, and drive him with his fellow workers from the country. The soldiers were talking of nothing else now. What anguish this was for the friars of San Fernando! What a crowning indignity for him who had been their leader! Yet had they worked so badly, they and he?

In the same letter to Father Sancho just quoted, he wonders: "If, for having administered more than 6,000 baptisms and 5,307 confirmations in this population of unbelievers where the name of the Saviour had never been pronounced, for having done so much ploughing and so much building, the holy College has earned the recompense of being henceforth deprived of all missions, let it endure it with patience! We must all accept our suffering. By that means, at least, all envy will cease. . . . Meanwhile, I submit myself to the will of God and to that of my Superiors, who in my eyes are but one."

To cite the exact figures, Junípero and his colleagues had baptized 6,410 persons since their arrival in Upper California, as follows: at San Diego, 1,046; San Capistrano, 472; San Gabriel, 1,019; San Buenaventura, 53; San Luis Obispo, 616; San Antonio, 1,127; San Carlos del Carmelo, 1,014; Santa Clara, 669; and Dolores de San Francisco, 394.

The Indult granted for ten years by Pope Clement XIV expired on July 16, 1784. "It was on this day," writes Palou, "that Junípero received within himself the notice that death was near." He had just confirmed the 938th neophyte at the Mission.

On this same date, July 16, the frigate arrived at San Francisco. No friar was aboard. Father Sancho promised two for the following year. The community of San Fernando, he explained, had never been so reduced in numbers. Two of its members, Fathers Verger and Ramos, had become bishops; several had returned to Europe on the termination of their ten-year enlistment period; death was striking heavy blows among the older men, five of whom, including Father Pangua, had succumbed in the course of one month; no quota had assured them a relief force since 1770, and there was no word from the contingent that Father García was then recruiting in Spain.

Father Sancho's letter confirmed the old man's feeling that for him his task had come to an end. God was reserving for others— for the Dominicans or for his own colleagues—the charge of continuing it. Junípero wrote then to all his ministers. Those in the southern missions he exhorted always to labor tirelessly and well, and to welcome his successor—whoever he might be—as the envoy of God; and he promised a meeting with them in eternity. Those of San Antonio and San Luis, who must come to get the things the boat had brought them, he urged to hurry, since he wished to talk with them. He likewise sent for Francisco Palou, leaving him free to choose whether to make the journey by land or sea.

On July 27 he received a communication from the Governor, informing him that the Commandant General had ordered the establishment of a mission at Montecito, near the Santa Barbara Presidio. "Everyone knows that I have always considered this mission and several others to be necessary," Junípero replied. "How many Indians of Montecito and elsewhere would be in Heaven already if I had been listened to! Nothing, then, my very dear Señor, would be more agreeable to me than to set out with you this very day for the Channel. . . . But, alas, there are no ministers for this new work. All that I can do is write immediately to the College to get them. . . ."

He wrote on August 6 to Father Sancho, the last letter that we have from him.

I have suffered deeply in the death of so many of our Brothers [he wrote]. But I have been so happy to learn that your procession on Corpus Christi Day was so beautiful, and enhanced still further by the presence of our two Bishops. Happy Superior! Happy community! May its fine religious spirit flourish anew! Saints, saints—that is what we need! May God grant you the graces necessary for the right training and development of our new missionaries! May they not be like the old ones; the more one gave in to them, the more they redoubled their demands! And then, too many among them have gone away. . . . Now that you are few in number, that the lesson of the dead is still present to all, that there have been so many desertions, and that a new era is beginning with a new Superior, would this not be the moment to revive the original fervor? . . . But you know all this better than I do. In any case, I promise you my most complete obedience; and I ask your blessing.

He spoke again of the Custody:

Because no friar has come this year, it does not follow that none should come next year. On the contrary, I ask you to send for them, convinced though we may be that we are to be sent away from here. Twenty-five will leave as easily as eighteen, if so be that we must go. Let us serve well, for so long as we are permitted to serve. I am bearing in mind, moreover, that, in spite of his desire to favor the Reverend Fathers of the Dominican Order, His Lordship needs the consent of Señor Neve to carry out his idea, and that it will still be necessary, when they are both agreed, to have the approval of Madrid before they can achieve their ends. All that, in my opinion, is not going to work out so quickly.

However this may be, you are to take it as assured that all your injunctions will be obeyed. It is in all deference and religious submission that I shall hand the missions over to the Dominican Fathers —if they come. I shall merely beg them to give me a receipt, for us to keep, of the persons and goods which we shall have delivered to them. . . . May Your Reverence be neither saddened nor disquieted! God and His grace are present everywhere. I am confident that Our Immaculate Lady will permit us still to do good upon the earth, as we wait for her to open Heaven's door to us.

Twenty-nine

Junípero's Death
[1784]

Without waiting for the frigate to sail, the faithful Palou had set out overland. When he arrived at Carmel on Wednesday, August 18, he found his master still up and about, but breathing with great difficulty. At the evening service, when he heard him singing in his usual beautiful voice, he said to one of the soldiers of the escort, "The Father Prefect does not seem to be doing so badly, does he?"

"Do not deceive yourself," replied the soldier, who had known Junípero since 1769. "This saintly man is always in good voice when it is a matter of praying or singing, but I tell you that his condition is hopeless."

The next day, the sick man asked his guest to say Mass in his place. For some days he continued to go to the church, and to take part in the prayers and hymns; but from that time on he was not able to officiate.

"We began the conversations for which he had summoned me," Palou writes. The conversations took place in Junípero's cell. This room, to which one gained access through a large antechamber, was furnished with a bed, a table, a straight chair, some shelves of books, and a wicker armchair that had been there for only a short time. The bed had no mattress: it consisted of three unplaned boards, two blankets, and a pillow. On the pillow rested a crucifix a foot long. At night Junípero, sleeping on the bare boards, used to lay it upon his breast. Along with the blankets and pillow, he had always taken this great figure of Christ with him on his travels.

"Every time I went into his cell," writes Palou, "I found my master lost in thought, as if he were absent from this world. I learned from Father Noriega that this mysterious concentration, this gathering together of the life of the soul, had been going on since the day when the Indult of Confirmation expired."

Was this death that was drawing near? In any case the hour of separation for the two friends had come. It was settled, indeed, that Francisco Palou should take the frigate back to Mexico and go on from there to Madrid, to inform Galvez of what was afoot in regard to the missions.

"You want me to desert you, then, at this moment?" he asked.

"Let us offer this supreme sacrifice to God," Junípero answered. "While I am still alive, go!"

The hearts of these two faithful men, who had fought the good fight together for thirty-five years, were torn not only by the grief of final separation from one another, but still more by the great injustice and public humiliation that menaced their beloved College. They would have had less to suffer if they had known that Neve, whom they believed to be their adversary, was actually their ally, and that his letter of December, 1783, was now in Galvez' hands. Nor did they know that the Commandant General was in his death throes while they were deliberating. Felipe de Neve died, in fact, at Arispe on Saturday, August 21, 1784, at four o'clock in the afternoon. What were his last moments? . . . Let us hope that at the hour when the good deeds a man has done bring more cheer to his heart than do the honors and pleasures he has sought for, Neve congratulated himself on having done justice to the Fernandinos, and that he felt the effect of the "poor prayers" which Junípero continued to address to God in his behalf.

On Monday the twenty-third, the frigate dropped anchor in the port of Monterey. Canizares, who was now in command of it, immediately sent Juan García, the ship's doctor, to Carmel. The physician suggested applying red-hot irons to the sick man's flesh, in order to clear the congestion in the chest. "Do whatever you wish," Junípero responded. And he allowed his body to be cauterized without giving any sign of pain.

During the next two days, he made use of the respite his illness was granting him to cut out for the Indians the fabrics the ship had brought. Suddenly, in the midst of this, Palou recounts, an eighty-year-old Indian woman arrived—"the old chicken woman," who was thus known because in the early days, when the Mission had only one brood of fowl, she had been discovered ravaging the barnyard. Hidden with her grandson behind the hedge, she was pointing out the chickens; and the boy, already a good shot, was striking them down with his arrows. "They must have given themselves quite a treat at our expense," Palou writes, "for—through forethought, no doubt—they had spared only the sitting hen." Now Junípero laid aside his scissors and received the old woman kindly. She explained that she could not sleep at night because she was cold. He got her one of his two blankets, and she took it away with her. Palou goes on:

" 'Is it because she has come to settle for your chickens that you have made her this present?' I asked.

" 'Exactly so!' he answered, laughing."

On Wednesday, he expressed his regret that the Fathers from San Antonio and San Luis had not arrived. He was anxious to see them again, so that he might persuade them to give a good welcome to the Dominicans—if these should present themselves. Had the Fathers not received his summons? Palou sought information at the Presidio, and learned that with their usual insouciance the couriers had left the Prefect's letters there. He sent them on by special messenger with an added word of alarm.

Junípero was more exhausted when he got up on Thursday morning. He had had a painful night. "There is nothing left for me," he said to Palou, "but to prepare myself to fulfill the divine will." He spent the entire day in the same state of recollection as before, and made his general confession again in the evening, "weeping with sorrow at the memory of his sins."

After taking a bowl of broth, he went to bed, refusing to allow anyone to sit up with him. The night that followed was no better than the last one had been, as he admitted on Friday morning to Father Palou, who had come into his cell before going to celebrate Mass, and found him reciting his breviary.

"Keep a consecrated host for me," he said. "As for the rest, we will consider that later."

After Mass had been said, Junípero announced that he wished to receive the Sacrament in the church. It was in vain that Palou offered to bring the holy Viaticum to him. "It is not for Our Lord to move from His place for me, but for me to go to Him, since I am able to do so," he answered.

They had to yield to his determined will.

The Indians formed in procession, which was joined by the Mission escort, and with them the Commandant of the Presidio and part of the Presidio troop. Junípero dragged himself along at the procession's end. When he reached the steps of the sanctuary, he knelt before the little table placed there for the occasion, and in his usual strong voice—but this time broken by sobs —he intoned the *Tantum Ergo*. Those present were so overcome by emotion that he sang it almost alone. Father Palou gave him Communion. The old padre offered his thanksgiving to God on the steps; then the procession took him back to the residence. Almost everyone was weeping. He went into his cell, sat down at the table, and continued his prayers.

"I was sitting in the anteroom, making sure that he was not disturbed," Palou writes, "when the carpenter from the Presidio arrived without warning and claimed the right to enter. I objected.

" 'The Father has sent for me, to take measurements for his coffin,' he declared.

"I burst into tears. The man insisted:

" 'I really must speak with him, so I may know how he wants it!'

" 'Make it just like the one you made for Father Crespi,' I said.

"He ended by going away."

Junípero spent the entire day in his armchair, not speaking a word, taking nothing to eat but a little broth; he was engrossed in God. In the evening, feeling more ill, he asked for the holy oils. He received them from Palou's hands, in his armchair. Then with the others who were present he recited the Litany of the Saints and the Penitential Psalms.

The following night he did not sleep. He was suffocating in this little cell filled with Indians. Sometimes he remained on his knees, his head and shoulders leaning against the bed; sometimes he sat on the floor, held up under the arms by two neophytes who thus helped him in his breathing. "I suggested that he should go to bed," Palou writes. "He replied that in this position he was not so suffocated. Dr. García, seeing that his condition was becoming worse, whispered in my ear that probably the revered Father wanted to die on the ground. I offered to give him absolution and the plenary indulgence proper to our Order; he knelt to receive them, and showed his joy when they had been received."

So passed this long night, when the little old man was a hundred times close to suffocation and never uttered one complaint.

The sunlight appeared at last through the narrow window. It was the last time that the sun would rise for him. It brought him one of those sudden restorations of strength which had so often occurred in the course of his life. Junípero sat down again in his armchair, close to the crucifix that lay on the pillow, and plunged once more into prayer.

Toward ten o'clock Captain Canizares presented himself at the house, accompanied by Cristobal Diaz, the frigate's chaplain, and the two men were immediately ushered in. As happy as a child, Junípero went to meet them, embraced them warmly, and had the bells rung in their honor. Together the three began to recall old memories.

As mate under Captain Vincent Vila in 1769, Canizares had refused to abandon Junípero on the beach of San Diego, and had offered him asylum on the *San Carlos;* in 1773, as mate under Captain Miguel Pino, he had in spite of Fages taken him aboard the same boat for San Blas. After that he had gone, with Cristobal Diaz, to Peru. The sick man had the two tell him the story of this voyage, taking a great interest in their narrative. Then suddenly he said:

"How good you are, to have come back from so far away to throw a handful of earth upon my head! . . ."

"We could hardly keep from bursting into sobs," Palou writes. "Finding him in such a good state, we had so little expected these words."

"What is this you are saying, Father Prefect?" cried Canizares, forcing back his tears. "We believe, on the contrary, that you are on the road to recovery, and that you will soon take up your apostolic work again."

"I beg you to do me the kindness of coming to throw a handful of earth upon my coffin," Junípero repeated. "It is an act of mercy for which I shall be grateful."

Palou continues:

"Then, turning toward me, he said, 'I ask you to bury me beside Fray Juan Crespi. When the stone church has been built, let them put me where they wish.'

"Emotion kept me from replying for a moment. Then I said, 'If it is the will of God to call you to Himself, beloved Father, we shall carry out your desire. On your part, for the sake of the tender affection you have always shown me, may I ask you, when you draw near the presence of the Holy Trinity, to offer adoration in my behalf, and, after that, never to forget me? Remember also these missions which you are leaving orphaned, and the persons here with you now.'

" 'I promise you that,' Junípero responded gravely. 'If God in His infinite mercy grants to the sinner that I am the eternal happiness which I so little deserve, I will pray for each one of you, and also for all those Indians whom I am leaving still unconverted.'

"A little later, at his request, I sprinkled the cell with holy water.

" 'Do you feel any uneasiness?' I asked.

" 'No! But it is to forestall it,' he answered.

"He remained silent for a long moment. Then suddenly, in the utmost agitation, he cried out, 'I am afraid! I am afraid!'

"Was this the devil? That spirit which is wicked from the beginning, and from which Jesus wishes us to pray the Father to deliver us; that spirit which hates God and the souls beloved of God—had that spirit come to terrify and tempt him now?

" 'I am in terror!' he cried, once more. 'Recite the Prayer for the Dying, and say it very loud, so I can hear!'

"All those present fell on their knees. In addition to Father Noriega and myself, there were Don José Canizares, Don Cristobal Diaz, Dr. García, several neophytes and sailors. I recited the prayers that commended the soul of the dying to God, and the revered Father responded, in his armchair, like a man in good health. As soon as we had finished, he said, with an air of joy,

" 'God be praised! God be thanked, that He has brought me back to peace! All my fears have vanished!'

"He rose from his chair and went into the anteroom with us. We were as amazed as we were happy over what we already called his cure.

" 'You see, Father Prefect, what my dear St. Anthony can do,' Canizares said then. 'He always answers my prayers. I had prayed to him to cure you. Now all that remains, as I ask, is for him to send you forth on travels for the establishment of new missions.'

"Junípero did not reply, but his smile indicated that he had no longer any expectation of taking to the road. Picking up his diurnal, he sat down at the table that was in the room, to recite his office. When he had finished, I observed that it was past one o'clock, and that he would do well to have something to eat. He drank a cup of broth, thanked me, and suddenly took leave of us.

" 'Let us go and rest now!' he said, as he went back to his cell.

"That was indeed the first time that he had been heard to speak of rest. We were not surprised, however, inasmuch as he had not slept at all during the preceding night. Everyone went away, then, for lunch."

Junípero lay down, fully dressed, on his bed.

It is said that at the moment of quitting this world the dying see their entire existence spread out before them, as in a lightning flash.

Was the lowly house at Petra before Junípero's eyes now, with his mother who had endowed him with such a beautiful soul and such a strong constitution, and who used always to talk to him about God's will? Did he see his little sister Juanita, of whom he did not know whether she was still alive; and his old father, who, on what he thought was his deathbed, had directed him always to be a good son of St. Francis?

He had fulfilled this vow, and realized the ideal of his youth. Putting himself in the hands of Him whom the Father had sent, he had, like the *Poverello*, followed the holy Gospel: poor in spirit; pure, gentle, and humble in heart; patient under infirmity and persecution; judging none, forgiving all; loving his friends and his enemies; making use of his talents; living in unceasing conformity to the good pleasure of God.

If the happy man is he who always has a good conscience, Junípero had been that man. He could thank God for giving him the gift of life, and, his task accomplished, he could fall asleep in the last sleep of the earth. Undoubtedly he prayed, one last time, for his parents, for the Indians, for the living and the dead whom he had loved, for that dear Francisco Palou who had shown himself so faithful to the very end. Then he closed his eyes.

Did the Virgin Mary come to seek him—she upon whom he was wont to depend to open Heaven's gate for his entrance? The devil, in any case, did not present himself again; for when Palou came back, softly, into the cell after the visitors had gone, he found his master's face relaxed, without a trace of conflict or anguish. Junípero seemed to have fallen asleep, the great crucifix that always accompanied him on his travels poised, as if by an angel's hand, upon his breast. But he was not breathing any longer, and already his body was beginning to grow cold.

Father Junípero had died in peace, on the twenty-eighth of August, 1784, at about a quarter to two in the afternoon, at the age of seventy years, nine months, and four days, after fifty-four years spent under the vows of religion and thirty-five in the missions.

A little later, while the passing bell was tolling, Father Palou, aided by Father Noriega, divested him of his hair shirt and his sandals; then, as he was—that is to say, with his cowl on his head, clad in the Franciscan homespun habit, with the triple-knotted cord about his waist—he laid him in his coffin.

His mortal remains were left exposed to view until the moment of burial. The Indians, weeping and bearing field flowers, had overrun his cell, lamenting the loss of "their holy father, their blessed father, the best man on earth," as they were wont to say.

When a saintly man passes from this earth, something of the divine takes its flight back to Heaven, and those who have been close to him, suddenly impoverished, have the feeling that they will be less protected henceforth. Those who have had little understanding of him, or none at all, are often the first to extol him and to call upon him.

The sailors of the Pacific, and the men over them, had always revered Junípero. No sooner had he closed his eyes than the soldiers of Monterey desired to equal them in devotion. Palou was beset by the votaries of relics. Canizares and Cristobal Diaz each carried away a sandal; Dr. García took a handkerchief, which, he said, would work cures for his patients; the frigate's crew fell upon the under-tunic, so that they might make scapulars from it; the soldiers of the escort and the garrison insistently pleaded with Palou to hand over to them the dead man's body-linen and any medals that were left.

Father Paterna was the first to experience the benefits bestowed by Junípero's hair shirt. He had been stricken with dysentery when he arrived at Carmel on the Tuesday following the Prefect's death. The 125 miles he had covered in this dog-day heat, traveling day and night in order to see Junípero again before he died, had completely exhausted him. The grief of not finding the sick man still alive had aggravated his illness. He took to his bed.

Was the minister of the San Luis mission going to die, too? Already, on the advice of Dr. García, Francisco Palou was preparing to administer the last rites. "As a preliminary," Father Palou recounts, "I advised him to put on the hair shirt of the servant of God. He did so, soon felt better, and a few days later, after the Mass celebrated a week after Junípero's death, he set out, wholly recovered, to return to his mission."

At twilight on that Saturday of August 28, the coffin had been placed in the church, opposite the altar, near the steps of the sanctuary. The church was crowded with people all night. The Indians were reciting the Rosary aloud. Two soldiers were standing guard to keep them from snipping off strands of the dead man's white hair and cutting his homespun robe to pieces.

The funeral took place the next day, the twenty-ninth of August. In the absence of Governor Fages, who was at a distance, the Inspector General of the two Californias, who was passing through, decided, in agreement with Captain Canizares, to pay Junípero the honors that were rendered to the King's generals. One is happy to think that Spain should have taken leave thus of the last and perhaps the most godly of its *conquistadores*. From sunrise on, throughout the day, the great cannon of the fort thundered forth every half-hour, alternating with broadsides from the frigate.

Francisco Palou sang the Mass. Father Noriega, Don Cristobal Diaz, and old Father Sitjar, who had arrived from San Antonio the evening before, assisted him at the altar. All the officers of the land and sea services in full uniform were present, and their men with them.

Toward four in the afternoon, Junípero made a tour of his mission for the last time, borne on the shoulders of the King's officers. They took turns in four separate crews, since no one of them was willing to be deprived of the honor of carrying his body. The priests in their black copes marched before the bier; behind, in two ranks, came the soldiers and the sailors with torches in their hands; they were followed by the Indians and colonists.

The procession went back into the church, where lauds were sung. During the last response Junípero was lowered into his tomb at the left of the altar, close by that of Father Crespi. "Then the weeping of the congregation drowned out the voices of the singers," Palou writes. Canizares, Cristobal Diaz, and all the others filed past the grave to throw a handful of earth into it. Then the church was emptied; the guns were stilled; the sun went down over the ocean; and soon, in the silence that had again fallen, the mission bells sounded the evening Angelus.

Thirty

Epilogue
The Communal Republic of California and Junípero's Glorification

Nothing of what Junípero had been in dread of came to pass. As a matter of fact, he had suddenly had the feeling, three days before his death, that his friend Galvez would prevent the expulsion of the Franciscans. "I do not believe," he had said to Palou, "no, I do not believe that these missions will fall into the hands of the Dominican Fathers." [1] And so it was: the Dominicans remained where they were; the San Gabriel Custody did not see the light of day; far from being obliged to leave the countryside where they had planted their missions, the Fernandinos lived on there for another half-century.

To the nine missions they already had, they added twelve more, which they located among the others in such a way as to bring the distance between one Christian community and the next within scope of a day's journey.

The difficulties of the early days had been left far behind. The College had taken confidence anew; there was no longer a dearth of soldiers; livestock, manual labor, agricultural and household implements—all were plentifully at hand. It was enough now that San Fernando should send two friars and the Governor should detach six men to found a new mission. . . .

Lasuen, who was Prefect from 1785 to 1803, established the Mission of Santa Barbara in 1786, La Purisima Concepción in 1787, Santa Cruz and Soledad in 1791, San José, San Juan Bautista, San Miguel, and San Fernando in 1797, and San Luis Rey in 1798. Santa Iñes was founded in 1804 by Father Tapis, San Rafaël in 1817 by Father Sarria, and San Francisco Solano in 1823 by Father Altamira.

[1] Letter from Francisco Palou to Father Sancho, September 13, 1784.

334

The machine was so well adjusted that it never got out of order; Junípero's methods were so perfect that nothing had to be changed. Less than twenty years after his death almost all the Indians, from San Diego to San Francisco and from the ocean to the eastward deserts, had embraced Christianity.

This was, one might have said, a vast monastic federation, covering a territory as large as Belgium and Holland together. A mission had no boundaries except those of its neighbor mission, and, here and there, those of the Spanish villages. Every mission was self-sufficient, with its workshops for weaving and tanning, its mill, its wine press, its forges, its slaughterhouses, and kitchens as large as those of Gamache in *Don Quixote*. At San Diego a masonry canal nearly six miles long brought water from a large dam to the Cosoy.

The yearly record books and balance sheets tell us almost to the single unit the number of sacraments administered, and almost to the single goat the size of the flocks.

There were from one thousand to fifteen hundred Indians in each Christian community, living within sound of the church bell, faithfully receiving the sacraments, singing the hymns as they went to their work, greeting one another with the *Amar a Dios* as on the island of Majorca; receiving each morning their daily food ration, with every Saturday their weekly quarter of meat; receiving clothing as they needed it, care in case of illness, and correction when correction was deserved.

A mission harvested, in good years and bad, from eleven to twelve thousand bushels of grain, and possessed an average of ten thousand head of cattle, twelve thousand sheep, and a thousand horses. Some were richer: notably San Gabriel, where the harvest in 1821 amounted to 29,000 bushels, and where the herds, in 1828, numbered 26,300 cows, 13,300 sheep, 125 pigs, and 2,037 horses.

During this same year, when it attained its apogee, the Indian republic possessed 252,000 head of cattle, 268,000 sheep, 3,500 mules, 34,000 horses, 8,300 goats, and 3,400 pigs. These last were all descended from the four sturdy swine, triumphant over scurvy, that had disembarked in 1769 from the ill-fated *San Carlos*.

In effect, it was indeed a Christian republic of the communal type which Junípero had founded.[2] If he had tried to introduce

[2] We use the term "communal" in preference to "communist" because since Marx and Lenin communism implies the denial of God.

private property in the Sierra Gorda, that never existed in Upper California. Both in their production and in their distribution, riches were held in common: all material goods belonged to the community; like the friars, the Indians possessed nothing of their own.

Only one other example of such a realized undertaking is known to history: the "Reductions" of the Jesuits in Paraguay (1610-1768). But between these two republican regimes there were many differences, one of which was especially to the advantage of the California Indians: these latter, their weapons of war taken away by their ministers, lived in peace from the time they became Christians, whereas the Guaranis of Paraguay remained bellicose even after they had been converted, and did not abstain from making cruel war when they had the opportunity.[3]

It was the place of the Spanish soldiers to guard against external danger and maintain internal order in California. In regard to the first point, no necessity for their intervention arose; and as for the second, the only beginnings of revolt were provoked by the *gente de razón* always ready to try to despoil the Indians. As this class never comprised more than ten per cent of the population, the Franciscans were successful to the end in keeping them at a distance and preventing their robberies.

In reading the accounts given by visitors to the Upper California of that era, one feels that one is dreaming. . . .

"There is such an excess of wealth here—especially in horned cattle and wool-bearing animals—that the Saturday slaughterings do not succeed in reducing it," the malevolent Tamaris wrote, in 1814, to the King of Spain.

"You would never imagine what orange trees, olive trees, vines, and fruit trees of all kinds are growing behind the high orchard walls of San Luis Obispo," wrote Ewin Bryant.

"Looking at these mills, these workshops, these machines, these roads, these bridges, these canals, and all these well-constructed buildings, how can one believe that it is the natives, without aid from the white men, who have done all this!" wrote Duflot de Mafras.

"I had never seen a country without its poor, but I have discovered one," Dy Gastan recounted. "Does a traveler arrive with-

[3] What Voltaire says in Chapters XIV and XV of *Candide* is nevertheless exaggerated and unfair.

out any horse to ride? Someone gives him a fine steed, someone
else gives him saddle and bridle. Does he want milk? They make
him a present of a milch cow. Is he hungry? They get him a beef
to kill."

Vancouver, La Pérouse, the Anglican W. Colton, the Calvinist
H. Rogers, the Huguenot Nelly van de Grift, the Catholic Guadalupe Vallejo, the trapper Dy Gastan, the Russian official Langsdorff, and a great many others are of one voice in their excla-
mations of admiration and wonder.

According to some, "it is the return of the Golden Age." In
the expression used by others, this is "the Spanish Arcadia." "This
is the happiest people that I have ever seen," proclaimed Heath
Davis; and Dy Gastan carried his comment a step further: "the
happiest in the world." As for the earnest and conscientious Bancroft, he averred that "existence here is like a long festival day,
without care and almost without toil."

"Are they working or playing, these natives?" Nelly van de
Grift and Guadalupe Vallejo wondered. "Everything, to them, is
a pretext for enjoyment. . . . It is a festivity for the women to
go and wash the linen in common, to eat together under the trees,
then to come home at night in the big ox-carts, singing beneath
the stars, while their children sleep in their arms. . . . It is another festival for the men who, when the harvest is finished, bring
home the last heads of grain braided together in the form of a
cross and go in procession to place them on the altar."

"To what is this unprecedented wealth due," wrote Vancouver,
"if not to the stern economy and the sacrifices which the friars
imposed upon themselves from the beginning?"

And they kept this up in everything that concerned their own
existence. The Fernandinos were always satisfied with their poor
sinodos, fasting one day out of two,[4] avoiding contact with money,
diverting no share of it to the profit of their College.

In a world-famous book that appeared in 1516, Thomas More
propounded the question, "What is the ideal political system, and
the one which can make sure the happiness of mankind?" He answered, with Plato, that it was the communal regime. Before pub-

---

[4] They fasted during the regular Lent of the Church (from Ash Wednesday
to Easter), during the Lent of their Order (from the first of November to
Christmas), and every Friday of the year. In addition, most of them observed
the Lent of the Epiphany (from January 6 to Septuagesima Sunday), which
the Franciscan Rule declared to be optional.

lishing his book, however, he took care to give it the title of
Utopia, to show clearly that it was a dream, and that he deemed
the system impracticable.

From the testimony cited, have we not reason to believe that
once at least, thanks to the genius and the saintliness of Father
Junípero Serra, this impossible ideal was achieved, and the Utopia
of St. Thomas More was realized?

This republic lasted for half a century.

From 1821 on, Mexico was rejoicing in its independence and
living in chaos.

Among the innumerable guerrilla leaders who presided over its
destinies, none is more picturesque than General Santa Anna. From
1828 to 1858 he appeared and reappeared unceasingly upon the
scene of his country's national life. Sometimes he is seen legislat-
ing and parading in the capital; sometimes he is pursuing his rivals
into the mountains; sometimes he returns to play cards and organize cockfights on his ranch at Manga del Clavo, near Veracruz. Often, also, to escape being killed, he goes abroad, as a political refugee, and enjoys life on his savings. He had lost a leg
in combat. The grateful crowd carried it in procession to the
cathedral of Mexico. In the sequel, turned thankless, they took
it out, dragged it through the streets at the end of a rope, and
threw it nobody-knows-where. In his memoirs, Santa Anna returned again and again to mention of this "sacrilege," and could
not be consoled for not knowing where his leg was.

He certainly knew where Upper California was. But neither he
nor anyone else among the ruling spirits of the country had time,
at first, to go and plunder that distant province. It was Vice President Farias who, in 1833, judged that the moment had come to
give it some attention.

Gomez Farias was an Indian whose possession of a few drops
of white blood had the effect of making him all the more anti-
Christian and of intensifying his adherence to his ancient tribal
morality, which was disposed to murder, theft, and hypocrisy. As
the Mexican Constitution granted the Vice President the responsibility for making laws in the President's absence, Farias had considerable leeway: and in 1833 Santa Anna went four times on vacation to Manga del Clavo, leaving opportunity in the Vice President's hands.

Among the decrees promulgated by Farias, one suppressed the three-hundred-year-old University of Mexico; another abolished the vows of religion; a third expelled all the Spaniards who remained in Mexico; and finally a fourth, under date of May 7, 1833, "secularized" the California missions.

The "secularizers" and their friends took about twelve months to draw up inventories and to divide among themselves what there was to make away with.

Since 1769 one hundred and forty-six Fernandinos, all told, had carried on their activity in the country. They had performed one hundred thousand baptisms, blessed twenty-eight thousand marriages, celebrated seventy-four thousand burial rites—all of which goes to show that they had not been lacking in zeal.

Nor had they been unkind or inconsiderate in their treatment of the Indians. "The irrefutable proof of this," wrote the Protestant A. Forbes, who was at that time in California, "lies in the affection, the attachment, the unimaginable veneration, which the neophytes manifested toward their ministers. Not only did they obey them like children, but their devotion to them bordered upon adoration."

St. Francis ordained that his sons should "not resist evil, and if they were persecuted in one place, *fugiant in aliam terram*—go and do penance elsewhere."

The friars did not put up any resistance, and slipped quietly away aboardship. One of them, however, Father Peyri, who had been minister of San Luis Rey for thirty years, was seen by some of his flock at the moment when the *Pocahontas* was casting off. The Indians jumped upon their horses and rushed headlong, with cries, toward the sea. Two of them reached the ship, which received them and took them to Spain with their old minister.

The California missions were thus destroyed. Their riches went where we have said; their empty buildings remained the property of the State; the missionaries returned to Europe. As for the Indians, they vanished, to rejoin other savages and become savage once more with them. Our Lady of Good Harvests was herself exiled from a region on which she had lavished so many blessings over a period of seventy years.

It was for those who had banished her now to encourage her return; it was for those who had transformed this Eden into a desert to bring back its prosperity.

War broke out between Mexico and the United States. After having tried eight Presidents and Vice Presidents in the course of two years, the Mexican Congress once more entrusted the destinies of the fatherland to President Santa Anna and Vice President Farias. The first immediately set out for the north with his army; the second at once decreed a new confiscation of the goods of the Church. He sent a copy of his decree to Santa Anna, who, in his letter of reply, wrote him, "How can you sleep peacefully, when I have nothing with which to feed the twenty thousand soldiers of my army? You have not sent me even one peso in the month that you have been in charge of the country's affairs! . . ." [5]

Santa Anna was defeated. While he was a fugitive in Colombia, Farias and the Congress were obliged to subscribe, on February 2, 1848, to the conditions imposed by the conqueror. Against a payment of $15,000,000, the United States took possession of Texas, New Mexico, and Northern California—that is to say, more than half of the territory of Mexico. [6] When the news of the treaty reached Paradise, Junípero must surely have felt that at $18.00 per square mile, the United States had not paid dearly for his former missions.

Certainly at the time when he was succeeding in planting the missions in such good situations he did not know that they would one day produce so much fruit, wine, and varied foodstuffs that these would be sent as exports throughout the world; he did not know that the ground over which he dragged his bad leg contained gold and oil, or that the huts in which he celebrated Mass would later be replaced by giant factories and by buildings that soared into the sky; he did not know that San Buenaventura was to have a population of some twenty-three thousand souls, San Diego four hundred thousand, San Francisco seven hundred and seventy-five thousand, and that ships would come annually by tens of thousands to anchor in San Francisco Bay; he had not foreseen that this land where twenty thousand Indians were not finding enough to eat would later be feeding fourteen million inhabitants. Yet he had some slight anticipation of this prodigious future. His letters from 1771 to 1773 bear witness to his perspi-

---

[5] Bravo Ugarte, *Historia de Mexico* (Mexico, 1946), III, 204.
[6] Texas had been admitted into the Union on December 29, 1845, but Mexico had not resigned itself to its loss.

cacity, if not to an actual spirit of prophecy. There are, for example, the following notes to his Guardian:

"To make as much wine as Father Noah is something that will depend entirely on us. . . . There will be large towns roundabout here. . . . The farm of San Gabriel is capable of supporting all our missions, if it is properly managed. . . . The famous port of Monterey is nothing compared to what that of our Father St. Francis will become. . . ."

And, again, there is what he said to Bucareli:

"Get me a few more mules and a few teams of oxen, revered Señor; I am asking you for them for the last time. Afterwards, we shall be self-sufficient. Were the King to send us out then to establish missions to the ends of the world, he would no longer have to give us anything." (*June 21, 1774.*)

GLORIFICATION OF JUNÍPERO

Except for Sulpitius Severus, who got matters under way while St. Martin was still alive, no disciple was ever in greater haste than was Francisco Palou to see his master canonized.

No sooner was Junípero's tomb sealed than Palou returned to San Francisco and set to work on his biography.

A book of about one hundred thousand words, in sixty chapters, it was finished on February 28, 1785. A few months later the author, leaving to Lasuen the administration of the missions, took ship for Mexico. The next year, he was elected Guardian of the College, succeeding Father Sancho. And in 1787 the *History of the Life and Apostolic Works of the Venerable Father Fray Junípero Serra* was published by Felipe de Zuñiga in the City of Mexico.

The book, bearing the seal of approval of four theologians, was printed on indestructible paper and embellished with maps, landscapes, and "portraits"—notably one of Rivera seizing the Christian Carlos—and in the course of its development it had been augmented by the addition of a twenty-five-thousand-word chapter on "The Virtues of Junípero, Servant of God." This supplementary chapter defined the ambitious aims of the author.

In foreword, epilogue, and various notes, Francisco Palou told his readers: "Do not expect to find in this book the style of a Bossuet or a Fléchier. I do not possess that kind of talent. Moreover, that was not necessary for the carrying out of the plan to which I set myself."

Succinctly, Palou wrote:

Three days before his death, as my revered master was lamenting in my presence that the insufficiency in the number of friars was preventing the establishment of the new Missions of Santa Barbara and Purisima Concepción, I observed that if the expected recruits were not arriving from Spain, it was perhaps because there were none to be found there. He responded, with a sigh:

"Ah, if the friars of our holy Province had Father Crespi's diaries of his apostolic travels in their hands, I am sure that the mere reading of them would send several on their way to us. Transmit those diaries to them, I beg of you."

I have not failed to do that, and I have added, also, his own. But my thought has been that this was not enough: that there would be the desire to know the fruits of these journeys, and that nothing would be more likely to incite men to apostolic vocations than the record of Junípero's own work. My companions urged me, furthermore, to write this. . . . Then when they read it, they observed that a chapter was needed in which the reader could see that God's servant Junípero had practiced all the virtues of the saints. I judged that they were right, and acceded to their desire.

Since my necessary activities as missionary and Guardian have not permitted me to give this work all the care it deserved, I wanted to send it, as it was, to Majorca, counting on the Father who is Historian of the Province to make it better. But I was assured that it could appear in its original state, just as I had written it; and since those who told me that offered to pay for the printing, I have followed their advice. Here, then, is my book.

It is, I know, far from perfect. But it possesses one quality which has its value in history: it is accurate. Almost everything that I have reported I have myself seen or heard; the rest, which is very little, I have learned from witnesses whose veracity I guarantee.

I beg you none the less, reader, to excuse my imperfections. No one is without those. Even Homer, Demosthenes, Aristotle, and Solon had their imperfections. You also, doubtless, have yours; and by reason of them, thus, I hope that you will be willing to pardon mine. Meanwhile, *vale!* Good health to you, reader!

The supplementary chapter on "The Virtues" was intended to facilitate the task of the future postulators of Junípero's cause. It was made up of eight "articles": the first set forth "the profound humility of God's servant"; the next four dealt with his cardinal virtues of prudence, justice, strength, and temperance; the last three were concerned with his theological virtues of faith, hope, and charity. The whole was supported by veridical and convincing citations of characteristics and deeds.

Unfortunately, the author had neither revelations, prophecies, nor miracles to report; and "he was too honest a man to invent them." Besides, he added, "that is not what makes saintliness, as has been very well said by Alexander of Hales, Suarez, and Viguer, and as, at Rome itself, the promoter of the Faith recalled during the discussion of the beatification of St. Vincent de Paul."

Francisco Palou was a voice crying in the wilderness.

Galvez, who loved the poets and the saints, died June 17, 1787, at the time the *Life* was appearing; and Charles III, who devoted earnest effort toward the canonization of Spaniards, died in 1788; Palou himself died suddenly on April 6, 1789, at Querétero, in the course of a suit he was bringing against Pedro Fages.

He got the better of the Governor, inasmuch as the latter handed in his resignation that year. But he was less happy as an author than as a litigant; no one took any interest in his book or his projects. Some people even went so far as to accuse him of having fabricated legends to exalt his hero. For more than a century Junípero was left in the shade, and "the admirable Lasuen," as he was called, was extolled at his expense.

Beginning with the year 1910, however, documents were brought to light which proved that Palou's *Vida* was telling the truth, indeed that it fell considerably short of saying enough about its subject.

The idea of obtaining Junípero's beatification was then taken up anew. The American Catholics continue to occupy themselves zealously with it. Not a week goes by in which their periodicals do not inform us of the progress of these activities. It may be hoped that they will be successful.

No one will be less surprised than Francisco Palou the day when his master ascends to the altars. "I had always thought so," he will say. "Is my supplementary chapter on 'The Virtues' not the proof of that?"

But what would have astonished him enormously a few years ago—if the elect are still subject to astonishment—is the honor accorded Junípero by a predominantly non-Catholic country. What monk ever received such a tribute?

This glorification took place in 1927, when, in conformity with the judgment of the Congress of the United States, President Calvin Coolidge moved to set up memorials to the Fathers and Founders of the American Nation in the Capitol in Washington. Each State was asked to designate its two most glorious heroes as representatives. California named Thomas Starr King and Junípero Serra. From then on, Junípero took his place among the country's tutelary geniuses.

He is there in his robe of rough homespun, his feet bare in their sandals, raising aloft in one hand the great crucifix that accompanied him everywhere, holding in the other the model of one of those Churrigueresque churches he used to build. On the high marble pedestal on which his bronze statue stands are the simple words, in gold letters:

JUNÍPERO SERRA
CALIFORNIA

Nor would Palou have foreseen that the coreligionists of the captain who had tried to strangle his master would one day be going on pilgrimage to his tomb. Of the hundreds of thousands of individuals who visit the California Missions every year the majority are, in fact, non-Catholic.

It is a pilgrimage unique of its kind in the length of the route and the diversity and beauty of the sites visited. Cars follow the same *Camino Real* (the King's Highway) along which Junípero urged on his mule. In the towns with their Franciscan names traversed by the pilgrims everything speaks of him. The word "Mission" is found even on the hotel signs and at the refreshment counters. Here and there, in a public square, appears a statue of Junípero. Millions of post cards and leaflets reproduce what are assumed to be his features.

Of the actual establishments he founded, very little is left; the earthquake of 1812 razed them almost all. But everything that was later reconstructed, everything that escaped Farias' barbarism, has now become a relic, and has been kept up with pious devotion. At these missions there are well-tended lawns, gardens, fountains, thick fortress walls, cemeteries with their crosses, flagged corridors, vaulted galleries, little rooms that were used by the friars, large halls where the Indians used to assemble. There are also doves that seem to have lived there, in well-accustomed intimacy, since almost two hundred years ago, and come to perch on your shoulder as if to bid you welcome in behalf of the former hosts.

These friars of old rest beneath the stone flooring of the churches which have all been reopened for worship. The name of each is graven in the stone, followed by the date of his death. At San Diego we again find Fray Juan Figuer, 1784; at San Juan Capistrano, Fray Vicente Fuster, 1800; at San Gabriel, Fray Antonio Cruzado, 1804, Fray Miguel Sanchez, 1804, Fray Francisco Dumetz, 1811; at San Buenaventura, Fray Vicente Santa María, 1806; at Santa Barbara, Fray Antonio Paterna, 1793; at San Antonio, Father Buenaventura Sitjar, 1808; at San Luis Obispo, Father Joseph Cavaller, 1789; at Carmel, finally, Crespi, Lasuen, and Junípero himself. One is not much surprised over the failure to encounter Benito Cambon, who in 1791 felt the need of going to see once more what was happening in Mexico and, the year after, in Spain; but one regrets that the ashes of Francisco Palou should not yet have been transferred from Querétaro to San Francisco.

As it would not be possible to fill the "Junípero Serra Museums" with what was left by a man who possessed nothing, one finds in them ploughshares, earthen kettles, old furniture, and, along with these, donkeys' packsaddles, yokes for oxen, horseshoes, and other objects bequeathed to posterity by the good beasts that helped Junípero to convert the Indians. At San Gabriel, however, one is shown the thick breviary in which he used to read his office; at Carmel, the liturgical vestments he used, his poor cell, and the three boards on which he reposed for a few minutes before his death.

One day—it was an afternoon of torrid heat—a group of schoolgirls, under the guidance of their teacher, made their way, like a breath of fresh air, inside the old walls. There was concentration, and reflection, to be seen on those young and charming faces. After a long visit, the girls came back to bend over a panorama in relief which had been explained to them when they entered; they listened to a phonograph record of the *Alabado* that the Indians used to sing every morning and evening; after that, they drew up around a bust of Junípero. Then the teacher read them—as one recites a psalm—the following passage from the address delivered by Senator I. B. Dockweiler at the unveiling of the statue in the Capitol in Washington:

This man, whose memory is indissolubly one with the epic of California, was great in his humility;

He triumphed by his courage, when everything would have appeared bound to discourage him and beat him down;

He is one who is worthy of first place among the immortal heroes who created our nation;

So his memory will never die, and his name will be blessed from generation to generation.

CHRONOLOGY

1713:
> November 24: Birth and baptism of Michel Joseph (Miguel José) Serra, at Petra on the island of Majorca, Spain.

1719-29:
> He has his elementary schooling and receives a classical education from the Franciscans of Petra.

1729-30:
> He begins the study of philosophy with the Franciscans of Palma.

1730:
> September 14: He enters the Franciscan novitiate of Jesus-outside-the-Walls, Palma.

1731:
> September 15: He takes his vows of religion with the name of Junípero.

1731-34:
> He studies philosophy. On December 21, 1731, he is admitted to minor orders.

1734-37:
> He studies theology. On December 18, 1734, he is ordained subdeacon, and on March 17, 1736, he is ordained deacon.

1737:
> He is ordained priest a little before Christmas.

1740-49:
> He teaches philosophy at St. Francis of Palma (1740-43), takes his degree as Doctor of Theology (1742), and occupies the "first chair of Scotist theology" at the University of Palma (1744-49).

1749:
> April 13: With Francisco Palou he embarks at Palma for Cadiz. August 29: He embarks at Cadiz for Veracruz.

October 18-November 2: He preaches a mission in Puerto
   Rico.

December 6: He arrives at Veracruz.

December 16: He leaves Veracruz for Mexico.

1750:

   January 1: He arrives at Mexico City.

   May 31: He sets out for the Sierra Gorda with Francisco Palou.

1750-58:

   As Prefect, he directs the missions of the Sierra Gorda.

   In September, 1758, Junípero and Palou, having been assigned
      to work among the Apaches of Texas, return to Mexico.

1759:

   October: The victory of the Apaches over the Spaniards pre-
      vents the two friends from reaching their post.

1759-67:

   Junípero devotes himself to preaching in the central and south-
      ern portion of Mexico.

   July 14, 1767: Appointed Prefect of Lower California, he sets
      out for San Blas.

1768:

   March 12: He sails from San Blas, and on April 1 he lands at
      Loreto.

   July 6: Galvez arrives in Lower California and sends for Juní-
      pero.

   September 28: Junípero leaves Loreto to answer Galvez' call.

   October 29: He joins Galvez at La Paz, and together they
      make the preparations for the expedition to the north.

1769:

   January 10: Galvez and Junípero conclude their conference
      and separate.

   March 28: Junípero leaves Loreto and sets out on the road
      north.

   May 14: He founds the Mission of Velicata, a little above the
      30th parallel.

   July 1: He arrives at San Diego, near the 33rd parallel.

   July 16: He founds the Mission of San Diego.

   August 15: The Redskins attack the Mission, and five men are
      killed.

1770:

February 11: Rivera leaves San Diego to search for food supplies in the Peninsula. Portola decides that the expedition will abandon Upper California on March 15, if the ship does not arrive with provisions before that. Junípero succeeds in having the date of withdrawal put off until March 20.

March 19: The ship appears, and the order for withdrawal is canceled.

End of May: Galvez returns to Mexico. Father Verger brings forty-nine friars from Spain.

June 3: Junípero founds San Carlos Mission at Monterey.

July 9: Portola quits Upper California, the command of which he leaves to Pedro Fages.

August 16: Galvez announces to the world that Spain occupies the Pacific coast as far north as the 38th parallel.

1771:

May 21: Ten Fernandinos disembark at Monterey.

July 14: Junípero founds the Mission of San Antonio.

August 5: He transfers San Carlos Mission from Monterey to Carmel.

September 8: Foundation of the Mission of San Gabriel.

1772:

April: No ships arrive, thus there is famine in Upper California.

April 13: Juan Crespi deserts Junípero, who remains alone at Carmel for five months.

August 22: Junípero and Fages set out for the south.

September 1: Foundation of the Mission of San Luis Obispo.

September 16: Fages and Junípero arrive at San Diego. Their lack of agreement prevents establishment of San Buenaventura. Junípero decides to see the Viceroy, Bucareli.

October 20: He sails from San Diego.

November 4: He lands at San Blas.

November 7: He arrives at Tepic, and learns that the Dominicans have supplanted the Fernandinos in Lower California.

December: He falls gravely ill at Guadalajara and is given Extreme Unction.

1773:

January: Junípero has a relapse at Querétaro.

February 6: He arrives "half dying" at San Fernando.

February 13: He delivers his first *Memorandum* to Bucareli. Their conversations give rise to measures assuring the future of New California.

May 17: Palou leaves Loreto for Monterey.

October 10: Junípero arrives at Guadalajara on the way to San Blas.

1774:

January 24: Junípero sails from San Blas.

March 13: He lands at San Diego.

April 27: South of San Luis Obispo, he encounters Anza, who has just established connection by land between Sonora and Upper California (first expedition).

May 11: Junípero returns to Carmel.

May 23: Rivera replaces Pedro Fages at Monterey.

1775:

June: Father Lasuen arrives at Carmel to intrigue against Junípero.

August 13: Establishment of San Capistrano is decided upon, and Lasuen is appointed its minister.

November 5: The Indians attack the Mission of San Diego and murder Father Luis Jaume.

1776:

January 4: Anza arrives at San Gabriel (second expedition).

March: Anza delivers to Junípero a License that deprives him, in part, of his powers. Rivera is excommunicated.

June 29: Junípero leaves Carmel.

July 11: He lands at San Diego, and begins to restore the Mission.

August 8: Rivera obliges him to interrupt the work; it is begun again on the first of October.

October 9: Palou founds the Mission of San Francisco.

November 1: Junípero re-establishes San Capistrano.

The end of 1776: Monterey replaces Loreto as capital of the two Californias, which are removed from the jurisdiction of the Viceroy and placed under that of the Commandant General de Croix, with residence at Arispe (Sonora).

1777:

January 12: Foundation of the Mission of Santa Clara.

January 15: Junípero returns to Carmel.

February 11: Neve establishes himself at Monterey as Governor and Rivera is sent back to Loreto.

Beginning of June: Lasuen and Paterna come to Carmel to make their submission.

1778:

In June: Junípero receives authority to administer confirmation.

September 16: He arrives at San Diego to begin his first circuit of confirmations. He returns to Carmel December 24.

1779:

April 6: Death of Bucareli. He is replaced as Viceroy by Mayorga.

September: Neve forbids Junípero to administer confirmation.

October 15: Junípero arrives at San Francisco, where he performs confirmations in spite of this prohibition.

1780:

June 15: On the occasion of the American War of Independence, Junípero addresses a circular letter to his ministers.

September 5: Neve leaves for the Peninsula.

December 26: De Croix lifts the interdict on Junípero's confirmations.

1781:

April: San Fernando refuses to send friars to found missions of the Santa Barbara Channel.

July 18: Rivera is murdered by the Yumas.

August 16: Neve notifies Junípero that the interdict has been lifted.

October 25: Junípero, accompanied by Father Crespi, administers confirmation at San Francisco and Santa Clara.

November 22: Both men return to Carmel.

December: Foundation of Los Angeles.

1782:

January 1: Death of Juan Crespi.

March 31: Junípero founds the Mission of San Buenaventura.

April 19: Foundation of the village-presidio of Santa Barbara.

May 19: Junípero returns to Carmel.

September: Neve is named Inspector General of the Interior Provinces and Fages Governor ad interim of the Californias.

October 12: Fages installs himself at Monterey.

The end of 1782: Junípero decides that, beginning with 1783, the ministers will no longer serve as chaplains to the presidios.

1783:

June 2: Junípero learns that there is danger of the Dominicans' supplanting the Fernandinos in Upper California.

August: Neve replaces De Croix as Commandant General and Fages is confirmed in office as Governor.

About August 15: Junípero sails for San Diego, where he begins his third and last circuit of confirmations.

1784:

January: He returns to Carmel.

April: He administers confirmation at Santa Clara and San Francisco.

May: He makes a retreat at Santa Clara to prepare for death.

August 21: Death of Neve at Arispe.

August 28: Death of Junípero at Carmel.

SOURCES[1]

The documentation made use of in the production of the present work would come to some fifteen thousand pages, of which about four thousand are the writings of Junípero himself, and the rest are drawn from his contemporaries.

Junípero's Writings

About a third of Junípero's output consists of Latin commentaries on Aristotelian and Scotist doctrines which he wrote during his professorial career (1740-49). The larger part, written in Spanish and dating from the years of his apostolic work (1749-84), includes a travel diary, five important *Memoranda,* and about one hundred eighty letters, some fifty of which are addressed to his superiors, about forty to his relatives and colleagues, and the others to various representatives of the King, Charles III. To these must be added about fifty entries in the Mission Registers.

The Writings of His Contemporaries

The contemporaries whose writings supply us with information about Junípero are his superiors who sent him their orders, his colleagues who lived with him, the Crown representatives with whom he had dealings, and, finally, various individuals who were involved in the events of his life.

His superiors. A considerable portion of the correspondence of the Guardians of San Fernando—Verger, Pangua, Sancho—has been rediscovered, as well as *Memoranda* addressed by them to the Court of Madrid and to that of Mexico City.

His colleagues. Letters written by Palou, Crespi, Lasuen, and other companions of Junípero's labors have also been discovered. From Crespi we have in addition seven travel diaries. As for Palou,

[1] We sum up here in a few lines the long survey of the sources published in the French edition of this work (Paris, Plon, 1956). See also the Bibliography, below.

who knew Junípero for more than forty years, he published a Life (*Vida*) of his master in 1787 and left voluminous chronicles (*Noticias*) of the California missions.

Representatives of the Crown. From the Minister Galvez; the Viceroys Charles de Croix, Bucareli, and Mayorga; the Commandant General Teodoro de Croix; the Governors Armona, Barri, Fages, Neve, and Rivera, we have reports, instructions, ordinances, and official correspondence, as well as a certain number of the letters they wrote to Junípero. The Galvez file alone, which is in the Archives of Seville, fills 2,627 pages.

Various individuals. From the military leaders Escandon, Velasco, Labra, Portola; the marine officers Juan Perez, Vila, Quiros, Canizares, and others; the explorers Anza, Costanso, Garces, Diaz, Pedro Font, and others, we likewise have numerous reports and travel diaries in which Junípero appears.

Most of these documents are still unpublished.[2] Almost all are in Mexico (*Archivo General de la Nación, Biblioteca del Museo Nacional, Biblioteca Nacional,* Mexico City), or in Spain (*Archivo de Indias,* Seville; *Biblioteca Conventualis,* Palma and Barcelona). The few scattered pages to be found elsewhere are in Washington (Library of Congress), New York (Public Library), Austin, Texas (Library of the University of Texas), Santa Barbara (Mission), Fresno and San Francisco (Episcopalian Chancery).

To these sources others will certainly be added in the future. New letters of Junípero, in particular, will be brought to light, for he wrote four or five times as many as we are acquainted with. But nothing that is yet to be discovered, it appears, will be capable of altering the portrait that can be drawn of him at the present time; he has in fact revealed himself wholly in his writings cited above, and no one ever changed less, in inner nature or in conduct.

[2] The only ones published to date are the few *Diarios* and *Noticias* mentioned in the Bibliography, below.

BIBLIOGRAPHY

Acceptance and Unveiling of the Statues of Junípero Serra and Thomas Starr King presented by the State of California. Washington, 1932.

Administración de . . . Bucareli y Ursua. 2 vols. Mexico, 1936.

The Americas, III (1947), 102-14, 234-43, 368-81; IV (1948), 65-82, 141-50, 287-93; V (1949), 48-60; VI (1950), 3-31, 291-333, 467-86; VII (1951), 267-80; IX (1953), 291-314.

Apostle of California. Quarterly review published since 1943 at Santa Barbara.

ARRICIVITA, Juan Domingo. *Cronica . . . del Colegio . . . de Querétaro en la Nueva España.* Segunda parte. Mexico, 1792.

BAEGERT, Johann Jakob. *Observations in Lower California.* Translated by M. M. Brandenburg and Carl L. Baumann. Berkeley, 1952.

BANCROFT, Hubert H. *History of Mexico.* 6 vols. San Francisco, 1883-87.

―― *History of California.* 7 vols. San Francisco, 1886-90.

―― *History of the North Mexican States and Texas.* 2 vols. San Francisco, 1884-89.

BEECHEY, Frederick M. *Narrative of a Voyage to the Pacific and Beering's Strait . . . in the Years 1825-26-27-28.* 2 vols. London, 1831.

BOLTON, Herbert Eugene. *Anza's California Expeditions.* 5 vols. Berkeley, 1930.

―― (ed.) *Fray Juan Crespi, Missionary Explorer . . .* Berkeley, 1927.

―― (ed.) *Historical Memoirs of New California by Francisco Palou.* 4 vols. Berkeley, 1926.

―― *Guide to Materials for the History of the United States in the Principal Archives of Mexico.* Washington, 1913.

BOLTON, Herbert E., and MARSHALL, Thomas M. *The Colonization of North America, 1492-1783.* New York, 1920.

BUENO, j. g. Cabrera. *Navegación especulativa y practica.* Manila, 1734.

CASAS, Augusto. *Fray Junipero Serra . . .* Barcelona, 1949.

CASTAÑEDA, Carlos E. *Guide to the Latin American Manuscripts in the University of Texas Library.* Cambridge, 1939.

CASTAÑEDA, Carlos E. *Calendar of the Manuel E. Gondra Manuscript Collection.* Mexico, 1952.

CHAPMAN, Charles E. *The Founding of Spanish California.* New York, 1916.

—— *A History of California* . . . New York, 1921.

CLAVIJERO, Francisco Javier. *The History of [Lower] California.* . . . Translated and edited by Sara E. Lake and A. A. Gray. Stanford, 1937.

CLINCH, Bryan J. *California and Its Missions* . . . 2 vols. San Francisco, 1904.

COOK, Sherburne F. *The Conflict between the California Indian and White Civilization.* 4 vols. Berkeley, 1943.

CUEVAS, Mariano. *Historia de la Iglesia en Mexico.* 5 vols. Tlalpan, 1921; El Paso, 1928.

CULLETON, James. *Indians and Pioneers of Old Monterey.* Fresno, 1950.

DUFLOT DE MAFRAS, Eugène. *Exploration* . . . *des Californies.* . . . 2 vols. Paris, 1844.

DUHAUT-CILLY, Auguste. *Voyage autour du monde principalement à la Californie.* . . . 1826-1829. 2 vols. Paris, 1834-35.

ELDREDGE, Zoeth S. (ed.). *History of California.* 5 vols. New York, 1915.

ENGELHARDT, Zephyrin. *The Missions and Missionaries of California.* 5 vols. San Francisco, 1908-16.

—— *The Franciscans in California.* Harbor Springs (Mich.), 1897.

—— *San Diego Mission.* San Francisco, 1920.

—— *San Luis Rey Mission.* San Francisco, 1921.

—— *San Juan Capistrano Mission.* Los Angeles, 1922.

—— *San Francisco or Mission Dolores.* Chicago, 1924.

—— *San Gabriel Mission and* . . . *Los Angeles.* San Gabriel (Calif.), 1927.

—— *San Fernando Rey.* Chicago, 1927.

—— *San Antonio de Padua.* Santa Barbara, 1929.

—— *San Miguel Arcangel.* Santa Barbara, 1929.

—— *Mission N.S. de la Soledad.* Santa Barbara, 1929.

—— *San Buenaventura.* Santa Barbara, 1930.

—— *Mission la Concepción Purisima.* Santa Barbara, 1932.

—— *Mission San Carlos.* Santa Barbara, 1934.

ERNEST and COWAN. *A Bibliography of the History of California 1510-1906,* Columbus (Ohio), 1952.

Estado General de las fundaciones hechas por D. José de Escandon. . . . 2 vols. Mexico, 1929-30.

FAGES, Pedro. *Extracto de Noticias* (1770), *Diario historico* (1772). Translated and edited by Herbert E. Bolton. Berkeley, 1927.

Fages, Pedro. *A Historical, Political, and Natural Description of California*. Translated by H. I. Priestley. Berkeley, 1937.

Forbes, Alexander. *California: a History of Upper and Lower California*. . . . San Francisco, 1919.

Galvez, José. *Plan for the Establishment of a Government and Comandancía General which Includes the Peninsula of the Californias and the Provinces of Sinaloa, Sonora and Nueva Viscaya*. San Francisco, 1934.

—— *Informe general que . . . entregó El Excmo Señor Marques de Sonora al . . . Virrey Bucareli.* . . . Mexico, 1867.

Garces, Fray F. T. H. *Diario 1773-74, Diario 1775-76*. New York, 1900.

Geary, Gerald J. *The Secularization of the California Missions (1810-1846)*. Washington, 1934.

Geiger, Maynard. *Calendar of Documents in the Santa Barbara Mission Archives*. Washington, 1947.

—— (trans. and ed.) *Palou's Life of Fray Junipero Serra*. Washington, 1955.

Gleeson, William. *History of the Catholic Church in California*. 2 vols. San Francisco, 1872.

Graham, Cunningham. *A Vanished Arcadia*. London, 1901.

Hawes, Horace. *The Missions in California* . . . San Francisco, 1856.

Hayes, Benjamin. *Missions of California*. Bancroft Library, 1873.

Herrera Carrillo, Pablo. *Fray Junipero Serra, civilizador de las Californias*. Mexico, 1950.

Hittell, T. *History of California*. 4 vols. San Francisco, 1898.

Instrucciones que los Virreyes de Nueva España dejaron a sus succesores. Mexico, 1867.

Jiménez-Rueda, Julio. *Historia de la cultura en México*. Mexico, 1950.

Joyce, T. A. *Mexican Archaeology*. 1914.

Kotzebue, Otto von. *A New Voyage round the World, in the Years 1823-26*. 2 vols. London, 1830.

Langsdorff, G. H. von. *Voyages and Travels . . . during the Years 1803, 1804, 1806 and 1807*, London, 1803-1814, 2 vols.

Lapérouse, Jean-François de. *Voyage . . . autour du monde*. Paris, 1798.

Lowery, Woodbury. *The Spanish Settlements within the Present Limits of the United States, 1513-61*. New York, 1901.

Maas, Otto (ed.). *Las Ordenes Religiosas de España y la Colonización de America*. . . . 2 vols. Barcelona, 1918-29.

Mecham, J. Lloyd. *Church and State in Latin America*. . . . Chapel Hill (N. C.), 1934.

—— (ed.) *Memorias de Relaciones*. Mexico, 1922.

MENDIZÁBAL, Miguel Othón de. *Ensayos sobre las Civilizaciones Aborigines Americanas.* Mexico, 1924.

Las Misiones de la Alta California. Mexico, 1914.

MORRELL, B. *A Narrative of Four Voyages to the South Sea, North and South Pacific Ocean, 1822-31.* New York, 1832.

PALOU, Francisco. *Relacion historica de la Vida . . . del V.P. Fray Junipero Serra.* . . . Mexico, 1787.

—— *Noticias de la Nueva California.* Mexico, 1857. (See also under Bolton and Geiger entries.)

PIETTE, Charles J. G. M. *Evocation de Junipero Serra.* . . . Montréal, 1946.

—— *Le secret de Junipero Serra.* . . . 2 vols. Bruxelles, 1949.

PRESCOTT, William E. A. *The Conquest of Mexico.* 3 vols. New York, 1843.

PRIESTLEY, Herbert I. *José de Galvez, Visitor-General of New Spain (1765-1771).* Berkeley, 1916.

Provincial Annals (Santa Barbara, Calif.), IV, V, VI, VII, VIII, IX.

Publications of the Historical Society of Southern California. Vol. II. Los Angeles, 1891.

Publications of the Academy of Pacific Coast History. Vols. II and III. Berkeley, 1911-13.

Recopilación de leyes de los reinos de las Indias. 4 vols. Madrid, 1681.

RICARD, Robert. *La "conquête spirituelle" du Mexique . . . de 1523 à 1572.* Paris, 1933.

RICHMAN, Irving Berdine. *California under Spain and Mexico.* Boston, 1911.

ROBERTSON, James A. *List of Documents in Spanish Archives Relating to the History of the United States.* Washington, 1910.

ROBINSON, Alfred. *Life in California.* New York, 1846.

SANTA ANNA, Antonio Lopez de. *Mi historia militar y politica, 1810-1874.* Mexico, 1952.

SANCHEZ, Nelly Van de Grift. *Spanish Arcadia.* San Francisco, 1929.

SHEPHERD, William R. *Guide to the Materials for the History of the United States in Spanish Archives.* Washington, 1907.

STODDARD, Charles Warren. *In the Footprints of the Padres.* San Francisco, 1902.

THOMAS, Alfred B. (trans. and ed.). *Teodoro de Croix and the Northern Frontier of New Spain.* Norman (Okla.), 1941.

TORRENS Y NICOLAU, Francisco. *Bosquejo histórico del . . . V.P. Fray Junipero Serra.* Felanitx (Spain), 1913.

VANCOUVER, George. *A Voyage of Discovery.* . . . 6 vols. London, 1801.

VISCHER, Edward. *Missions of Upper California.* San Francisco, 1872.

WAGNER, Henry R. *The Cartography of the Northwest Coast of America to the Year 1800.* Berkeley, 1937.

—— *Spanish Voyages to the Northwest Coast of America—Sixteenth Century.* San Francisco, 1929.

WATERS, Willard O. *Franciscan Missions of Upper California as Seen by Foreign Visitors and Residents 1786-1848.* s.l.n.d.

WEBB, Edith B. *Indian Life at the Old Missions.* Los Angeles, 1952.

INDEX

SACRAMENTO R.

San Francisco

Santa Clara

SAN JOAQUIN R.

San José

SAN FRANCISCO

Monterey

SALINAS R.

Carmelo

JUNÍPERO SERRA PEAK

San Antonio

KING R.

L. TULARE

CARMELO

CALIFORNIA

San Luis Obispo

SANTA MARIA R.

SAN ANTONIO

Pacific Ocean

Concepcion · Santa Barbara

San Buenaventura

Canal Santa Barbara

SAN LUIS OBISPO

Miles

0   50   100   200

palacios